Protecting the Environment

PRIVATELY

Protecting the Environment

PRIVATELY

Edited by

Jeffrey Bennett

Australian National University, Australia

World Scientific

NEW JERSEY • LONDON • SINGAPORE • BEIJING • SHANGHAI • HONG KONG • TAIPEI • CHENNAI

Published by

World Scientific Publishing Co. Pte. Ltd.
5 Toh Tuck Link, Singapore 596224
USA office: 27 Warren Street, Suite 401-402, Hackensack, NJ 07601
UK office: 57 Shelton Street, Covent Garden, London WC2H 9HE

Library of Congress Cataloging-in-Publication Data
Protecting the environment, privately / [edited by] Jeffrey Bennett.
pages cm
ISBN 978-9814675437
1. Environmental protection--Economic aspects. 2. Environmental policy--Economic aspects.
3. Environmental economics. I. Bennett, Jeff, 1954–
HC79.E5P6955 2015
333.72--dc23
2015009300

British Library Cataloguing-in-Publication Data
A catalogue record for this book is available from the British Library.

In-house Editors: Dipasri Sardar/Philly Lim

Typeset by Stallion Press
Email: enquiries@stallionpress.com

Printed in Singapore by B & Jo Enterprise Pte Ltd

Contents

Contributors

Sven Anders is an Associate Professor of Agricultural Economics in the Department of Resource Economics and Environmental Sociology at the University of Alberta. His research interest lies in the economics of vertical food marketing and retailing, with a focus on consumer and firm behaviour along agri-food value chains. His research includes work on food standards, food trade, and food policy. Sven has published in the area of third-party certification in food systems, food–nutrition–health, and he conducts research on the impact of food-health related product differentiation on manufacturer-retail competition.

Terry L. Anderson is the William A. Dunn Distinguished Senior Fellow at the Property and Environment Research Center (PERC), Bozeman, Montana, and the John and Jean DeNault Senior Fellow at the Hoover Institution, Stanford University. His is author or editor of 38 books, including, *Free Market Environmentalism for the Next Generation* and *Environmental Markets: A Property Rights Approach*. Anderson holds a Ph.D. in economics from the University of Washington (1972) and is an avid outdoorsman accomplished at archery hunting, fly fishing, skiing, and horseback riding.

Jeff Bennett is Professor in the Crawford School of Public Policy at the Australian National University. He is a Distinguished Fellow of the Australian Agricultural and Resource Economics Society and a Fellow of the Academy of Social Sciences in Australia. Jeff is widely published in environmental, natural resource and agricultural economics and is an internationally recognised leader in the fields of environmental valuation and private-sector involvement in environmental protection.

Anthea Coggan is an Environmental Economist with the Commonwealth Scientific and Industrial Research Organisation (CSIRO) Australia. Anthea's research is focused on designing and evaluating innovate ways to change the incentives faced by land managers such that they provide public goods such as biodiversity conservation to a level that is socially desirable. One particular economic instrument which has captured Anthea's attention is biodiversity offsetting. Anthea has a number of publications focused on efficient and effective offset design, as well as publications on environmental policy design more broadly.

Lin Crase is Professor of Applied Economics and Director of the Centre for Water Policy and Management at La Trobe University. He has published extensively on water resource management, water property rights and the intersection between public policy and resource management objectives.

Dustin Garrick is Assistant Professor and Philomathia Chair of Water Policy at McMaster University in Ontario, Canada. His comparative water policy research examines water allocation institutions and climate change adaptation in transboundary rivers of western North America and Southeast Australia, where he completed a Fulbright Fellowship in 2011. He currently serves on the OECD/Global Water Partnership task force on water security and sustainable growth, and as Colorado River Basin chair of the Food, Energy, Environment and Water (FE2W) network.

Robert Gillespie is the Principal of Gillespie Economics, an environmental and resource economics consultancy business. He has extensive experience in the application of welfare economics to a diverse range of public and private-sector policies and projects and a particular interest in the valuation of environmental, social and cultural impacts using non-market valuation techniques.

Ellen Goddard is a Professor holding the Co-operative Chair in Agricultural Marketing and Business in the School of Resource Economics and Environmental Sociology at the University of Alberta, Canada. Professor Goddard's research interests include: agricultural marketing; trade and policy; consumer demand for foods in Canada; impact of advertising and other media information on consumer demand; and agribusiness co-operatives. She has also published extensively in these areas. Professor Goddard is the Program Leader, Consumer and Market Demand Policy Research Networks, Agriculture and Agri-Food Canada, and Member of the AVRI Council.

R. Quentin Grafton is Professor of Economics at the Crawford School of Public Policy at the Australian National University. He is Chairholder of the United Nations Educational, Scientific and Cultural Organization (UNESCO) Chair of Water Economics and Transboundary Water Governance, Director of the Food, Energy, Environment and Water Network and is also a Fellow of the Academy of Social Sciences of Australia and a Society Fellow of the Asia Pacific Policy Society.

Suzie Greenhalgh leads the environmental policy and governance research at Landcare Research NZ. She is an applied researcher working with national and regional level government, business and communities to address pressing and emerging environmental challenges. Suzie spent a number of years in the USA working on US and global environmental issues and now predominantly works in New Zealand and the Pacific. Her primary areas of expertise are water policy and governance and the use of ecosystem service concepts to underpin decision-making.

Laure Kuhfuss is a Post-Doctoral researcher in the department of Geography and Sustainable Development at the University of St Andrews, Scotland, United Kingdom. Her research is in the area of agricultural and environmental economics, with a special focus on payment for environmental services schemes. Her Ph.D. work, carried out at the University of Montpellier 1, focused on the evaluation and design of innovative agri-environmental contracts in France.

Philippe Le Coent is a Ph.D. student in Environmental Economics conducting research on innovative incentive systems for farmers to adopt pro-environmental practices, mobilizing behavioural and experimental economics. He started his career as an agronomist in international agricultural Development for 10 years, mostly at the Food and Agriculture Organization of the United Nations (FAO).

Erin O'Donnell is an Environmental Water Law and Policy Specialist. She has worked in the Australian water sector for the past decade, where she developed and implemented policies to manage environmental water in the context of a water market. Erin is currently completing her Ph.D. at the University of Melbourne Law School, on the water markets and environmental water management organizations of south-eastern Australia and the western USA.

Sue O'Keefe is an Associate Professor in the School of Economics and Finance and a member of the Centre for Water Policy and Management at La Trobe University. Her research interests are in water policy and management.

Raphaële Préget is permanent researcher in Applied Economics at the French National Institute for Agricultural Research (INRA). She holds a Ph.D. in Economics from the University of Paris I. Her research is in the field of environmental economics, public economics and behavioural economics.

John Rolfe is Professor of Regional Economic Development and Deputy Dean Research in the School of Business and Law at the CQ University at Rockhampton. John has a number of research interests, but specialises in non-market valuation, regional development, and environmental, resource and agricultural economic issues. He is currently the Editor-in-Chief for the *Australian Journal of Agricultural and Resource Economics*.

Gabriela Scheufele is a Research Fellow in the Crawford School of Public Policy at the Australian National University. She completed a Ph.D. in Environmental and Resource Economics investigating changes in non-market values and non-market-valuation techniques across time at the Australian National University in 2011. Her current research interests focus on Payments for Environmental Services (PES) scheme design; non-market environmental valuation; design of conservation auctions; and incorporating environmental economic research into policy development.

Kathleen Segerson is a Board of Trustees Distinguished Professor of Economics at the University of Connecticut. She serves on the National Academy of Sciences/National Research Council Board on Agriculture and Natural Resources, is a co-editor of the *Journal of the Association of Environmental and Resource Economists*, and is a Fellow of both the Association of Environmental and Resource Economists (AERE) and the Agricultural and Applied Economics Association (AAEA).

Mindy Selman is a Senior Associate in the World Resources Institute's Water Program. Her current research covers a variety of issues including environmental markets, eutrophication, and agricultural policy. She is an internationally recognized expert in water quality trading and has led work to develop nonpoint source estimation tools and registries for the Chesapeake Bay water quality markets. Before joining World Resource Institute (WRI), Mindy completed her MS in Sustainable Development and Conservation Biology from the University of Maryland; she holds her undergraduate degree in International Relations from Mary Washington College.

Dale Squires is Senior Scientist with US National Oceanic and Atmospheric Administration (NOAA) Fisheries and Adjunct Professor of Economics at the University of California San Diego. He serves on the Scientific Advisory Committee of the International Seafood Sustainability Foundation and the Scientific and Technical Advisory Committee of the International Pole and Line Foundation.

Luca Tacconi is Professor in the Crawford School of Public Policy at the Australian National University. His research focuses on the economic, political, and social factors that drive environmental change — resulting in loss of biodiversity and climate change — and their implications for rural livelihoods and poverty. He is conducting research on environmental governance, social and economic aspects of deforestation and climate change, PES, and research methods for environmental management.

Michael 't Sas-Rolfes is an independent conservation economist based in Cape Town, South Africa. With an academic background spanning business, environmental resource economics and biodiversity policy, he has been actively involved in wildlife conservation for most of his life, as a practitioner, researcher, consultant, writer and presenter. His areas of specialist expertise include wildlife trade policy and innovative mechanisms for financing and managing protected areas, with a strong focus on the role of the private sector and markets in conservation.

Sophie Thoyer is Professor in Agricultural and Environmental Economics and Head of the department of social, economic and management science of Montpellier Supagro (France). She publishes in the field of public economics applied to agri-environmental issues. She has worked extensively on water management and biodiversity protection issues with a special interest in the design of optimal agri-environmental schemes.

Wendy Umberger is an Associate Professor in Agricultural Economics and Food Policy and the Director of Global Food Studies Centre at the University of Adelaide. Umberger's research focus is in the area of behavioural economics. She uses innovative methods to understand drivers of consumer and producer behaviour related to agricultural and food technology adoption, food quality, food safety, nutrition and claims related to quality (credence) attributes. She has published extensively on these issues and has been invited to present her work internationally to a variety of global audiences, including the agricultural and food industry, government and academia.

Lawrence R. Watson is the Executive Director at PERC, the PERC in Bozeman, Montana. He also directs PERC's Enviropreneur Institute, an educational program and launchpad for environmental entrepreneurs. Watson's research focuses on the implementation of market-based solutions to natural resource conflicts. He holds a J.D. and M.A. in Environmental Economics from Duke University and a B.S. in Economics from Clemson University.

Ken Willis is Emeritus Professor of Environmental Economics in the School of Architecture, Planning and Landscape, at the University of Newcastle-upon-Tyne. His research interests include environmental and non-market valuation, environmental regulation, choice behaviour, and cultural economics, and has published extensively in these fields. Ken is Editor of the *Journal of Environmental Economics and Policy*.

Acknowledgements

For a long time I have wanted to put together a book that demonstrates the power and potential of markets to achieve environmental protection goals. This interest goes back to my initial meeting with Terry Anderson at a Mont Pelerin Society conference in Christchurch, New Zealand in 1989 and prior to that, faculty tea room discussions with Wolfgang Kasper when we were both at the University of New South Wales. These friends/colleagues were instrumental in encouraging me to think beyond the standard environmental economics paradigm of 'market failure' and opened my eyes to the prospects of property rights as a means of generating incentives for more efficient use of environmental resources. This book is dedicated to Terry and Wolfgang.

I'm grateful to World Scientific Press for the opportunity to fulfil my goal and, of course, to my fellow authors who have joined me in this quest. The Property and Environment Research Centre (PERC) is also acknowledged for providing me with a Lone Mountain Fellowship that allowed me some time to work on this volume. Thanks are also due to Ngaire Bennett who provided assistance in proofing the chapters and to Chris Ulyatt for his fastidious copy-editing.

Jeff Bennett

1. The Principles and Practice of Protecting the Environment Privately

Jeff Bennett

There is no question that the environment is important to human society: so much so that without the environment, the human race could not exist. As a species, humanity is dependent on the environment, at the most basic of levels, for its sustenance and its shelter as well as providing a liveable 'habitat'. Humanity also enjoys the environment as a source of cultural identity and as a venue for recreation.[1] Yet there are frequently expressed concerns that the condition of the environment is in decline and that future generations of humanity will face a situation where the ability of the environment to meet the needs of society is compromised to the point where well-being will deteriorate. This is broadly expressed as a risk to the 'sustainability' of society.[2]

[1] See Millennium Ecosystem Assessment (2005) for a comprehensive documentation of the values of the environment that are enjoyed by humanity.

[2] The exact definition of what constitutes 'sustainability' is the subject of considerable conjecture. Pezzey (1992) contends that there are at least 400 competing definitions.

What must be questioned, therefore, is why something that is so valuable to society is at risk. Given that there is a strong and evident demand for the goods and services provided by the environment, why cannot society organise itself to ensure that demand is met?

The first point to be recognised in addressing this question is that 'the environment' is, in most circumstances, not an asset that you either have or you do not. Rather it is experienced across a range of conditions and capacities to supply the services which are of value to humanity. Furthermore, the environment is an asset that people generally do not want to experience either in its entirety or in its complete absence. Having a completely unspoilt environment means that humanity could not exist because its existence causes some environmental damage. Nor could humanity exist if there was no environment. This conflict between using the environment (so causing its deterioration) and protecting it for on-going use demonstrates that the environment is scarce. There is not enough of it to satisfy all the competing uses of it. The upshot of scarcity is the need to make choices.

The implication of environmental scarcity is that the sustainability risk faced by humanity results from poor choices: people make choices involving the environment such that its condition declines to the point where further losses would create costs to society that are greater than the benefits so enjoyed. In other words, the costs to society in terms of lost environmental services would be greater than the benefits enjoyed from using the environment.

Concerns about the sustainability of humanity are thus best characterised as questions about the ability of society to organise itself so that the choices about the use of the environment made by the billions of individuals that constitute humanity are in the best interests of the whole of society over the long term. This organisational task is remarkably complex. Not only are there billions of people involved but they are staggeringly heterogeneous in their tastes. Furthermore, there is a constellation of different types of environmental assets. It is hardly surprising that there may be a lack of coordination between those in society who want the goods and services provided by the environment in a protected state and those 'competitors' who want to use it in ways that cause it to decline.

The reason for this relates to the amount of information required to achieve coordination. To know whether or not one competing use for the environment is more valuable to society than another — as is required to ensure society is using the environment to best effect — knowledge regarding the availability of the environmental assets, the alternative uses that can be made of them, the people who would like to use them, how badly they would like to use them, etc., is required. For people to make choices, they need to gather and make sense of all this complex information. That is a costly process and, as a result, decisions are likely to be made without full knowledge. Because of the costs of collecting and dealing with information, decisions will never be made with full information and the coordination process will never be complete. However, the lower the costs of knowledge, the better the coordination process will be. A key goal of society should therefore be to develop mechanisms of coordination that keep knowledge costs as low as possible.

The logic regarding lower knowledge costs is not specific to choices regarding the environment. Wherever resources — such as labour and capital, as well as natural resources — are scarce and choices must be made, coordination across society is required. Information is the pre-requisite for successful coordination. The predominant mechanism used in the world today for coordinating individual choices regarding the use of resources is the market. People come together in markets to buy and sell: those who have a resource in excess of their requirements exchange with those who do not have enough. Through the process of voluntary exchange, resources move from lower valued uses to higher valued uses and all parties are advantaged. That means society as a whole is made better off.

But with every exchange there are knowledge costs involved. In the market context, these are often referred to as 'transaction costs'. Markets mostly work exceptionally well to the benefit of all parties because of their capacity to generate knowledge at low cost. Each party to a market transaction has an incentive to do better for themselves and through their actions delivers information regarding the strength of their preferences. Knowledge regarding relative benefits and costs becomes available to all. The timely free flow of information about who has what, and how much they value what they have, is voluntary, it facilitates exchange and generates gains for all. When the transaction costs exceed the expected gains from exchange, people withdraw from the exchange. This in turn is socially beneficial because if the costs of exchange are greater than the benefits, continuing to exchange would effectively be a waste of resources.

Markets do not eliminate transaction costs, they act to lower them. Exchange provides an incentive for individuals to divulge information. Furthermore, because there are gains to be enjoyed from exchange and transaction costs act as a barrier to achieving those gains, market participants have an incentive to develop ways of bringing those transaction costs down.

Markets involve exchange between individuals. But it is important to note that what is being exchanged in a market is the right to the use of a resource, commonly referred to as a property right. Unless a buyer has confidence in their rights to a resource, they are unlikely to engage in exchange. Likewise, a seller will not part with a resource unless they are confident of receiving the rights to compensation. Gaining that confidence involves transaction costs: buyers and sellers who are unfamiliar with each other will need to establish trust or engage in formal agreements involving penalties for any breach. Property rights therefore need to be well defined, closely defended and readily divestible. As the costs of defining, defending and divesting property rights increase, the chance of exchange occurring decreases.

The ability of markets to perform well as coordinating mechanisms is dependent on information. Property rights are important in determining the costs of gathering and processing that information. Hence, the processes involved in the formation of property rights are therefore worth investigating.

The first prospect for the formation of property rights is that individuals considering exchange get together as part of the exchange to define the rights over the resources involved and take measures to defend them. This type of formation is largely reliant on informal institutions (where 'institutions' refer to the 'rules of the game' as defined by North, 1990) such as trust, respect and honesty that are held in common amongst the parties involved in the trade. Where communities are relatively small and homogeneous in terms of their shared values, this type of property right formation process can be very low cost and precipitate welfare-improving exchange and well-coordinated societies (Ostrom, 1990).

However, when societies grow in size and heterogeneity, as Olson (1965) noted, such informal arrangements are likely to break down. More formal, externally driven institutions then become important in the process of property right formation (Kasper, Streit and Boettke, 2012). Centralised organisations such as elected governments, dictatorships, monarchies or central planning councils may form to enact laws that define rights to property (titles, contracts, fraud, etc.) as well as constitute other organisations to adjudicate over disputes (courts) and to enforce the laws (police, jails). In doing this, elements of the total transaction costs are born more generally (perhaps by the tax-paying base) to facilitate exchange. Greater certainty regarding exchange outcomes is afforded to buyers and sellers. Confidence is expanded, at least when the formal institutions are themselves trusted. The creation of such centralised formal institutions also allows a society to enjoy economies of scale in bearing transaction costs, given that the same institutions can underpin trillions of exchanges. As a result of the development of strong and reliable institutions, the exchange of formally held and enforced property rights, societies based on markets have prospered to unprecedented levels over the last 200 years. The success of this style of social coordination has been recognised through its adoption — in various manifestations — by almost every nation in the world.

Notwithstanding this success, it remains the case that some resources have not been included in the social coordination process that is characterised by the market exchange of property rights. In some cases, the complexities of establishing and policing rights are such that the transaction costs become prohibitive. Even the centralised process of defining and defending property rights cannot generate sufficient economies of scale to bring the transaction costs down to the point where they are less than the potential gains that could be enjoyed from the exchange of those rights. Such resources are therefore 'open access' because, without rights being defined and defended, anyone can use the resource without compensating those who bear the costs of that use.[3]

The consequence of open-access is overuse. People will exploit an open-access resource to the point where the additional value enjoyed from use falls to zero even though other potential users could gain positive values. The values of the forgone uses of a resource are ignored as people race to use the 'free' goods and services it provides.

Furthermore, because an open-access good is effectively 'free' to users, there is no incentive for anyone to go to the trouble of supplying the good. If a potential supplier knows that they will not be able to stop anyone from using their good or service, they also know that they will be hard-pressed to collect any revenue from their operation. Without revenue, there is no way that the costs they bear in supplying the good can be met, let alone enjoying any profit for their efforts. Without this profit incentive, supply will fall to zero. The process of social coordination provided by market exchange, whereby resources are allocated to their highest value uses, is lost.

Aspects of environmental resources — particularly where the environment must be in its protected state — have this open-access characteristic. There are considerable complexities in defining and defending rights to environmental assets such as the gene pool supplied by the biodiversity of a protected natural area and services such as the knowledge people enjoy from the continued existence of endangered species. It is either impossible or very costly to establish and to police such rights to ensure that people pay for their use of the resource so that those who bear the costs of supplying it are compensated for their efforts.

Consequently, some environmental resources will suffer from over use and others will simply not be supplied.

---

[3]This is the 'non-excludability' characteristic of a 'public good'.

For example, the air and waterways will be over-used as venues for the disposal of wastes. As 'free' resources people will use them irrespective of the costs imposed on others and their condition will progressively decline. Other environmental resources will not be supplied or existing supplies will be run down. For instance, endangered species will be hunted for their meat, feathers, tusks, etc., over which property rights are defined (so providing a supply incentive) without recognition of the values forgone as a result of their death. The latter are the existence benefits and gene pool assets for which rights are so complex and hence costly to define and defend. Species extinction is then possible given the lack of an incentive to supply.

This is where the concerns regarding the sustainability of the environment come to the fore. Without markets working to provide social coordination, the risk is that open-access elements of the environment will decline to levels that are not desirable from a society-wide perspective. The choices being made by individuals are leading to outcomes that are making society as a whole worse off.

In the mainstream of economic analysis, this situation is known as 'market failure': markets fail to deliver socially optimal allocations of environmental resources. With markets so 'discredited', analysts have looked for non-market alternatives to the social coordination challenge. Following the thinking of Pigou (1932), governments have moved away from the decentralised, market-based system of social coordination toward the centralised process of government action. This action involves centralised agencies developing interventions that range from the levying of taxes on activities that pollute waterways and the air, to the payment of subsidies to people who jointly provide open-access environmental goods alongside profit-generating goods right through to the direct provision of environmental goods and services by government. So, around the globe, governments have instituted pollution taxes and emissions trading schemes, payments to farmers who protect stream banks from erosion, restrictions on the production or consumption of environmentally harmful substances such as ozone-depleting chemicals, and have become the owners/managers of national park and nature reserve estates. Some of these interventions display some characteristics of markets or are supplanted onto market processes in order to modify the outcomes of markets. Others are more 'command and control' orientated, whereby governments regulate the activities of individuals. Others, still, involve government agencies becoming producers of environmental goods and services. In all cases, governments have supplanted or supplemented the market-based system of social coordination in an attempt to redress the susceptibility of the market process to produce 'unsustainable' outcomes.

What must not be forgotten in considering the centralised alternative to the decentralised, property rights, market-based process of social coordination is that it does not avoid the challenge of collecting and assimilating the information necessary to perform the coordination task. The difference is that the central authority responsible for developing and implementing the government's policy bears some of the information or transaction costs. Questions such as 'What should the tax rate be for nitrous oxide emissions?' and 'How many hectares of eucalypt forest should be set aside from logging and declared a National Park?' emerge in the policy process. And answers to these questions require information on the costs and benefits of alternative resource use strategies, if they are to result in policies that deliver net improvements in society's well-being. Essentially, the same type of information generated in a decentralised fashion by market processes has to be collected by government at a centralised level. The transaction costs of the market process have not been avoided. Rather they have been transferred. They have also transformed because while the information-generation process of the market place is voluntary and stimulated by self-interest, the centralised process faces a range of difficulties because it is imposed on people.

These difficulties lead to the first reason why the centralised approach to social coordination of environmental resource allocation can also be considered to 'fail'. The information collected and processed by central government agencies is likely to be far from 'complete'. Individuals may have incentives to misrepresent information to government in an effort to gain advantage from policy initiatives. Individuals may simply refuse to cooperate with government data-collection activities for fear of being disadvantaged. Put simply, the task of gathering information relating to the strength of peoples' preferences for different resource uses when they have no incentive to reveal them is complex and hence costly.

Collecting and processing information centrally is also time consuming. That means government actions will be informed by information that is out-of-date. With alternative resource allocations (and the values people hold for them) evolving and changing constantly, the risk is that government policy measures may not secure the goals intended for them.

If governments believe they have the capacity to overcome market 'failure' and deliver outcomes that are socially superior, they run the risk of developing the 'fatal conceit' that Hayek (1991) warned of in his arguments against the rise of socialism. The prospect of government 'failure' is at least as real as that of market 'failure'.

The informational deficit faced by government is only the first potential cause for government 'failure'. The argument regarding information makes an implicit assumption that the motives of centralised government are focused on improving the well-being of society. There are arguments that suggest this is not always the case. These arguments relate to the concept of 'rent-seeking'.

Where centralised authorities have the power to determine the allocation of resources, there is the prospect that groups of people or individuals will seek to gain profit from the use of those resources by influencing the decision-making process. That may be through the payment of bribes, the promise of political support or through the threat of harm. Given that those with responsibility for making decisions in government have motives that relate to their personal well-being (perhaps in addition to, or instead of, motives relating to the well-being of society) the likelihood is that the resource allocation choices they make will be influenced by the bribes and promises of support or harm. Hence, democratically elected officials seeking to stay in power are likely to support claims on resources made by interest groups that can increase their probability of re-election. Unelected officials may be more responsive to lump-sum payments into foreign bank accounts or fully funded luxury holidays. Even advisers in government agencies may not be exempt from rent-seeking. For instance, people employed in government agencies responsible for the environment may seek such jobs because they have a personal interest in protecting the environment and, when appointed, use their powers to achieve their personal goals. Those personal goals may not be consistent with achieving the greatest net social well-being. Rent-seeking is not just the province of those who seek to gain profit from the use of the environment: environmental conservationists also seek to influence government decisions by lobbying both elected and unelected officials.

Hence, centralised coordination faces the danger of committing to meet the demands of vested interest groups either through facilitating or restricting access to resources. Often when policies are implemented that cause costs to influential vested interest groups, governments will pay compensation to offset the costs borne. Because governments have the power to raise funds from taxpayers in ways that cause the burden to be shared widely (and hence not felt strongly by any individual) and the power to allocate those funds to groups that will benefit in significant ways, there is an on-going temptation to redistribute. Where governments can borrow funds cheaply, the temptation is further extended. The result can be a burgeoning public sector and a growing fiscal deficit. This situation is in marked contrast to that faced under the decentralised market-based coordination system which relies on the discipline provided by the need to match a buyer with a seller so that they achieve mutual gain every time a resource allocation decision is made.

What society faces, therefore, is a complex dilemma. The decentralised coordination process characterised by the voluntary exchange of property rights in competitive markets works well but not necessarily always, especially when environmental 'open-access' resources are concerned. The alternative, centralised process characterised by governments intervening to reallocate environmental resources so that 'sustainability' issues are avoided is also flawed: the motives of elected and un-elected officials may not be aligned with the best interests of society at large and even if they were, the informational challenges facing them are of great complexity.

This dilemma can be viewed as a continuum of alternative social coordination mechanisms for environmental resource allocation given that there are flaws apparent in both the decentralised and centralised models.

At one extreme is the individually-based model where there is no government intervention in allocating environmental resources. At the other extreme is the centralised 'command and control' model where all decisions affecting the environment are made by the government/dictator/central council, etc. In between there is a myriad of alternative mixtures of the two, with varying combinations and emphases placed on centralised and decentralised coordination. The history of environmental policy-making over the past century has been one in which the dominant paradigm has been toward centralisation. The economic arguments associated with 'market failure' (Pigou, 1932) were predominant. Hardin's (1968) 'The Tragedy of the Commons' coupled with Carson's (1962) *Silent Spring* gave intellectual credence and populist momentum, respectively, to the push toward centralised control. Public awareness of environmental issues grew steadily with both increases in income and educational attainments across the whole of society. In democracies, this stimulated political action to increase government intervention in the name of environmental causes. Even in totalitarian states, public disquiet regarding deteriorating environmental conditions could not always be ignored by those in power for fear of civil disobedience. The shift toward centralisation that resulted largely ignored concerns regarding 'government failure'.

However, more recently, there has been a growing recognition both of the potential perils of moving too far toward the centralised, 'public sector' extreme and the potential advantages of shifting environmental resource use coordination more towards the decentralised, 'private sector' end of the coordination spectrum. The fall of the Berlin Wall and the recognition that environmental conditions in the former Soviet Union and its eastern European allies were demonstrably worse than in the West, gave recognition in environmental circles to the Hayekian arguments against centralised control.

Conceptual thinking in support of decentralised coordination was also advanced by the work of Coase (1960) who pointed out the reciprocal nature of issues arising from the over-use of open access resources. While Pigou (1932) framed over-use in terms of one party's use of a resource causing uncompensated 'externality' costs for another party, the Coasian position is to view the situation as two parties competing for access to the same resource. For example, pollution of a waterway would be viewed in Pigovian thinking as the polluter creating a cost to swimmers (who, therefore, should be compensated), the Coasian approach is to see the waterway as a resource that can be used either by swimmers or polluters. If swimmers have the rights to the waterway, their use of the resource causes a cost to the polluter who has to use a more expensive means of disposing of their wastes (Anderson, 2004). What the Coasian way of thinking does is to highlight the prospect of negotiated solutions to the use conundrum. In particular, the Coase Theorem states that it does not matter who has the right to the waterway, the outcome of the negotiations between polluters and swimmers will be an efficient use of the resource. The caveat on that rule is that there are no transaction costs. In this way, Coase was also responsible for recognising the importance of transaction costs in the negotiation process.

Coase's thinking was complemented by Ostrom's (1990) work on common property resources.[4] Using evidence from around the globe, Ostrom demonstrated that communities can develop coordinating (governance) mechanisms for managing open access resources where it would be otherwise expected that the 'tragedy of the

[4] Common property resources are open access resources which are 'rival' in consumption. This means that anyone can access a resource and that access means the resource is no longer available to others. An example would be a forest that is accessible to all, but once trees in the forest are harvested, they are no longer available to anyone else. This is in contrast to a 'public good' that is not only open access (non-excludable) but 'non-rival' in consumption: anyone can use a public good and its use by one person does not preclude others from enjoying it. An example is the knowledge that an endangered species continues to exist.

commons' would prevail. In particular, Ostrom showed that the types of coordination structures that have evolved to manage open access resources vary considerably in response to the particulars of each resource use context (Ostrom, 2010). The conclusion is that one size does not fit all. However, the research has yielded some common characteristics of successful community-based governance arrangements. These revolve around the mechanisms used to define rules of exclusion and use within the relevant community group. Limits to the effectiveness of community-based rules in achieving successful open access resource use are also noted and these reflect Olson's (1965) conclusions relating to the size and heterogeneity of the group that constitutes the community.

The significance of property rights in negotiations between parties competing for access to open access resources was made apparent by Demsetz (1967). He recognised the importance of transaction costs in achieving successful outcomes in those negotiations and concluded that property rights emerge when the transaction cost savings they allow are greater than the costs incurred in their establishment. This sets the parameters for the establishment of property rights, either informally as part of negotiations between competing parties or more formally by centralised authorities.

These fundamental understandings — along with contributions from many other scholars — form the foundations of 'new institutional economics' (NIE). With its blending of contributions from the disciplines of law and economics NIE is used to analyse the consequences of different institutional and organisational arrangements particularly in circumstances involving open access resources such as elements of the environment.

The results of this shift in thinking from centralised social coordination of environmental resource use toward more decentralised resource allocation processes are evident across a wide array of contexts.

Community-based natural resource management (CBNRM) along Ostrom's line of thought has emerged to take over roles formerly taken by government authorities: for instance, Suich, Child and Spenceley (2009) provide examples from southern Africa where the transition from colonialism has been accompanied by an evolution of wildlife and habitat management. Private companies and clubs and societies have been established, or have extended the range of their activities, to supply environmental services by buying land to be set aside as protected areas (Bennett, 2012).

In other contexts where property rights have not existed, efforts have been made to extend the definitions and defence of property rights. There are on-going changes in the costs associated with defining, defending and trading property rights. Often these changes arise because of technological advances. For instance, grazing lands in the western US ceased to be open access once barbed wire was invented, providing a cheap and effective way of excluding stock. In more recent times, satellite-based Automatic Identification Systems (AISs)[5] have been developed to allow fishing vessels to be tracked and penalised for fishing outside allocated waters. The prospect is, therefore, that transaction costs can be reduced over time and more environmental resources shifted from open access to market allocated.

Governments have also sought ways to make a shift away from command-and-control style regulations in environmental resource management. In the context of pollution control, regulations on the extent of emissions have been replaced by emissions trading schemes (Stavins, 1998). These schemes effectively involve the definition of new property rights — the right to pollute an air space or waterway. The controlling authority sets the maximum amount of emissions to establish scarcity of the resource and then the parties responsible for the pollution must seek to buy a right to pollute if they do not develop ways to control their pollution. Trading in these rights takes place amongst polluters to ensure that cost-effective pollution control is achieved. With the establishment of property rights to the resource that is being polluted, market forces are used to improve environmental resource allocation.

In the context of natural resource management, Payment for Environmental Service (PES) schemes have been introduced in

[5] See http://www.imo.org/OurWork/Safety/Navigation/Pages/AIS.aspx [accessed 15 June 2014]

various formats, but fundamentally in an attempt to provide greater market discipline in the payment of subsidies to parties with a capacity to provide environmental services who otherwise would not (Tacconi, 2012). In PES schemes, central authorities seek to act as intermediaries or brokers to lower the transaction costs that separate buyers and sellers of environmental services. Actions can include the provision of research results that demonstrate the relationships between prospective sellers' natural resource management actions (for instance tree planting along a river) and outcomes that a buyer would value (improved water quality downstream), so assisting in establishing property rights. Alternatively, the authority may act as a clearing house of proposed actions to allow buyers a low-cost way of searching for potential sellers. All the various formats essentially involve (to a greater or lesser degree) the introduction of market elements into an otherwise centralised allocative process.

*****

The chapters of this book contribute to a better understanding of the trend toward greater decentralisation of the environmental resource use coordination process: the shift away from the dominant position of the public sector toward achieving protection of the environment by private-sector action.

The following chapters are divided into two parts. The first includes chapters that focus on environmental protection initiatives that involve a minimal role for the public sector. While the fundamental role of government in providing the underpinning institutional structures for the operation of society is acknowledged, these chapters explore the prospects for the private sector to initiate and sustain nature conservation. The chapters in the second part pay attention to collaborative arrangements between the public and the private sector, mostly in cases where governments have sought to harness the strengths of private-sector incentives in achieving environmental policy goals.

The first part of the book begins with a contribution from **Anderson and Watson.** They make it clear in **Chapter 2** that the challenges posed by economists who favour the 'market failure' approach to environmental issues are in fact opportunities. They advance the view that dynamic markets coupled with dynamic ecological systems leave open the space for environmental entrepreneurs to achieve environmental and financial advantage. Using a range of examples to illustrate their points, they argue that governments should make the most of 'enviropreneurs' in achieving the environmental protection goals of society by removing regulatory obstructions that act to inhibit their innovative approaches to defining, enforcing and trading property rights in environmental assets and services.

Two types of private-sector provision of terrestrial ecosystem protection are set out by **Bennett** in **Chapter 3**. Using Australian and German examples, he shows how not-for-profit enterprises have been able to achieve significant holdings of conservation land. His example from the United States involves for-profit businesses undertaking the management of protected areas. There, the areas remain in public ownership, however private companies are contracted to, and pay for the right to, perform significant management tasks. Bennett argues that these examples demonstrate that the traditional 'public good' arguments used to justify public-sector provision of environmental goods and services are too generalised. Private-sector opportunities exist but can be 'crowded out' by relatively inefficient public-sector operations.

Fisheries are the focus of **Chapter 4**. The role of technological change in delivering improvements in the environmental impacts of both capture and culture fisheries is considered by **Grafton, Segerson and Squires**. They look at the drivers of that technological change and conclude that profit-motivated market forces, both for buyers and sellers, are important contributors to 'green innovation'. While stressing the potential role for public policy in stimulating change, they also point to the significance of private–public partnerships. Included in this is the role to be played by civil society. Examples of measures taken to reduce bycatch are used to illustrate their arguments.

Michael 't Sas-Rolfes tackles the issue of markets for biodiversity in **Chapter 5**. He draws on his experience of protecting rhinos in game reserves in southern Africa to make the point that the bottom-up approach to conservation, facilitated by institutions such as private property rights, has been far more successful than the top-down approach epitomised by CITES regulations regarding the trade in endangered species. However, he makes it clear that private nature reserves are by no means an Africa-only phenomenon and makes mention of the Australian cases detailed by Bennett in Chapter 3. He also highlights the significance of technological advances in the definition and defence of private property rights in a similar vein to that described by Grafton *et al.* in Chapter 4.

Water is increasingly being recognised as a resource that has significance for environmental values as well as extractive or consumptive uses. The ways in which the private sector has emerged as a buyer and seller of environmental services from water in the Murray–Darling River Basin in Australia is reviewed by **O'Keefe and Crase** in **Chapter 6.** While the review indicates some private-sector action in the Basin, the conclusion drawn is that it is limited and faces barriers resulting from the complexity of the coordination task involved in achieving basin-wide goals. However, precedents have been established for expansion.

In **Chapter 7, Willis** considers the case of cultural and historic assets. He points out that around the world there are numerous examples of such assets being protected by private owners. However, he notes the dilemma regarding the pricing of public access to stately homes, art collections and the like when it is the revenue from visitors that enables their continued protection. If there is no congestion at the site, marginal costs of provision are zero and any positive price charged by a private owner will mean that some will be excluded from enjoying use of the asset. The choice may be between this welfare loss and that which would be associated with inefficient or non-existent public sector supply.

Chapter 8 is the last chapter in the first part of the book. Its focus is on the potential for buyers and sellers in markets for food to deliver improvements in environmental management. **Umberger, Anders and Goddard** provide a comprehensive review of initiatives being undertaken in the food sector to link consumer demand for food that is produced in an environmentally sustainable way through to suppliers. They consider strategies such as eco-labelling and environmental 'foot-printing' right through to the 'de-marketing' of products by which suppliers encourage customers to buy less in an attempt to capture market share through enhanced reputation. Their conclusion is that 'private-sector initiatives can lead to positive environmental outcomes' but they are unwilling to deny the prospect of some environmental promotions being 'greenwash'.

The extent to which the public sector plays a more direct role in protecting the environment is more prominent in the cases considered in the second part of the book. The emphasis is more on the relative importance of the private and the public sectors in securing environmental improvements when the institutional precursors to private-sector engagement (such as well-defined and defended property rights) are in some way compromised.

The first chapter in this part focuses on PES schemes. These have achieved some degree of prominence over the last two decades as avenues for private-sector involvement in the protection of the environment. They have been implemented in developed and less-developed countries with the additional goal of supporting the incomes of people living in environmentally sensitive areas. **Scheufele** provides an overview of such schemes in **Chapter 9**. She draws the conclusion that the performance of most PES schemes leaves much to be desired, yet they offer considerable promise if designed to release the efficiency incentive advantages of markets. The limit to the potential offered is in the extent of the transaction costs required to establish and sustain the PES market.

The emphasis that Scheufele gives to transaction costs in the formation of PES schemes is taken up by **Garrick and O'Donnell** in **Chapter 10**. They investigate the role of the private sector in the acquisition and management of water for environmental flows in the contexts of the western US and the Murray–Darling Basin in Australia. In part they provide an alternative analysis to that provided by O'Keefe and Crase in Chapter 6, but their approach is to consider the role of the private sector in providing 'legitimacy' to water trades for the environment. The dual concepts of transaction costs and environmental governance are advanced as the means to understand best how private-sector entities have become involved in the environmental water stories of both jurisdictions.

Transaction costs are also a key point of departure for **Coggan** in **Chapter 11.** Brokers, or market intermediaries, are common in modern economies. They exist as a means of facilitating trade by lowering transaction costs through specialisation. Coggan argues that there is a role for brokers in the formation of markets for environmental goods and services. She illustrates the types of roles brokers can play in a number of different market contexts, making note of the distinctive role played by private-sector entities even when markets have been structured under government direction.

The specific use of auctions to distribute government funds to private sector suppliers of environmental services is the focus of **Rolfe** in **Chapter 12.** He outlines the concepts that underpin conservation auctions and gives examples from the array of experience generated from applications in Australia. The chapter thus builds on the material on the more generic notion of PES schemes presented in Chapter 9. Rolfe concludes that while the Australian experience is extensive, relative to the total amount of public funds expended on environmental conservation, it is minor and is in decline. The 'thinness' of the markets that have been established under the auction schemes would suggest that private-sector suppliers have not been overly enamoured by the schemes.

Kuhfuss, Le Coent, Préget and Thoyer investigate the concept of conservation auctions in the European context. Specifically, in **Chapter 13** they consider the performance of European Union (EU) initiatives to contract farmers to change their management strategies toward more environmentally orientated options. They conclude that many of the desired outcomes of the contracts have not been achieved. The solution they suggest for this performance deficit is to shift the focus of private-sector involvement from the individual farmer to groups of adjacent farmers. The goal is to ensure changes in on-farm management are coordinated across multiple farms and that contracts are written with a focus on outcomes. The point made is that private action to protect the environment need not be limited to single individuals taking action. Rather, 'collective' action may be required to achieve goals that depend on change across a broader geographical region.

Tacconi's contribution in **Chapter 14** focuses on global climate change as a driver for private sector environmental initiatives. He specifically considers the issue of deforestation in developing countries as a source of greenhouse gas emissions and the actions of firms to curb those emissions. His prognosis is that markets for carbon emissions are thinly traded and that the only action that has come about has been precipitated by non-government organisations' (NGOs') 'name and shame' campaigns or collaborative industry/ NGO arrangements. Tacconi concludes that government initiatives have not been successful in curbing deforestation in developing countries. But he also has concerns about NGO activities in terms of the impacts on forest-dependent communities.

Governments can effectively trigger a demand for environmental protection from the private sector by imposing conditions on resource development projects. By requiring companies to 'offset' harm done to the environment as a result of developments, a demand for off-site environmental protection or restoration is created. **Gillespie** critically reviews the offsetting policy of the New South Wales Government in **Chapter 15**. He acknowledges the offset mechanism as a means of rewarding private-sector land managers for their environmental management initiatives. However, he points to flaws in the design of the policy and suggests reforms that could be implemented to improve the interaction between environmental services supply and demand.

Greenhalgh and Selman turn their attention to the protection of water resources in **Chapter 16**. They outline the ways in which water quality trading schemes have been developed in a number of contexts through public-sector agencies setting pollution level 'targets'. The flexibility in achieving those targets that is afforded by trading between polluters is applauded: The cost effectiveness of pollution control achieved through trading is beneficial to the private-sector operators as well as to the community at large.

Bibliography

Anderson, T. (2004). Donning Coase-Coloured Glasses: A Property Rights View of Natural Resource Economics, *Australian Journal of Agricultural and Resource Economics*, 48(3), pp. 445–462.

Bennett, J. (2012). Coase Rules OK? Exploring Prospects for Private Sector Environmental Protection, *Economic Record*, 88(281), pp. 165–302.

Carson, R. (1962). *Silent Spring*, Houghton Mifflin, Chicago.

Coase, R.H. (1960). The Problem of Social Cost, *Journal of Law and Economics*, 3(1), pp. 1–44.

Demsetz, H. (1967). Toward a Theory of Property Rights, *American Economic Review*, 57(2), pp. 347–359.

Hardin, G. (1968). The Tragedy of the Commons, *Science*, 162(3859), pp. 1243–1248.

Hayek, F.A. (1991). *The Fatal Conceit: The Errors of Socialism*, The University of Chicago Press, Chicago.

Kasper, W., Streit, M. and Boettke, P. (2012). *Institutional Economics: Property, Competition, Policies*, Edward Elgar, Cheltenham.

Millennium Ecosystem Assessment (2005). *Ecosystems and Human Well-Being: Synthesis*, Island Press, Washington.

North, D. (1990). *Institutions, Institutional Change and Economic Performance*, Cambridge University Press, Cambridge.

Olson, M. (1965). *The Logic of Collective Action: Public Goods and the Theory of Groups*, Harvard University Press, Cambridge.

Ostrom, E. (1990). *Governing the Commons: The Evolution of Institutions for Collective Action*, Cambridge University Press, Cambridge.

Ostrom E. (2010). Beyond Markets and States: Polycentric Governance of Complex Economic Systems, *American Economic Review*, 100(3), pp. 641–672.

Pezzey, J. (1992). Sustainability: An Interdisciplinary Guide, *Environmental Values*, 1, pp. 321–362.

Pigou, A.C. (1932). *The Economics of Welfare*, 4th edition, Macmillan and Co., London.

Stavins, R. (1998). What Can We Learn from the Grand Policy Experiment? Lessons from SO_2 Allowance Trading, *The Journal of Economic Perspectives*, 12(3), pp. 69–88.

Suich, H., Child, B. and Spenceley, A. (2009). *Evolution and Innovation in Wildlife Conservation: Parks and Game Reserves to Transfrontier Conservation Areas*, Earthscan, London.

Tacconi, L. (2012). Redefining Payments for Environmental Services, *Ecological Economics*, 73(C), pp. 29–36.

2. Dynamic Ecology and Dynamic Markets: The Role of Environmental Entrepreneurs

Terry L. Anderson and Lawrence R. Watson

Entrepreneurs are relegated to a black box in economics because most economic models focus on equilibrium conditions, whereas entrepreneurs thrive in and often create disequilibrium. Leaving the entrepreneur out of the analysis is particularly inappropriate regarding environmental issues because nature is constantly changing, as are the demands society places on nature. The purpose of this chapter is to bring environmental entrepreneurs — enviropreneurs — to the analysis of private environmental protection by integrating them into free market environmentalism.

Markets and nature are both subject to dynamic forces that are never in equilibrium. Regarding nature, ecologists increasingly recognise that there is no 'state of nature' which would exist in the absence of humans or to which nature would return if left alone by humans. Whether it is cosmic or geological forces that would alter the earth's resources — air, water, land, flora and fauna — or Darwinian evolutionary forces, nature is in a perpetual state of flux. Similarly, Austrian economists recognise that there is no stable market equilibrium because markets are an amalgamation of individual human actions dependent on subjective valuation of demand and opportunity costs.[1] Both nature and markets are also continually changing along with the particular circumstance of time and place that make local knowledge indispensable (Hayek, 1945). In this context, efforts to maintain balance in the environment or the marketplace are nonsensical and usually counter-productive in that they stifle creativity, innovation and inevitable change.

Ecologist Daniel Botkin has been particularly influential in recognising that ecological models have oversimplified ecological systems and ignored the importance of dynamic organisms. In Botkin's (2012, p. 3) words, 'We have tended to view nature as a digital camera's still life, much like a tourist-guide illustration of La Salute; but nature with and without people is and always has been a moving-picture show, much like the continually changing and complex patterns of the water in the Venetian lagoon.' Botkin asks, 'How real is the concept of a balance of Nature? What is the connection between people and nature? What are our roles in and obligations to nature ... ?' (2012, p. 8).

In the economics profession, Schumpeter (1934) is noted for having brought entrepreneurs into the mix by arguing that they create 'winds of destruction', but it is also appropriate to think of them in a Darwinian sense, filling niches created by changing human values and changing environmental conditions. Entrepreneurs avoid well-established markets where profits have been competed away, instead searching for nascent markets where others have not ventured. For the entrepreneur, the lure of new products, new production processes, and new resource uses is the driving force. As Ridley (2009) puts it, markets driven by entrepreneurship are 'spontaneously

[1] For a concise discussion of the fundamentals of Austrian economics, see Boettke, P. J. Available at http://www.econlib.org/library/Enc/AustrianSchoolofEconomics.html [Accessed 15 September 2014].

self-ordered through the actions of individuals, rather than ordained by a monarch or a parliament'.

The provision of environmental goods and services is a space rife with the potential for entrepreneurial rewards. Rising incomes have increased the demand for environmental quality and environmental amenities generally known as ecosystem services. Such amenities and services include clean air and water which reduce illness, wetlands which reduce water filtration costs, forests which sequester carbon, and open space which provides recreation. In addition to new demands flowing from and shaping dynamic markets, dynamic environmental conditions continually open up new opportunities for enviropreneurs. Whether it is changing relative prices of natural resources — for example, cheap natural gas causing a shift away from coal — or changing human values — for example, demand for wildlife habitat causing a shift from livestock production — enviropreneurs see environmental problems as environmental opportunities. To capture those opportunities, enviropreneurs must acquire: (i) the scientific and local knowledge necessary to respond to dynamic ecological conditions; (ii) the economic knowledge imbedded in prices; and (iii) the control of resources, either by purchasing existing property rights or by creating new ones, and shift those resources from lower to higher valued uses.

Consider the production and marketing of ecosystem services. Production requires a scientific understanding of what inputs are necessary to provide the service, as well as an understanding of the local conditions under which provision of the service is most profitable. For example, if forest carbon sequestration is the goal, is it young or old forests which sequester the most carbon and how will this change over time? If it is young forests, what are the trade-offs between carbon sequestration and the potential for greater biodiversity in mature forests or greater lumber production? On the marketing side, who will buy the ecosystem services, and how will contracts for the provision of those services be written and enforced? Will wealthy people in the United States pay for carbon sequestration in the Amazon? If they do pay, what happens if those forests burn or are cut down? Because the answers to these questions are not simple — indeed, if they were, the potential for entrepreneurship would be nil — answering them provides fertile ground for the enviropreneur.

The purpose of this chapter is to better integrate entrepreneurship into environmental markets and thereby create a better understanding of the tools necessary for enviropreneurs to produce environmental goods and services in the presence of dynamic ecology and dynamic markets. The chapter begins by emphasising how important property rights are to environmental entrepreneurship; without clearly defined, enforceable, and transferable property rights, contracting for environmental goods and services is impossible. Contracts describe how and whether resource owners capture gains from trade and define the voluntary distribution of those gains between the contracting parties.

After describing a theoretical framework for environmental entrepreneurship, the chapter then applies the framework to several case studies of enviropreneurs harnessing property rights and contracts to produce environmental goods and services. The important lessons derived from this chapter are:

(1) Property rights must exist before enviropreneurs can act, and where they are lacking, entrepreneurs play a key role in defining and enforcing them;
(2) Enviropreneurs contract with resource owners to reallocate resources to higher valued and often new uses; and
(3) Enviropreneurs find innovative ways of measuring, monitoring, and marketing environmental goods and services to protect the environment privately.

2.1. Contracting for the Environment

Nobel laureate Coase (1937) was one of the first modern economists to focus attention on the ways in which firms reduce transaction costs by supplanting market contracts with hierarchical, internal management decisions. Although Coase did not discuss how the entrepreneur fits into the firm, Barzel (1997) picked up where Coase left off by suggesting that entrepreneurs are the actors who recognise and capture the returns associated with transaction cost savings. The motivation and reward for the entrepreneur come in the form of his or her claim on the residual, the return left after other input owners have been paid for their contributions to the production process. In addition, as emphasised by Alchian and Demsetz (1972), the entrepreneur must measure and monitor contributions of other input owners to collective firm output. Hence, the entrepreneur, as the 'residual claimant', is the person whose challenge is to measure and monitor new input combinations, measure and monitor the marketing of new goods and services, or both.

Because entrepreneurs are producing new goods and services and using new input combinations, contracting presents new risks and challenges, and this is especially true for environmental entrepreneurship. Consider a simple example of land used for agricultural production. Suppose that an individual is leasing land for crop production, an activity which has been well established on the land, for which the production process is well understood, and from which the returns are well known because the price of the output is determined in an open and competitive market. In such a case, the entrepreneur can only gain by differentiating her product or changing the production process so as to reduce costs and earn additional rents. In new markets, such as those for environmental goods and services, the enviropreneur has a much broader range of activities because neither the products nor the production process have been refined through competition.

Contrast agricultural production in a competitive market like wheat with leasing land for producing ecosystem services, such as endangered species habitat. For ecosystem service production the entrepreneur wanting to lease land for ecosystem service production must define what she wants to produce and then determine the 'production function' for that use; in other words, she must be able to estimate and measure the relative contributions of land, labour, and capital to the final output. She must determine what the final output will be worth and develop contracts for marketing that final output, whether directly to individual consumers, not-for-profit (non-governmental) firms, or governmental agencies. Finally, she must recognise the dynamic nature of both ecology and markets. For example, if climate change causes the species of interest to move to a new location, owning land in the old location will be of little value. Moreover, if people no longer value the species for which preservation efforts have been undertaken, it may not be possible to afford the resources necessary for protection. In short, dynamic ecology and dynamic markets require that the enviropreneur be nimble.

If property rights are well-defined and enforced, the entrepreneur can contract with the owners to get them to change how resources are used or purchase the resources from those owners and change resource use. If they are not, the entrepreneur must create them, meaning he must define the boundaries of the property and exclude others from using it. Water rights provide a quintessential example (Anderson, Scarborough and Watson, 2012). Where water is abundant riparian water rights, giving all landowners along a stream rights to an undiminished quantity and quality of water, work well. However, if water is scarce, an upstream water user can affect the flow for those downstream. To resolve conflicting or competing uses, property rights must be defined, and enforced, lest the tragedy of the commons results in overuse. This explains why pioneers coming to the arid western United States abandoned the riparian system of the East and adopted the prior appropriation system (Anderson and Hill, 2004).

Contracting issues are particularly important for enviropreneurs, because many environmental goods and services are subject to the free-rider problem. That is to say, goods such as clean water or air, endangered species preservation, or greenhouse gas reduction can be enjoyed by people who do not pay for it. Once clean air and water are produced, anyone in the vicinity can enjoy it; once endangered species are preserved, people can get satisfaction out of knowing those species continue to exist; and greenhouse gases reduced in one location reduces them worldwide. Enviropreneurs trying to capture rents in producing such goods will be under-compensated for their efforts if they cannot find ways of contracting — privately or collectively through government — with potential free-riding consumers.

By bundling a private good, such as housing, with a public good, such as open space protected by a nearby conservation easement, environmental entrepreneurs can overcome at least some of the free-rider problem. Thus, the question is not whether the enviropreneur can force every beneficiary to pay, but whether the provision of the environmental good or service is optimal. The relevant question is whether enviropreneurs can devise, draft, and enforce contracts with enough beneficiaries to cover their costs.

2.2. Enviropreneurship in Action

To the enviropreneur, ill-defined or non-existent property rights, contracting, and negotiation are not problems, but are opportunities. Whether the enviropreneur can profit from environmental opportunities will depend on the costs and benefits of better defining and enforcing property rights and contracting for those rights (see Demsetz, 1967; Anderson and Hill, 1975; Anderson and Hill, 2004; Libecap, 1989). Rising environmental values, whether due to higher incomes or changing preferences, attract entrepreneurial attention. But high asset values and emerging demands may not be sufficient if the costs of defining rights and enforcing contracts cannot be overcome. The following examples illustrate the potential for environmental entrepreneurship.[2]

2.2.1. *Contracting for land conservation*

One of the fastest growing areas where environmentalists have been entrepreneurs is land conservation. In 2008, approximately 1,700 land trusts held more than 37 million acres (14,973,369 ha) under conservation easements, up from 867 land trusts holding 866,000 acres (350,458 ha) under easements in 1990. These easements are

[2] This section was adapted from Anderson (2009).

contractual arrangements between landowners and land trusts placing limits on how land can be used. Operating like any business, land trusts provide a good — open space, forest preservation, endangered species habitat, or cultural and historic preservation, to mention a few — which they market to members, landowners, and public agencies.

The challenge for the land trust is to find ways of optimising the costs of supplying the conservation values. Doing so requires that land conservation entrepreneurs focus on the production function for the good and the costs of monitoring contracts with owners. Hence all of the characteristics of entrepreneurship described earlier come into play.

To understand the production function question, contrast the preservation of open space with provision of habitat for an endangered species. Open space typically means that land does not have buildings on it. Hence the land trust need only write an easement that limits the number of buildings. Measuring and monitoring that contract is quite simple, requiring only an occasional drive-by or aerial survey.

Endangered species habitat, in contrast to open space, is more likely to require land with specific characteristics, if not specific parcels, and stricter limits on land use. Indeed, if this were not the case, the species would not likely be endangered in the first place. The environmental entrepreneur wanting to save an endangered species will have to carefully specify the habitat requirements, monitor land use, and measure results. Given that inputs are likely to be unique, the potential for post-contractual opportunism is greater. For these reasons, any land trust interested in protecting endangered species in addition to open space will have more contractual entrepreneurial functions to perform and is more likely to become a residual claimant by owning the land. Research by Parker (2002) supports these hypotheses. He concludes that land trusts providing scenic values or preserving working lands tend to hold conservation easements and land trusts providing recreational amenities or engaging in active management tend to own land outright. These findings are consistent with a theory of entrepreneurship which suggests that residual claimancy disciplines the entrepreneur in his monitoring function and reduces the potential for post-contractual opportunism. In Parker's (2002, p. 15) words:

> The findings suggest that land trusts reduce their costs of providing environmental amenities by considering transaction costs and specialization in their decision to own land or hold conservation easements... . Though land trusts are not-for-profit organizations, they face budget constraints that give them incentives to search for ways of reducing costs.

The dynamic nature of ecology, particularly in the context of projected climate change and species migration, further complicates the ownership versus easement analysis. Conservation easements that restrict land uses in perpetuity could produce little in the way of conservation outputs if, for example, a particular species of concern migrates out of the region or if development pressure subsides. Nonetheless, the land trust would be contractually bound to monitor and enforce the easement terms, thus incurring significant economic costs for little conservation gain.

Dynamic ecology requires that the enviropreneur consider these possibilities and write contractual terms that efficiently allocate the dynamic risks. Because perpetual easements cannot account for dynamic changes over time, some entrepreneurial land trusts are already exploring ways to sell development rights back to landowners and using the proceeds to generate and capture higher conservation returns elsewhere. Option contracts offer another way to share dynamic risks.

2.2.2. *Bees for water*

Another example of innovative contracting for ecosystem services comes from Bolivia (see Asquith, 2006). In the Los Negros Valley, Natura Bolivia is a non-governmental organisation led by environmental entrepreneur Maria Teresa Vargas. The organisation found a contractual way of paying upstream land users to change their land use practices to provide downstream farmers with more, cleaner water. The farmers raise vegetable crops such as carrots, tomatoes, and lettuce for local markets using irrigation water from the Los Negros River. In the upstream catchment basin, officially designated a national park with abundant flora and fauna, illegal land incursions, mainly for logging, have reduced the cloud forest cover. This resulted in lower water flows in the river, as well as impacts on wildlife habitat. Because of the remoteness of the park and the lack of enforcement resources, the downstream farmers could not rely on the government to guarantee their water supply.

Natura Bolivia had to find an alternative. As Asquith (2006, p. 6) put it, 'Natura's challenge was therefore to try to provide security of contracts and markets and clarify property rights in a situation where neither security, clarity, or the resources needed to provide them existed.' Its solution was to provide the upstream land users with an alternative way of making money from the land, a way that reduced logging and increased downstream water quantity and quality. The alternative was to provide one beehive to the upstream land users in return for their pledge to stop logging on 10 ha. From 60 beehives protecting 600 ha in 2003, the project grew to 210 beehives protecting 2,100 ha in 2006.

The beauty of this form of payment is that the contract has self-enforcing elements. Because the bees require forest for honey production and the honey production is more profitable than logging, upstream land users, illegal though their land claims may be, have an incentive to protect the cloud forest which ensures adequate flows in the river. Additionally, with the land more valuable for beekeeping, the upstream land users are trying to better define and enforce their rights to the land. To do this, they have sought Natura Bolivia's help demarcating land boundaries so that they can better control land use. They are using Global Positioning System (GPS) to identify boundaries, plotting the boundaries on a satellite image-based land use map, and fencing the parcels with barbed wire once all of the neighbours agree on the boundaries. Again quoting Asquith (2006, p. 6), 'The farmers explained that in addition to allowing them to keep their cattle out of environmentally sensitive areas, enclosing their land with barbed wire would help them strengthen their existing land claims.'

Given that the ultimate goal is more, cleaner water in the river, measurement and monitoring of flows is required. Farmers undertake twice-weekly measurements of water depth, periodic calibrations of velocity, and daily measurements of rainfall. Asquith reckons that having the landowners take the measurements helps 'to minimise data collection costs, to increase local credibility in the data, and to try to ensure the scheme's self-sustainability.' If water did not increase because upstream loggers did not continue protecting the land, sanctions would be imposed locally and beehives would be taken back.

To get this project started, Vargas added one more element of entrepreneurship, namely a funding mechanism to overcome the potential free-rider problem. Initial funding for the project depended on a charitable contribution to Natura Bolivia from international foundations. The initial grants provided a return to her on her entrepreneurship as well as funds for the initial purchase of beehives. To more closely connect farmers with upstream loggers, she was able to convince farmers to impose taxes on themselves through the local government water agency. The proceeds were then used to buy beehives and barbed wire and to help with contractual enforcement.

In summary, Natura Bolivia, along with Vargas's entrepreneurship, developed a way of paying for ecosystem services where property rights were not clear, and contracts between suppliers and demanders were non-existent. The innovative contractual arrangement whereby beehives and barbed wire were traded for more, cleaner water:

(1) Made both downstream farmers and upstream loggers residual claimants to the rents on both sides of the contract;
(2) Provided a way of measuring and monitoring the ecosystem services provided; and
(3) Encouraged self-enforcement to help minimise transaction costs.

Drawing an analogy with the American West, Asquith concludes that Bolivian environmental entrepreneur Maria Teresa Vargas is 'developing and strengthening local property rights — this time not through a posse, but through institution building, an innovative conservation and development scheme, and good old-fashioned barbed wire' (Asquith 2006, p. 6).

2.2.3. *Buy that fish a drink*

The old adage that whiskey's for drinking and water's for fighting has become increasingly true as environmental demands compete more with agricultural, municipal, and industrial ones. Whether it is clean water for drinking, more water for aquatic life such as endangered salmon, or instream flows for recreation, battle lines have been drawn. Examples include the contentious fight over water for Mono Lake in California, where environmental groups used the public trust doctrine to deny Los Angeles the right to continue diverting water for urban citizens, or over water for the Klamath River in Oregon, where environmental groups used the *Endangered Species Act* to shut off flows to farmers for irrigation. In both of these examples, and many others like them, the resultant gains for the environment must be compared to the legal costs of fighting, not to mention the wear and tear on the social fabric.

Recognising these costs, some environmental entrepreneurs are using property rights and contracting to achieve better results for the environment, the economy, and society (see Scarborough and Lund, 2007). The first problem these entrepreneurs have had to overcome is changing the legal constraints on water marketing. Because water in the American West is scarcer than in the East, western frontier entrepreneurs devised a system of water allocation very different from that in the East. Known as the prior appropriation doctrine, this system allocates water rights on the basis of first in time-first in use; in other words, the first people to divert water for use in their gold mining operations or for irrigating their fields have priority over later claimants. It is important to emphasise that diversion was a requirement for establishing a water right. Diversion ensured that water would be put to a 'beneficial use,' which meant water was applied to commodity production or municipal demands in order to prove and maintain that users had a legitimate right. In short, as the prior appropriation system was established, water had to be diverted in order to maintain a right to it.

The rising demand for environmental uses centres around instream flows that do not require diversion; therein lies the necessity of changing the diversion requirement for establishing and maintaining water rights. In order to lease or buy water for instream purposes, environmental entrepreneurs had to change state laws requiring diversion so that they could keep the water where they wanted it. With entrepreneurial leadership from the Oregon Water Trust, an organisation devoted to improving spawning habitat for salmon and steelhead, Oregon became the leader in changing its laws so that environmental entrepreneurs could lease water, leave it instream, and not forfeit the water right for non-use (meaning it was not diverted). Other states have followed suit allowing similar organisations to form in Washington, Montana, Idaho and Colorado, while allowing existing organisations, such as Trout Unlimited, to lease, purchase, or keep donated water rights instream for environmental purposes. Scarborough and Lund (2007, p. 58) conclude that

> With stream flows in decline throughout the West, there is an increasing need to find viable and effective means to preserve instream flows for fish and wildlife habitat while maintaining a productive agricultural sector… . Since 1998, more than 1,000 transactions have been initiated by federal, state, and private entities in the region, restoring nearly two million acre feet (around 3,015 GL) to instream flows.

These transactions have required several important elements of environmental entrepreneurship, not the least of which is measuring and monitoring contract performance. Once environmental demanders have negotiated with diverters to leave water in the stream, they must measure flows to see that the water is being delivered. They must also determine whether the instream flows are achieving their desired result, which for the Oregon Water Trust is more spawning salmon and steelhead. Therefore, they take periodic stream flow measurements and count returning fish. If they are getting enough bang for their buck, they continue the leases; if they are not, they move their resources elsewhere.

Instream flow entrepreneurs must overcome the free-rider problem, because many of the ecosystem services they provide — for example, more fish in the ocean or river — are available to others who may not have paid for the services. Charitable contributions are a partial solution to this problem, but the main source of funding has come from governments. Especially in the Northwest, where many of the instream issues centre around endangered species, state and federal governments have taxed uses which impact the species, mainly hydroelectric power generation. They then make some of the funds available to organisations using markets to increase instream flows.

2.2.4. *Farming for the birds*

The toughest problems facing enviropreneurs are those that involve mobile resources, especially when those resources move across political boundaries. Local air emissions are simple compared to global; local water management is simple compared to international rivers; and non-migratory wildlife management is simple compared to migratory fish and birds. But, as we emphasised at the outset of this chapter, for enviropreneurs, these are not problems, they are opportunities.

The Nature Conservancy (TNC), one of the most entrepreneurial conservation organisations, saw an opportunity to provide more habitat for migratory shorebirds on their annual journey from South America and Mexico to the Arctic. This journey takes many of the birds through California's Central Valley where water engineers have altered the natural systems to provide water for agricultural, municipal and industrial uses. In the process, 95 per cent of the original wetlands have disappeared.[3]

---

[3] For a complete discussion, see eBird (2014).

An innovative market transaction, called BirdReturns, between bird lovers and farmers is bringing some of the wetlands and birds back. It begins by asking bird watchers to use a smartphone app, eBird, to record shorebird sightings, which are then used by the Cornell University Ornithology Lab in New York, to map where water is needed.

TNC then uses private donations to pay farmers to flood fields — which normally would have been drained — most directly in the migratory bird flight path. Given that the birds are only there for a short time, TNC does not have to purchase the water outright; it only needs to 'rent' it when the birds are in residence. TNC uses a reverse auction in which farmers submit bids and the lowest bidder wins. Through this competition, TNC keeps the costs of achieving its goal down.

The first season of the programme ended in April 2014, with birders reporting sighting all of the birds they hoped to attract in, what they call, 'pop up' wetlands, 10,000 acres owned by 40 farmers. The hope is to increase the number of shorebirds stopping in California from 170,000 to 400,000 in both the spring migration north and the fall migration south. Although it is too soon to assess the programme's overall success, its potential is summed up by Mark Reynolds, the TNC scientist who heads the programme: 'Migratory birds are a daunting challenge. It's a hemispherical scale, and it's seasonal, and every species has a different life history. ... This program allows us to be strategic with scarce conservation dollars' (as cited in Robbins, 2014). Because the challenge is even more complicated in light of projected climate variation, innovative contracting of this sort offers great hope for conservation interests, especially in a dynamic world.

The flexibility offered by innovative contractual arrangements is most apparent — and needed — when resources are mobile. Aside from migratory birds, enviropreneurs have used leases and other spot contracts to increase stream flows during droughts (Scarborough, 2010) and to reduce bottom-trawling for groundfish in California while maintaining the economic performance of local fisheries (TNC, 2014). In a dynamic environment and a dynamic marketplace, voluntary contractual arrangements offer enviropreneurs more flexibility and therefore more opportunities to achieve their desired conservation outcomes than does costly litigation or inflexible regulations.

2.2.5. *Reorganising resources, profitably*

The environmental entrepreneurs described earlier were not motivated by profits, *per se*, but rather value the pragmatism of specifying rights and harnessing contracts for environmental returns. In recent years, however, a different breed of enviropreneur has been investing in conservation for the express purpose of making money. For these individuals and organisations, the profits generated by conservation are not incidental; they are the necessary and expected return from carefully selected conservation investments. By reorganising environmental inputs to meet new and emerging demands, some enviropreneurs are generating — and capturing — significant rents. A prime example is the private investment firm of Beartooth Capital.

Like other investment firms, Beartooth raises money from private investors to purchase undervalued assets in the marketplace. When the asset appreciates in value, Beartooth sells it and returns a profit to its investors. It is the traditional buy low, sell high strategy — with a twist. Instead of tech stocks or credit default swaps, Beartooth's portfolio contains ranch properties in the Western United States. And rather than a passive investment strategy of anticipating an increase in their portfolio value, Beartooth purchases and restores untapped ecological potential and environmental amenities on degraded ranch properties. Typically, Beartooth partners with conservation groups, government agencies, and private companies to restore and enhance a property's environmental values while enhancing its agricultural productivity. As the owner and residual claimant, Beartooth earns a profit — or loss — after it reorganises and restores a ranch's environmental amenities and sells it on the open market.

To be sure, Beartooth properties are neither hobby farms nor unmanaged wilderness preserves. The firm's founding partners, Robert Keith and Carl Palmer, view agriculture as an economic engine for stewardship and an integral component of the restoration strategy. As they explain on the firm's website (beartoothcap.com), 'It used to be assumed that once a piece of land was protected it could be left alone, but we now know differently. We can't remove agricultural activity from the land and expect it to thrive; we can't walk away.'

One of the properties in Beartooth's portfolio which strikes a balance of agricultural and environmental production is the Big Springs Creek Ranch in Central Idaho. There, Beartooth has partnered with TNC of Idaho and several state and federal agencies to restore stream flows and enhance spawning habitat for trout, Chinook salmon and steelhead — all while expanding the property's alfalfa production.

They conserved water by switching from flood irrigation to new centre-pivot sprinklers — a much more efficient irrigation technique. They also changed the point of diversion for their major water right out of Big Springs Creek, thereby leaving 7 cubic feet per second (cfs) (198.2 litres per second) of water instream, more water than had ever before been dedicated to instream flow in the Pahsimeroi Valley. To improve the quality and access of the spawning habitat on the property, Beartooth and its conservation partners replaced an irrigation diversion, which previously prevented fish passage up Big Springs Creek, and rested the riparian bottom from grazing for more than four years, which significantly enhanced bank stability and creek health. Lastly, the Beartooth team reconnected Duck Creek, a small spring creek that now provides excellent habitat for young fish to find shelter and food as they grow and prepare to return to the sea.

The results have been nothing less than amazing. Prior to their restoration work, wild salmon seldom made it to spawning beds where the highest number of fish ever counted was two in a single year. According to Beartooth's website, however, in the two years since restoration, Idaho Fish and Game has counted more than 60 salmon spawning sites on and above the ranch.

Keith and Palmer, Beartooth's founders, have measured the firm's environmental impact on the Big Springs Creek Ranch and the other properties in their portfolio. According to their website, the firm has restored over 37 miles (60 km) of rivers and creeks and placed more than 15,000 acres (6,070 ha) of land under conservation easement, including 6,000 acres (2,428 ha) with globally rare, threatened or endangered species. At Beartooth, however, there is no 'triple bottom line' accounting that separates the company's environmental and financial performance. If they sell a restored property for a premium over its acquisition costs plus the costs of its restoration actions, their fund makes money. For these enviropreneurs, environmental and financial returns are inextricably linked. What helps fish, helps their financials. By reorganising and restoring the environmental amenities on western ranch properties, they epitomise the new, profit-focused breed of enviropreneurs.

2.3. Dynamic Enviropreneurship

Entrepreneurship offers a new lens through which environmental problems become environmental opportunities. By focusing on how property rights are produced and what contractual arrangements allow the exchange of those property rights, we can better understand the potential for free market environmentalism. Equilibrium models of the environment or of markets leave little room for enviropreneurs because they leave out the dynamic elements of both. Concepts of carrying capacity, maximum sustained yield, and balance of nature suggest that environment problems are engineering problems. Similarly, the concepts of equilibrium prices and quantities, optimal resource allocation, and maximum social welfare all suggest 'market failures' can be corrected by governments getting the prices right.

Dynamic ecology and dynamic economics, on the other hand, suggest that the moving picture show requires actors who gather the knowledge necessary to understand the interface between nature and human demands on it. The dynamic nature of ecology and economics also requires actors who can create property rights to unowned resources and then harness contracts to maximise ecological and economic outputs by trading those rights. The actors in this dynamic world are enviropreneurs, who represent the next generation of environmentalists.

To further unleash the creative and dynamic potential of enviropreneurs, we need to eliminate policies that inhibit their ability to contract with competing resource users. For instance, until western states added 'instream flows' to the list of beneficial uses, conservationists hoping to leave more water instream for fish habitat had no means of legally acquiring water rights from ditch companies and other diverters. This change in the law, the elimination of an unnecessary and counter-productive diversion requirement, opened the door for enviropreneurs to begin contracting with agricultural water users, rather than fighting with them. Similar changes could and should occur in legal structures governing endangered species, conservation easements, public lands management, and water quality. By giving enviropreneurs the flexibility to define rights and write contracts, we enable them to pair the demands of a dynamic economy with the resources of a dynamic environment.

Bibliography

Alchian, A.A. and Demsetz, H. (1972). Production, Information Costs, and Economic Organization, *American Economic Review*, 62(December), pp. 777–795.

Anderson, T.L. (2009). 'Unlocking the Black Box of Entrepreneurship: Applications for the Environment', in Libecap, G.D. (ed.), *Frontiers in Eco-Entrepreneurship Research, Advances in the Study of Entrepreneurship, Innovation and Economic Growth*, Emerald Group Publishing Ltd., Bingley, pp. 39–52.

Anderson, T.L. and Hill, P.J. (2004). *The Not So Wild, Wild West: Property Rights on the Frontier*, Stanford University Press, Stanford.

Anderson, T.L. and Hill, P.J. (1975). The Evolution of Property Rights: A Study of the American West, *Journal of Law and Economics*, 18(1), pp. 163–179.

Anderson, T.L., Scarborough, B. and Watson, L.R. (2012). *Tapping Water Markets*, Routledge, Taylor and Francis Group, Florence.

Asquith, N. (2006). Bees & Barbed Wire for Water, *PERC Reports*, 24(4 December), pp. 3–6.

Barzel, Y. (1997). *Economic Analysis of Property Rights*, 2nd edition, Cambridge University Press, New York.

Botkin, D.B. (2012). *The Moon in a Nautilus Shell: Discordant Harmonies Revisited*, Oxford University Press, Oxford.

Coase, R.H. (1937). The Nature of the Firm, *Economica*, 4(3), pp. 386–405.

Demsetz, H. (1967). Toward a Theory of Property Rights, *American Economic Review: Papers and Proceedings*, 57(2), pp. 347–359.

eBird (2014). BirdReturns — A Pilot Shorebird Habitat Enhancement Program of The Nature Conservancy and the California Rice Commission. Available at: http://ebird.org/content/ebird/news/tnc_birdreturn/ [Accessed 10 December 2014].

Hayek, F. (1945). The Use of Knowledge in Society, *American Economic Review*, 35(4), pp. 519–530.

Libecap, G.D. (1989). *Contracting for Property Rights*, Cambridge University Press, New York.

Parker, D.P. (2002). Cost-Effective Strategies for Conserving Private Land, PERC, Bozeman.

Ridley, M. (2009). 'The Natural Order of Things,' *The Spectator*, January 7. Available at: http://www.spectator.co.uk/features/3213246/the-natural-order-of-things/ [Accessed 31 March 2014].

Robbins, J. (2014). 'Paying Farmers to Welcome Birds,' *New York Times*, April 14. Available at: http://www.nytimes.com/2014/04/15/science/paying-farmers-to-welcome-birds.html?_r=0 [Accessed 8 December 2014].

Scarborough, B. (2010). *Environmental Water Markets: Restoring Streams through Trade*, PERC, Bozeman.

Scarborough, B. and Lund, H.L. (2007). *Saving Our Streams: Harnessing Water Markets*, PERC, Bozeman.

Schumpeter, J.A. (1934). *The Theory of Economic Development*, Harvard University Press, Cambridge.

The Nature Conservancy (TNC) (2014). 'Developing Economically and Environmentally Sustainable Fishing Techniques.' Available at: http://www.nature.org/ourinitiatives/regions/northamerica/unitedstates/california/howwework/central-coast-groundfish-project.xml [Accessed 10 December 2014].

3. Protected Areas: Public, Private or Partnerships

Jeff Bennett[1]

Terrestrial ecosystems, when set aside from consumptive/extractive uses as 'protected areas', provide a range of goods and services. Species that are rare and endangered are protected from development threats and so have an increased chance of continued survival. People can enjoy the experiences gained from visiting such areas — be they interested in learning, thrills, vistas, exercise or relaxation. Scientists can use the ecosystems as laboratories in which to gain a better understanding of life on earth. The gene pool embedded in the ecosystem may offer the potential for discoveries of compounds that have beneficial pharmaceutical properties.

Different protected areas offer these goods and services in differing proportions. Some ecosystems in remote areas that are rarely visited by the general public will not generate much by way of recreational benefits. Yet as habitats of species that are endangered by developmental activities in the adjacent region, they may generate more scientific and gene pool benefits. Alternatively, areas that are

[1] The assistance of Gabriela Scheufele and Marc Carter in the preparation of material for this chapter is greatly appreciated. Remaining errors are the responsibility of the author alone.

adjacent to population centres or are famous internationally for some notable geographic feature may attract many visitors and potentially face pressure on their capacities to protect species from the adverse impact of humans and so deliver other types of benefits. Different strategies for managing protected areas, as well as their physical characteristics, have an impact on the mix of goods and services they provide.

The different goods and services produced also have different economic characteristics. These are best described in terms of two features: the good's ability to be supplied exclusively to those who pay for it (often called their 'excludability'); and, whether or not the good can be consumed by a person without precluding others from their use (called 'rivalry' in consumption).

For example, consider the recreational benefits of a protected area. A person who is required to pay an entrance fee when visiting a protected area (with the reasonable prospect of a fine if they try to evade the fee) is enjoying an excludable benefit. If the area is uncrowded and their visit does not cause anyone else to experience a loss of enjoyment, then there is no rivalry in consumption. That recreational good falls into the economic category of a 'club good': it is excludable and non-rival. If however, the extra visitor causes existing visitors to experience a loss of enjoyment through congestion, then the good becomes both excludable and rival. That makes it a 'private good'. And if the person is visiting a remote area where there is no-one collecting an entry fee and there are no other visitors then the good being enjoyed is both 'non-excludable' and 'non-rival'. This classifies the good as a 'public good'. Hence, the recreational goods and services provided by a protected area can take a range of different economic forms.

Other protected area products have similarly divergent characteristics. For instance, the knowledge that a rare species is secure from extinction by its habitat being set aside from development as a protected area has public good characteristics: users cannot be prevented from enjoying it and one person's use does not deplete others' enjoyment. Another and contrasting example involves the genetic material from a plant that is endemic to a protected area. That material may be 'excludable' initially if the area's owners police access to it. Furthermore, any resultant pharmaceutical compounds that are discovered may be patented to prevent use by those who do not pay. If the compounds can only be extracted from the plant and not synthesised in a laboratory, then rivalry is introduced and the good becomes purely private. If access to the plant is non-excludable but the good is rivalrous — that is, no-one can be stopped from harvesting the plant for its compounds but the harvesting process destroys the plant — then the good is known as 'common property'. Alternatively, if the compound can be readily synthesised and no patent laws pertain, then the plant's compounds take on public good status. The relevant good becomes the knowledge of the compound and this is both non-excludable and non-rival.

All of these different economic characteristics give rise to different incentive structures for both users and suppliers of protected area goods and services. Where private goods are involved, profits are the incentive that will encourage suppliers to act to protect ecosystems. In a competitive market, a price for the private goods equal to the marginal costs of production will be charged and those users who anticipate a marginal benefit in excess of the price charged will purchase the protected area product. In this way all users experience a value that is greater than the costs of provision and the market is effective in the process of allocating resources between protecting and developing ecosystems.

However, wherever goods and services derived from ecosystem protection have elements of non-excludability or non-rivalry, then the allocative process offered by market forces starts to face some additional challenges. For instance, there is no incentive for a profit motivated supplier to provide the public goods offered by protected areas. This is because of the non-excludability characteristic: without the capacity to prevent non-payers from using the good, 'free-riding' behaviour will prevail on the part of the good's users. Supplies of public goods from protected areas are therefore likely to be restricted to what would be offered through users' altruistic (non-profit) motives. The same conclusion can be drawn regarding common property goods, with the additional conclusion that any existing supplies of such goods would be used without replenishment, given that users would use the (rivalrous) good for their personal profit, knowing that if they didn't, someone else would.

A slightly different conclusion can be drawn regarding 'club goods' produced from protected ecosystems (such as uncongested visits to a protected area that has an entry fee). Once the asset on which the club good is based has been provided (for example, a protected area has been declared and the infrastructure to allow visitation has been established) then because there are no congestion costs, the costs of allowing an extra user to visit are effectively zero. The implication of this is that the price that should be charged for visitors is zero. If a non-zero price was charged, some users would be excluded. Those excluded visitors would enjoy a benefit that is greater than the costs of letting them visit. Hence a loss is generated for society when they are not permitted to visit. The quandary then is, if zero is the right price to charge as a reflection of the marginal costs of a visit, then again there is no incentive for a profit-motivated supplier to take on the role of protected ecosystem producer. So while a private-sector supplier has an incentive to protect ecosystems for their club goods because they are excludable, requiring a positive price for their provision means that some users will be excluded when they could have enjoyed a net benefit from free access.

All this implies that simply allowing private market forces to operate to supply protected areas is likely to meet some difficulties in ensuring that society has enough of these areas and enough of the goods and services they provide.

But that is not to say that the private sector has no role to play in protected ecosystem provision. A number of points need to be recognised in developing the conclusion that indeed the private sector has a valuable role to play.

First, there is no guarantee that the public sector will perform the task any better than leaving it to the private sector. Government 'failure', due to both informational constraints and the prospects of rent-seeking, may cause significant deficiencies in protected area provision and management. For instance, corrupt government officials may turn over access to a nation's entire protected area network to logging interests in order to gain personal financial advantage. Alternatively, a government may be swayed by environmental lobby groups to over-expand the area set aside from development. This would mean that the marginal benefits enjoyed from conservation exceed the benefits of development. However, the motivation for over-expansion of the conservation estate rests in the government's interest in a return to power at the next election and that could depend on the support of 'green' voters.

Second, it is misleading to conclude that private-sector provision of protected areas would amount to zero. Because protected areas produce a mixture of all four types of goods and services (public, private, club and common) there are circumstances where the incentives to produce private and club good elements are sufficient to see public and common property goods supplied as co-products. In this way, non-excludable goods are 'piggy-backed' on the production of the excludable, profit-generating goods. An example would be a protected area supplied by a profit-motivated entrepreneur because it offers a popular recreational site and co-incidentally, is the habitat of a rare species of insect that is unaffected by visitation.

Third, it is also misleading to assume that the profit motive is the only driving force for protected area suppliers and that free-riding is pervasive across all protected area users. The prospect is that not-for-profit organisations have sufficient motivation to organise sufficient altruistic donors to allow for protected area uses to compete effectively against extractive users in markets for the rights to land resources. This type of private-sector action can therefore be targeted at public goods alone as it is not reliant on the exclusion of users. Resultant protected areas may be set aside from any human visitation, in order to secure, for example, the future of endangered species.

While protected areas may offer co-production of public, club, common property and private goods, thinking that these elements may not be separated in the management of such areas is also misguided. That opens the prospect for partnerships between public- and private-sector interests in the provision and management of protected areas. For instance, a protected area may have been purchased by the state because of its public good characteristics (a rich source of biodiversity perhaps) but the private good and club good elements of the area could be managed by private-sector interests. Hence, private-sector concessionaires could lease the rights to manage camp sites and hostels/hotels, run kiosks, lead guided walks, etc., in the protected area. Users would pay commercial prices for these services, and the concessionaire would provide the state owner a fee for the right to operate. Competitive tendering for the right to operate would ensure competitive pricing for the services offered and contract conditions would ensure that the activities of the concessionaire did not jeopardise the area's capacity to meet its public good/species protection goals.

The rest of this chapter is devoted to demonstrating the practicalities of all of these private-sector alternatives to the simple public-sector provision/public-sector management model that has been prominent in the first century of protected area history. It does so by reviewing examples of private-sector protected area actions across a number of different countries: Australia, Germany and the United States.

3.1. Private Supply of Public Goods

Two not-for-profit organisations have developed in Australia over the past two decades to provide protected areas. Australian Wildlife Conservancy (AWC) and Bush Heritage Australia (BHA)[2] use essentially the same formula in their operations: funds are raised from tax-free donations and are spent on the purchase of land to be set aside as conservation reserves. Together, their networks of protected areas amount to around four million ha; approximately half of one per cent of the nation's land area.

The two organisations operate under the same economic logic: public good environmental services are supplied without the incentive of profit, using funds that deny the free-rider hypothesis. They are,

[2] Information reported in this section is based on the annual reports of AWC (2013) and BHA (2013).

however, dissimilar in a number of respects so it is worth considering them as separate entities.

AWC was founded by Martin Copley, a Western Australian businessman in 1991. At the end of the 2013 financial year, it owned and managed 23 properties covering around 3 million ha. Some of the AWC estate had its origins in an earlier founded not-for-profit conservation company, Earth Sanctuaries Pty Ltd., which was forced to downsize its portfolio of reserves due to financial difficulties.[3] The total assets of AWC, valued on an historic cost basis, amount to nearly $70m, with the properties and associated plant and equipment making up approximately two-thirds of total assets.

Annual receipts from donations and grants to AWC amounted to $13.7m in 2013: $11.6m of this came from donations and the remainder from government grants. In addition, revenues came from sanctuary income — primarily from visitors — ($1.8m) and returns on financial investments ($0.3m). That makes annual revenues equal to $15.89m. In the same year, total costs were $12.12m. This comprised administrative costs ($1.12m) fund-raising costs ($0.93m) and operational costs ($10.06m). No land purchases were made in 2013 by AWC. The organisation employed 80 staff, 80 per cent of whom were field-based.

In contrast, BHA was founded by environmental activist and former Australian Senator, Bob Brown, also in 1991. By 2013, the BHA estate comprised 35 reserves amounting to almost one million ha. The initial properties protected by BHA were donated by Bob Brown, who remains as the organisation's patron. The assets of BHA are in the order of $41.4m, with two-thirds of that sum being accounted for by the properties and their associated assets.

---

[3]The history of Earth Sanctuary's operations is detailed in Aretino *et al.* (2001) and Bennett (2012). In part, those difficulties arose when Earth Sanctuaries sought listing on the Australian Stock Exchange in order to access more capital. Meeting the reporting requirements for listing proved problematic because of difficulties in estimating a commercial value for the native species protected in the estate given that they are legally the property of the crown and not tradeable.

BHA generated revenue from contributions of $13.5m in 2013. The organisation claims to have 15,000 active donors. Additional revenue was sourced from reserve income ($0.25m) and financial asset returns ($0.63m) making a total for revenues of $14.18m. Total expenditures in the same year amounted to $11.65m. Operational costs amounted to $6.3m, including payments made relating to the purchase of Naree Station as a new reserve. Other costs included those for administration ($2.1m) and fundraising initiatives ($3m). BHA employs 65 staff, 30 per cent of whom are part-timers and 50 per cent of whom are located in the field. They also use the services of volunteers: In 2013, 403 people volunteered a total of 2,200 hours.

So while both organisations raise around the same amount of money each year, clearly AWC has the larger and more valuable portfolio of land. Both have significant financial resources on top of their land assets. Their expenditure patterns are different. AWC devotes 83 per cent of its costs to operational expenses while 54 per cent of BHA expenses are operational. There are consequential differences in the overhead costs: administrative costs for AWC are around 9 per cent, around half of BHA's percentage; fund-raising accounts for 7.6 per cent of AWC's costs compared to 26 per cent for BHA.

These different cost profiles reflect different operational practices by the two organisations. The higher costs of raising funds for BHA reflects its larger, more diffuse donor base, in contrast to AWC's concentration on philanthropic trusts and corporate donors. It also suggests the higher administrative costs associated with BHA's move toward protecting ecosystems through engagement with private sector (and government) partners. AWC has also relied more heavily on relatively large government grants to assist with its estate purchases.

On top of its one million hectares of reserves, BHA claims to have a further 2.5 million ha of protected areas due to partnership arrangements. In particular, BHA supports ecosystem protection on aboriginal-owned land through partnership arrangements. Most recently, it has raised funds sufficient to establish a capital fund called the Midlands Conservation Fund that will earn sufficient income to pay ten landowners in central Tasmania to protect

2,600 ha. Negotiating and then implementing such partnerships involves greater administrative rather than operational expenses.

That is not to say that AWC is not involved in the development of partnership agreements. In 2014, its recommendation to the NSW Government was to contract private-sector conservation groups to provide feral[4] proof fencing (of the type already employed successfully in a number of AWC sanctuaries) for areas of up to 4,000 ha each in three National Parks. If AWC is successful in securing the contract, the cost and revenue implications will be revealed in future years. However, given that the fencing activity will be an operational expenditure for AWC, the proportions of costs may not change significantly.

Another distinction between the two organisations is in their revenue streams. Because AWC has more sanctuaries that are open to the public for commercial visitation, they raise a greater proportion of their total revenue from sanctuary income ($1.8m of $15.89m; 11 per cent for AWC compared to $0.25m of $14.18m; 2 per cent for BHA). For instance, AWC offers twin share dorm-style accommodation with shower and toilet facilities for up to 40 people with full kitchen and BBQ facilities available at its Yookamurra sanctuary in South Australia. However, BHA does encourage their donors to visit their reserves and some visitation involves payment. For instance, 'tag-along-tours' for four-wheel-drive vehicles are arranged for some reserves (for example, Bon Bon Station, Naree Station and Yourka) and a per-person fee is charged, with the reserve managers acting as guides. Other options for visitation such as walking tours and overnight camping are offered at no charge, but a donation is requested.

It is notable, however, that neither organisation is strongly dependent on income arising from the direct use of its protected area assets. Rather, their attention is more focused on providing the public good, species protection benefits: Hence their relatively heavier reliance on donations from the general public who enjoy the 'existence value' of the reserves rather than visitors who enjoy 'use values' that result in entrance fee revenues.

---

[4] Notably, cats, foxes and rabbits.

It must also be acknowledged that the public sector does play a role in the success of AWC and BHA. Fundamentally, the state provides the necessary institutions — particularly those relating to land ownership — within which they operate. Additionally, the tax treatment of donations, effectively amount to a public-sector subsidisation of their activities. Because donors can deduct donations from their taxable income, the government agrees to forgo an income stream as a result of the decision to allow tax deductible status for both organisations. The amounts of the deductions involved do not appear on the balance sheets of either the companies or the government. However, the deductions provide indirect benefits to AWC and BHA because their revenues from donations are enhanced. Donors gain the advantage of lower tax bills as well as the satisfaction enjoyed from supporting the conservation initiatives. In effect, donors 'buy' conservation services from AWC or BHA at a 'price' that is subsidised by government to the extent of their marginal tax rate. Tax deductibility also results in indirect costs to taxpayers, as forgone revenues must be raised from other sources, or potential expenditures given up. However, by permitting tax deductibility, governments can achieve lower expenditures on environmental protection because the private sector takes on a greater role. In this way, the burden of supplying environmental protection public goods is partially shifted away from the taxpaying public to those in the community that donate to the cause.

A variation on the AWC/BHA model of private-sector nature protection has developed in Germany. The *Landesbund für Vogelschutz* (LBV)[5] is a private-sector 'club' that operates in Bavaria to protect birdlife. It does so by the purchase/leasing and management of land: around 2,100 ha are currently owned by the LBV with a further 800 ha leased. Consistent with the densely settled characteristics of Bavaria, the total holding is made up of 450 separate areas of land. The LBV lands are managed under formally designated preservation plans. These include restrictions to fertilisation, the use of pesticides, the construction of dams and dykes and building limitations. Easements to enforce these restrictions are included

[5] See Naturshutz in Bayern http://www.lbv.de/ [Accessed 8 August 2014].

in the land title of each land holding. The LBV has targeted purchases within Flora–Fauna-Habitat Directive Areas, as designated by the European Union, so that 50 per cent of holdings are within these zones. A component of the management plan for each area is an active monitoring programme designed to check on the success or otherwise of the biodiversity protection strategies in place.

The value of the LBV's nature reserve estate at the end of 2012 was over EUR22m,[6] as calculated on an historic cost basis. During 2012, out of a total expenditure on its core nature protection activities of nearly EUR8.5m, LBV spent EUR1.12m on land purchases for nature protection reserves. A further EUR3.5m was spent in the planning and management of its existing reserve network. Other draws on its finances came from its environmental education activities (EUR1.38m) and the management of its member base, public relations and administration (almost EUR2m).

The LBV cannot raise any revenue from visitation to their reserves, as German law specifies an unrestricted right to access nature. Hence there is no financial incentive to encourage use. Some less ecologically vulnerable reserves are publicly promoted in order to further the organisation's goal of public education. However, those reserves with high ecological value and with greater sensitivity to use are not publicly promoted in order to remove pressure from threatened species, especially at breeding times.

Without a stream of revenue from visitation, the LBV has sourced its funds for land purchase (as well as its operational expenses) from a range of other providers from both the private and the public sectors. In 2012, total revenues received by LBV in the form of 'goodwill' (payments not directed at the explicit provision of services) amounted to EUR8.16m. The primary components of this were membership fees (25 per cent), donations (22 per cent), bequests (6 per cent) and government subsidies (45 per cent). A further EUR2m (gross) was sourced from off-reserve commercial business operations — ranging from a kindergarten to financial portfolio management — conducted by the LBV.

---

[6] See LBV (2013).

Government contributions clearly make up an important component of LBV's revenues. It has worked in collaboration with the 'Bayerischer Naturschutzfonds' (Bavarian Nature Fund), operated by the Bavarian state government to purchase land, with up to 85 per cent of the purchase price being sourced from the Fund. Some acquisitions have been made with 100 per cent of funds coming from 'Landkreise' (local councils). Specific issue funds such as the 'Klimaprogamm Bayern 2020' (Bavarian Climate Programme 2020) have also been accessed.

In contrast to the activities of the LBV, the Deutscher Alpinverein (DAV)[7] does not own any land but is a private club that has responsibility for the maintenance of a network of around 30,000 km of hiking trails, predominantly in the Bavarian Alps. That responsibility extends to a legal duty of care to maintain the safety of hikers using the tracks. The task is achieved largely through the actions of volunteers who are members of the DAV. With around one million members, around 50,000 hours of voluntary track maintenance work is carried out each year. The DAV also spends around EUR1m per annum in supporting the volunteers' work. Those funds are sourced primarily from membership fees but with around 30 per cent coming from government grants.

3.2. Public–Private Partnerships[8]

Over the last 150 years,[9] the public sectors of countries around the world have acquired land for the purpose of establishing National Parks[10] and nature reserves. While the protected areas so created

[7] See Deutscher Alpenverien, DAV, http://www.alpenverein.de/ [Accessed 10 August 2014].

[8] The material presented in this section has benefited from discussions with Meyer (2014). Available at: *pers. com*, 1 July 2014. Warren Meyer is the founder and president of Recreation Resource Management of America, Inc. Supporting material is also drawn from Meyer (2013) and Gilroy, Kenny and Morris (2013).

[9] The first national park to be declared was Yellowstone National Park in the United States in 1871.

[10] Not all 'National' Parks are the responsibility of national governments. For instance, Australian national parks are managed by state governments.

have created a legacy of an on-going supply of environmental goods and services, they have also left taxpayers with a stream of on-going management costs. Competing demands for access to the public purse have often pushed spending on protected area management to a lower order. The result has been some run down of the asset base, a reduction in services provided and consequential public disquiet. Pressure for governments to address the gap between funding and public demands has led to their searching for alternative means of managing their protected area estates. One outcome has been the development of public–private partnerships in protected area management.

An example of such a partnership is the operation of Recreation Resource Management of America Inc. (RRMA). This for-profit, family-owned private corporation was founded in 1989 as a campground recreation provider for the United States Forestry Service (USFS)[11] and now manages almost 100 campground sites in Arizona and Colorado. In these campgrounds, RRMA acts as a concessionaire to the USFS, effectively leasing the campgrounds for a fixed cost plus a proportion of the revenues raised from charging a use fee to campers. Under this model, ownership of the protected area is held by the public sector (USFS) but the management of the recreation component of the management task is conducted by the private sector (RRMA). The management of the ecosystem remains the responsibility of the USFS.

The success of the RRMA–USFS partnership implies that the private-sector provider is able to generate more visitor revenue at a lower cost than the public-sector alternative: where the USFS was unable to cover the costs of servicing the recreational visitor market, RRMA has been able to make profits sufficient to keep them in business for 25 years. The differences in the operations of the private and the public-sector alternatives are illustrated by a comparison between two adjacent parks in Arizona: Red Rock State Park and Crescent

[11] The USFS is responsible for the management not only of state owned commercially logged forests in the United States. It also has responsibility for the recreational use of the lands under USFS control.

Moon Ranch, a USFS reserve where the camping facilities are managed by RRMA (Meyer, 2013). While the two protected areas share similar ecological and infrastructure features, in 2010, Red Rock State Park generated a loss of over $114,000[12] while Crescent Moon Ranch provided a return to the State of nearly $45,000.[13] The marked difference in financial performance is largely a result of different costs of operation.

Most of the differences in cost structures relate to labour costs. In RRMA managed sites, staff members are predominantly part-time, working only during the season when camping is popular. This applies to head-office staff as well as field staff. Many RRMA staff stay on-site, living in their own recreational vehicle (RV). Often the staff are retired people taking the opportunity to earn some income while travelling around the country. Wages are paid to reflect the skills required to collect rubbish, maintain roads, clean bathroom facilities and manage the visitors to ensure a pleasurable stay.

Public-sector managed areas, in contrast, usually employ full-time staff qualified in environmental science or similar, and likely to begrudge performing menial campground management activities. Furthermore, some agencies require their park management staff to have law enforcement certification, thus adding to the wages that must be paid. The inflexibility,[14] higher average hourly wage rates and the additional on-costs being paid by the public-sector operations go a long way to explain their higher cost structures.

However, the differences between public and private operators go beyond cost structures. Perhaps more importantly, the incentives faced by private operators are more closely aligned with delivering greater benefits to the park users. Given that their revenue stream is determined by the demand for the goods and services they offer,

[12] This loss does not take into account the proportion of park headquarter costs that relate to the management of Red Rock State Park.

[13] This total is made up of concession fees paid to the USFS, amounting to 18 per cent of gate takings at Crescent Moon Ranch less $10,000 paid to the RMMA as an 'oversight' fee for investment in park infrastructure improvements.

[14] Staff wages and conditions are generally negotiated on a whole-of-agency basis with consequential inflexibility to meet specific workplace requirements.

private operators (and their staff) have an incentive to ensure that their camp sites are clean and well presented, that the bathrooms are regularly serviced, that staff on-site are welcoming and informative, etc. In contrast, and particularly where gate takings are returned to the general revenue pool of government and not retained to fund park expenditure, the incentive of staff to provide good service to visitors is significantly diluted.

So great may the incentive be for a private-sector operator to commercialise the visitation aspect of a protected area that it may manage the area to the detriment of its capacity to supply some of its non-use environmental values such as species protection. Two factors (can) work against this prospect. The first is that the visitors to the area are attracted to it by its environmental features. Management actions that degrade those features would result in fewer of those current visitors returning. However, if the risk to non-use environmental goods and service supply comes from management that would attract a different type of visitor — perhaps one attracted to large-scale hotel development — then the second factor comes into play to prevent the change occurring. The operations of the private-sector concessionaire are subject to a 'lease' agreement. As part of that type of agreement between the USFS and RRMA, for example, conditions as to the type of operation and the extent of impacts are included. Not only does the public sector retain ownership of the asset being managed but it also retains control over the broad parameters of the private-sector operator's operations. Put simply, 'use' activities in a protected area that are promoted by the concessionaire can be controlled so that 'non-use' derived goods and services are not compromised.

Another potential danger of private-sector management of protected areas is that profit-motivated interests may be interested in managing only those recreational sites that have visitation rates that generate the best returns, leaving the less popular sites to be managed by the public sector. The USFS has overcome that problem in its dealings with RRMA by letting out concessions that are regionally based rather than for individual camp sites. Concession agreements therefore cover both high and lower use sites. This has some 'up-side' for the concessionaire as it permits some sharing of fixed costs across a wider region, thus providing some economies of scale.

Importantly, the costs and operations of the concessionaire are not only subject to the incentives created by users. They are also driven by competition between alternative suppliers. RRMA competes with five other corporations of a similar scale[15] when tendering for the rights to manage a campground. Smaller scale operators also compete for locally specific tenders. The tendering process involves competition across a number of elements. The first is the proposed operational plan for the site in question. The plan must specify aspects of operations as broad ranging as staff uniforms and equipment through to customer grievance procedures. A business plan must also be included. The components of the operational plan become the clauses of the contract entered into by the successful tenderer. The second element is the financial capability/security of the tenderer to ensure the stability of the operator. The last two elements relate to financial matters: the fees to be charged for visitation and the amount of money to be paid back to the USFS. Hence, competition is across operational and financial matters.

Contracts between RRMA and the USFS are for a period of five years with the option of a further five years. This rotation of contracts ensures that the pressure of competition between suppliers is maintained, but it does not give the private supplier a strong incentive to improve or even maintain the built infrastructure of the area. To combat that problem, the USFS quarantines the payments made by RRMA into a fund that is dedicated to capital investment. Furthermore, expenses incurred by RRMA in the maintenance of the sites being managed may be taken in lieu of concession payments. Plans for investment and maintenance activities require strong cooperation between the USFS and RRMA much as they would be between a 'landlord and the tenant'. This is achieved through an annual planning process that establishes a strategy of action for the

---

[15] Each operation holds between 10 to 40 contracts, with each firm managing between 50 and 400 sites.

summer period (in a climate where winter construction and maintenance is problematic). Collaboration also ensures that the full suite of environmental goods and services provided by the protected area are accounted for.

The public–private partnership that has been established between USFS and RRMA serves as a useful example of how such arrangements can ensure the continued supply of high quality use services in protected areas while simultaneously relieving pressures on the public purse and not depleting the goods and services provided by the areas for 'non-use' goods and services. By enlisting the strengths of the private-sector operation in controlling costs and ensuring visitor satisfaction, while constraining activities to protect other environmental values, the partnership agreements make sure that private and public goods are simultaneously produced.

The potential exists for this style of partnership to be extended to cover the management of all aspects of protected areas. This would entail the extension of private management activities to encompass ecosystem protection. By implication, costs would rise without any additional revenues from gate takings. For some areas, this would mean no possibility of profitable operations for a private operator. Two alternatives deserve consideration. The first is to group protected areas into conglomerations within which there is sufficient overall profit-making potential to ensure the viability of a private concessionaire. Where this strategy is unavailable — perhaps because of low levels of overall visitation in a relatively remote region — the second option would be for the public sector to conduct a reverse auction for the right to manage a protected area. This would mean that prospective managers would provide an operational plan along with an amount that the government would need to pay for services so specified. Both options would take advantage of the cost and service advantages offered by a competitive private sector, but would ensure that the protected area estate stayed in public hands and be managed in an overall way that produced use and non-use benefits to society.

Of paramount importance to the success of such public–private partnerships is the establishment of procedures within the public sector that allow revenue streams generated by visitation to each protected area to be held in an account that is managed specifically for that area. Not only does this provide a pool of funds for the area's management but it also establishes positive incentives for its managers. Furthermore, it removes the funding of protected area operations from the whims of political processes: approvals for expenditures on protected area management actions need not endure the delays and dangers of rent-seeking that are inherent in those processes.[16]

3.3. Conclusions

The goal of this chapter has been to draw on a range of experiences internationally to demonstrate the practical potential for private-sector engagement in the provision of terrestrial nature protection. What is apparent from the cases presented is that rarely will the private sector be active in nature protection without some public-sector interaction. In the Australian and German cases, public subsidies support the private-sector operators. In the US case, ownership of the ecological resource remains in the hands of the public sector.

However, in each case, there is clearly room for a move toward greater responsibility being entrusted to the private sector with consequential resource use efficiency improvements. For example, governments, through their own acquisitions of land for national parks, can act to 'crowd out' private-sector initiatives to protect the environment such as BHA and AWC. A government policy to declare that the national park estate would not be further extended would signal to nature lovers that any further expansion would only come from their individual donation to a private-sector operator.

Governments can also facilitate the formation and operation of private nature protection estates by ensuring that the transaction costs associated with land title exchange are as low as possible.

[16] Leal and Fretwell (1997) set out the rationale for park 'self-sufficiency'.

For instance, exemptions from stamp duty on the transfer of land for nature protection could add to the incentives offered by tax deductibility. While such actions may be seen by governments to increase their fiscal load, taking elements of nature protection off the public balance sheet and putting them into private hands would help to relieve that load over time.

The USFS management case demonstrates the potential for private-sector management of existing protected areas in jurisdictions that currently involve only public-sector organisations in the management tasks. Scope exists for the synergistic operation of commercial enterprises in protected areas to take advantage of the willingness to pay of visitors to those areas. Budgetary pressures on public-sector agencies may force change in this direction faster than may be expected given the historical aversion shown by conservation lobby groups to in-park commercial operations. Continued ownership by the public sector of the reserve estate will help to mitigate that opposition, as will guarantees of operational standards afforded by strong contractual agreements between the state owner and the private manager. Such agreements are commonplace in private–public-partnerships in the fields of transportation, health and education. The lessons learnt from that experience are readily transferred across to the nature protection realm.

Bibliography

Aretino, B., Holland, P., Peterson, D. and Schuele, M. (2001). Creating Markets for Biodiversity: A Case Study of Earth Sanctuaries Ltd., *Productivity Commission Staff Research Paper*, AusInfo, Canberra.

Australian Wildlife Conservancy (AWC) (2013). *Annual Report 2013*. Available at: http://www.australianwildlife.org/media/20774/AWC-Concise-Financial-Report-2013-FINAL.pdf [Accessed 2 July 2014].

Bennett, J. (2012). Coase Rules OK: Exploring Prospects for Private Sector Environmental Protection, *Economic Record*, 88 (281), pp. 278–287.

Bush Heritage Australia (BHA) (2013). *Annual Report 2013*. Available at: https://interactivepdf.uniflip.com/2/62222/308571/pub/ [Accessed 2 July 2014].

Gilroy, L., Kenny, H. and Morris, J. (2013). Parks 2.0: Operating State Parks Through Public Private Partnerships, *Policy Study 419*, Reason Foundation and The Buckeye Institute, New York.

Landesbund fur Vogelshutz (2013). *Jahresbericht 2012/2013*, http://www.lbv.de/jahresberichte/2012-2013/ [Accessed 10 August 2014].

Leal, D. and Fretwell, H. (1997). *Back to the Future to Save Our Parks*, PERC Policy Series, PS–10, Property and Environment Research Centre, Bozeman.

Meyer, W. (2013). A Tale of Two Parks, *PERC Case Studies*, Property and Environment Research Centre, Bozeman.

4. Promoting Green Growth in Fisheries

R. Quentin Grafton,[1] Kathleen Segerson and Dale Squires

Fisheries and their governance are at a crossroad. The market failures inherent in the exploitation of capture and culture fisheries are increasingly resolved for target species as a result of institutional innovation, but substantial biodiversity loss and ecosystem externalities nonetheless remain (Grafton *et al.*, 2010). A major challenge and opportunity facing seafood supply is to maintain or increase food production from marine resources while maintaining healthy ecosystems and conserving biodiversity. Meeting this challenge requires expanding the range of successfully applied management instruments and promoting technologies. It demands processes, and institutional and market design, that mitigate bycatch and to conserve stocks. We call this green growth. Green innovation that supports natural capital stocks will serve as a lynchpin to green growth through that complements conventional and incentive-based marine conservation and fisheries management approaches.

[1] Grafton is grateful for partial funding from the OECD under contract SRM#:PO0500025148 in support of this research.

To foster green growth, the private, civil society, and public sectors can develop markets and other institutions to address market failures in fish harvesting that affect both target and non-targeted species and habitats. The goal of such growth is to provide an economically efficient supply of the public goods of biodiversity, ecosystem services, knowledge, and information that promotes sustainable capture and culture fisheries (Squires and Vestergaard, 2013b; Grafton, 2014; Squires and Garcia, 2013; Squires, Clarke and Chan, 2014). We contend that institutional innovation that more closely aligns collective and individual incentives is fundamental to overcoming the 'tragedy of the commons' and promoting green growth in fisheries and marine conservation.

In this chapter we examine fisheries innovation that contributes to green growth, notably incentive-based, flexible approaches that encourage capture and culture fishers to act in ways consistent with the public good. Green growth, or economic development that promotes the sustainable use of natural capital stocks or endowments, can either be diminished or supported by innovation. Green innovation may include productivity growth, technologies that reduce or mitigate adverse environmental impacts, institutional design, and organisational processes that are consistent with sustainable methods of production and consumption. In the absence of the full internalisation of technological externalities, whereby costs or benefits imposed on others are fully accounted for in all individual decisions, green innovation with common resources and multiple public goods requires collective action. Ideally, this action should occur through private–public partnerships to establish the appropriate incentives or information and knowledge interventions.

Our key conclusion is that capture and culture fisheries innovation and the development of policies, and institutions that support and induce it, will be the single most important approach to achieve green growth: i.e., addressing sustainable fisheries while conserving biodiversity and healthy ecosystems. Section 4.1 reviews the innovations that enhance biodiversity and ecosystems and also increase the economic efficiency of capture and culture fisheries. Section 4.2 considers technology, biodiversity and ecosystem services as public goods. Section 4.3 examines five types of fisheries innovations. Section 4.4 discusses three pillars of green growth. Section 4.5 outlines conclusions to the chapter.

4.1. Product, Process and Institutional Innovation

Technological change describes the overall process of invention, innovation, and diffusion of technology (Schumpeter, 1942). *Invention* describes a set of actions that result in the development of new products, technologies or processes. *Innovation* is the deliberative process of adapting or using inventions and better practices and putting them into practical use, be it at an individual (producer or consumer), organisational or national level. *Diffusion* refers to the spread of innovations through a society or industry. Diffusion is costly, because firms must learn about new technology, often purchase new gear and equipment, and adapt it to their particular circumstances.

Process innovations are new production processes. *Product innovations* affect the physical properties of the product, including the development of entirely new products and require some consumer adjustment. The distinction between process and product innovations is not always clear. Figure 4.1 illustrates process, product, and institutional innovations (Grafton, 2014).

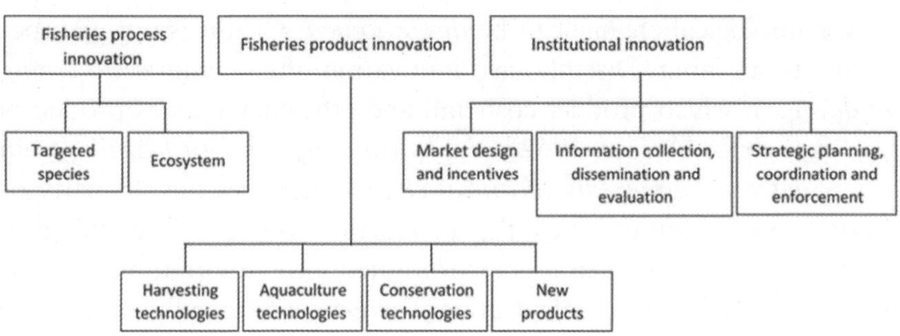

Figure 4.1: Fisheries innovation: Process, product and institutional
Source: Grafton (2014).

Exogenous technological change occurs when technological change is largely independent of economic forces, and in modern fisheries, largely reflects progress in science and technology in general. Much innovation in capture and culture fisheries is exogenous due to its military, aerospace and information technology antecedents, and is then adapted and diffused within the fishing sector (Squires and Vestergaard, 2013b). For example, technological developments in the defence industry led to sonar that was adapted by fishers to locate schools of fish and geo-positioning technology that allows fishers to have a precise global location helping them to return vessels to particular locations of fish abundance, such as submerged sea mounts.

Endogenous technological change is the result of activities within the economic system that respond to the economic incentives of the system. Thus, endogenous technological change is due to intentional actions by firms that respond to changes in knowledge or conditions in markets and the environment, often arising from intentional investment decisions made by profit-maximising agents. Examples include the development of fishing gear and fishing operations that reduces sea turtle bycatch and post-hooking mortality. These include circle hooks and mackerel type bait to replace J hooks and squid bait in shallow set pelagic longlines (Watson *et al.*, 2005), eco-Floating Aggregating Devices (FADs) (Dagorn *et al.*, 2013) or the Medina panel and backdown procedure to reduce dolphin mortality for tropical tuna purse seine fisheries.

Technological change can be *disembodied* when it is not incorporated into an input. Disembodied innovation often comprises *learning by doing*, in which product costs fall and efficiency rises as producers gain experience (Arrow, 1962), and *learning by using* or *learning from others*. *Factor augmenting technical change* increases the efficiency or productivity of inputs into the production process. Technological change is *embodied* when it is incorporated into an input, notably the physical capital stock, only through investment, thereby raising the efficiency of each unit of technology-embodied input. Technology then evolves endogenously within fisheries as a result of these private investment decisions and learning by doing and using then follows.

An increase in a firm's physical capital stock leads to a parallel increase in its stock of knowledge, which is a public good with an external benefit that any other firm can access at zero or low cost and which creates 'dynamic increasing returns' (Romer, 1986, 1990; Squires, Clarke and Chan, 2014). The value of a new technology to one user may depend on how many other users have adopted the technology, where users are generally better off the more others adopt the same technology (Arthur, 2009). An example of this network external benefit and dynamic increasing returns is the increasing use of buoys with acoustic sensors and GPS attached to drifting FADs, where the more these buoys are used, the lower their cost and the more knowledge and information are created and shared. Clearly, the overall state of technology is determined in part by these knowledge spillovers or network external benefits and dynamic increasing returns through investment-specific technological change.

Biased technological change refers to technological change that alters the relative proportions of inputs or outputs (Hicks, 1932). We define *biodiversity saving technological change* as those actions that reduce the relative proportions of bycatch to target species, or more generally, undesirable outputs such as adverse biodiversity and ecosystem impacts, relative to capture and culture target outputs (Squires and Vestergaard, 2013b; Squires and Garcia, 2013; Squires, Clarke and Chan, 2014; Grafton, 2014). *Resource augmenting technical change* for wild stocks allows more effective use of the entire, existing resource stock, such as exploitation of a previously inaccessible stock, but does not increase the size of the wild stock (Squires and Vestergaard, 2013a).

The profit motive, and more generally, responding to market incentives, is the primary reason why technologies are developed and diffused (Romer, 1990; Acemoglu, 2002). Non-profit factors also play a role in diffusion (Romer, 1990). For example, fishers may 'satisfice' rather than optimise across all margins, especially in the context of innovation (Nelson and Winter, 1982; Grafton, 2014). Vessel owners and skippers might choose to deploy/adopt a particular harvesting technology to improve safety or reduce human physical effort, whether or not it contributes to higher profits.

Innovation responding to marketplace needs is *demand-pull* and to new research opportunities provided by knowledge advances is *technology-push* (Jaffe, Newell and Stavins, 2005). For example, biased technical change that reduces bycatch induced by new market demands for eco-friendly and eco-labelled products is demand-pull innovation. Biodiversity saving technical change induced by increased scientific knowledge about how to reduce bycatch and information technology embodied into the physical capital stock such as acoustic sensors is technology-push.

Induced or directed technological change is a form of biased, endogenous technological change that changes the proportions of inputs used or outputs produced (Hicks, 1932; Acemoglu, 2002). Profit incentives affect both the amount and direction of technical change. They include: (i) the impacts of increasing relative input supplies and their scarcity; (ii) profits and output prices; (iii) cost minimisation and relative input prices; and (iv) increasing returns to scale due to external benefits from knowledge and networks. This directed technical change is a key form of technical change in conserving biodiversity and ecosystems (Squires and Vestergaard, 2013b; Squires and Garcia, 2013; Squires, Clarke and Chan, 2014; Grafton, 2014).

Two important components of directed technological change are the *price effect* and the *market effect* (Acemoglu, 2002). Both can direct the five types of fisheries innovation we discuss in the following paragraphs. The price effect occurs if there are stronger incentives to innovate when goods command a higher price or inputs are relatively scarce with corresponding higher relative prices. The market effect, which can potentially outweigh the price effect, occurs when it is more profitable to develop technologies that have a larger market and more abundant inputs. Biased technological change that reduces the proportion of forage fish in cultured fish diets in response to market imperatives is demand-pull and can be responding to the market effect. It could also be technology-push when there is new knowledge about cultured fish diets or in response to the price effect if the relative price of forage fish increases relative to prices of substitutes such as soybeans.

4.2. Technology, Biodiversity and Ecosystem Services as Public Goods

The broad economics problem can be viewed as increasing the supply of the pubic goods (goods that can be consumed without excluding others from their consumption and without reducing the amount available to others for consumption, of biodiversity and ecosystem services), while sustainably harvesting the common resources of capture and culture seafood (Tisdell, 1991; Grafton *et al.*, 2010; Squires and Garcia, 2013; Grafton and Squires, 2013; Kronbak, Squires and Vestergaard, 2013; Squires, Clarke and Chan, 2014). This twin goal of increasing public goods and sustainability when harvesting common resources entails public and private policies that address two linked externalities or market failures (unintentional and uncompensated effect of one producer or consumer upon another). These are the public good ecosystem externality (Crocker and Tschirhart, 1991) and the resource stock externality. Users of one part of the ecosystem create an ecosystem externality by changing the flow of ecosystem services in another part on which other uses depend.

Technology is a second public good. This is because existing technology and technological change affect how, when and what is harvested it necessarily affects green growth. Thus, a third externality or source of market failure exists: the knowledge externality of developing and diffusing new technology (Jaffe, Newell and Stavins, 2005; Squires and Vestergaard, 2013b; Squires and Garcia, 2013; Grafton, 2014; Kronbak, Squires and Vestergaard, 2013; Squires, Clarke and Chan, 2014). In Schumpeter's third component of technological change, diffusion, an increase in a firm's physical capital stock through embodied technical change, leads to a parallel increase in its stock of knowledge, which is a public good with an external benefit that any other firm can access at zero or low cost (Romer, 1986, 1990; Arthur, 2009). The cost or value of a new technology to one user may depend on how many other users have adopted the technology. Technology diffusion rates depend on the strength of economic incentives for technology adoption and create dynamic increasing returns through network effects as other firms adopt the innovation.

Technology, like any other public good, is underprovided because new technology creates external benefits and incentives for free riding (Jaffe, Newell and Stavins, 2005). A firm that invests in or implements a new technology typically creates benefits for other producers along with spillovers of value or consumer surplus while the innovating firm incurs all the costs. Firms and markets left to their own devices therefore lack the incentives to increase those benefits by optimally investing in any of the five forms of fisheries innovation set out in the next section.

Due to the free riding and under-provision of these public goods, there is a role for collective action through the public sector and public–private–civil society partnerships in conservation and developing and diffusing green innovations. The public sector can help finance or even directly supply the public goods (such as providing new technology or marine protected areas) due to the external benefit that all of society can enjoy. The private sector can similarly directly supply the public goods, such as biodiversity offsets (Kotchen, 2009). In fisheries, as we discuss in the next section, there are also private–public–civil society partnerships supplying public goods, such as the current development of biodiversity saving eco-FADs that involve private industry, governments, and the International Seafood Sustainability Foundation (ISSF), itself an industry–civil society partnership.

4.3. Five Types of Fisheries Innovations

Fisheries innovations can be classified by their application or point of implementation (Grafton, 2014):

(1) Harvesting or fishing technologies, which are process innovations leading to more effective ways to find or harvest fish and are typically associated with improvements in catch per unit of effort;
(2) Conservation technologies, which are process innovations that are usually biased and that reduce the bycatch or the impacts of

fisheries on marine habitats and are typically bycatch or biodiversity saving;

(3) Product innovations, such as the development of surimi as a crabmeat substitute;
(4) Aquaculture technologies, which are process innovations that more effectively culture fish; and,
(5) Institutional innovations intended to improve how fisheries are managed to help mitigate market failures and to better deliver on desired outcomes of management, such as ecosystem-based fisheries management.

Fishing, conservation, and aquaculture technologies can be disembodied and/or embodied, exogenous or endogenous, biased or Hick's neutral, and directed (induced).

Any of the five forms of fisheries innovation may support green innovation, but it is most likely to be closely associated with the development and adoption of conservation technologies (Grafton, 2014). For example, these include processes and technologies that promote the development of Low Impact and Fuel Efficient (LIFE) fishing (Suuronen *et al.*, 2012), biodiversity saving technical change, and institutional innovations that can support the provision of public goods, such as marine spatial planning or marine protected areas. We now focus on the five types of technologies.

4.3.1. *Harvesting technologies*

Innovations in harvesting technologies, when there are uncorrected market failures, can exacerbate ecosystem externalities and diminish the public goods of biodiversity and ecosystems and their benefits (Squires and Garcia, 2013; Grafton, 2014; Squires, Clarke and Chan, 2014). This can generate undesirable outcomes in three principal ways. First, innovations in harvesting technologies that increase catch per unit of effort and economic efficiency can increase economic welfare in the presence of sustainable harvest or effort targets, such as Total Allowable Catches or Total Allowable Effort, or incentives that fully internalise stock externalities for targeted species.

However, they can further exacerbate the resource stock externality, overfishing, overfished resource stocks and reduce economic welfare in their absence (Smith, 1972; Smith and Krutilla, 1982). Harvesting innovations can be process, such as fish finding electronic technologies, or product innovations, such as flash frozen refrigeration of harvested fish, thereby changing the product form from fresh to frozen, which allows vessels to receive higher prices and fish longer.

Second, in the absence of controls or incentives to limit the harvest of bycatch or the effects on habitat, innovation in harvesting technologies can reduce biodiversity and the abundance of unpriced, but nevertheless positively valued non-targeted species, and the services they provide. This may be described as unresolved ecosystem externalities in fisheries (Kronbak, Squires and Vestergaard, 2013). Third, overfished target species also reduce the biodiversity and ecosystems services that these species provide below optimal levels (Kronbak, Squires and Vestergaard, 2013).

4.3.2. *Green technologies*

Conservation technologies can be characterised in at least three ways (Grafton, 2014). First, biased technical change reduces the relative proportions of undesirable bycatch or more broadly, biodiversity loss and environmental degradation as discussed earlier. These innovations can be disembodied, such as changes in areas and time fished, or embodied in the physical capital stock, such as Tori lines to reduce seabird bycatch with pelagic longlines or nets and pens that prevent escapement of cultured fish. These process innovations include not just innovations in the harvesting process, but also post-catch handling procedures, such as line cutters to reduce post-hooking sea turtle mortality with shallow set pelagic longlines, a form of embodied technological change accompanied by learning by doing.

Second, conservation technologies can be associated with monitoring and information, and are both disembodied and embodied (Grafton, 2014). Examples include satellite vessel monitoring systems or video monitoring. The intent of these embodied conservation technologies is to measure and monitor the direct harvesting impacts of fishing that may include both targeted and non-targeted species and/or provide a control or an incentive to fishers to mitigate their ecosystem externalities.

The third type of conservation technology is not directly related to mitigating ecosystem externalities, but addresses another information externality (Grafton, 2014). It is intended to improve the information, evidence and data on the life history, movement and abundance of marine populations, and also the quality of habitat. A description of some of these technologies is provided by Godo (1998) and can include data storage and data transmission technologies that facilitate real-time information sharing and data access (Food and Agriculture Organization (FAO), 2010, pp. 157–167) as well as instruments for monitoring fish populations (Wall, Anderson and McLean, 2014).

4.3.3. *Product innovations*

One of the most important dynamic incentives for product innovation occurs through the market effect, in which the expectation of increased profits provides the primary motivation for the development of new fish products and markets. Some innovations are exogenous to the fishing industry, such as in food technology and food processing, and can allow for a greater range of fish products (Grafton, 2014). Such products can add value and provide additional revenue sources, such as the sale of fish oil as a dietary supplement. An important incentive for new product innovation originates in consumer markets and the supply chain, and may be especially strong with vertically integrated fishing or aquaculture companies that have the opportunity to multiply the gains along the seafood value chain (Squires and Garcia, 2013; Grafton, 2014). Retail companies selling final fish products, and processors, are particularly vulnerable to consumer concerns about unsustainable fishing practices if they supply a recognisable consumer-branded product, such as UK retailers of canned tuna sourced from FADs, inducing shifts to pole-and-line or free school caught skipjack tuna.

Market access provides important incentives for green growth (Squires and Garcia, 2013; Grafton, 2014). Securing and enlarging markets for fish products is the key motivating factor for fishing industries to obtain eco-certification and secure eco-labels, an instance of the market effect of directed innovation. Two sets of externalities are present:

(1) The familiar set of linked common resource-public good externalities, resulting from firms using the environment as a costless input into their production process; and,
(2) An externality related to imperfect information (Kotchen, 2013).

The dynamic incentive to innovate from eco-certification and eco-labels is market or demand-pull driven and responding to the information externality, where consumer preferences for sustainable fish products provide an access advantage for certified products. Potentially attractive wholesaler and retailer margins on fish products may also encourage supermarket chains to promote conservation practices to preserve these margins into the future. For example, the need to maintain market access to the US provided financial incentives for tuna fishers in the eastern Pacific Ocean to adopt 'dolphin free' tuna practices while sustainable certification is a requirement to be able to sell fresh fish at a premium price in high-end markets. The price effect further induces biodiversity-saving technological change as regulations and changing public opinions increase the shadow price of bycatch, or more generally the shadow price of biodiversity and ecosystem services.

4.3.4. *Aquaculture technologies*

Aquaculture technologies refer to the entire value chain of the production and marketing of captive or cultured marine fisheries; i.e., aquaculture. They represent an important type of innovation in fisheries that has allowed for an enormous expansion in production over the past three decades, so that aquaculture now accounts for around half of total seafood for human consumption.

To the extent that wild, capture fisheries have greater unresolved market failures, including stock, information and ecosystem externalities, the increase in aquaculture production may support green growth. On the other hand, unresolved and localised ecosystem externalities may be exacerbated by aquaculture (Naylor *et al.*, 2000). These externalities may include: organic waste contamination from the permanent co-location of large numbers of fish or the destruction of valuable ecosystems, such as mangroves, when establishing some forms of aquaculture such as shrimp farm; the escape of captive fish that poses disease risks and may diminish genetic diversity; and the physical space used by aquaculture enterprises. In the absence of negative feedbacks on the profitability of aquaculture operations causing the external costs through price or market effects, or public policies, these types of ecosystem externalities will continue (Asche and Bjorndal, 2010).

Indirect effects of aquaculture technologies include added fishing pressure on some low trophic fish stocks — forage fish, which provide the source of much of the aquaculture feed in the form of fish meal (Tacon and Metian, 2008). This has been called the 'fish meal trap'. It arises because of market failures in wild, marine capture fisheries where there is a divergence between the private and social cost of harvesting fish. In part, sustainability concerns, and especially rising fish meal prices (Asche and Bjorndal, 2010), have induced biased-innovation in aquaculture feeds, as the consequence of the price effect. This, in turn, has stimulated the development of aquaculture feeds with modified vegetarian diet and new feed technologies (Bowdy *et al.*, 2012). Increasing competition for fish oil from cosmetic and pharmaceutical companies has also provided incentives to research and innovate to reduce the fish oil component in fish feedstocks.

Bowdy *et al.* (2012) provide a comprehensive review of emerging technologies led by the expansion of aquaculture. For decades fish genetic improvements have been studied, although their application in aquaculture have been limited (Dunham, 2004, p. 4). While only about 10 per cent or less of aquaculture output is based on genetically improved stocks from resource augmenting innovation

(Gjedrem, Robinson and Rye, 2012) there has been sustained productivity growth in aquaculture that explains about one-third of the reduction in production costs in salmon aquaculture over the 1990s (Tveteras and Heshmati, 2002).

Improvements in managing the health of cultured fish have also emerged and are directly associated with green growth. This biased technological change has focused on diagnostic technologies, epidemiology and disease exclusion (Bowdy *et al.*, 2012). These efforts have helped to reduce drastically the use of antibiotics in some cultured fish in response to consumer health concerns, an example of the market effect and incentives directing technical change originating from the consumer market and supply chain. The market effect from improved market access and the price effect from regulations internalising environmental impacts raising relative input prices both induced these biased innovations.

4.3.5. *Institutional innovations*

Institutional innovation is a key to promoting green growth in fisheries (Jaffe, Newell and Stavins, 2005; Squires and Vestergaard, 2013b; Squires and Garcia, 2013; Grafton, 2014; Squires, Clarke and Chan, 2014). Institutional innovation in the context of fishing and green growth refers to the myriad of policy initiatives that:

(1) Internalise the external costs of actions by fishers on either target species or non-target species and habitat; and/or,
(2) Create dynamic incentives that have significant effects on the path of product, conservation, and aquaculture innovations, all of which lead to biodiversity conservation and healthier ecosystems.

The relevant forms of market failure or externalities are for the common resource stock, biodiversity and ecosystem services, technology, and information, where the latter three are public goods externalities. These externalities are to various degrees linked, but nonetheless require multiple policy instruments, since a single policy instrument is insufficient to address all externalities.

Important sector-specific factors affecting fisheries innovation include (Grafton, 2014):

(1) Types of fishery regulation (input versus output controls, use of spatial planning, etc.), and whether these are 'command-and-control', such as quotas, time-and-area closures, and technology standards (mandated gear and operating procedures, such as minimum mesh sizes and avoidance of biodiversity hot spots) or market- or incentive-based, such as transferable bycatch property rights or bycatch taxes;
(2) The characteristics of the fisheries (pelagic or benthic, subsistence or industrial, coastal or deep water, recreational or commercial, atomistic);
(3) The property rights structure in the harvesting sector (access versus harvesting rights, individual versus community rights, etc.) and property rights over technology and more generally knowledge (patents, licenses) in the general economy;
(4) Harvesting-supply chain-consumer retail markets industry structure (large-scale producers and processors with a strong and active industry association and substantial economic surplus for investment and innovation, such as the ISSF and International Pole and Line Foundation for tunas or many small producers and atomistic processors, such as for many coastal fisheries with limited collective organisation and limited economic surplus), well organised and extensive consumer markets with well established brands such as tunas versus indistinguishable product from multiple sources such as cultured tilapia; and,
(5) Public policies towards innovation and its diffusion (public support for research and development, or a legal structure supporting strong fisheries regulation, including for conservation, and supporting innovation, or laws on eco-labelling and eco-certification).

Collectively these factors determine the nature of the public goods, the market failures and individual and collective dynamic incentives for different types of innovation.

Green innovation, especially for conservation technologies, can be voluntarily supplied by the private sector. Incentives for innovation include rewards for their own sake, earning a market premium or gaining market access, securing a competitive advantage through product differentiation, deterrence of boycotts in consumer markets and to lessen the scrutiny of environmental authorities. Voluntary approaches in many instances respond to potential regulatory threats and depend on several factors that include the incentives to participate; clear standards of performance; and, adequate monitoring of behaviour of those fishers undertaking the desired actions and those who are not so engaged (Segerson, 2010). Voluntary provision of a public good, biodiversity offsets of nesting site conservation for sea turtles, by the major US tuna processors through ISSF provides an example (Gjertsen *et al.*, 2014).

4.4. Three Pillars to Green Growth

The three pillars that support green innovation in fisheries include (Grafton, 2014):

(1) The international and national innovation framework;
(2) Institutional and market design to achieve ecosystem goals; and,
(3) Knowledge creation, transfer and diffusion supported by fisheries innovation networks (FINS).

4.4.1. *International and national frameworks for green innovation*

A nation's incentives and framework to innovate can be called its national framework for green innovation that encompass all the public and private organisations, incentives, regulations and structures that foster or promote the sustainable use of natural capital stocks (Grafton, 2014). Moreover, international frameworks for green innovation are increasingly important, because the globe is increasingly interconnected by markets, knowledge, biodiversity and ecosystem services are global public goods. Transboundary fisheries, biodiversity, and ecosystem issues cut across national boundaries (Squires and Garcia, 2013). The organisation of international innovation and international frameworks, due to the sovereignty of states and absence of a global government, require formal cooperation through treaties and conventions, such as the Convention on Biological Diversity or the Regional Fisheries Management Organizations (Barrett, 2003). However, many conservation innovations are 'one-shot' public goods, in that the benefits to the provider are sufficiently high so that free riding is immaterial and only a single provider is required. With one-shot conservation innovations, the requirement is the more informal coordination of activities among nations, civil society, and the private sector, such as the development and subsequent testing around the world of circle hooks to replace J hooks and Tori lines to lower seabird bycatch for shallow set pelagic longline fisheries (Squires and Garcia, 2013). Once a nation, civil society, or industry provides the conservation technology, other parties can simply test and adapt them to their own circumstances.

In the broadest sense, the public sector's role is to overcome the market failures that exist and to provide the incentive (positive and negative) structure for innovation and to avoid any adverse impacts of innovation in the presence of unresolved common resource externalities (Jaffe, Newell and Stavins, 2005). This involves two key strategies:

(1) Mitigation or removal of market failures inherent in the exploitation of common resources by internalising the external costs associated with stock, congestion and ecosystem externalities; and,
(2) Mitigation of the market failures inherent in the under-provision of knowledge, information diffusion and technological innovation because of their positive externalities.

While much harvesting technology is exogenous in origin, most conservation and product innovations in fisheries are endogenous, often induced responding to the price or market effects, or endogenous in response to R&D. As a public good, technology's availability is unaffected by the numbers that employ it. Most conservation and product innovations are path dependent, in that the mix of technologies and institutions in place at any time depends upon the path taken by technological evolution and is thereby influenced by particular decisions and chance events along the way (David, 1985). For example, the current public–private–civil society R&D partnership for bycatch saving technological change with tuna purse seine fishing setting on FADs is in response to the market effect and organised on a model emerging out of the tuna–dolphin issue. The mix and interaction of public policies to correct for the common resource and ecosystem externalities and the knowledge and information externalities with innovation is complex.

4.4.2. *Institutional/market design and fisheries innovation*

A key question is the relationship between the two sets of institutional innovations, where their relative importance and relationship to one another can vary over time in general environmental issues (Orr, 1976; Jaffe, Newell and Stavins, 2005) and in fisheries in particular (Squires and Vestergaard, 2013b; Squires and Garcia, 2013; Grafton, 2014). Policy instruments can be chosen on the basis of two factors:

(1) The impact upon the market failures of the resource stock externality and the ecosystem externality and related knowledge and information externalities; and,
(2) The dynamic impact upon incentives to innovate and adopt green technology.

In both cases, incentives have to be aligned at the individual, group and collective level and to address both the target and bycatch species (or more generally biodiversity and habitat). Market-based instruments may also support more efficient technology adoption decisions that are environmentally friendly compared to command-and-control instruments, such as time-area closures or mandated performance and technology standards (Jaffe, Newell and Stavins, 2005). Malueg (1989) provides evidence for this efficiency in terms of the adoption of substitutes for lead in gasoline in the US and also with the adoption of cleaner air technologies in terms of sulphur dioxide allowance trading. In the fisheries context, there is evidence that market-based instruments have promoted process innovations at the fisher level that support green growth.

Policy instruments chosen only for their short-run impact and without regard for their long-run or dynamic impacts through incentives directing biodiversity saving technological change may not be optimal when these dynamic incentives plus the direction and amount of biased technical change are jointly considered. Some institutional innovations create more specific and targeted innovation and diffusion and adoption than others in harvesting. For example, traditional time-and-area closures may have minimal impact upon dynamic incentives to innovate, and technology standards, such as gear and operating requirements like pingers in drift gillnets to reduce whale interactions, can even freeze technology in place and reduce incentives to innovate. The placement of institutional innovations within the consumer retail market-supply chain-harvesting sector nexus is also important. For example, consumer incentives created in retail markets, supported by eco-labelling and eco-certification that address information externalities, can have powerful impacts upon innovation, such as occurred in canned tuna markets and dolphin-safe labels (Ward and Phillips, 2010).

4.4.3. *FINs*

The institutional question that addresses the market failures in the creation and diffusion of new technology is the third pillar supporting green innovation, FINs, illustrated by Figure 4.2 (Grafton, 2014). These networks provide the structure and links between the private, public and civil society sectors. These links are valuable for knowledge diffusion via network mechanisms that are characteristics of atomistic industries, such as in fishing or agriculture (Minh *et al.*, 2011).

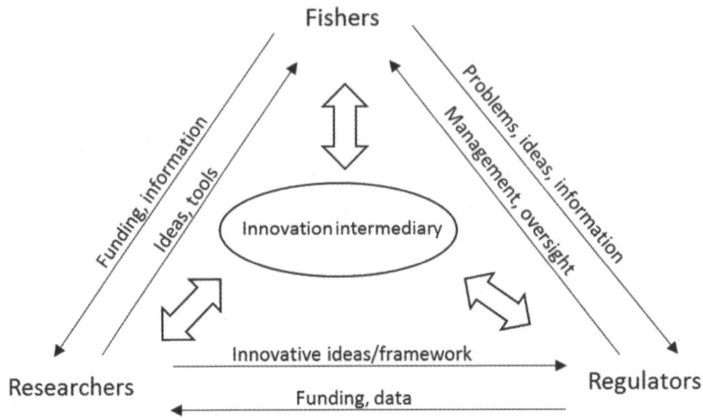

Figure 4.2: FINs
Source: Grafton (2014).

FINs also have value beyond diffusion (Grafton, 2014). The interaction of persons with complementary knowledge provides a 'bridge' across disciplinary or experiential divides that can provide benefits to all in that non-rival knowledge can be created that otherwise would not have occurred (Grafton, Kompas and Owen, 2007). When this arises within the fisheries sector, this can be characterised as endogenous innovation. Examples include a range of fisheries-specific technologies, such as eco-FADs and aquaculture with lower per unit demands for forage fish and reduced effluents.

The importance of information sharing and individual interactions is consistent with theoretical and country-level studies on productivity that combines three ideas:

(1) Cooperation and group interaction enabling economic actors to take advantage of large amounts of specialised knowledge;
(2) While knowledge is non-rival its creation and transfer, especially tacit knowledge, is not and depends on interactions across social groups; and,
(3) Individuals communicate at lower cost the greater the similarity between them (Grafton, Kompas and Owen, 2007).

The public sector's role is to facilitate the exchange by supporting FINs that include knowledge platforms for diffusion and exchange, and, where relevant, contribute to the knowledge and information base.

4.5. Concluding Remarks

Innovation in capture and culture fisheries is a key contributor to green fisheries growth. These product, process and institutional green innovations, many of them endogenous and biased towards saving bycatch, or more generally biodiversity and ecosystems, and responding to regulations and market and price effects, create more balanced harvesting, conserve biodiversity, and lead to healthy ecosystems and their services. Any of the five forms of fisheries innovation — harvesting, aquaculture, conservation, product and institutional — may support green innovation, but it is most likely to be closely associated with the development and diffusion of conservation innovations.

Meeting the green growth challenge in fisheries requires expanding the range of successfully applied management instruments and promoting technologies, processes and institutional and market designs. Green innovation that supports natural capital stocks and underpins ecosystems-based fisheries and aquaculture management provides a complementary strategy to conventional and incentive-based management approaches. Green innovation can provide a 'win–win' approach by inter-temporally reducing the costs of mitigating adverse ecological and biodiversity impacts from both capture and culture fisheries.

Green growth requires addressing the market failures or externalities associated with exploiting common fisheries resources and the public goods of biodiversity, ecosystem services, technology, and information. The multiple policy instruments required to address these multiple market failures not only directly create static incentives, but also dynamic incentives to innovate and adopt green technology. Three pillars that support green innovation in fisheries include the national innovation framework, institutional and market design to achieve ecosystem goals, and knowledge creation, transfer and diffusion supported by FINs.

Bibliography

Acemoglu, D. (2002). Directed Technical Change, *The Review of Economic Studies*, 69(4), pp. 781–809.

Arrow, K.J. (1962). 'Economic Welfare and the Allocation of Resources for Invention', in Nelson, R. (ed.), *The Rate and Direction on Inventive Activity*, Princeton University Press, Princeton, NJ, pp. 609–626. Available at: http://www.nber.org/chapters/c2144.pdf [Accessed 12 December 2014].

Arthur, W.B. (2009). *The Nature of Technology: What it is and How it Evolves*, Free Press, New York.

Asche, F. and Bjorndal, T. (2010). 'Aquaculture: Production and Markets', in Grafton, R.Q., Hilborn, R., Squires, D., Tait, M. and Williams, M.J. (eds.), *Handbook of Marine Fisheries Conservation and Management*, Oxford University Press, New York, pp. 60–71.

Barrett, S. (2003). *Environment & Statecraft: The Strategy of Environmental Treaty-Making*, Oxford University Press, Oxford.

Bowdy, C.L., Hulata, G., Liu, Z., Allan, G.I., Sommerville, C., Passos de Andrade, T., Pereira, R., Yarish, C., Shpigel, M., Chopin, T., Robinson, S., Avnimelech, Y. and Lovatelli, A. (2012). 'Novel and Emerging Technologies: Can they Contribute to Improving Aquaculture Sustainability?' in Subasinghe, R.P., Arthur, J.R., Bartley, D.M., De Silva, S.S., Halwart, M., Hishamunda, N., Mohan, C.V. and Sorgeloos, P. (eds.), *Proceedings of the Global Conference on Aquaculture 2010: Farming the Waters for People and Food*, Food and Agriculture Organization, Rome, pp. 149–191.

Crocker, T. and Tschirhart, J. (1991). Ecosystems, Externalities, and Economies, *Environmental and Resource Economics*, 2(6), pp. 551–567.

Dagorn, L., Holland, K., Restrepo, V. and Moreno, G. (2013). Is it Good or Bad to Fish with FADs? What are the Real Impacts of Drifting FADs on Pelagic Marine Ecosystems?, *Fish and Fisheries*, 14(3), pp. 391–415.

David, P. (1985). Clio and the Economics of QWERTY, *American Economic Review*, 75, pp. 332–337.

Dunham, R.A. (2004). *Aquaculture and Fisheries Biotechnology: Genetic Approaches*, CABI Publishing, Wallingford.

Food and Agriculture Organization (FAO) (2010). *The State of World Fisheries*, FAO Fisheries and Aquaculture Department, Rome.

Gjedrem, T., Robinson, N. and Rye, M. (2012). The Importance of Selective Breeding in Aquaculture to Meet Future Demands for Animal Protein: A Review, *Aquaculture*, 350–353, pp. 117–129.

Gjertsen, H., Squires, D., Dutton, P.H. and Eguchi, T. (2014). Cost-Effectiveness of Alternative Conservation Strategies with Application to the Pacific Leatherback Turtle, *Conservation Biology*, 28(1), pp. 140–149.

Godo, O.R. (1998). What can Technology Offer the Future Fisheries Scientist — Possibilities for Obtaining Better Estimates of Stocks Abundance by Direct Observations, *Journal of Northwest Atlantic Fishery Science*, 23, pp. 105–131.

Grafton, R.Q. (2014). 'Fisheries Innovation and how this can contribute to Green Growth', Report prepared for the OECD.

Grafton, R.Q. and Squires, D. (2013). Theory and Practice of Fisheries and Water Economics, in *Encyclopedia of Energy, Natural Resource and Environmental Economics*. Available at: http://ac.els-cdn.com/B9780123750679001637/3-s2.0-B9780123750679001637-main.pdf?_tid=992b7e96-81af-11e4-93df-00000aab0f26&acdnat=1418355371_d29752da2008f05347b7db2c93c9069c [Accessed 12 December 2014].

Grafton, R.Q., Kompas, T. and Owen, P.D. (2007). Bridging the Barriers: Knowledge Connections, Productivity and Capital Accumulation, *Journal of Productivity Analysis*.

Grafton, R.Q., Hilborn, R., Squires, D. and Williams, M.J. (2010). 'Marine Conservation and Fisheries Management: At the Crossroads', in Grafton, R.Q., Hilborn, R., Squires, D., Tait, M. and Williams, M.J. (eds.), *Handbook of Marine Fisheries Conservation and Management*, Oxford University Press, New York, pp. 3–19.

Hicks, J. (1932). *The Theory of Wages*, Macmillan, London.

Jaffe, A.B., Newell, R.G. and Stavins, R.N. (2005). A Tale of Two Market Failures: Technology and Environmental Policy, *Ecological Economics*, 54, pp. 164–174.

Kotchen, M.J. (2009). Voluntary Provision of Public Goods for Bads: A Theory of Environmental Offsets, *Economic Journal*, 119, pp. 883–899.

Kotchen, M.J. (2013). Voluntary- and Information-Based Approaches to Environmental Management: A Public Economics Perspective, *Review of Environmental Economics and Management*, 8(1), pp. 276–295.

Kronbak, L.G., Squires, D. and Vestergaard, N. (2013). Recent Developments in Fisheries Economics Research, *International Review of Environmental and Resource Economics*, 7(1), pp. 67–108.

Malueg, D.A. (1989). Emission Credit Trading and the Incentive to Adopt New Pollution Abatement Technology, *Journal of Environmental Economics and Management*, 16, pp. 52–57.

Minh, T.T., Neef, A. and Hoffmann, V. (2011). Agricultural Knowledge Transfer and Innovation Processes in Vietnam's Northwestern Uplands: State-Governed or Demand-Driven?, *Southeast Asian Studies*, 48(4), pp. 425–455.

Naylor, R.L., Goldburg, R.J., Primaver, J., Kautsky, N., Beveridge, M., Clay, J., Folke, C. and Lubchenco, J. (2000). Effects of Aquaculture on World Fish Supplies, *Nature*, 405(29), pp. 1017–1024.

Nelson, R. and Winter, S. (1982). *An Evolutionary Theory of Economic Change*, The Belknap Press of Harvard University Press, Cambridge.

Orr, L. (1976). Incentives for Innovation as the Basis for Effluent Charge Strategy, *American Economic Review*, 66, pp. 441–447.

Romer, P. (1986). Increasing Returns and Long-Run Growth, *Journal of Political Economy*, 94, pp. 1002–1037.

Romer, P. (1990). Endogenous Technological Change, *Journal of Political Economy*, 98 (5), pp. S71–S102.

Schumpeter, J. (1942). *Capitalism, Socialism, and Democracy*, Harper, New York.

Segerson, K. (2010). 'Can Voluntary Programs Reduce Sea Turtle Bycatch? Insights from the Literature in Environmental Economics', in Grafton, R.Q., Hilborn, R., Squires, D., Tait, M. and Williams, M.J. (eds.), *Handbook of Marine Fisheries Conservation and Management*, Oxford University Press, New York, pp. 618–629.

Smith, V.K. (1972). The Implications of Common Property Resources for Technical Change, *European Economic Review*, 3(4), pp. 469–479.

Smith, V.K. and Krutilla, J. (1982). 'Reformulating the Role of Natural Resources in Economic Models', in Smith, V.K. and Krutilla, J. (eds.), *Explorations in Natural Resource Economics*, Johns Hopkins University Press, Baltimore.

Squires, D. and Garcia, S. (2013). A Multidisciplinary Workshop to Address Ecosystem-Level Impacts of Fisheries Bycatch on Marine

Megafauna: Biodiversity Conservation through Mitigation, Policy, Economic Instruments, and Technical Change, *International Union for the Conservation of Nature*, 10–13 September, Gland, Switzerland.

Squires, D. and Vestergaard, N. (2013a). Technical Change in Fisheries, *Marine Policy*, 42, pp. 286–292.

Squires, D. and Vestergaard, N. (2013b). Technical Change and the Commons, *The Review of Economics and Statistics*, 95(5), pp. 1769–1787.

Squires, D., Clarke, R. and Chan, V. (2014). Subsidies, Public Goods, and External Benefits in Fisheries, *Marine Policy*, 45, pp. 222–227.

Suuronen, P., Chopin, F., Glass, C., Lokkeborg, S., Matsushita, Y., Queirolo, D. and Rihan, D. (2012). Low Impact and Fuel Efficient Fishing — Looking Beyond the Horizon, *Fisheries Research*, 119–210, pp. 135–146.

Tacon, A.G.J. and Metian, M. (2008). Global Overview on the Use of Fish Oil in Industrially Compounded Aquafeeds: Trends and Future Prospects, *Aquaculture*, 285 (1–4), pp. 146–158.

Tisdell, C. (1991). *Economics of Environmental Conservation*, Elsevier Publishing Co., Amsterdam.

Tveteras, R. and Heshmati, A. (2002). Patterns of Productivity Growth in the Norwegian Salmon Farming Industry, *International Review of Economics and Business*, 49(3), pp. 367–393.

Wall, C.C., Anderson, C. and McLean, S.J. (2014). Getting More for Less: Increasing the Accessibility of Water Column Sonar Data for Fisheries Management, *Journal of the Acoustical Society of America*, 135, p. 2153. Available at: http://dx.doi.org/10.1121/1.4876978.

Ward, T. and Phillips, B. (2010). 'Seafood Ecolabelling', in Grafton, R.Q., Hilborn, R., Squires, D., Tait, M. and Williams, M.J. (eds.), *Handbook of Marine Fisheries Conservation and Management*, Oxford University Press, New York, pp. 608–617.

Watson, J., Epperly, S., Shah, A. and Foster, D. (2005). Fishing Methods to Reduce Sea Turtle Mortality Associated with Pelagic Longlines, *Canadian Journal of Fisheries and Aquatic Sciences*, 62, pp. 965–981.

5. Markets for Biodiversity

Michael 't Sas-Rolfes

Along with climate change, the continuing loss of the earth's biological diversity (biodiversity) is a major contemporary environmental concern (Barnosky *et al.*, 2011; Wilson, 2013). At the 1992 Rio Earth Summit, the world's governments established the Convention on Biological Diversity (CBD) to address this issue at a global level. The text of the CBD provides a definition of biodiversity that includes diversity within species, between species, and of ecosystems, thereby broadening the scope of previously narrower concerns relating to species conservation and protected areas.

The CBD followed various previous conservation governance initiatives at national and international levels, including the establishment of organisations such as the International Union for the Conservation of Nature (IUCN) and treaties such as the Convention on International Trade in Endangered Species (CITES). However, despite all these efforts, recent assessments claim that governments are still not doing enough or spending enough to halt biodiversity decline, with possible serious consequences for humanity (Millennium Ecosystem Assessment, 2005; Rockström *et al.*, 2009; Secretariat of the CBD, 2010; Waldron *et al.*, 2013).

The causes of biodiversity loss have been examined in some detail by both scientists and economists, sometimes working in collaboration (Swanson, 1998). One economic perspective argues that biodiversity is a global 'public good', and therefore not supplied in sufficient quantities by the market (Ferraro and Kiss, 2002). This implies that biodiversity loss is a consequence of market failure and that government-based solutions are required. However, this notion is simplistic because it ignores the role of government failure.

Biodiversity loss results from a complex set of interacting human and biophysical factors, in which institutions[1] — the rules of the game that define social interaction — play a vital role. Contemporary institutional analysis recognises that governance is an increasingly complex undertaking, involving both conventional government bodies and elements of civil society such as community structures, corporations and non-profit organisations. Economists such as North (1990) and Williamson (2000) have highlighted that institutions create the incentives that guide human behaviour and lead to varying economic outcomes; recent work by Acemoglu and Robinson (2012) provides strong empirical support for this.

Further specific work on natural resource management integrates insights of institutional theory with ecosystems science, and has generated the concept of 'socio-ecological systems'. As a leading pioneer in this type of research, Ostrom argues that there are no panaceas — no single type of governance system will resolve all environmental problems — and that simple distinctions between market and state are increasingly irrelevant: complex human systems relating to the management of common pool natural resources require polycentric or 'hybrid' forms of governance (Ostrom, 2010; Ostrom, Janssen and Anderies, 2007).

This analysis implies that markets can and do play a role in biodiversity conservation. But what is that role and what should it be? What scope is there for that role to be enhanced, so as to improve the current performance of existing conservation efforts? This chapter considers these questions by examining the historical and

[1] In this context, institutions can be defined as 'the humanly devised constraints that shape human interaction' (North, 1990, p. 3).

contemporary context of conservation, including the role of private initiatives and markets, and then highlighting some recent developments. It also includes an illustrative case study of rhino conservation in South Africa, before concluding with a few comments about the likely future role of markets for biodiversity and some associated challenges and opportunities.

5.1. History of Conservation

When did our human ancestors start to conserve biological resources? Increasingly, research is showing that, contrary to romantic notions of noble savages living in harmony with ecosystems, the spread of *Homo sapiens* out of Africa had disastrous consequences for large mammal and bird species in Eurasia, Australasia and the Americas. Although climate change may partially account for some extinctions, increasingly the evidence suggests that our ancestors exterminated most of these species for food (Barnosky *et al.*, 2004). Through the selective use of fire, and by removing important nutrient-dispersing large animals, they also radically transformed the earth's ecosystems. For example, it is now thought that the Amazon region of South America was a more fertile mosaic woodland area before losing all of its megafauna to probable human predation (Doughty, Wolf and Malhi, 2013).

It appears that humans co-evolved with ecosystems, changing their diets and lifestyles in response to changes in climate and habitats. Some communities discovered agriculture and gradually assumed agrarian and urbanising lifestyles, whereas others remained hunter-gatherers (Harari, 2014). Some may have evolved institutions to regulate overharvesting or other forms of environmental degradation, whereas others simply moved on or went to war with their neighbours when vital biological resources became scarce (Diamond, 1999).

The concept of private property appears to have emerged as a consequence of agriculture and urbanisation, and was not initially applied to wild nature, which continued to serve largely as an open access commons until recent times. To the extent that private conservation institutions existed, these most likely took the form of nobles claiming exclusive hunting rights in designated areas. Outside such areas, animals continued to be slaughtered on a large scale, especially with the spread of growing numbers of European colonists with guns and horses in North America and Africa during the 18th and 19th centuries (Beinart and Coates, 2002).

By the year 1800, early settlers in South Africa became aware that they had hunted at least one indigenous antelope, the bluebuck, to extinction. A second, the bontebok, teetered on the brink. This prompted a farmer, Alexander van der Bijl to enclose an area to protect the last remaining specimens in 1837 (Skead, 1980). The bontebok was thus saved by private initiative, not directly by the state: the state simply provided the legal framework that allowed both the enclosure of land and private property right claims. Elsewhere, where wild animals remained open access property (*res nullius* or *ferae naturae*) they continued to be hunted toward extinction — for example, the North American bison and passenger pigeon were both heavily hunted in the late 19th century, and the latter species became extinct in the early 20th century (Beinart and Coates, 2002).

Historical accounts reveal that early conservation concerns were essentially utilitarian: they mostly related to maintaining stocks of biological resources for future use (Adams, 2004; Beinart, 2008). However, during the late 19th and early 20th century, changing perceptions of the human-nature relationship caused public interest in conservation to increase dramatically (Jepson and Whittaker, 2002), with two noteworthy features. The first is that such interest emanated largely from social movements in the West (Europe and the USA), with policy changes driven by elite societies. The second is that the underlying social values driving public conservation concerns started to diversify. For example, in the USA, Theodore Roosevelt and Gifford Pinchot's more tangible and pragmatic concerns with ethical hunting and wise use could be contrasted against the more spiritual and aesthetic interests of John Muir and Henry David Thoreau.

As wildlife conservation policy developed, two distinct approaches emerged: (i) laws seeking to regulate the harvest of certain species through quotas, term limits or complete bans, and (ii) laws seeking to designate specific 'protected areas' (Jepson and Whittaker, 2002). These laws helped to save certain species and habitats from overexploitation, but were also supplemented by private initiatives. For example, in addition to the bontebok, private landowners and individuals also played a significant (if not exclusive) role in protecting the last remaining specimens of endangered large mammals such as the American bison, Arabian oryx, Przewalski's horse and Père-David's deer. Private landowners also voluntarily retained large areas of natural habitat — so-called private protected areas.

According to Phillips (2004), the protected area concept has historical roots dating back some two millennia, but the modern protected areas movement originated in the USA, Australia, New Zealand, and South Africa during the late 19th century, spreading fairly rapidly to other countries. Although the state rapidly assumed the key role as guardian of protected areas, Africa's first designated nature reserve, Rooiport, was a private hunting refuge, established by the De Beers mining company in South Africa in 1893. By 1933, protected areas had gained acceptance as the principal means to conserve nature, as recognised by the London Conference on African Wildlife (Jepson and Whittaker, 2002). That same conference saw the first attempt to set international standards by developing a system for categorising protected areas.

The late 1940s saw the establishment of the IUCN, which assumed a key role in guiding global conservation governance, in part through its World Commission on Protected Areas (WCPA). During this period, the state played the principal role in establishing and managing protected areas. However, in 1951, a group of ecologists in the USA formed The Nature Conservancy, a non-government organisation (NGO) that sought to purchase properties for the sake of conserving them (Smith and Mark, 2009) and from the early 1960s, private landowners in South Africa started to show an interest in wildlife ranching and providing wildlife-based tourism products (Carruthers, 2008). Elsewhere, governments continued to dominate conservation efforts, with a growing emphasis on scientific-based management and preservationist approaches, which allowed for non-consumptive tourism, but which typically excluded harvesting or commercial use of wildlife products.

The early 1970s saw further intensified state activity at a global level, coincident with the rise of the environmental movement and the 1972 United Nations Conference on the Human Environment in Stockholm (Dauvergne, 2011). This conference also saw the launch of the United Nations Environment Programme (UNEP). The USA government promulgated the *Endangered Species Act* (ESA) in 1973, and the world's governments launched CITES in the same year (Rosendal, 2014).

Both the ESA and CITES employ top-down restrictive measures to conserve endangered species, rather than provide positive economic incentives for conservation. However, this protectionist approach to conservation was challenged by the concept of sustainable development, first presented in the World Conservation Strategy (IUCN, 1980), and subsequently developed further by the 1987 Brundtland Report (World Commission on Environment and Development, 1987) and 1992 Earth Summit that spawned the CBD. The CBD significantly reframed global conservation policy, by broadening the scope of conservation to 'biodiversity', and emphasising both the use of biological resources and the sharing of economic benefits relating to such use (Rosendal, 2014).

The concept of biodiversity emerged concurrent with the development of conservation biology, a broader interdisciplinary approach to conservation science, in the mid-1980s (Soulé, 1985). Popularised following a seminal conference in 1988 (Wilson, 1988), the term emphasises diversity, not only between species, but also within species and of ecosystems, and has now become mainstream. However, as Maier (2012) points out, it is a problematic concept to specifically define or measure, and thus presents some significant challenges to contemporary conservation policy.

Reviewing the history of conservation, we can observe that it began with a simple utilitarian concern for species facing extinction, and then evolved via an interest in protecting natural areas to contemporary concerns over the role of biological resources in maintaining life support processes. We can also observe that private initiatives preceded state action in the 19th century, whereas the state played the most dominant role in conservation throughout the 20th century. However, recent developments suggest that private conservation initiatives will play an increasingly vital role in the 21st century.

5.2. Contemporary Conservation

Recent demographic, environmental, geopolitical, and technological developments are reshaping the context in which contemporary biodiversity conservation initiatives must take place. Rapid human population growth and spreading economic prosperity are placing added strain on biological and other resources, and growing economic inequality presents a further challenge. Concern over the consequences of potential future climate change is reshaping government policy and business practices. The global balance of political and economic power is shifting from west to east, and the power and role of the state is dwindling relative to that of market institutions, corporations and other NGOs, all of which play an increasingly significant role in environmental governance (Agrawal and Lemos, 2007). Finally, a range of innovations in biotechnology, communications and information technology present both new opportunities and challenges for conservation (Hoekstra, 2014; Rosendal, 2014).

These changes are all contributing to a heated debate between two schools of thought in contemporary conservation. At the core of these discussions is the question of whether the biodiversity conservation agenda should be determined by anthropocentric goals or by notions that nature has an intrinsic value, separate from any instrumental or utilitarian value to humans. The latter view is expressed by Soulé (1985) as a fundamental normative postulate of conservation biology.

The motivation for the former view arises from evolving ecological ideas (Worster, 1994), especially relating to emerging conceptions of more dynamic, chaotic and interconnected global ecosystems (Botkin, 1992), from which humans are not readily separable, and in which 'nature' is a profoundly human construct

(Cronon, 1996). Combined with more recent insights relating to the concept of the 'Anthropocene' (Crutzen, 2002) and associated global environmental change, these ideas are developing concurrently with a range of conservation management innovations, including 'radical rewilding', assisted migration, and forward-thinking engagements with exotic species in novel and designer ecosystems (Marris, 2011; Mallon and Stanley Price, 2013).

Karieva, Marvier and Lalasz (2012) play a leading role in this debate, by advocating conservation 'for' people rather than 'from' people. Along with related writings in a similar vein (Marris, 2011; Shellenberger and Nordhaus, 2011), their position has drawn a strong reaction from other conservation scientists, who disagree with several of their specific propositions (Miller, Soulé and Terborgh, 2014) and contend that conservationists should not be concerned with promoting human interests and economic prosperity (Doak *et al.*, 2014). This debate appears to be linked to fundamentally different approaches in conservation science, that can be labelled as 'compositionalist' and 'functionalist' respectively (Callicott, Crowder and Mumford, 1999). Compositionalist approaches are based on evolutionary ecology and regard humans as separate from nature, whereas functionalist approaches are based on ecosystems ecology and consider humans as an embedded part of nature.

Further disagreements among conservationists abound. Although species diversity can be positively correlated with ecosystem productivity and stability (Cardinale *et al.*, 2012), not all scientists agree on which elements of biodiversity are more important or why — scientists have diverse values, and their opinions even differ on to what extent this is so, or whether this is a good thing or not (Sandbrook *et al.*, 2011; Rudd, 2011). Competing international conservation NGOs have also adopted different methods for classifying the world's different ecological regions and pursue different global prioritisation strategies (Redford *et al.*, 2003). Opinions also vary on which types of measures are most appropriate for conserving biodiversity, ranging from area-based protection to species-centred regulation.

Conservationists thus face multiple trade-offs (Leader-Williams, Adams and Smith, 2010) and the need for these is further highlighted by persistent serious deficits in funding for state protected areas in developing countries (James, Gaston and Balmford, 2001; McCarthy *et al.*, 2012), which undermines their effectiveness (Bruner, Niesten and Rice, 2010; Pimm *et al.*, 2014). The extent to which protected areas are considered effective by scientists' standards has received very little attention until a recent systematic review (Geldmann *et al.*, 2013), which reaches mixed conclusions and calls for increased monitoring of sites and greater application of adaptive management techniques.

The question of what constitutes effective or successful conservation typically looks to science for input, but the answers typically extend beyond science. Redford *et al.* (2011) suggest guidelines for establishing species conservation effectiveness, but acknowledge that there are no single empirical answers and that scientists' opinions on this are also value-laden. Trudgill (2001) finds that value-laden terms are pervasive in ecosystem science and questions the conflation of science and emotion in conservation, but concludes that they are inseparable. Jepson and Canney (2003) assert that there is a role for values-led conservation, to link scientific concerns to public concerns.

Public concerns extend to social, economic and political issues. Many protected areas bear a legacy of colonialism and dispossession of local communities (Adams and Hutton, 2007; Dowie, 2011). Even with the withdrawal of colonialism, in most developing countries neo-colonial attitudes to conservation prevail along with imbalances in geopolitical power, and western views of conservation frequently conflict with those of indigenous people and the poor (Guha, 1989; Goldman, Nadasdy and Turner, 2011). The political economy of state protected areas is under increasing scrutiny (Anderson and James, 2001; Child, 2013), as is the role of large international conservation NGOs and their relations with corporations, celebrities and the elite (Chapin, 2004; Brockington and Duffy, 2011).

It is thus apparent that science alone cannot determine conservation goals and that people's preferences must be taken into account. We cannot separate the question of how to 'conserve' from the question of for whom we are 'conserving'. As the renowned conservationist Bill Adams asserts: 'Conservation is never anything but social and never anything but political' (Jepson and Ladle, 2010). To be effective, conservation must therefore accommodate multiple, diverse (and sometimes competing) objectives. This is a task for which directly democratic, bottom-up and market institutions are well suited.

5.3. Biodiversity Markets and Privately Protected Areas

The early 21st century has seen a proliferation of market-based approaches to biodiversity conservation. Following earlier development of economic incentive-based approaches to conservation (McNeely, 1988) and techniques for the attempted valuation of non-market ecosystem services (Daily, 1997), there have been various attempts to create market-based mechanisms that confer biodiversity conservation benefits (Alvarado-Quesada, Hein and Weikard, 2014; Pirard, 2012). Such attempts include the establishment of biodiversity offset schemes, of which the literature is largely critical (Bull *et al.*, 2013; Walker *et al.*, 2009).

Thompson (2000) draws a distinction between what he terms 'regulatory markets' and genuine 'markets for nature', where the former constitute transactions designed and constrained in a specific regulatory framework, whereas the latter entail direct voluntary transactions relating to the underlying resource. As a clear example of the latter, Cashore (2002) describes the evolution of 'non-state market-driven' governance systems, in which NGOs and consumers take the lead in pressuring companies to improve social and environmental management practices, employing tools such as voluntary standards, certification and product labelling. The most well developed and studied example of this is sustainable forestry certification through the Forestry Stewardship Council, in which the state plays no direct role. Other examples include the Marine Stewardship Council and the FairWild Standard.

Aside from improved public and corporate engagement with supply chain management, perhaps the most promising avenue for market-based biodiversity conservation takes the form of 'privately protected areas'. A recent IUCN–WCPA review of protected area governance types identified this category as distinct from state, co-managed and community-based protected areas, where the latter refers to areas under the jurisdiction of traditional indigenous communities. According to the WCPA definition, privately protected areas may be owned and managed by a range of entities, including private individuals, corporations and NGOs.

Recognising the growing importance of this governance type, the IUCN also recently commissioned an international pilot study of the extent of privately protected areas, the results of which were presented at the World Parks Congress held in Sydney in late 2014. This study consists of detailed reviews of 17 countries, and reveals a diverse range of preferred approaches, partly dictated by the constraints of national legal frameworks (Stolton, Redford and Dudley, 2014). These approaches vary from conservation easements to outright land ownership, by entities ranging from high net worth individuals to land trusts. Most countries note a dramatic recent expansion in the land area conserved by non-state entities.

Among the individual country reports, Australia records 137 private conservation properties covering about 4.6 million ha of land, plus a further 4.5 million ha under covenants; Brazil reports more than 1,000 privately protected areas, accounting for 153 million ha; Chile reports 308 private conservation initiatives, covering some 4 million ha; the UK records that environmental NGOs and land trusts own or manage 3,630 properties covering some 475,000 ha; and the USA has poor data, but estimates that between 2 and 6.7 million ha are privately protected.

In numerous developing countries, state protected areas have failed due to a lack of funding (Rosendal, 2014). In recent years, some of these have been privatised or contracted out to private entities, such as African Parks, a South African based non-profit company that manages National Parks in several African countries (Brockington, Duffy and Igoe, 2008). In other instances, high net worth individuals have attempted to revive failed parks on their own, such as American Greg Carr's initiative to re-establish the defunct Gorongosa National Park in Mozambique.

Elsewhere, high net worth individuals have acquired farms and rangelands and converted them to conservation estates or mixed-use areas in which sustainable land use practices and conservation feature heavily. Examples include Ted Turner's extensive ranches and bison-breeding projects in the USA, the Tompkins brothers' initiatives in Patagonia, Paul Tudor Jones' large-scale wildlife conservation projects in Zimbabwe and Tanzania's Serengeti, and Danish entrepreneur Anders Povlsen's land acquisitions in Scotland, Denmark and Romania. In the USA, a group of philanthropic investors is working toward establishing the American Prairie Reserve, which aims to consolidate a large expanse of private and public lands to create an open system in which bison and other native species can roam freely: 'a wildlife spectacle to rival the Serengeti'.

Private investors and philanthropists also continue to protect and breed highly endangered species. Save China's Tigers is a project aimed at re-establishing wild populations of the Chinese tiger subspecies that is now extinct in the wild. Individuals from Chinese zoos were moved to a facility in South Africa, to breed up and rewild a founder population for reintroduction into newly established Chinese protected areas. In Texas, ranchers have provided refuge to *ex situ* populations of highly endangered North-African antelope species such as the *addax*, *dama gazelle* and *scimitar oryx*, successfully raising their numbers through breeding, while allowing trophy hunting as a sustainable means of financing and expanding their operations.

Private conservation initiatives are not necessarily philanthropic. In South Africa, wildlife ranching has become a big business and has emerged as an economically viable form of land use that outcompetes conventional agriculture over large parts of the country, especially in more arid areas. Wildlife ranching can generate income from ecotourism, meat production and the sale of hunting opportunities, as well as profits from breeding and the resale of live animals. The development of this industry has been facilitated by three vital factors: the ability to enclose areas by fencing, technological advances that enabled the large-scale capture and translocation of large mammals, and legal innovations that allow for private ownership rights to be established over valuable free-ranging ('wild') animals.

According to industry sources, there were only three private wildlife ranchers in 1960; today the number of private reserves and ranches exceeds 13,000, and numbers of game have increased 20-fold.

South Africa's experience can be contrasted with that of Kenya, in which the state retains ownership of wildlife and hunting of big game has been banned since the 1970s. According to Kenyan economist Norton-Griffiths (1998) the consequences for conservation have been disastrous: wildlife has no value to local people and Kenya has lost more than 70 per cent of its big game as locals quietly exterminate it and replace it with domestic livestock and crops from which they can benefit directly.

Kenya does allow a limited degree of private land stewardship in one part of the country, in which high net worth individuals have invested substantially in protecting big game, including endangered species such as both black and white rhinos. Largely thanks to these efforts, Kenya provides a haven for just over 1,000 rhinos. By contrast, South Africa harbours more than 20,000 rhinos, some 80 per cent of Africa's continental population. This was not always so: in 1900, South Africa's rhinos had been reduced to only a few dozen animals, while hundreds of thousands of rhinos roamed freely across other African countries, including Kenya. This reversal of fortune presents an interesting case study of the potential for private and market-based conservation.

5.4. Case Study: Rhino Conservation in South Africa

At the start of the 20th century, the southern white rhino was the world's most endangered rhino variant,[2] reduced to a single population of less than 50 animals in a single protected area in South Africa, the Hluhluwe-iMfolosi Park, under the jurisdiction of the Natal Parks Board (NPB). By the early 1960s, the park had reached

[2] A separate population of northern white rhinos is now extinct in the wild; there is some debate over whether the northern white rhino should be considered as a sub-species or a different species altogether.

its full carrying capacity for white rhinos and, following the development of new translocation technologies, the NPB decided to adopt a bold strategy to expand the range for the species. At first rhinos were moved to the Kruger National Park and other state protected areas, but from the late 1960s some animals were also moved to private properties on which managed trophy hunting was allowed.

Commercial rhino trophy hunts grew in popularity, and by the early 1980s the NPB faced a long waiting list of private owners seeking allocation of surplus animals to hunt. At the time, the NPB charged a nominal fee to landowners to cover the costs of moving the animals, but the hunts were sold at a 600 per cent mark-up, providing an opportunity to make a quick and substantial profit. The NPB was essentially subsidising the distribution of rhinos to private landowners; however, this provided little incentive to breed them, as the law did not recognise full ownership rights over game ('t Sas-Rolfes, 1990).

This situation changed during the late 1980s with two new developments. The first was the passing of new legislation, the *Theft of Game Act*, which provided explicit recognition of the right to own free-ranging game animals. The second was the implementation of auctions as a means to trade live rhinos. These two developments had a dramatic effect on the private rhino market. Prices of live white rhinos increased 10-fold in just four years and the gap between the live and trophy price narrowed considerably. A live rhino became far more commercially valuable in relation to a trophy, and this created incentives for private landowners to reinvest the proceeds from trophy sales and take rhino breeding seriously. The privately owned rhino population increased dramatically in the following years, and today some 25 per cent of South Africa's rhino population survives on private land.

The southern white rhino represents one of the world's great conservation success stories — it is now way more abundant than all other rhino species put together. Although the NPB played an important initial role in protecting the species and initiating a bold management strategy, private ownership and the development of markets (for live animals and trophy hunts) created strong incentives for added rhino protection, population growth and range expansion. State agencies such as South African National Parks and NPB also benefited significantly from the proceeds of rhino sales to the private sector. Since those agencies are empowered to retain their own funds, live rhino sales finance other conservation activity that is not so easily provided by the market.

Unfortunately, South Africa now faces a challenge. Under CITES, rhino horn trade has been banned since the late 1970s. The ban precludes the further development of legal markets for rhino horn, despite the fact that South Africa and other countries have built up substantial stockpiles of collected horn from natural mortalities, and despite the fact that entrepreneurs have developed techniques to safely and sustainably harvest horn (which regrows) from live animals. Persistent consumer demand for rhino horn products in Asian consumer markets has driven black market prices to all-time highs, fuelling aggressive poaching activity that now threatens South Africa's conservation success. Preventing poaching requires significant spending on security, which is increasingly unaffordable to both state agencies and smaller private rhino owners. The resolution of this challenge remains to be seen, but has wide-ranging implications for both the South African wildlife ranching industry and African conservation policy in general ('t Sas-Rolfes, 1995; 't Sas-Rolfes and Fitzgerald, 2013).

5.5. The Future of Private Conservation

Increasingly, both theoretical and empirical work suggests that the key to successful conservation involves creating appropriate incentives for local people whose lives are closely linked to nature. Institutions that empower relevant communities both politically and economically create the right conditions for sustainable stewardship. Building on the work of Ostrom, theorists such as Pennington (2013) and Araral (2014) argue a strong case for 'bottom-up' approaches to resource management that involve private and community initiatives and market institutions. Having identified that funding shortages for state protected areas undermine their potential effectiveness and constrain the potential of achieving stated biodiversity conservation targets (Leverington *et al.*, 2010; McCarthy *et al.*, 2012), organisations such as the IUCN also increasingly recognise and embrace private and market-based approaches to conservation (Bishop *et al.*, 2008; Stolton, Redford and Dudley, 2014; TEEB, 2010).

Market-based approaches to conservation have their critics and sceptics (Brockington, Duffy and Igoe, 2008; Büscher, Dressler and Fletcher, 2014). Some concerns relate to issues of political economy: neo-colonial practices and inequality. For example, the purchase of large tracts of wild-lands by high net worth individuals and other private entities for exclusive use is seen by some as 'land-grabbing' (Fairhead, Leach and Scoones, 2012; Pearce, 2012). Other concerns relate to the commodification of nature, which is regarded as unethical. Commercial captive breeding of wild species raises concerns over animal welfare and the consequences of potential genetic manipulation and modification. These concerns are relevant in South Africa, where lions are bred in captivity to be trophy hunted under so-called 'canned' conditions, and other animals are selectively bred to achieve extraordinary trophy sizes or rare colour variants.

Notwithstanding these concerns, the evolution of property rights and markets over elements of biodiversity is a natural institutional response to their increasing scarcity (Anderson and Hill, 1975) and property rights approaches offer great promise in the design of effective environmental management institutions, as long as distributional concerns are taken into account (Anderson and Libecap, 2014). The alternatives of top-down approaches, such as those employed by CITES and the ESA, have been proven to have shortcomings, often even leading to perverse effects (Hutton and Dickson, 2000; Lueck and Michael, 2003).

Non-state, market driven approaches to biodiversity conservation provide significant advantages over ageing and less flexible bureaucratic approaches that are increasingly challenged by global environmental change and constrained government budgets. By potentially allowing a diversity of locally relevant competing institutions and techniques, market approaches can be more scale-relevant and adaptable than top-down approaches and can effectively supplement or even replace the latter. Technological innovations further enhance the potential for creating, monitoring and enforcing more effective property rights regimes that create appropriate local incentives to conserve; they also enable greater transparency, accountability and grassroots democracy. Market approaches to biodiversity management thus offer significant benefits for people and nature alike and may serve to improve their interactions.

Bibliography

Acemoglu, D. and Robinson, J.A. (2012). *Why Nations Fail: The Origins of Power, Prosperity and Poverty*, Profile Books, London.

Adams, W.M. (2004). *Against Extinction: The Story of Conservation*, Earthscan, London.

Adams, W.M. and Hutton, J. (2007). People, Parks and Poverty: Political Ecology and Biodiversity Conservation, *Conservation and Society*, 5, p. 147.

Agrawal, A. and Lemos, M.C. (2007). A Greener Revolution in the Making?: Environmental Governance in the 21st Century, *Environment: Science and Policy for Sustainable Development*, 49, pp. 36–45.

Alvarado-Quesada, I., Hein, L. and Weikard, H.-P. (2014). Market-Based Mechanisms for Biodiversity Conservation: A Review of Existing Schemes and an Outline for a Global Mechanism, *Biodiversity Conservation*, 23, pp. 1–21.

Anderson, T.L. and Hill, P.J. (1975). The Evolution of Property Rights: A Study of the American West, *Journal of Law and Economics*, pp. 163–179.

Anderson, T.L. and James, A. (2001). *The Politics and Economics of Park Management*, Rowman & Littlefield, Lanham.

Anderson, T.L. and Libecap, G.D. (2014). *Environmental Markets: A Property Rights Approach*, Cambridge University Press, New York.

Araral, E. (2014). Ostrom, Hardin and the Commons: A Critical Appreciation and a Revisionist View, *Environmental Science & Policy*, 36, pp. 11–23.

Barnosky, A.D., Koch, P.L., Feranec, R.S., Wing, S.L. and Shabel, A.B. (2004). Assessing the Causes of Late Pleistocene Extinctions on the Continents, *Science*, 306, pp. 70–75.

Barnosky, A.D., Matzke, N., Tomiya, S., Wogan, G.O.U., Swartz, B., Quental, T.B., Marshall, C., McGuire, J.L., Lindsey, E.L., Maguire, K.C., Mersey, B. and Ferrer, E.A. (2011). Has the Earth's Sixth Mass Extinction Already Arrived?, *Nature*, 471, pp. 51–57.

Beinart, W. (2008). *The Rise of Conservation in South Africa: Settlers, Livestock, and the Environment 1770–1950*, Oxford University Press, Oxford.

Beinart, W. and Coates, P. (2002). Environment and History: *The Taming of Nature in the USA and South Africa*, Routledge, London.

Bishop, J., Kapila, S., Hicks, F. and Vorhies, F. (2008). *Building Biodiversity Business*, Shell International Limited, London.

Botkin, D.B. (1992). *Discordant Harmonies: A New Ecology for the Twenty-first Century*, Oxford University Press, Oxford.

Brockington, D. and Duffy, R. (2011). *Capitalism and Conservation*, Wiley-Blackwell, Chichester.

Brockington, D., Duffy, R. and Igoe, J. (2008). *Nature Unbound: 'Conservation, Capitalism and the Future of Protected Areas'*, Earthscan, Abingdon.

Bruner, A., Niesten, E. and Rice, R. (2010). 'Misaligned Incentives and Trade-offs in Allocating Conservation Funding', in Leader-Williams, N., Adams, W.M. and Smith, R.J. (eds.), *Trade-Offs in Conservation: Deciding What to Save*, Wiley-Blackwell, Chichester, pp. 197–214.

Bull, J.W., Suttle, K.B., Gordon, A., Singh, N.J. and Milner-Gulland, E.J. (2013). Biodiversity Offsets in Theory and Practice, *Oryx*, 47, pp. 369–380.

Büscher, B., Dressler, W. and Fletcher, R. (2014). *Nature Inc.: Environmental Conservation in the Neoliberal Age*, University of Arizona Press, Tuscon.

Callicott, J.B., Crowder, L.B. and Mumford, K. (1999). Current Normative Concepts in Conservation, *Conservation Biology*, 13, pp. 22–35.

Cardinale, B.J., Duffy, J.E., Gonzalez, A., Hooper, D.U., Perrings, C., Venail, P., Narwani, A., Mace, G.M., Tilman, D., Wardle, D.A., Kinzig, A.P., Daily, G.C., Loreau, M., Grace, J.B., Larigauderie, A., Srivastava, D.S. and Naeem, S. (2012). Biodiversity Loss and its Impact on Humanity, *Nature*, 486, pp. 59–67.

Carruthers, J. (2008). 'Wilding the Farm or Farming the Wild'? The Evolution of Scientific Game Ranching in South Africa From the 1960s to the Present, *Transactions of the Royal Society of South Africa*, 63, pp. 160–181.

Cashore, B. (2002). Legitimacy and the Privatization of Environmental Governance: How Non–State Market–Driven (NSMD) Governance Systems Gain Rule–Making Authority, *Governance*, 15, pp. 503–529.

Chapin, M. (2004). A Challenge to Conservationists, *World Watch Magazine*, pp. 17–31.

Child, B. (2013). *Parks in Transition: 'Biodiversity, Rural Development and the Bottom Line'*, Routledge, London.

Cronon, W. (1996). *Uncommon Ground: Rethinking the Human Place in Nature*, W.W. Norton, New York.

Crutzen, P.J. (2002). Geology of Mankind, *Nature*, 415, p. 23.

Daily, G. (1997). *Nature's Services: Societal Dependence On Natural Ecosystems*, Island Press, Washington, DC.

Dauvergne, P. (2011). 'Globalization and the Environment', in Ravenhill, J. (ed.), *Global Political Economy*, Oxford University Press, Oxford, pp. 450–480.

Diamond, J. (1999). *Guns, Germs, and Steel: The Fates of Human Societies*, W.W. Norton, New York.

Doak, D.F., Bakker, V.J., Goldstein, B.E. and Hale, B. (2014). What is the Future of Conservation?, *Trends in Ecology & Evolution*, 29(2), pp. 77–81.

Doughty, C.E., Wolf, A. and Malhi, Y. (2013). The Legacy of the Pleistocene Megafauna Extinctions on Nutrient Availability in Amazonia, *Nature Geoscience*, 6, pp. 761–764.

Dowie, M. (2011). *Conservation Refugees: The Hundred-Year Conflict between Global Conservation and Native Peoples*, MIT Press, Cambridge.

Fairhead, J., Leach, M. and Scoones, I. (2012). Green Grabbing: A New Appropriation of Nature?, *Journal of Peasant Studies*, 39, pp. 237–261.

Ferraro, P.J. and Kiss, A. (2002). Direct Payments to Conserve Biodiversity, *Science*, 298(5599), pp. 1718–1719.

Geldmann, J., Barnes, M., Coad, L., Craigie, I.D., Hockings, M. and Burgess, N.D. (2013). Effectiveness of Terrestrial Protected Areas in Reducing Habitat Loss and Population Declines, *Biological Conservation*, 161, pp. 230–238.

Goldman, M.J., Nadasdy, P. and Turner, M.D. (2011). *Knowing Nature: Conversations at the Intersection of Political Ecology and Science Studies*, University of Chicago Press, Chicago.

Guha, R. (1989). Radical American Environmentalism and Wilderness Preservation, *Environmental Ethics*, 11, pp. 71–83.

Harari, Y.N. (2014). *Sapiens: A Brief History of Humankind*, Harvill Secker, London.

Hoekstra, J. (2014). Networking Nature: How Technology Is Transforming Conservation, *Foreign Affairs*, 93, p. 80.

Hutton, J. and Dickson, B. (2000). *Endangered Species, Threatened Convention: The Past, Present and Future of CITES, the Convention on International Trade in Endangered Species of Wild Fauna and Flora*, Earthscan, London.

IUCN (1980). *World Conservation Strategy: Living Resource Conservation for Sustainable Development*. Available at: https://portals.iucn.org/library/efiles/html/WCS-004/cover.html [Accessed 8 November 2014].

James, A., Gaston, K.J. and Balmford, A. (2001). Can We Afford to Conserve Biodiversity? *BioScience*, 51, pp. 43–52.

Jepson, P. and Canney, S. (2003). Values-Led Conservation, *Global Ecology and Biogeography*, 12, pp. 271–274.

Jepson, P. and Ladle, R.J. (2010). *Conservation: A Beginner's Guide*, Oneworld, Oxford.

Jepson, P. and Whittaker, R.J. (2002). Histories of Protected Areas: Internationalisation of Conservationist Values and their Adoption in the Netherlands Indies (Indonesia), *Environment and History*, 8, pp. 129–172.

Karieva, P., Marvier, M. and Lalasz, R. (2012). Conservation in the Anthropocene — Beyond Solitude and Fragility. Available at: http://thebreakthrough.org/index.php/journal/past-issues/issue-2/conservation-in-the-anthropocene/ [Accessed 19 January 2014].

Leader-Williams, N., Adams, W.M. and Smith, R.J. (eds.) (2010). *Trade-Offs in Conservation: Deciding What to Save*, Wiley-Blackwell, Chichester.

Leverington, F., Costa, K.L., Pavese, H., Lisle, A. and Hockings, M. (2010). A Global Analysis of Protected Area Management Effectiveness, *Environmental Management*, 46, pp. 685–698.

Lueck, D. and Michael, J. (2003). Preemptive Habitat Destruction under the Endangered Species Act, *Journal of Law & Economics*, 46, pp. 27–60.

Maier, D.S. (2012). *What's So Good About Biodiversity?: A Call for Better Reasoning About Nature's Value*, Springer Science & Business Media, Dordrecht.

Mallon, D.P. and Stanley Price, M.R. (2013). The Fall of the Wild, *Oryx*, 47, pp. 467–468.

Marris, E. (2011). *Rambunctious Garden: Saving Nature in a Post-Wild World*, Bloomsbury, New York.

McCarthy, D.P., Donald, P.F., Scharlemann, J.P.W., Buchanan, G.M., Balmford, A., Green, J.M.H., Bennun, L.A., Burgess, N.D., Fishpool, L.D.C., Garnett, S.T., Leonard, D.L., Maloney, R.F., Morling, P., Schaefer, H.M., Symes, A., Wiedenfeld, D.A. and Butchart, S.H.M. (2012). Financial Costs of Meeting Global Biodiversity Conservation Targets: Current Spending and Unmet Needs, *Science*, 338(6109), pp. 946–949.

McNeely, J.A. (1988). *Economics and Biological Diversity: Developing and Using Economic Incentives to Conserve Biological Resources*, IUCN, Gland.

Millennium Ecosystem Assessment. (2005). *Ecosystems and Well-Being: Biodiversity Synthesis*, World Resources Institute, Washington, DC.

Miller, B., Soulé, M.E. and Terborgh, J. (2014). 'New Conservation' or Surrender To Development?, *Animal Conservation*. Available at: http://onlinelibrary.wiley.com/doi/10.1111/acv.12127/full [Accessed 8 November 2014].

North, D.C. (1990). *Institutions, Institutional Change and Economic Performance*, Cambridge University Press, Cambridge.

Norton-Griffiths, M. (1998). 'The Economics of Wildlife Conservation Policy in Kenya', in Milner-Gulland, E.J. and Mace, R. (eds.), *Conservation of Biological Resources*. Blackwell Science, Oxford, pp. 279–293.

Ostrom, E. (2010). Beyond Markets and States: Polycentric Governance of Complex Economic Systems, *The American Economic Review*, 100(3), pp. 641–672.

Ostrom, E., Janssen, M.A. and Anderies, J.M. (2007). Going Beyond Panaceas, *PNAS*, 104, pp. 15176–15178.

Pearce, F. (2012). *The Land Grabbers: The New Fight over Who Owns the Earth*, Eden Project Books, London.

Pennington, M. (2013). Elinor Ostrom and the Robust Political Economy of Common-Pool Resources, *Journal of Institutional Economics*, 9, pp. 449–468.

Phillips, A. (2004). A History of the International System of Protected Area Management Categories, *Parks*, 14(3), pp 4–13.

Pimm, S.L., Jenkins, C.N., Abell, R., Brooks, T.M., Gittleman, J.L., Joppa, L.N., Raven, P.H., Roberts, C.M. and Sexton, J.O. (2014). The Biodiversity of Species and their Rates of Extinction, Distribution, and Protection, *Science*, 344(6187), p. 987.

Pirard, R. (2012). Market-Based Instruments for Biodiversity and Ecosystem Services: A Lexicon, *Environmental Science & Policy*, 19–20, pp. 59–68.

Redford, K.H., Amato, G., Baillie, J., Beldomenico, P., Bennett, E.L., Clum, N., Cook, R., Fonseca, G., Hedges, S., Launay, F., Lieberman, S., Mace, G.M., Murayama, A., Putnam, A., Robinson, J.G., Rosenbaum, H., Sanderson, E.W., Stuart, S.N., Thomas and P., Thorbjarnarson, J. (2011). What Does it Mean to Successfully Conserve a (Vertebrate) Species?, *BioScience*, 61, pp. 39–48.

Redford, K.H., Coppolillo, P., Sanderson, E.W., Da Fonseca, G.A.B., Dinerstein, E., Groves, C., Mace, G., Maginnis, S., Mittermeier, R.A., Noss, R., Olson, D., Robinson, J.G., Vedder, A. and Wright, M. (2003). Mapping the Conservation Landscape, *Conservation Biology*, 17, pp. 116–131.

Rockström, J., Steffen, W., Noone, K., Persson, Å., Chapin, F.S., Lambin, E.F., Lenton, T.M., Scheffer, M., Folke, C., Schellnhuber, H.J., Nykvist, B., de Wit, C.A., Hughes, T., van der Leeuw, S., Rodhe, H., Sörlin, S., Snyder, P.K., Costanza, R., Svedin, U., Falkenmark, M., Karlberg, L., Corell, R.W., Fabry, V.J., Hansen, J., Walker, B., Liverman, D., Richardson, K., Crutzen, P. and Foley, J.A. (2009). A Safe Operating Space for Humanity, *Nature*, 461, pp. 472–475.

Rosendal, G.K. (2014). 'Global Biodiversity Governance: Genetic Resources, Species and Ecosystems', in Axelrod, R.S. and VanDeveer, S.D. (eds.), *The Global Environment: Institutions, Law, and Policy*, CQ Press, Los Angeles, pp. 283–304.

Rudd, M.A. (2011). Scientists' Opinions on the Global Status and Management of Biological Diversity, *Conservation Biology*, 25, pp. 1165–1175.

Sandbrook, C., Scales, I.R., Vira, B. and Adams, W.M. (2011). Value Plurality among Conservation Professionals, *Conservation Biology*, 25, pp. 285–294.

Secretariat of the CBD (2010). *Global Biodiversity Outlook 3*. Secretariat of the CBD, Montreal.

Shellenberger, M. and Nordhaus, T. (2011). *Love Your Monsters Ebook — Postenvironmentalism and the Anthropocene*. Available at: http://thebreakthrough.org/index.php/programs/philosophy/love-your-monsters-ebook [Accessed 24 August 2014].

Skead, C.J. (1980). *Historical Mammal Incidence in the Cape Province: Vol. 1 — The Western and Northern Cape*, Department of Nature and Environmental Conservation, Cape Town.

Smith, S. and Mark, S. (2009). The Historical Roots of The Nature Conservancy in the Northwest Indiana/Chicagoland Region: From Science to Preservation, *The South Shore Journal*, 3, pp. 1–10.

Soulé, M.E. (1985). What is Conservation Biology?, *BioScience*, 35(11), pp. 727–734.

Stolton, S., Redford, K.H. and Dudley, N. (2014). *The Futures of Privately Protected Areas: Developing Capacity for a Protected Planet*, IUCN, Gland.

Swanson, T.M. (ed.) (1998). *The Economics and Ecology of Biodiversity Decline: The Forces Driving Global Change*, Cambridge University Press, Cambridge.

TEEB (2010). *Mainstreaming the Economics of Nature: A Synthesis of the Approach, Conclusions and Recommendations of TEEB*. Available at: http://www.teebweb.org/publication/mainstreaming-the-economics-of-nature-a-synthesis-of-the-approach-conclusions-and-recommendations-of-teeb/ [Accessed 19 January 2014].

Thompson, B.H.J. (2000). Markets for Nature, *William & Mary Environmental Law & Policy Review*, 25, p. 261.

Trudgill, S. (2001). Psychobiogeography: Meanings of Nature and Motivations for a Democratized Conservation Ethic, *Journal of Biogeography*, 28, pp. 677–698.

't Sas-Rolfes, M. (1990). Privatizing the Rhino Industry, *FMF Paper*, Free Market Foundation, Johannesburg.

't Sas-Rolfes, M. (1995). *Rhinos: Conservation, Economics, and Trade-Offs*, IEA Environmental Unit, London.

't Sas-Rolfes, M. and Fitzgerald, T. (2013). 'Can a Legal Horn Trade Save Rhinos?', PERC Research Paper, Bozeman.

Waldron, A., Mooers, A.O., Miller, D.C., Nibbelink, N., Redding, D., Kuhn, T.S., Roberts, J.T. and Gittleman, J.L. (2013). Targeting Global Conservation Funding to Limit Immediate Biodiversity Declines, *PNAS*, 110, pp. 12144–12148.

Walker, S., Brower, A.L., Stephens, R.T. and Lee, W.G. (2009). Why Bartering Biodiversity Fails, *Conservation Letters*, 2, pp. 149–157.

Williamson, O.E. (2000). The New Institutional Economics: Taking Stock, Looking Ahead, *Journal of Economic Literature*, XXXVIII, pp. 595–613.

Wilson, E.O. (ed.) (1988). *Biodiversity*. National Academies Press, Washington, DC.

Wilson, E.O. (2013). Beware the Age of Loneliness, *The Economist*: *The World in 2014*. Available at: http://www.economist.com/news/21589083-man-must-do-more-preserve-rest-life-earth-warns-edward-o-wilson-professor-emeritus [Accessed 8 November 2014].

World Commission on Environment and Development (1987). *Our Common Future*, Oxford University Press, Oxford.

Worster, D. (1994). *Nature's Economy*: *A History of Ecological Ideas*, Cambridge University Press, Cambridge.

6. Non-Government Provision of Environmental Water: A Case from the Murray–Darling Basin

Sue O'Keefe and Lin Crase

6.1. Introduction

Increasingly in developed countries, stronger preferences for environmental goods have given rise to a range of conundrums relating to the reallocation of resources, particularly water. This is complicated by the fact that water is often regarded as a common pool resource with multiple competing users and uses that almost inevitably have resulted in resource depletion (Hardin, 1968). In that context water has historically been viewed as a vehicle for promoting agricultural production such that irrigation is now the main extractive user of water worldwide. Questions thus naturally arise about the extent and form of agricultural water use, especially in times of drought. The so-called Millennium Drought in Australia's Murray–Darling Basin (MDB) in the first decade of this century exemplifies the policy challenges of reallocating water for environmental ends and, likewise in California, the current drought has brought into sharp relief the tensions between environmental uses of water and other extractive demands.

Water management generally is plagued by the fugitive nature of the resource; it is not bound by man-made jurisdictional and administrative boundaries, and its interconnected nature makes it difficult to conceptualise in terms of distinct autonomous components (Bodin and Crona, 2009). Thus, reallocation decisions are no simple thing, partly due to the intense political elements that accompany them, partly because jurisdictions sharing water resources will often have competing interests but also because the science of ecological responses is inherently uncertain.

Environmental problems are usually attended by complexity, and this in turn relates to the issue of scale. Given a connected river system and the associated potential for third-party and flow-on effects, actions aimed at preserving one environmental asset may exacerbate the condition of another, and thus some form of coordination is crucial. This can be achieved by central action by the state, collective responses while preserving localised action, some form of coordinated market exchange, or some combination of these (Meinzen-Dick, 2007). In many jurisdictions the difficulty of securing coordination combined with the historical role of the state in promoting water development has meant that centralised decision-making features prominently in the delivery of environmental outcomes in large river basins. However, there is also a myriad of potential and real combinations of state agencies and individuals, some of which are polycentric or nested agencies. The balance between centralised control of water and localised management has also attracted the attention of numerous analysts at a theoretical level (Bennett, 2012; Crase, O'Keefe and Dollery, 2012) although relatively few cases of pure decentralised provision are available, at least in the case of environmental water.

In the case of the MDB, a series of ground-breaking reforms over the last three decades has culminated in the Basin Plan, released in 2012. This resulted in the establishment of a substantial environmental water holding, such that the Commonwealth Environmental Water Holder (CEWH) is now the single largest holder of water entitlements in the Basin. However, despite the emphasis on a hierarchically coordinated approach in the Basin Plan, the associated documents explicitly recognise the importance of harnessing local knowledge and participation. In pursuit of these objectives, there has been some support for increased devolution of the now-assembled Commonwealth's environmental reserve (see, for example, Crase, O'Keefe and Dollery, 2012), and others have suggested that an expanded role for the private sector might be preferable (Bennett *et al.*, 2010).

In this chapter, we present a case study that highlights the potential for non-government involvement in the provision and management of environmental water to achieve ecological ends. The emphasis is on understanding the nature of provision of environmental goods to support theoretical expositions offered elsewhere in this volume.

The chapter itself has three additional parts. In the following section, we briefly present a schema for disaggregating private involvement in environmental watering. This is followed by a case study covering the MDB, while some lessons and summary remarks make up the final section.

6.2. Some Conceptual Considerations

Riparian environmental goods represent non-use values that are both non-rival and non-excludable (Bennett, 2012). This poses obvious problems for any potential market-based activity, since these conditions preclude the establishment of a price for access or use. Some commentators have nonetheless raised the possibility of transforming the non-use value into a use value, thereby providing the means to exclude those who are not willing to pay or donate to the environmental good (Bennett, 2012). Others have suggested that the central issue is not whether or not a good is excludable, but rather what is the cost of making it excludable (Banzhaf, Fitzgerald and Schnier, 2013, p. 240).

Nevertheless, the question of the most efficient manner in which to deliver environmental outcomes is not a simple dichotomy; and the issue of scale is crucial in determining the preferred approach, especially in the context of water-related environmental goods. 'The optimal role of government is inextricably linked to the nature and scale of the environmental problem' (Banzhaf, Fitzgerald and Schnier, 2013, p. 252). Non-government collective action groups are innately likely to be more suited to smaller scale systems and a more localised approach, whereas state institutions are advantaged at higher spatial scales due to higher levels of authority and access to more resources to enable the coordination across large areas and many users (Meinzen-Dick, 2007).

The point is that it is not a simple question of government/public provision or non-government provision, there is a myriad of alternatives that are best placed along a continuum between these extremes. Further, the classification of public versus non-government can be of limited use, given that government consists of a number of interconnected layers within a hierarchical structure; notably, local, state, and commonwealth in the Australian milieu. The result is that there is a wide range of successful institutional arrangements to deal with environmental problems, many involving creative government and non-government solutions tailored to local and historical circumstances (Dietz, Ostrom and Stern, 2003).

To re-emphasise the importance of avoiding dichotomous choices, as a minimum, some level of public involvement is necessary to ensure the institutional framework is such that society's private rights can be enforced. In some cases, the main role of government is to remove legal barriers to exchanging property rights (e.g., establishment of the right to instream flows for water trusts (King, 2004)) whilst in other instances governments have created new property rights (e.g., land trusts in the US (Anderson and Parker, 2013)). Nonetheless, governments can also stand in the way by allowing special interests to create barriers to exchange (Anderson and Parker, 2013, p. 273). The consequences of getting this wrong are that too little government involvement will result in an incomplete market and too much will restrict market transactions and decrease efficiency (Banzhaf, Fitzgerald and Schnier, 2013). Beyond this most basic level of involvement, governments could coordinate environmental activities at federal, state and/or local scales and potentially engineer different forms of engagement and collaboration with a range of non-government interests.

Responsibility for water resources in the MDB was initially vested in the states prior to the establishment of the Basin Plan. The Plan is premised upon the transfer of power to the federal government in pursuit of superior coordination of environmental outcomes. And yet despite government calls for localised responses to environmental issues, local government itself has never expressed an appetite for involvement in this sphere. Thus, while the fiscal federalism literature draws attention to the theoretical gains from subsidiarity (Dollery and O'Keefe, 2011), the notion of 'localism' in environmental water management does not relate to local government — it invariably relates to local non-government organisations (NGOs). Perhaps this phenomenon is explained by the fact that, in Australia, protection of the environment has traditionally been seen primarily as the realm of the state and commonwealth governments (Productivity Commission, 2010), alongside some modest involvement from NGOs. Further, the Productivity Commission notes that there is potential for government activity to crowd out private activity. Until relatively recently, the scope for involvement from private individuals or entities in delivering environmental outcomes has not been seriously considered. Central to these arrangements has been the conceptualisation of the inter-connectedness of the basin, the attendant scope for third-party effects and the associated difficulty in individual appropriation of the benefits of environmental enhancements.

The upshot of this set of circumstances has been that:

- Localised response to environmental watering does not generally involve local government;
- Private provision of environmental watering might be more accurately characterised as non-government, including NGOs.

Just as public provision is much more nuanced than sometimes realised, so too is private or non-government activity. The latter could take the form of charitable giving, free exchange, private allocation and public funding, public–private partnerships and so on. To illustrate the range of 'private' involvement in environmental watering, in this chapter we employ a simple organising framework that focuses on the assignment of responsibility and choices across three dimensions that comprise the management of environmental water. We focus on three key questions and seek to locate the various examples of management structures along separate continua. These questions are:

- Who holds the water?
- Who applies or allocates the water to achieve environmental goods?
- And lastly, what is the nature of the payment(s) used to fund environmental outcomes?

In the case of 'holding' environmental water, at one end of this continuum is a central agency such as the federal government, say in the form of the Commonwealth Water Holder in Australia. At the other extreme are private individuals who might opt to purchase water to deploy on an environmental asset (e.g., a local wetland), or donate part of their existing water entitlements for an environmental cause.[1] Between these extremes exists more decentralised government agencies (e.g., state governments) and groups like water trusts.

Similarly, allocation decisions can be heavily centralised with a single basin-wide agency or the same decisions can be radically decentralised, as would be the case where an individual opted to independently deploy water to a private wetland. Again, variations can exist within these extremes, as will be noted in the case analysis.

In the case of financing there are at least two matters worth considering. First, the initial acquisition of environmental water often requires financing, unless the state opts simply to modify existing extractive rights without compensation. Second, the process of managing environmental water is itself costly and requires financing.

---

[1] For example, in Australia some farmers have donated allocations that accrue to irrigation entitlements through exchanges such as WaterFind (www.waterfind.com.au).

In the case of so-called 'regulated streams' in the MDB, costs generated from the management of infrastructure, planning and monitoring are all likely to pass to the holder or manager of water rights.[2] Meeting these costs via general revenues of the federal government would constitute a centralised approach, while individual donation or voluntary payment lies at the other end of this spectrum. Again, variants within these extremes are possible — in the case of the New South Wales River Bank Program, the water holding that attends this programme was initially purchased using funds accumulated by a levy on hard waste disposal in metropolitan Sydney. The costs of operating the programme are financed by trading the water allocations in the water market.

The point of this three-fold taxonomy is to emphasise that simple dichotomies between private and public (i.e., non-government) provisioning of environmental watering are unlikely to capture the extent of institutional variation in this context. We now turn to a case study in order to provide practical substance to this topic.

6.3. Environmental Watering and the MDB, Australia

6.3.1. *Background*

Almost every Australian and most international observers of water management have heard of the plight of the MDB. The Basin is Australia's most productive agricultural zone, accounting for around 40 per cent of national agricultural output, but it is also under environmental stress (Murray–Darling Basin Authority, 2012). A key reason for the stress is that the area comprises Australia's most extensive irrigation developments, containing about 60–65 per cent of the nation's irrigated lands (Ashton *et al.*, 2009; Australian Bureau of Agricultural and Resource Economics–Bureau of Rural Science, 2010; Murray–Darling Basin Authority, 2012), and is

[2] In a somewhat cruel irony, environmental water holders in Australia pay dam managers to release water to mimic flows that pre-date the dam.

simultaneously home to a range of important ecological assets that compete for water.

Community preferences for better environmental outcomes and emerging evidences of the environmental (and fiscal) ills of irrigation have resulted in successive calls to reduce water extractions from the Basin's rivers and aquifers. The resulting policy shifts have had several phases (Crase, O'Keefe and Kinoshita, 2012; Musgrave, 2008), with the most recent episode resulting in a Plan for the entire basin that foreshadows a significant reduction in average consumptive water use by irrigation from around 10,000 Gigalitres (GL) per year to less than 8,700 GL (Murray–Darling Basin Authority, 2012). This set of actions will take the environmental water holding to about 20 per cent of all water previously used for consumptive use (Productivity Commission, 2010).

The Basin Plan (Murray–Darling Basin Authority, 2012) passed through Federal parliament in 2013, and Basin States have committed to adopting and implementing all components of the Plan by 2019. Importantly, the Plan

> is intended to facilitate the ongoing shift from largely local-and state-scale water management to a coordinated, basin scale approach with strong local engagement [and] ... the growing focus on larger-scale actions is helping to improve efficiency and effectiveness of environmental water delivery as well as the ability to achieve larger scale environmental outcomes (CEWH, 2012, p. 6).

The Basin Plan's environmental watering plan is thus intended to 'Coordinate the planning, prioritization and use of environmental water; enable adaptive management; and facilitate consultation, coordination and cooperation between the Commonwealth and the states.' (The Department of Sustainability, Environment, Water, Population and Communities (DSEWPAC), 2013, p. 2). Clearly, the mantras of cooperation, coordination, adaptive management and localised responses are common themes. For example, the MDB Environmental Water Holders Report of 2013 specifically notes that 'Cooperation is the key ... to deliver ... water that will be returned to the environment' (DSEWPAC, 2013, p. 3) citing benefits such as increased knowledge, improved understanding of regional priorities and issues and the potential to develop new delivery and monitoring arrangements.

As noted earlier, the volume of water held as an environmental reserve is already significant. For example, the CEWH (CEWH, 2012) reported in September 2012 that it had already acquired 1,415 GL of water entitlement, equivalent to over 1,000 GL of long-term average supply, making it the single largest entitlement holder in the Basin.

Separate to so-called environmental 'held water', a variety of 'rules-based' allocations exist that can be combined to deliver environmental outcomes (National Water Commission, 2010, p. 8). Managing this different types of environmental water is complicated due to:

- Gaps in scientific knowledge about the responsiveness of different ecosystems to watering (Hone, Foster and O'Keefe, 2011);
- Fragmented holding of environmental water entitlements and potentially disconnected decisions relating to the activation of rules-based water (Crase, O'Keefe and Dollery, 2012);
- The sheer scale of the MDB with geographically separated ecological assets and variable hydrological connectedness between them;
- Rudimentary understanding of the links between water volumes and non-volume parameters, such as the timing of flows (Crase and Gawne, 2011; Crase, O'Keefe and Dollery, 2012);
- Differing and complex rules about the potential to carry-over and manage water between years, and dam release protocols (Crase, 2011); and
- Shifting societal values and uncertainty about future climates.

Regardless of these challenges, it is critically important that environmental water be managed efficiently. Total government expenditure on environmental restoration in the MDB is already estimated to have topped $25 billion since 1997 (Lee and Ancev, 2009), and there is a real risk that public confidence in government environmental programmes will be undermined if the environmental water reserve is not well-managed. Key to this will be getting the balance right between basin-wide and localised decision-making.

6.3.2. *Coordination*

Under the *Water Act 2007* the Basin Plan specifies a coordinated approach to water use across the Basin's four States and the Act. The Plan sets sustainable levels of take by determining the long-term average Sustainable Diversion Limits for water resources which are subject to adjustment to facilitate further improvements, along with a constraints management strategy. To achieve these goals the CEWH works with landholders, catchment management authorities, natural resource management boards, local groups, state governments and is committed to 'effective collaboration and stakeholder engagement' (DSEWPAC, 2013, p. 162), however defined. Its tasks include deciding where to apply environmental water, delivery of this water and monitoring its effects.

Water use proposals are made by catchment management authorities and local environmental reference groups who bring these forward through state agencies. These proposals are then prioritised with advice from a Scientific Advisory Committee and further consultation with the MDBA and local delivery managers.

On-site delivery, monitoring and reporting are managed by state agencies, Catchment Management Authorities, river managers, parks authorities and, in limited cases, community groups.

Despite this relatively orderly and structured approach, some concern has already been expressed about the potential disjunction between the need for coordinated responses on one hand and the importance of local involvement and cooperation. In the context of such a highly-connected river system, 'Cooperation is the key ... to deliver ... water that will be returned to the environment' and benefits such as increased knowledge, improved understanding of regional priorities and issues and the potential to develop new delivery and monitoring arrangements are also non-trivial (DSEWPAC, 2013, p. 3). Also critical in this context is the nature of the *Water Act 2007* itself which exclusively deals with water, even though environmental outcomes and optimising across them necessarily involves others resources, such as land. Regardless of the clear need for cooperation and integration at different scales, examples of on-the-ground partnerships to deliver environmental water are few and far between.

6.3.3. *Non-government environmental watering — Nature Foundation SA*

There has been some interest in the notion of water trusts in the MDB in recent years with several fledgling organisations such as Healthy Rivers, and the Murray Wetlands Working Group Ltd. emerging. The attractiveness of these organisations is that they can:

(1) More easily negotiate about the use of complementary resources in achieving environmental outcomes;
(2) Bring site-specific local knowledge to bear;
(3) Divert hostility away from the state; and,
(4) Broker more flexible and novel solutions (King, 2004; O'Neill, 1989).

Recognising these benefits, a Water Trust Alliance was established in 2010–2011, with the intention of generating interest in the use of localised non-government responses to environmental watering.

At a Water Trust Alliance Workshop in December 2011, representatives of the Commonwealth Environmental Water Office (CEWO)[3] invited attendees to express an interest in working directly with the CEWH to manage the environmental water held by the

[3]The Commonwealth Water Holder is supported by the CEWO in managing the Commonwealth's environmental water portfolio (www.environment.gov.au).

Commonwealth.[4] The Nature Foundation of South Australia (NFSA) was the only entity to take up this offer and details of the arrangements between CEWH and the Nature Foundation are described here by drawing heavily on personal communication from the Assistant Secretary, Environmental Water Delivery, CEWO, Benjamin Docker.

The NFSA is a not-for-profit charity that 'works with and inspires others to save, protect and restore South Australia's natural biodiversity' (NFSA, 2014). Historically, the Foundation has focussed on purchasing and managing land with significant conservation values. The Foundation has also undertaken discrete conservation projects, although again the focus has primarily been on land assets. Working to achieve environmental benefits, the Foundation partners with private land-holders, irrigators, the community, private sector and government departments including the South Australian Department for Environment, Water and Natural Resources.

Following negotiations between the CEWO and the NFSA, an Environmental Water Delivery Agreement was signed in 2012. Titled the 'Water for Nature' project, the agreement involves the NFSA partnering with the CEWO to deliver 50 GL of Commonwealth Environmental Water over the next five years to sites located near the River Murray (NFSA, 2014). NFSA began delivering water under this agreement in February 2013, having developed the watering action through partnership with an enthusiastic landholder to complement land management strategies such as weed and pest control and salt interception (DSEWPAC, 2013). In essence, the agreement provides access to a relatively small portion of CEWH's environmental water reserve.

Notwithstanding the role for the NFSA established by this agreement, all Commonwealth water use, including that involving the Nature Foundation, must contribute to the achievement of one or

---

[4] It is worth noting that CEWH uses its website (www.environment.gov.au) to invite other local input in the management of environmental water. It is not clear that this has resulted in formalised involvement of the form witnessed with the Nature Foundation SA.

more of the following high-level objectives, ascribed as part of the Basin Plan:

- To protect and restore water-dependent ecosystems of the MDB;
- To protect and restore the ecosystem functions of water-dependent ecosystems; and
- To ensure water-dependent ecosystems are resilient to climate change and other risks and threats (Murray–Darling Basin Authority, 2012, p. 1).

Thus, the NFSA must necessarily deploy water in a manner consistent with the broader planning framework. To achieve this consistency, the Foundation develops watering proposals in consultation with their advisory group and community members. These proposals are subsequently considered by the CEWO and assessed using the *Framework for Determining Commonwealth Environmental Water Use.*

The criteria for assessing such proposals are specified as:

1. The ecological value of the river, wetland or floodplain;
2. The expected outcomes from the watering;
3. The potential risks of the watering;
4. The long-term sustainability and management of the site;
5. The cost effectiveness and feasibility of the watering (CEWH, 2013, pp. 24–26).

To date, the environmental watering undertaken by the Foundation has been localised, albeit with the involvement of both state and federal governments to ensure coordination within a broader programme of watering. 'The smaller scale, off-stream watering is seen as complementary to the larger scale in-channel watering, particularly when operations to contribute to over-bank watering actions are limited' (Docker, 2014). In the context of the broad portfolio of water held by CEWH which, on average, yields about 1,500 GL per year, the volume influenced by the NFSA has not been sufficient enough to raise any concerns about potential trade-offs between local and basin-wide watering objectives.

Notwithstanding the modest amounts of water deployed by the NFSA to date, the CEWO notes several advantages to this approach. First, the arrangement is particularly helpful when dealing with the watering requirements that attend smaller and discrete areas of private land. Second, the engagement of local communities, landholders and other government organisations is seen as advantageous. Third, the approach is more akin to 'integrated land and water management by aligning water use with complementary Natural Resource Management project activities (e.g., revegetation; weeds and pest management)' (Docker, 2014).

Set against these advantages are several disadvantages that relate to this type of localised 'private' provision. First, the agreement involves small volumes of water and this could prove 'administratively costly if many more organisations sought similar arrangements' (Docker, 2014). Second, the nature of the current agreement can involve high delivery costs since pumps and other infrastructure can be required to deliver water to discrete sites. Third, the number of entities capable of involvement in partnerships with CEWO is necessarily limited. This arises because organisations must have access to 'alternative sources of funding for ongoing operations', since 'the Commonwealth can only provide funds to manage the delivery of environmental water associated with specific watering events'. In addition, partner organisations must 'have sufficient capacity to deliver on project objectives and meet standard administrative requirements, and it is not clear that there are many organisations that can do this'. In sum,

> there appear to be a very limited number of local non-government organisations that have an interest and the capacity to manage local environmental water delivery projects. Therefore, at present the approach is geographically constrained to the area in which the NFSA operates (Docker, 2014).

6.4. Lessons, Observations and Concluding Remarks

This case study is indicative of some progress towards the more localised approach to the delivery of environmental outcomes, albeit under the coordination of the CEWO and with a non-government entity. This is broadly consistent with other evidence of increased local and NGO involvement in the delivery of environmental outcomes; increased engagement with regional communities; and cooperation across jurisdictions. In addition, there has been more recognition of the potential to use alternative delivery mechanisms; for example, pumps, regulators, irrigation infrastructure and 'piggybacking' of flows within streams. Nonetheless, it has also been argued that the scope for expansion of this type of involvement is constrained by the propensity for government action in this space to crowd out private activity (Andreoni, 1990). Despite the acknowledged potential benefits of non-government and localised participation in environmental watering, these have only been realised in relatively specific circumstances. The scope for private and localised responses would appear to be greatest where several conditions are met: namely, the approach is most applicable to small-scale watering events that require negotiation and agreement with a range of individuals and groups as the contracted party with established local networks is best placed to facilitate this; this is particularly relevant to watering on private property; the approach is also more suitable to drier conditions, when small-scale watering using pumps and other infrastructure to deliver water to discrete wetlands is more ecologically appropriate (Docker, 2014).

In the context of the three-dimensional framework introduced earlier for contemplating the range of non-government arrangements for dealing with environmental watering, the case offered here stands a long way from atomistic private involvement and the expression of private preferences. Although some observers have invoked the subsidiarity principle to suggest that environmental water could be specified as entitlements and held by local entities (Young, 2012), there has been little real progress on this front. First, the water used for environmental purposes remains strictly held by the centralised CEWH. Whilst the Environmental Water Delivery Agreement with the NFSA implies some degree of control, there is little doubt that even this small amount of water continues to be the property of the central agency. Second, it is clear from the architecture designed to coordinate decisions that the allocation of environmental water remains strongly shaped by central priorities. Whilst localised decision-makers have a conduit for expressing preferences, it remains difficult to see how those local preferences would be weighed against central requirements. Finally, financing choices remain strongly influenced by central considerations and this may well explain why more localised and non-government arrangements are slow to emerge. In a somewhat bizarre turn of events, funding for monitoring the impacts of environmental watering has been recently reduced, and so it is difficult to discern how additional organisations might be able to fund the running costs of managing environmental water and the requirement to demonstrate beneficial outcomes from such arrangements.

In short, the expansion of so-called private and/or localised provision of environmental water seems unlikely in the short term in the MDB. Moreover,

> If agreements of this nature were to proliferate such that the volumes involved might impact significantly on the broader opportunities available to the Commonwealth, it may be necessary to limit the overall volume available for these types of actions and to undertake a more competitive selection process (Docker, 2014).

In sum, whilst there is some theoretical appeal for using private interests to deliver environmental water, the practical and historical hurdles remain non-trivial, at least in the MDB. Clearly, a useful extension would involve establishing the extent to which similar constraints bind private provision in other jurisdictions.

Bibliography

Anderson, T. and Parker, D. (2013). Transaction Costs and Environmental Markets: The Role of Entrepreneurs, *Review of Environmental Economics and Policy*, 7(2), pp. 259–275.

Andreoni, J. (1990). Impure Altruism and Donations to Public Goods: A Theory of Warm-Glow Giving? *Economic Journal*, 100, pp. 464–477.

Ashton, D., Oliver, M., Hooper, S., Mackinnin, D. and Mallawaarachchi, T. (2009). *Irrigated Agriculture in the Murray–Darling Basin: A Farm Level Analysis by Region and Industry*, ABARE, Canberra.

Australian Bureau of Agricultural and Resource Economics — Bureau of Rural Science (2010). *Assessing the Regional Impact of the Murray–Darling Basin Plan and the Australia Governments Water for the Future Program in the Murray–Darling Basin*, ABARE–BRS, Canberra. Available at: http://www.daff.gov.au/__data/assets/pdf_file/0011/1812971/regional-impact-mdba-2010.pdf [Accessed 15 April 2014].

Banzhaf, H., Fitzgerald, T. and Schnier, K. (2013). Non-Regulatory Approaches to the Environment: Coasean and Pigouvian Perspectives, *Review of Environmental Economics and Policy*, 7(2), p. 238.

Bennett, J. (2012). Coase Rules OK? Exploring Prospects for Private Sector Environmental Protection, *Economic Record*, 88(281), pp. 278–287.

Bennett, J., Kingsford, R., Norris, R. and Young, M. (2010). *Making Decisions about Environmental Water Allocations*, Australian Farm Institute, Sydney.

Bodin, Ö. and Crona, B. (2009). The Role of Social Networks in Natural Resource Governance: What Relational Patterns Make a Difference? *Global Environmental Change*, 19, pp. 366–374.

Commonwealth Environmental Water Holder (2012). *Commonwealth Environmental Water Holdings*, CEWH, Canberra. Available at: http://www.environment.gov.au/ewater/about/holdings.html [Accessed 10 February 2012].

Crase, L. (2011). The Fallout to the Guide to the Proposed Basin Plan, *Australian Journal of Public Administration*, 70(1), pp. 84–93.

Crase, L. and Gawne, B. (2011). Coase-coloured Glasses and Rights Bundling: Why the Initial Specification of Water Rights in Volumetric Terms Matters, *Economic Papers*, 30(2), pp. 135–146.

Crase, L., O'Keefe, S. and Kinoshita, Y. (2012). Enhancing Agri-Environmental Outcomes: Market-Based Approaches to Water in Australia's Murray–Darling Basin, *Water Resources Research*, 48, pp. 1–8.

Crase, L., O'Keefe, S. and Dollery, B. (2012). Presumptions of Linearity and Faith in the Power of Centralised Decision-Making: Two Challenges to the Efficient Management of Environmental Water in Australia, *Australian Journal of Agricultural and Resource Economics*, 56(3), pp. 426–437.

Dietz, T., Ostrom, E. and Stern, P. (2003). The Struggle to Govern the Commons, *Science*, 302(5652), pp. 1907–1912.

Docker, B (2014). *pers.com.*

Dollery, B. and O'Keefe, S. (2011). 'Institutional Considerations for Collaborative Behavior in Tourism and Recreation', in Crase, L. and

O'Keefe, S. (eds.), *Water Policy, Tourism and Recreation: Lessons from Australia*, Resources for the Future, Washington, pp. 82–99.

DSEWPAC (2013). *The Murray–Darling Basin Environmental Water Holders Report of 2013*, DSEWPAC, Canberra. Available at: http://www.environment.gov.au [Accessed 27 April 2014].

Hardin, G. (1968). The Tragedy of the Commons, *Science*, 162, pp. 1243–1248.

Hone, S., Foster, A. and O'Keefe, S. (2011). A Role for the Private Sector in the Provision of River and Riparian Goods?, *Economic Papers*, 30(2), pp. 157–166.

King, M. (2004). Getting our Feet Wet: An Introduction to Water Trusts, *Harvard Environmental Law Review*, 28, pp. 495–534.

Lee, L. and Ancev, T. (2009). Two Decades of Murray–Darling Water Management: A River of Funding, a Trickle of Achievement, *Agenda*, 16(1), pp. 5–23.

Meinzen-Dick, R. (2007). Beyond Panaceas in Water Institutions, *Proceedings of the National Academy of Sciences of the United States of America*, 104(39), pp. 15200–15205.

Murray–Darling Basin Authority (2012). About the Basin, MDBA, Canberra. Available at: http://www.mdba.gov.au/explore-the-basin/about-the-basin [Accessed 2 January 2014].

Musgrave, W. (2008). 'Historical Development of Water Resources in Australia: Irrigation Policy in the Murray–Darling Basin', in Crase, L. (ed.), *Water Policy in Australia: The Impact of Change and Uncertainty*, Resources for the Future, Washington, pp. 28–43.

National Water Commission (2010). *Australian Environmental Water Management Report*, NWC, Canberra. Available at: http://nwc.gov.au/__data/assets/pdf_file/0020/22169/Australian-environmental-water-management-framework-criteria.pdf [Accessed 4 May 2014].

Nature Foundation of South Australia (NFSA). [Website]. Available at: www.naturefoundation.org.au [Accessed 23 April 2014].

O'Neill, M. (1989). *The Third America: The Emergence of the Non-Profit Sector in the United States*, Jossey-Bass, San Francisco.

Productivity Commission (2010). *Market Mechanisms for Recovering Water in the Murray–Darling Basin, Final Report*, Melbourne.

Young, M. (2012). 'Chewing on the CEWH: Options for Improving Management of Environmental Water in the Murray–Darling Basin', in Quiggin, J., Mallawaarachchi, T. and Chambers, S. (eds.), *Water Policy Reform: Lessons in Sustainability from the Murray–Darling Basin*, Edward Elgar, Massachusetts, pp. 129–135.

7. Private Sector Protection of Cultural Heritage

Ken Willis

7.1. Introduction

Cultural heritage is the legacy of physical artefacts and intangible attributes of society inherited from past generations. Physical artefacts include works of art, literature, music, archaeological and historical artefacts, as well as buildings, monuments, and historic places. The demand for many aspects of cultural heritage can be measured and valued in the marketplace like any other economic good. People willingly pay to visit heritage sites; to see cultural artefacts, or to experience the cultural heritage of another country; just as they are willing to pay to see cultural events such as 'pop' concerts, films, drama, musicals, opera, ballet, comedy and other theatrical productions.

Many iconic cultural heritage sites are in government ownership, and are managed and operated by government departments or quangos. Some examples are the British Museum in London, the Louvre in Paris, the Colosseum, Roman Forum, and Castel

Sant' Angelo in Rome, the Acropolis in Athens, the Taj Mahal in Agra, the Red Fort in Delhi, the Pyramids in Giza, the Temple of Karnak, Luxor Temple, Valley of the Kings, and Temple of Hatshepsut in Luxor. Quangos such as English Heritage own and manage many archaeological sites, historic castles and gardens; whilst the National Trust in England owns and manages many historic houses, and land in cultural landscape areas, such as the Lake District in England.

However, there are numerous cultural heritage sites in private ownership. These vary from religious sites, to others owned and managed by charities, to those owned by individuals. These include iconic sites such as St Peter's and the Sistine Chapel in the Vatican; Westminster Abbey in London; Jain temples at Ranakpur and Sravanabelgola; the Sikh Golden temple at Amritsar; the Hindu temples at Somnath (Gujarat), Mamallapuram (Tamil Nadu), Minakshi Sundareshvara Temple in Maduri, the Brihadishvara Temple at Thanjavur, and the temple towns of Srirangam and Kumbakonam in Tamil Nadu. Other sites include the hundreds of ancient churches through Europe; and less well known temples in Asia.

7.2. Market Protection

The potential for private ownership and protection through the private market is greater for cultural heritage sites than for many other environmental terrestrial, aquatic and marine ecosystem services. Many cultural heritage sites attract large numbers of visitors, exclusion of non-paying visitors can be enforced, and hence revenues generated. Most of the stately homes of England and Scotland are in private ownership, such as Chatsworth House, Derbyshire; Burghley House, Lincolnshire; Blenheim Palace, Oxfordshire; and, Mellerstain House, Scotland. There are numerous similar sites throughout the world. The market can also provide a leading role in completing cultural heritage buildings. Progress on Gaudi's art nouveau cathedral, Sagrada Familia, in Barcelona, commenced in 1882, progressed slowly and intermittently until an entrance charge was introduced in the 21st century providing much needed funding to complete the building.[1]

Many more smaller sites, such as the exquisite and poignant sculptures in the di Sangro family chapel Cappella Sansevero in Naples, are also protected and managed through private ownership. These are all point sources, and are capable of being more profitable and generating more income compared to private ownership of larger terrestrial and aquatic areas where exclusion is more difficult to practice.

A substantial quantity of cultural heritage is in the hands of millions of small private collectors throughout the world. These typically include smaller items, easy to acquire, trade, and store, such as postage stamps, post cards, coins, paintings, military, railway and other memorabilia. Prominent industrialists have also acquired significant private collections of art and antiquities. Most notable of these include Paul Getty (1892–1976), an avid collector of art and antiquities, who established the J. Paul Getty Museum in California to display his works of art, and the Getty Villa dedicated to the study of arts and cultures of ancient Greece, Rome, and Etruria; and Calouste Gulbenkian (1869–1955) whose art collection is displayed in the Museu Calouste Gulbenkian in Lisbon. Numerous other private collectors amassed collections, such as the Davies sisters, Gwendoline (1882–1951) and Margaret (1884–1963), who bequeathed their art collection to the National Museum of Wales; and John Bowes (1811–1885) who built a French chateaux at Barnard Castle, in the countryside of northern England, to house his collection of paintings, ceramics, glass, automata, tapestries etc. (Bruce, 2014a) and the anthropological artefact collection of Augustus Pitt-Rivers (1827–1900) (Bruce, 2014b).

---

[1] At Gaudi's death in 1926 only a quarter of the project was complete. The Spanish Civil War and lack of funding meant construction only passed the midpoint in 2010. Progress increased immensely after the introduction of an entrance charge. In 2014 the entrance charge to the Sagrada Familia cathedral was EUR14.80 per person. The Sagrada Familia attracts around 3m visitors per year. Entrance fees pay most of the EUR25m a year cost of continuing construction. The Sagrada Familia is due to be completed in 2026.

Is private ownership of cultural artefacts profitable? Pommerehne and Feld (1997) suggested the average real rate of return on paintings to private investors did not seem particularly large, only amounting to about 0.6 to 1.5 per cent, depending on the country, sample and time period. They argued that, compared with investments in financial markets, particularly investments in high security assets (government securities), this implied an opportunity loss in real terms of 1.6 to 2.0 per cent per year, since the annual average real rate of return on financial investments was as high as 2.5 to 3.0 per cent from 1650 to 1987. The risk on paintings was also estimated to be much higher than the risk for government securities. Thus, in profitability terms, paintings did much worse on average than financial assets.

Frey and Pommerehne (1989) pointed out that the financial rates of return on paintings show a large variance. In their sample the highest real rate of return on a painting was +26 per cent per year and the lowest −19 per cent, with a mean rate of 1.5 per cent per year and a median rate of 1.8 per cent.[2] All studies showed that the real rate of return on paintings was below that of financial assets, suggesting private individuals purchase paintings for psychic and consumption reasons as well as financial ones. There may be additional reasons for investment in art as a way of minimising or avoiding tax.

Art is subject to risks in addition to uncertainty about future prices. These include attribution of paintings, fakes and forgeries and material risks (risk of individual pieces of art being destroyed by fire, stolen, or looted in war). These risks affect public institutions such as art galleries and museums, as well as private individuals.

---

[2] Tracy Ermin's 'My Bed', an unmade bed and a floor littered with empty vodka bottles, cigarette butts and condoms, short listed for the Turner prize in 1999, and bought by the art collector Charles Saatchi for £150,000 in 2000, was sold in July 2014 at Christie's art auction in London for £2.2m to Count Christian Duerckheim an industrialist and art collector from Cologne. This represents a continuous rate of return of 19.2 per cent on the initial investment.

A cultural heritage good may either be a private market good or a 'public good'.[3] Where excludability (producer rights) exists, a price can be charged and the private sector can be an effective mechanism in protecting and conserving the cultural heritage good. Where producer property rights can be established, such as entrance to museums, and historic buildings, or copyright over artistic works such as books and music scores, then a price can be charged and the market system can operate.

However, some cultural goods, such as heritage sites, differ from private goods in two respects by:

(1) Being immobile: people must travel to experience the good or culture, rather than taking the good to the market as occurs with most private goods. This means that the market for the good is established by how far people are willing to travel to experience the cultural good.
(2) Having 'public good' elements. A 'public good' is one whose consumption by one person in no way detracts from its availability to others (it is non-rivalry, i.e., has zero opportunity cost of consumption); and consumers cannot be excluded from consuming the good (it is non-excludable, i.e., producers of the good have no property rights over it). Thus, whilst it is possible to charge for entry into the interior of Edinburgh Castle (excludability can be practised), visitors to Edinburgh can enjoy the exterior views of the Castle, and its contribution to the character of the city and its skyline, free of charge.

A cultural heritage good may be (i) rival and excludable, i.e., a market good; (ii) rival and non-excludable: a public good with congestion costs; (iii) non-rival and excludable: an excludable good but

---

[3] A pure public good is a good with zero opportunity cost of consumption (i.e., it costs no more for X+1 people to consume the good as X number of people), no producer rights (i.e., non-excludability, it is not possible to exclude person X, so no price can be charged), and no consumer rights (a person has to consume the good whether s/he likes it or not).

one with zero opportunity cost of consumption; and (iv) non-rival and non-excludable: a pure public good.

There are examples of cultural heritage sites in all of these four categories. Whether the private market can protect a heritage site depends on whether people can be excluded and a price charged to protect and maintain the good.

7.3. Non-Rival and Excludable Goods

Many cultural heritage sites are excludable, and either rival or non-rival in consumption. Many government-owned heritage sites charge an admission fee, e.g., to the Colosseum in Rome and the Taj Mahal in Agra, as a means of not only raising income but also of optimising visitor utility by avoiding excessive congestion costs. However, in the UK there is free admission into most national museums (e.g., British Museum, National Gallery, Natural History Museum, Science Museum, Tate, V&A, in London, and the National Railway Museum in York). Free admission to make culture available to all means that consumer surplus comprises all of the benefit to visitors. Free admission also means that, for the last marginal visitor, consumer surplus is zero. Where there are zero opportunity costs of admission, and no congestion, then zero pricing is economically efficient.

In the absence of congestion (i.e., rival consumption), it costs no more to admit $X+1$ visitors to the British Museum as X visitors. The marginal cost of the additional visitor is zero; so that any non-zero price will produce an inefficiency. However, the cost to the government as the supplier of the British Museum is positive; whilst the optimal price to the consumer of the (undepletable) externality is zero. If the price charged for entry is zero (as in the case of the British Museum, London) then government must supply the good, and pay the costs.

7.4. Rival and Excludable Goods

Free access to cultural goods such as the British Museum in London leads to congestion and loss of utility to intra-marginal visitors at certain periods during the day (see Maddison and Foster, 2003). An entrance charge can reduce congestion costs and optimise utility to visitors.

Private-sector heritage sites avoid the economic problems of public-sector provision of cultural heritage by charging prices to cover costs, and also to manage congestion. This raises the issue of what admission price should be charged. Clearly the admission price needs to cover the cost of operating the site, after grants and sponsorship have been taken into consideration. But should they charge more, say, a revenue-maximising price?

Raising revenue to maintain cultural heritage goods is important to private-sector organisations. Stated preference techniques such as contingent valuation (CV) can be used to determine admission prices as well as the consumer surplus on a heritage site. The desired admission price might be a price to cover the costs of managing the site, or a revenue-maximising price. Willis (2003) used CV to determine the revenue-maximising prices that could be charged for access to the Bosco di Capodimonte, a historic park and royal hunting ground surrounding the Palace of Capodimonte, Naples, Italy.

Visitors were interviewed at the two entry gates into the Bosco. A total of 494 visitors completed questionnaires. The demand curve, relating visits to price, was derived from the bid curve, recording the bid amount (P), the proportion accepting that bid amount, and the number of visits at that bid amount (Q). The analysis is based upon the aggregate demand curve.[4] The functional relationship between visits and price represented by the demand curve was of the form:

$$Q = b_0\, e^{-b1P}.$$

The exact parameters for this curve were estimated by fitting a nonlinear regression model to the function $Q = b_0/(\exp(b_1 {}^* P))$, which searched for a best fit over possible ranges of parameters of the model, with respect to the specified derivatives of the function

[4] The analysis did not seek to model the number of visits each individual would make at different prices; but aggregated individuals' visits at different prices to derive an aggregate demand curve for the 'average' visitor in the sample.

specified in the model. The procedure first examined the starting value specifications in the parameters and evaluated the residual sum of squares for each combination of values specified in the grid of values. The parameters which produced the best fit function for the Bosco data were $b_0 = 29.8643$ (standard error = 1.6287), and $b_1 = 0.1979$ (se = 0.0173); with confidence intervals for b_1 of 0.1594 and 0.2363 at 95 per cent level.

The conditions for determining the maximum revenue point on a demand curve for a good are:

(1) First-order condition: $f'(P) = 0$, $dq/dp = 0$,
(2) Second-order condition: $f'(P) < 0$, $d^2q/dp^2 < 0$,

where q = quantity or number of visits, and p = price per visit.

The optimal price that achieves maximum revenue was derived from the model $Q = b_0\, e^{-b1P}$, where $Q = 29.8643\, e^{-0.1979P}$. Differentiating this function, and setting $dq/dx = 0$, the maximum revenue point, is achieved when $P = 5{,}053$, i.e., the entry charge is 5,053 lira per visit for all visitors.[5] This is statistically the 'best estimate' but it is subject to statistical error. This maximum revenue price is where $dq/dp = -1$, i.e., where the elasticity of demand with respect to price is –1. The upper and lower confidence limits suggest that the revenue maximising price lay between 4,232 lira and 6,474 lira.

The analysis of the Bosco data indicated that price discrimination would increase revenue above that of a single admission price of 5,053 lira. A lower price for economically 'inactive' (non-employed such as retired people and student) visitors of 3,802 lira, and a higher admission price for economically 'active' (employed wage earning) visitors of 10,893 lira would increase revenue by 44.2 per cent compared with a single admission price of 5,053 lira applied to all visitors.

The National Trust in England charges one price for admission by adults to each of its sites. This is probably not a revenue-maximising

---

[5] In 1999, the year of the survey, EUR1 = 1,936 lira. The euro replaced the Italian lira in 2002 as the currency in Italy. 5,053 lira is EUR2.61.

strategy if willingness to pay (WTP) varies across market segments. Many private cultural heritage sites seek to maximise revenue by price discrimination. Lower prices are often applied to students and people who are retired and have pensions, i.e., those with lower ability and WTP. Declining marginal utility of consumption implies that WTP for each additional marginal visit admission will decline. Some private heritage sites try to capture the greater utility on the first visit by charging a higher price for this visit (e.g., tourists from distant parts of the country and from abroad who wish to visit the site but who are unlikely to return again that year) and a lower price for subsequent visits within the year. Thus, the adult admission charge to Westminster Abbey is £18 (GBP, 2014), but for £40 an individual can purchase an annual pass which allows unlimited visits within a 12-month period. Similarly, the adult admission price to Castle Howard, York, a house designed by the great architect Sir John Vanbrugh in 1699, is £14 (GBP, 2014), but an annual pass to the house, gardens and grounds is £40.

Private cultural heritage sites need to be responsive to visitor demands to maximise visitor numbers and revenue. The same incentive does not exist for public museums and heritage sites, although public museums with free admissions often have targets for visitor numbers to each museum and archaeological site (see Tyne & Wear Archives and Museums, 2010) to justify government subsidies. In the past, public museums and art galleries simply displayed the same material year after year. But now they place greater emphasis on changing displays and organising special temporary exhibitions to attract more visitors.

Private heritage sites have been more conscious of the need to be innovative to survive by attracting paying visitors. Vindolanda, a Roman fort close to Hadrian's Wall in Northern England, funded entirely by paying visitors, took the decision quite early after the charitable trust was founded in 1970, to promote archaeological research and excavation, develop scale replicas of the fort wall and a gate, buildings and temple, and to display material excavated in a museum (Birley, 2013), including the Vindolanda writing tablets found on the site. The tablets are the oldest surviving handwritten documents in Britain. Written on fragments of thin, post-card sized wooden leaf-tablets with carbon-based ink, the tablets date to the 1st and 2nd centuries AD, and are probably the best source of information about life on Hadrian's Wall (a World Heritage Site).

Stated preference methods can be used to assess visitor preferences for the attributes of a cultural heritage site. Managing archaeological and heritage sites requires information on visitor preferences to guide displays of cultural exhibits. Willis (2009) used a CE to investigate visitor preferences for the attributes of Vindolanda. The study assessed visitor preferences, utility, and value of attributes of the site: excavation and research, interpretation information, museum displays, reconstructions, visitor amenities and admission price, including interaction effects between attributes. The analysis revealed a preference for the *status quo*; and greater choice uncertainty associated with alternative hypothetical attribute bundles, e.g., the development of a children's play area. Neighbouring substitute Roman forts affected the price visitors were willing to pay for entry. Colombino and Nese (2009) experimented with normal, uniform and triangular distributions in a CE to assess management policy (opening times, audio guides, guided tours, café, exhibitions, events, laboratory, audio–visual, documentation centre and price of admission) at the exceptionally well preserved archaeological site at Paestrum, Solerno, Italy, originally founded as a Greek city before being taken over by the Romans in 273 BC. They found a negative WTP for the development of a café on site; but that visitor preferences were heterogeneous across attributes with, for example, 46 per cent of respondents having a positive utility for a café.

Museum and gallery displays are rival: only a small proportion of artefacts owned by a museum or gallery can be displayed at any one time. Non-display items are held in storage, and many of these items, especially in public-sector museums and galleries are never displayed. The Smithsonian Museum Support Center is a storage and conservation facility in Maryland housing collections which are not on display. More than 54 million items are housed there, comprising 40 per cent of the Smithsonian collection which is not on display. The remaining 60 per cent not on display are artefacts housed behind-the-scenes in the Smithsonian museums themselves or at other off-site storage facilities. Preserving and maintaining cultural heritage is expensive, especially buildings. But even artefacts in museums, which are not displayed, require storage space, cleaning, and temperature and humidity control.

Private-sector suppliers may make more rational decisions about which cultural heritage artefacts to preserve and protect, and which to discard or not maintain. The private sector has an incentive to optimise the amount of cultural heritage it protects. In the private sector, there is an incentive to only keep artefacts, displayed or in storage, as long as the increase in their value exceeds the opportunity cost of the investment. The optimal holding time is time t, where the rate of growth in the value of the artefact (g) equals the rate interest (r). This is the save or savour question which is a prominent issue in wine storage (Jaeger, 1981), and antique furniture (Graeser, 1993) for example. The problem with the optimal holding concept for cultural heritage goods is predicting g over time.

Public sector museums may be constrained by the terms of the gift of the artefact,[6] or a policy not to dispose of artefacts. This can lead to the protection and preservation of objects of little or zero value to society; with preservation costs exceeding the value of the artefact.

7.5. Donations and Charitable Giving

Private cultural heritage sites can also be preserved in ways other than funding by visitors. Seaman (2013) recounts the experience of the Fox Theatre in Atlanta, Georgia. This theatre of Moorish and Egyptian architectural design, now on the National Historic Register in the USA, struggled for decades in various private for-profit manifestations, and was almost demolished in 1974 to make room for a headquarters building for Southern Bell telecommunications company. It was saved by an outpouring of both local and non-local private citizen activism and fundraising, and eventually lavishly

[6] For example, stipulating that the item cannot be sold by the museum.

restored and rejuvenated in 1987 by another highly visible private non-profit fundraising campaign. It is now a successful theatre, and a ballroom which also hosts everything from Sweet 16s to weddings and corporate events.

In many countries numerous stately homes, museums and archaeological sites are registered as 'charities' or 'trusts' to take advantage of tax breaks and grants from sponsors and government. In the UK, Gift Aid allows a charity to maximise the value of donations. The charity can reclaim tax from HM Revenue & Customs (HMRC) on the 'gross' equivalent of donations, that is their value before tax was deducted at the basic rate, currently 20 per cent. This means that for every £1 donated, the charity can claim an extra 25 pence. Some heritage sites ask visitors to sign a gift aid when purchasing their admission ticket, so that admission payments as well as other donations qualify as gift aid.

In the UK, gift money to a charity by a private company is deductible from total company profit when calculating Corporation Tax. Such gift sponsorship by private companies to cultural heritage venues can be an important source of revenue. Entry to the Faraday[7] Museum at the Royal Institution London is free of charge, but is heavily supported by donations from private firms, corporate supporters, Trusts and Foundations, and legacies.

Whilst Value Added Tax (VAT) is payable on repairs and maintenance of listed buildings, under harmonisation of VAT rules across the European Union, in the UK a grant up to the value of the VAT paid can be claimed from the government for listed places of worship.

Grant aid and donations, including tax breaks, account for a significant proportion of funding to private heritage sites. Admission charges typically account for only a minor proportion of total income of private sector heritage sites. A study of the independent

[7] Michael Faraday FRS (22 September 1791–25 August 1867) was an English scientist who contributed to the fields of electromagnetism and electrochemistry. His main discoveries were those of electromagnetic induction, diamagnetism and electrolysis.

museum[8] sector in the UK, by DC Research (2010), revealed that from a sample of 73 museums, only 22 per cent of revenue was derived from admission charges. Catering, and special events accounted for 10 per cent of revenue; retail sales for 17 per cent of revenue; functions, conferences and corporate hospitality 5 per cent; grant funding 36 per cent of revenue; and donations 10 per cent. So, grant and donation income accounted for almost half (46 per cent) of revenue to the independent museum sector.

7.5.1. *Charitable giving*

The importance of donations and charitable giving by individuals and private firms to the revenue of cultural heritage sites raises the issue of whether the donations fully reflect the value of the cultural heritage site to the donor, or whether donations are under-bequeathed as a result of the free-rider problem.[9]

Foster (1999) quantified the extent to which charitable organisations may have succeeded in overcoming the free-rider problem, and provided an empirical analysis of the different devices to counteract the free-rider tendency of potential philanthropists. Her results suggested that UK charities captured 50 per cent to 70 per cent of the full economic value in voluntary donations. The research also showed the two issues in determining the success of fund-raising were the choice of contact method, and the information used to define the target group. Direct face-to-face contact between the fund raiser and potential donor are more successful in securing donations, compared to remote methods. However, the higher the ratio of marginal fund-raising costs to the subscription fee, the greater the extent

[8] Independent museums represent over half the museum provision in the UK. They range from small local organisations, mainly operated by volunteers, to large institutions, many operating as charitable trusts.

[9] The free rider refers to someone who benefits from resources, goods, or services without paying for the cost of the benefit. It was first used in the economic theory of 'public goods'. A free-rider problem occurs when it leads to under-provision of a public good, or to overuse or degradation of a common property resource.

to which the charity should engage in targeting effort towards specific segments of the population.

7.5.2. *Crowding out effects*

If private and public sector cultural heritage sites raise revenues themselves, e.g., through entrance charges and charitable giving, will this affect grant aid from government? Maddison (2004) found evidence that this was the case: the extent of charitable giving, and non-grant income, significantly influenced changes in the level of government grants to museums. Using a Granger causality econometric model, Maddison (2004) estimated, across 18 public museums in England, that every additional £1 of revenue from non-grant sources served to reduce grants by £0.30. However, increases in capital expenditure and expenditure on new acquisitions both increased future grants by £0.27 and £0.52 for every £1 respectively (Maddison, 2004).

7.6. Indirect Use Value

Where excludability can be practised and a price can be charged, the private sector can provide for the protection and conservation of cultural heritage goods. However, in addition to direct use value to visitors, some cultural heritage goods may have indirect use value, option value, and existence value.

Indirect use values are benefits that are received from a good or service without the need to directly use it. An example is the enjoyment gained from being able to see the exterior of the heritage good without having to pay an entry charge to gain access to the interior of the heritage site. The visual externality of the heritage good, e.g., Edinburgh Castle, adds to the historic character and amenity profile of an area or city, such as Edinburgh. Option values relate to the potential for future use, for oneself, for others (altruism) or for future generations (bequest). For heritage goods, option values derive from conserving them for future use. Existence values reflect the benefits that derive purely from the existence of a cultural good.

For example, an iconic historic property may add to the status of an area providing benefits to local individuals which they value even if they have no intention of visiting the property.

Buildings of historic and architectural interest in Edinburgh are mainly located in the designated World Heritage Site area, comprising the old town (Castle, Royal Mile, Grassmarket, Calton Hill) and the Georgian New Town commenced in 1767 (Newtown, Dean Village, Stockbridge areas).[10] The historic buildings of the old and new towns are extremely expensive to maintain, a cost which is principally borne by their occupants. However, residents and visitors to Edinburgh can enjoy the ambience of the Old Town and New Town free of charge in an uncongested walk around the area. The fact that residents of the Old Town and New Town cannot charge visitors for entry to these areas means that buildings attract a lower rate of return from their private use, compared with their total value to society, and that too little is probably spent on their maintenance, and the maintenance of the roads, pavements and street furniture in the area.

A number of studies have used environmental valuation techniques to assess the indirect use values of cultural goods. Navrud and Strand (2002) used open-ended CV questions to assess people's WTP to protect cultural buildings and monuments in Norway, and to protect Nidaros Cathedral. An open-ended CV was also used by Mourato, Kontoleon and Danchev (2002) to value the conservation of Bulgarian monasteries by Bulgarian citizens. Pollicino and Maddison (2002) used a double-bounded CV approach to value the cleaning of Lincoln Cathedral to remove the effects of air pollution. A CV payment ladder was used by Maddison and Mourato (2002) to estimate the benefits of eliminating road noise and visual intrusion to Stonehenge, a stone circle built some 2,400 BC, by changes to the local road system. The value of reducing acid deposition damage to 100 marble monuments in Washington DC was estimated by Morey and Rossmann (2003) using a CE. Passive use values appeared to be

[10] Information on Edinburgh's World Heritage Site, including the Old and New Towns, can be found on the Edinburgh World Heritage Trust site: www.ewht.org.uk.

a more important component of WTP than direct-use values (Morey *et al.*, 2002).

This poses the dilemma for such cultural heritage goods: what is the 'public good' element of these goods worth?; and how should they be financed? Inevitably the indirect value element of cultural goods, whether public or even private cultural goods, will need to be financed through general taxation. Garrod *et al.* (1996) used CV to assess public preferences and WTP extra local taxes towards the renovation and restoration of private buildings in the historic Grainger Town area of Newcastle. People had a strong preference for renovating the historic area and preferred to contribute towards renovation in the most degraded areas.

7.7. Valuation Methods and Validity

Stated preference, (CV and CE) have been widely used to value cultural heritage goods. The increasing sophistication of the application of these methods (see Willis, 2014) will ensure that the assumptions of the model adopted conform to the characteristics of the data being analysed. The introduction of greater incentive compatible mechanisms should also ensure that consumers not only bear the cost but also derive the benefit of their actions, and hence produce more accurate, reliable and robust estimates of people's WTP for cultural heritage goods.

Nevertheless, there are concerns that stated preference (CV and CE) may over-estimate how many people will pay, and over-estimate how much they will pay; because they are based on what people say they will do, rather than what they actually do when a real decision has to be made. The accuracy and reliability of WTP and market share predictions are particularly important for private firms and individuals supplying cultural heritage goods: they need to know with some accuracy whether the revenue the cultural good is likely to generate will exceed the cost of their investment in its conservation.

Some studies have shown that CV can over-estimate value. For example, Neill *et al.* (1994) conducted two experiments to compare hypothetical and actual WTP for a small framed painting of a south-western USA rural scene by an unknown Navajo Indian artist. The first experiment compared CV maximum WTP estimates with those of a Vickrey auction in which subjects were actually required to pay for the painting out of their own pocket if their bid was successful. The average valuations were \$37.04 ($n = 41$) for the CV, and \$9.49 ($n = 16$) for the Vickrey auction; with medians of \$30 and \$6, respectively. The null hypothesis of no significant different between the two distributions was rejected. In a second experiment the results of a hypothetical Vickrey, and an actual Vickrey auction in which the bid involved a financial commitment, were compared. In this experiment, the average and median bids in the hypothetical Vickrey auction were \$301 and \$60 respectively ($n = 51$); and in the real auction \$12 and \$5 ($n = 60$). Again the null hypothesis of no significant difference between the two bid distributions was rejected.

Some CEs, such as that by Train (2003) for the Bay Area Rapid Transit around San Francisco, have been shown to accurately predict commuter percentages by transport mode; and others CE studies such as that by Carlsson and Martinsson (2001) have revealed insignificant discrepancy between marginal WTP for donations in hypothetical and actual experiments. However, some studies suggest that participants and visitor numbers can be over-estimated in stated preference experiments. In an experiment by Seip and Strand (1992), 101 Norwegians were asked in a CV study whether they would pay an annual amount equal to the annual membership fee of the Norwegian Association for the Protection of Nature to support the work of the Association. The 64 individuals who stated they would pay this amount later received a membership application to join the Association, but only 6 actually joined. Seip and Strand (1992) ascribed this discrepancy to interviewer bias, starting point bias, payment vehicle bias, hypothetical bias, unfamiliarity bias, and 'part-whole' bias.

Most of these biases did not apply to an experiment by Willis and Powe (1998) of potential visitors to Warkworth Castle. Potential visitors, who parked their car and walked up to the castle gate and looked at the entrance price, but did not enter, were asked in a CV experiment their maximum WTP to enter the medieval castle. They were then offered an entrance ticket at their stated CV price. This provided a real monetary test of behavioural intention. Only 40 per cent of potential visitors at the castle gate took up the offer of a ticket at their stated price, and made a real economic commitment immediately following their stated CV WTP response. The study revealed that even when the CV survey stage is juxtaposed to the behavioural intention stage, a substantial proportion of stated CV WTP values are not translated into real economic commitments and purchases. Perhaps this should not be so surprising from knowledge of the actual market place. Individuals often make purposeful trips to towns to purchase a good (new clothes, furniture, or whatever), only to inspect the good closely and decide not to buy. The problem is that CV surveys treat such individuals as valid respondents and count their WTP as an element of the total utility of a cultural good.

There is some concern that CEs tend to produce higher estimates of WTP for a good than CV methods. Why this is the case is not exactly known. It may result from the fact that in a CE price (or cost) is just one attribute amongst a number of others to be weighed against each other; whereas in CV the bundle of attributes are described on one side to the scales and against price on the other side. Thus, in CV price is more prominent.

The application of stated preference, CV and CEs, can over-estimate the value of heritage goods through the independent valuation and summation of WTP values, and the failure to take substitution effects into account (see Santos, 1999). This can result in too many proposals passing the benefit–cost test (Hoehn and Randall, 1989).

7.8. Conclusions

The majority of cultural heritage artefacts are protected by private-sector ownership. Public-sector protection of cultural heritage is, however, often more visible, because it involves many of the iconic paintings, buildings, and archaeological sites and because these treasures are more accessible to the general public.

Market incentives ensure that private-sector protection is more responsive to market demands, for rival and excludable heritage goods. Private-sector protection of these cultural heritage sites is more efficient, with higher benefit/cost ratios than many public museums and galleries. The private sector also often offers more interactive visitor experiences than at publicly owned heritage sites.

However, the private sector is less efficient at managing heritage sites where there are indirect use values and where the heritage site produces environmental externalities.

Economic techniques, such as CV and CE, can be used to estimate the demand and WTP for cultural heritage preservation in both the private and public sectors, and as a tool in managing cultural heritage sites. It is important to derive accurate estimates of the value of cultural heritage sites where indirect use and environmental externalities exist to ensure these elements are afforded suitable public-sector protection and funding.

Bibliography

Birley, A. (2013). 'Vindolanda', in Walker, C. and Carr, N. (eds.), *Tourism and Archaeology*, Left Coast Press, Walnut Creek, CA, pp. 127–141.

Bruce, F. (2014a). Less a Castle than a Cabinet of Curiosities: A Durham Museum Houses Treasures from One of History's Greatest Spending Sprees, *The Daily Telegraph*, April 5, 2014.

Bruce, F. (2014b). The Pitt-Rivers Museum Oxford, *The Daily Telegraph*, February 5, 2014.

Carlsson, F. and Martinsson, P. (2001). Do Hypothetical and Actual Marginal Willingness to Pay Differ in Choice Experiments? *Journal of Environmental Economics and Management*, 41, pp. 179–192.

Colombino, U. and Nese, A. (2009). Preference Heterogeneity in Relation to Museum Services, *Tourism Economics*, 15(2), pp. 381–395.

DC Research (2010). *The Economic Value of the Independent Museum Sector*, Report to the Association of Independent Museums, DC Research, Carlisle.

Foster, V. (1999). *On the Voluntary Financing of Public Goods*. PhD thesis, Department of Economics, University College, London.

Frey, B.S. and Pommerehne, W.W. (1989). Art Investment: An Empirical Enquiry, *Southern Economic Journal*, 56(2), pp. 396–409.

Garrod, G., Willis, K.G., Bjarnadottir, H. and Cockbain, P. (1996). The Non-Priced Benefits of Renovating Historic Buildings: A Case Study of Newcastle's Grainger Town, *Cities*, 13(6), pp. 423–430.

Graeser, P. (1993). Rate of Return to Investment in American Antique Furniture, *Southern Economic Journal*, 59(4), pp. 817–821.

Hoehn, J.P. and Randall, A. (1989). Too Many Proposals Pass the Benefit Cost Test, *American Economic Review*, 79, pp. 544–551.

Jaeger, E. (1981). To Save or Savor: The Rate of Return to Storing Wine, *Journal of Political Economy*, 89(3), pp. 584–592.

Maddison, D. (2004). Causality and Museum Subsidies, *Journal of Cultural Economics*, 28, pp. 89–108.

Maddison, D. and Foster, T. (2003). Valuing Congestion Costs at the British Museum, *Oxford Economic Papers*, 55(1), pp. 173–190.

Maddison, D. and Mourato, S. (2002). 'Valuing Different Road Options for Stonehenge', in Navrud, S. and Ready, R.C. (eds.), *Valuing Cultural Heritage*, Edward Elgar, Cheltenham, pp. 87–104.

Morey, E. and Rossmann, K.G. (2003). Using Stated Preference Questions to Investigate Variations in Willingness to Pay for Preserving Marble Monuments: Classic Heterogeneity, Random Parameters, and Mixture Models, *Journal of Cultural Economics*, 27, pp. 215–229.

Morey, E.R., Rossmann, K.G., Chestnut, L.G. and Ragland, S. (2002). 'Valuing Reduced Acid Deposition Injuries to Cultural Resources: Marble Monuments in Washington DC', in Navrud, S. and Ready, R.C. (eds.), *Valuing Cultural Heritage*, Edward Elgar, Cheltenham, pp. 159–183.

Mourato, S., Kontoleon, A. and Danchev, A. (2002). 'Preserving Cultural Heritage in Transition Economies: A Contingent Valuation Study of Bulgarian Monasteries', in Navrud, S. and Ready, R.C. (eds.), *Valuing Cultural Heritage*, Edward Elgar, Cheltenham, pp. 68–86.

Navrud, S. and Strand, J. (2002). 'Social Costs and Benefits of Preserving and Restoring Nidros Cathedral', in Navrud, S. and Ready, R.C. (eds.), *Valuing Cultural Heritage*, Edward Elgar, Cheltenham, pp. 31–39.

Neill, H.R., Cummings, R.G., Ganderton, P.T., Harrison, G.W. and McGuckin, T. (1994). Hypothetical Surveys and Real Economic Commitments, *Land Economics*, 70, pp. 145–154.

Pollicino, M. and Maddison, D. (2002). 'Valuing the Impacts of Air Pollution on Lincoln Cathedral', in Navrud, S. and Ready, R.C. (eds.), *Valuing Cultural Heritage*, Edward Elgar, Cheltenham, pp. 53–67.

Pommerehne, W.W. and Feld, L.P. (1997). The Impact of Museum Purchases on Auction Prices of Paintings, *Journal of Cultural Economics*, 21, pp. 249–271.

Santos, J.M.L. (1999). 'Valuing Alternative Bundles of Landscape Attributes', in Willis, K.G., Button, K. and Nijkamp, P. (eds.), *Environmental Valuation: Volume 2: Multi-Attribute Programmes, Validity, Allocation Issues, And Case Studies*, Edward Elgar, Cheltenham, pp. 361–386.

Seaman, B.A. (2013). 'The Role of the Private Sector in Cultural Heritage', in Rizzo, I. and Mignosa, A. (eds.), *Handbook on the Economics of Cultural Heritage*, Edward Elgar Publishers, Cheltenham, pp. 111–128.

Seip, K. and Strand, J. (1992). Willingness to Pay for Environmental Goods in Norway: A Contingent Valuation Study with Real Payments, *Environmental and Resource Economics*, 2, pp. 91–106.

Train, K.E. (2003). *Discrete Choice Methods with Simulation*, Cambridge University Press, Cambridge.

Tyne & Wear Archive and Museums (2010). *Corporate Plan 2009–2014*, Tyne & Wear Archive and Museums, Newcastle-upon-Tyne.

Willis, K.G. (2003). Pricing Public Parks, *Journal of Environmental Planning and Management*, 46 (1), pp. 3–17.

Willis, K.G. (2009). Assessing Visitor Preferences in the Management of Archaeological and Heritage Attractions: A Case Study of Hadrian's Roman Wall, *International Journal of Tourism Research*, 11, pp. 487–505.

Willis, K.G. (2014). 'The use of Stated Preference Methods to Value Cultural Heritage', in Ginsburgh, V.A. and Throsby, D. (eds.), *Handbook of the Economics of Art and Culture*, Elsevier, Amsterdam, pp. 145–181.

Willis, K.G. and Powe, N.A. (1998). Contingent Valuation and Real Economic Commitments: A Private Good Experiment, *Journal of Environmental Planning and Management*, 41, pp. 611–619.

8. Can Food Markets Result in Environmental Benefits?

Wendy Umberger, Sven Anders and Ellen Goddard

8.1. Introduction

The global food system is experiencing dramatic transformation as a result of diverse but interrelated economic, social and environmental factors (Pereira, 2013). These developments include issues such as globalisation, consolidation and integration of food businesses, increasing disposable incomes, changing governance (from primarily public to increasingly private as a result of more powerful multi-national food retailers and food processors), food price volatility, food insecurity, climate change, and increasing public concerns about the 'sustainability' of food systems (Desai and Ringler, 2013). Concerns about future food security as a result of climate change, environmental degradation and water pollution are perhaps some of the most significant drivers of recent changes occurring in the food industry. As a result, firms all along the food chain are creating new or adapting current business models to achieve more environmentally and socially sustainable practices (Bradbear and Friel, 2011;

Massoud *et al.*, 2010; Pereira, 2013; Reardon *et al.*, 2003; Smith, Lawrence and Richards, 2010; Thompson and Scoones, 2009).

Since 2008, when the United Nations Environment Programme (UNEP) developed the notion of a 'green economy', there has been a significant push for agricultural firms and the food industry to consider ways to improve '... human well-being and social equity while significantly reducing environmental risks and ecological scarcities' (Desai and Ringler, 2013, p. 31). Additionally, since 2008, agencies such as the The Organisation for Economic Co-operation and Development (OECD) and the World Bank have suggested that the private sector must begin to bear the full costs of sustainable or 'green' food production and consumption for longer term economic growth to continue (Desai and Ringler, 2013).

More recently, in 2012, world leaders from the private sector, government, non-government organisations (NGOs), and other groups converged for the United Nations Conference on Sustainable Development held in Rio de Janeiro (called the Rio+20 Conference). The focus was broadly on 'sustainable development' or how stakeholders can work together to simultaneously achieve economic growth, 'environmental sustainability', and food security. The two broad goals resulting from the Rio+20 Conference:

(1) Zero Net Land Degradation; and,
(2) Zero Hunger,

are especially relevant to the food industry (Desai and Ringler, 2013).

Ultimately, issues such as climate change, food security, poverty reduction, food waste, human and animal welfare, and maintaining natural resources must now be considered by the private sector as they are embedded in discussions about 'sustainability' and food systems. The food industry is now confronted with the enormous and difficult task of profitably producing plentiful amounts of food that meet market demands for products that are affordable, nutritious, safe, high quality and convenient. Firms must rise to this challenge while simultaneously ensuring their activities are environmentally sustainable and equitable (Godfray *et al.*, 2010; Desai and Ringler, 2013; Mazzanti, 2014; Pereira, 2013).

The broad aim of this chapter is to address the question of whether or not private actions by stakeholders in the food sector — including input suppliers, producers, manufacturers and processors, retailers and consumers — aimed at addressing environmental concerns are yielding environmental benefits. The chapter first provides an overview of how food systems are inherently linked to the environment. This is followed by a summary of recent private-sector initiatives by firms along the food chain to address environmental concerns with a discussion of ways in which these initiatives may lead to positive environmental outcomes. The final section of the chapter attempts to address the question of whether or not these initiatives are actually leading to positive environmental outcomes.

8.2. Linking the Global Food System and the Environment

Food systems are increasingly closely linked both positively and negatively with the environment. On the one hand, food production provides positive environmental externalities, for example keeping land in agricultural production may protect ecosystems and provide environmental services. On the other hand, food system activities, ranging from production to consumption, are increasingly linked to negative environmental externalities, including: pollution from inefficient use of water and agricultural inputs (e.g., fertiliser and pesticides, growth promotants and antibiotics), increasing greenhouse gas emissions, deforestation, desertification and soil degradation. Agricultural and food production activities account for the largest share (70–80 per cent) of global fresh water use (Desai and Ringler, 2013; Huffaker, 2014).

Environmental externalities result when private markets fail to internalise or account for the full costs of food production and consumption (Huffaker, 2014). Although government intervention through agricultural and food policies may help to address environmental concerns, there is growing pressure on the food industry, including food consumers, to be more environmentally responsible and to consider the broader longer-run impacts, both intra-generational and inter-generational, of food production and consumption decisions. There is now a general global consensus among public and private stakeholders in the agri-food sector that all players in the food industry must 'align the economic bottom line with social and environmental factors' (Pereira, 2013, p. 1234). This presents an enormous challenge for the food system. Some broad social issues, for example, providing abundant and affordable food, may actually in the short-run have a negative impact on the environment (Desai and Ringler, 2013). For example, Kotler (2011) and Jones, Hillier and Comfort (2013) discuss the inconsistencies inherent in firms attempting to achieve sustainability while also seeking to maintain profit margins and sales growth.

8.3. Strategies Food Industry Firms Use to Enhance Environmental Sustainability

There is increasing evidence to show that the motives for many private-sector food industry environmental initiatives are profit-driven. Firms may participate or develop environmental initiatives to increase their market share, protect the firm's reputation and brand equity, reduce production costs, or to limit and manage various types of financial, market, and/or production risks, both in the short- and long-run. The first part of this section focuses on private-sector strategies, such as eco-labelling, which are more 'market-driven'. The focus of these business-to-consumer approaches tends to be on either protecting firms' reputations and brand images or differentiating brands and products from competitors. This discussion is followed by examples of private-sector initiatives that require business-to-business information sharing, such as environmental management systems (EMSs), life cycle analysis, environmental footprinting, and environmental standards. Finally, we discuss other private-sector initiatives, such as online food retailing, and more environmentally-friendly packaging, which may have reduced the environmental impact of post-production food system activities.

8.3.1. *Eco-labelling*

Some of the most recognised food industry initiatives to address environmental concerns are food-labelling programmes, often termed eco-labelling. The number of private-sector initiatives focusing on communicating information related to environmental sustainability of food products has increased dramatically over the past decade (Grunert, Hieke and Wills, 2014). In 2014, the Ecolabel Index (ecolabelindex.com), an online global directory of eco-labelling, listed 148 different labelling schemes for food products alone. Most of the food eco-labelling schemes listed on the Ecolabel Index website provide information about a range of attributes related to social responsibility, including the environment, human health and welfare, and animal welfare. Broad marketing claims listed on food products range from general terms such as 'environmentally friendly', 'environmentally sustainable', 'clean and green' to 'carbon footprints'.

8.3.1.1. *Food industry motives for eco-labelling*

Initiatives such as environmental or eco-labelling of food products and certification schemes are attempting to address concerns of a certain segment of consumers in the market who value products with such 'clean and green' attributes (Chang and Kristiansen, 2006). The private-sector motivations for participating in independent (e.g., third-party certification) eco-labelling programmes, or developing their own proprietary (first-party certification) environmentally-oriented food label or certification scheme is nearly always related to a desire to protect the reputation of the firm or to differentiate the brand in order to gain market share in a competitive market. For example, supermarkets, food manufacturers and food wholesalers have attempted to differentiate themselves from their competitors in the marketplace through various gate-to-plate food certification schemes that demonstrate sustainable and/or socially responsible sourcing. These firms use a range of different strategies for signaling environmental information to their customers and consumers (Peschel *et al.*, 2014).

Manufacturers, distributors and retailers may choose to promote the environmental attributes of their products to influence consumers' food purchases using self-endorsed environmental claims, front-of-package statements or advertisements in their competition for the attention of environmentally conscious consumers and category markets shares. Typically focused on a single attribute (e.g., environmentally friendly), such self-endorsed claims typically remain unverified and make it difficult for product users to objectively evaluate the true environmental value or impact of the product or to compare it to a range of similar goods (Horne, 2009).

The voluntary labelling of 'verified' or 'certified' environmental credentials of food products dates back to the late 1970s with the introduction of the Blue Angel label in Germany (Jordan *et al.*, 2003). However, formal labelling systems that certify producers' or manufacturers' adherence to defined environmental standards were established in the wake of the 1992 'Rio Conference', the United Nations Conference on Environment and Development (UNECD). This was in response to pressures from consumer NGOs demanding a transformation of attitudes, behaviours and government actions to preserve scarce natural resources (Bernstein and Cashore, 2007).

Given one of the main objectives of pursuing environmental sustainability may be protecting the reputation of the firm, it is worth providing an example of how food firms may be undertaking strategies to do that. The reputational aspects of environmental sustainability are linked to interactions with consumers and citizens. Citizens, through NGOs and through public agencies, can make their concerns about environmental issues (and other corporate social responsibility (CSR) issues such as animal welfare, fair labour standards) well known. Strategies include targeting specific actions of individual firms and attempting to have regulations imposed on industries. One of the earliest examples of this was the 'dolphin-safe' tuna case where, in the 1980s, one NGO brought the unintended capture of dolphins to the public eye through a Dolphin Safe programme (Leadbitter and Benguerel, 2014). The programme had three strategies, namely:

(1) To publically shame companies which sold tuna which was caught in a manner which endangered dolphins;

(2) Distinguish, through the use of a label, food companies which sold 'dolphin-safe tuna'; and,
(3) Use the legal system to impose a ban on the sale of tuna which was produced using methods that could harm dolphins (Leadbitter and Benguerel, 2014, p. 418).

Eco-label systems have further developed to now include multi-issue, multi-sectoral certification systems devoted to sustainable food production and trade, to more recently introduced sophisticated standard enforcement and traceability systems at the helm of complex retail value-chains. These schemes now dictate price premiums and producer market access (Waldman and Kerr, 2014).

Modern eco-labelling schemes, such as the International Federation of Organic Agriculture Movements (IFOAM), Fairtrade Labelling Organizations International (FLO), Rainforest Alliance, UTZ (UTZ Kapeh), Marine Stewardship Council (MSC), The Global Partnership for Good Agricultural Practices (GlobalGAP), or the Common Code for the Coffee Community (4C), present commodity specific 'hybrid' labels, often built around the three core dimensions of sustainability — environmental, social and economic. They comprise the major independently certified voluntary standards that stand out due to their stringency in the monitoring of multiple explicit environmental criteria as part of determining the overall sustainability of a specific production system or an entire value-chain. Despite their mostly global scope, these certified eco-labelling schemes tend to be driven by the geographical distribution of production systems for a range of predominantly tropical agricultural commodities such as coffee, tea, bananas, cocoa, and seafood products (Barry *et al.*, 2012).

Eco-labelling schemes are increasingly not limited to assessing the environmental externalities of food production. A growing number of eco-label standards use proprietary environmental, social and economic benchmarks, which have led to fierce competition between different eco-labelling programmes in terms of capturing supply shares in producing countries as well demand in major consumer markets (Reinecke, Manning and Von Hagen, 2012). Moreover, through continuous improvements, complex standards have been developed which define implementation, monitoring, and communication practices and for customers, and especially final consumers, assure transparency, objectiveness and credibility of procedures (Roe and Teisl, 2007).

Ultimately, all credible food eco-labelling systems for food products now have in common their reliance on third-party certification approaches that take into account differences in geographical and product-specific parameters between value-chains and outcomes, a common characteristic of many international food markets. Table 8.1 summarises levels of market penetration for major eco-labels and certified food products.

8.3.1.2. *Can food consumers yield positive environmental outcomes?*

The extent that eco-labelling initiatives influence consumers' food purchase decisions and subsequently lead to tangible, positive environmental outcomes is a question mired in the complexities of modern food markets and the international value-chains underpinning them. Pedersen and Neergaard (2006) and Grebitus, Steiner and Veeman (2013) suggest that if consumers are to make environmentally-conscious food choices, then product labels, product and process information and communication by firms and agricultural stakeholders needs to be in line with consumer attitudes and perceptions regarding the link between specific food value chains and their environmental implications.

Without credible and easily obtainable information, consumers who are concerned about the environmental impact of food production and consumption will not be able to make choices at the supermarket. Consumers cannot judge the presence of intrinsic environmental attributes in food products unless information is provided through signals such as food labels. This is because environmental attributes are determined by the methods involved in production, processing and transportation of food products. Therefore, environmental attributes are 'credence' attributes, meaning that consumers

Table 8.1: Indicators of Market Penetration for Select Eco-labels.

Coffee	**Tea**	**Cocoa**	**Fish**
8 per cent of global exports certified to eco-label standards. 17 per cent of global coffee production in compliance. 77 per cent of eco-label coffee produced in South America. Price premium (lb.) \$0.05–\$0.10.	7.7 per cent of global tea exports sustainability certified (Fairtrade, Organic, Ethical Tea Partnership, Rainforest Alliance, GlobalG.A.P., UTZ). 70 per cent certified tea produced in Africa. Price premium (kg) \$0.50–\$1.38.	1.2 per cent of global cocoa trade sustainability certified (UTZ, Rainforest Alliance, Fairtrade, Organic). 3 per cent certified cocoa comes from major cocoa exporters (Ghana, Ivory Coast, Dominican Republic, Peru). Price premium (kg) \$0.07–\$0.29.	7 per cent of global wild caught fish is certified. 2.6 per cent of global aquaculture production certified. 60 per cent of U.S. fishery landings are certified. 252 global fisheries are certified. Price premium (kg) insignificant.

Source: Adapted from Barry *et al.* (2012).

cannot verify their existence at the point of purchase without a credible extrinsic cue or signal such as certification or label (Darby and Karni, 1973; Peschel *et al.*, 2014).

Ultimately, to make food purchases that reflect their values and concerns about the environment, consumers must have information so they can identify environmentally sustainable products (Grebitus, Steiner and Veeman, 2013). In some cases, firms may provide this information because they believe there is an economic incentive to do so. However, the costs of measuring, tracing and providing information about environmental attributes can be high and this may induce firms to cheat or make false marketing claims (Grolleau and Caswell, 2006).

Sønderskov and Daugbjerg (2011) and Carter (2007) suggest that several necessary conditions must be met for environmental initiatives to be successful in the marketplace:

(1) A high level environmental awareness amongst consumers;
(2) Consumers' willingness to incorporate pro-environmental thinking when making purchase decisions;
(3) Sufficient information to reliably substantiate eco-claims made on products; and,
(4) Consumers' willingness to pay price premiums for eco-labeled products.

The following paragraphs shed light on whether these four conditions are met.

Environmental awareness amongst consumers is undoubtedly high. The public, political and media debate over climate change, droughts in key food-producing regions around the world, the loss of productive farmland due to poor farming practices as well as urbanisation and food security are leading to increasing consumer interest in environmental attributes when choosing food products. According to Euromonitor International (2014), environmental issues summarised under the umbrella term of 'sustainability', ranked third in the top 10 global consumer trends for 2014.

While awareness of environmental issues is high, a study by Grunert, Heike and Wills (2014) conducted in France, Germany,

Poland, Spain, Sweden, and the UK found that even though consumers had medium-to-high levels of concerns about sustainability, it was not clear from the study whether concerns about sustainability influenced consumers' food choices.

Grunert, Heike and Wills (2014) point out that environmental or 'sustainability' labels will not necessarily influence even highly concerned consumers' food purchasing behaviour. This may be due to other factors playing a more important role when it comes to purchasing food (Grunert, Heike and Wills, 2014). For example, previous research has shown that other dimensions of food quality may supersede the influence of environmental attributes when purchasing food (e.g., food safety, price, taste, freshness, other social attributes such as human and animal welfare) (Caswell and Mojduszka, 1996; Umberger and Mueller, 2010; Norm, Cerf and Krishnan, 2011; Tully and Winer, 2014).

Additionally, consumers may be overloaded with information and may become confused about how to interpret environmental labels or certifications, which results in limited use of eco-labels at the marketplace (Grunert, 2011; Grunert, Heike and Wills, 2014; Horne, 2009). Most of the research exploring consumers' understanding and use of environmental labels has been conducted in the UK and Europe, where labelling schemes have existed for over 30 years. For example, Grunert, Heike and Wills (2014) found that understanding and use of labels with environmental information (e.g., Rainforest Alliance, Carbon Footprint) was generally low among consumers in the UK and European Union (EU). Research conducted by Ipsos and the London Economics Consortium (2013) indicated that while 70 per cent of EU consumers were familiar with organic labelling, labels that signal fair trade, short supply chains, or explicit eco-labels were only recognised by 44 per cent, 30 per cent and 25 per cent of consumers, respectively.

Consumer uptake of eco-labels is a function of whether the certified product is easy to distinguish from alternative products and is thus subject to search cost and moral hazard issues commonly encountered in products with credence attributes (Darby and Karni, 1973; Caswell and Mojduszka, 1996). In order to encourage environmentally-friendly food consumption, consumers need to have knowledge, experience and understanding of and trust in environmental labels and certification schemes (Gleim *et al.*, 2013; Peschel *et al.*, 2014).

Consumers are forced to trust available eco-label and related certification systems that indicate the product has been produced according to applicable standards in line with consumer perceptions of what constitutes environmental stewardship. Hence, firm reputation or brand recognition for 'good environmental behaviour' based on its credible adherence to self-imposed standards may be a more effective and cost-efficient identifier of favourable environmental behaviour for consumers, making independently certified eco-labels obsolete (Maloni and Brown, 2006).

For eco-label certification to be an effective environmental tool and to be economically viable, its objectives need to carefully balance benefits and costs. Meeting the cost of eco-label standards has been identified as a major barrier to their adoption and long-term success (Barry *et al.*, 2012). For example, meeting comprehensive sustainability targets set by Fair Trade or Organic standards can require costly, upfront investments, especially for small-scale chain stakeholders. While low-cost producers may adopt the standard, higher cost producers may not, regardless of their potential contribution to environmental improvements (Waldman and Kerr, 2014).

Bacon (2005) reports that although coffee producers able to access Fair Trade and Organic markets had an opportunity to get higher product prices, higher production costs and quality assurance costs often exceeded market price premiums. Thus, the pathway to carrying environmental labelling systems is on the basis of consumer demand. However, willingness to pay may be limited in its effectiveness compared to alternatives such as business-to-business focused incentive schemes (SustainAbility, 2011). While eco-labelling directed at consumers may be important in the initial promotion of favourable production practices, over time it may become less suitable to communicate diverse and complex sets of environmental production attributes that consumers are less likely to notice and be willing to pay for individually (Leiserowitz, Kates and Parris, 2006).

When it comes to evaluating whether existing eco-labelling systems are designed to meet consumer perceptions, demands, and willingness to pay, the lack of consistent empirical evidence is a major limitation. Barry *et al.* (2012), in a review of certification and supply-chain standards for environmental protection, find some evidence of improvements in production practices resulting from environmental certification in agriculture, but quantifiable, lasting impacts are hard to identify.

Consumer willingness to pay has been the workhorse in the literature attempting to assess preferences for a variety of environmental product and process attributes along food chains. Case studies involving eco-labels have been published on topics ranging from sustainable fishery management (Wessells, 2000; Teisl, Roe and Hicks, 2002), to fair-trade coffee (De Pelsmacker, Driesen and Rayp, 2005), and organics (Loureiro, McCluskey and Mittelhammer, 2001; Kiesel, Buschena and Smith, 2004; Janssen and Hamm, 2012). The results of these studies suggest that demand, market shares, and willingness to pay vary widely across the globe. Further, the circumstances under which eco-labels can command price premiums in retail markets are not well understood (Delmas and Grant, 2014) as many previous studies rely on stated rather than revealed preference methods (Loureiro and Lotade, 2005; Loureiro, McCluskey and Mittelhammer, 2001).

MSC's label for sustainably managed fisheries has received the majority share of research inquiry with respect to measuring consumer willingness to pay and environmental impact (Parkes *et al.*, 2010). Whether the MSC label can yield a retail price premium has been interpreted as one important indicator of the programme's effectiveness (Roheim, Asche and Santos, 2011). Tully and Winer (2014) conducted a meta-analysis of 81 consumer willingness-to-pay studies for socially responsible production practices, including those which considered environmental sustainability. An average of 60 per cent of respondents across studies stated a positive willingness to pay for food products labeled with eco-labels. The analysis confirmed an average consumer was willing to pay an average price premium of 16.8 per cent for food products with either an eco-label with either a certified or uncertified claim related to environmental benefits. Interestingly, willingness to pay for socially responsible practices (e.g., labour practices or animal welfare), an integral part of many eco-labels pursuing broader sustainability goals, was higher compared with those that only benefitted the environment.

Evidence of revealed consumer behaviour regarding eco-labels is still limited (Bjorner, Hansen and Russell, 2004; Teisl, Roe and Hicks, 2002). Thus, even if consumer awareness of certification and willingness to pay for certified environmental attributes in food exists, it varies by country and system investigated. Further, the continuous proliferation of environmental claims and labels with often contradictory signals can exacerbate uncertainty and confusion amongst consumers otherwise committed to the objectives of environmental protection (Treves and Jones, 2010).

Consumer demand for labelled products alone is unlikely to support a large-scale shift toward environmentally sustainable food value chain practices. Yet, perceived benefits to food industry firms from participation in eco-labelling initiatives may not be limited to price premiums alone. They may also include issues of market access or competitiveness, access to regulated resources (e.g., a fishery), or less tangible longer-term objectives such as reputation building. This has been emphasised in the growth of EMSs and related CSR initiatives with distinct environmental protection mandates. The following sections discuss some of these initiatives.

8.3.2. *Additional private-sector environmental initiatives*

A recent report in the UK highlights the linkages between businesses and environmental sustainability (Aldersgate Group, 2014). For a variety of sound economic reasons, companies, including food companies such as Nestle, Marks and Spencers and ASDA, are highlighting the fact that they understand their bottom line can be reinforced through a commitment to environmental sustainability. The factors driving food businesses to consider environmental sustainability as a business objective include beliefs that these practices are '(i) beneficial for business, (ii) in line with the firms core values, and (iii) in response to government intervention' (Ramirez, 2013, p. 2204).

The examination of how sustainable practices are beneficial for business has identified outcomes such as the ability to provide 'long term growth and financial security for all stakeholders and to enhance the firm's market position and reputation' (Jones, Hillier and Comfort, 2013, p. 39). These same issues around growth, market position and reputation are repeated through much of the literature, including in the context of sustainable tuna (Leadbitter and Benguerel, 2014) where the drivers of sustainable behaviour are described as public risk mitigation (avoiding the risk of reputational damage and boycott), market opportunity (first mover advantage in capturing premia for desired credence attributes), business obligation (protecting the safety and reliability of the supply chain to avoid fraud) and business ethics (CSR — very similar to the characteristic 'in line with the firm's core values' as identified by Ramirez, 2013).

Jones, Hillier and Comfort (2013) evaluated, through external documentation, the environmental activities of 10 of the UK's major food retailers. They found that food firms throughout the supply chain were addressing several environmental issues including: 'climate change and carbon emissions; energy consumption; water management; waste management; logistics; conserving natural resources; environmentally friendly products; and land and property holdings' (Jones, Hillier and Comfort, 2013, p. 26). Retailers find the profit motive to be an excellent driver for decisions such as the recent decision by Marks and Spencer to change all lighting to light-emitting diode (LED) (Farrell, 2014). Reported reasons for undertaking such a change include improving the consumer experience and becoming more environmentally sustainable but as with many of the sustainability initiatives undertaken it will also be cost effective for Marks and Spencer.

Jones, Hillier and Comfort (2013) suggest that, frequently, the creation of firm sustainability agendas may come through activities that improve their own 'commercial interests'. This may lead to the exclusion of other important agendas such as the 'viability of natural ecosystems' (Jones, Hillier and Comfort, 2013, p. 37) and in ways that do not threaten consumption (this issue of incompatibility between increasing or maintaining consumption and environmental sustainability being raised by numerous researchers).

8.3.2.1. *EMSs*

EMSs are business management tools that provide a framework for agricultural producers and other firms operating in the food system to continuously improving their environmental management practices and to reduce their impact on the environment (Cary, Bhaskaran and Polonsky, 2007; Cary and Roberts, 2009; Chang and Kristiansen, 2006). EMSs are usually accredited using the International Standard for Environmental Management, ISO 14001, which began in the 1990s. They often underpin the eco-labelling programmes and private food standards discussed in the previous section and add credibility to claims of 'clean and green', 'environmentally friendly', and 'environmentally sustainable' (Chang and Kristiansen, 2006).

Several factors have limited the widespread adoption of EMSs in the food industry. A major concern is whether the costs of these systems exceed private and/or public benefits. The requirements necessary for firms to implement an EMS are considered by many to be overly burdensome, particularly for small-scale agricultural producers. Thus, Cary, Bhaskaran and Polonsky (2007) contend that firms will only adopt an EMS if one of the following conditions holds:

(1) There is an opportunity to get a significant price premium;
(2) Government regulation is inevitable; and/or,
(3) It is a requirement to enter the market.

There is little evidence in the literature to suggest that EMS lead to private benefits that are large enough to cover the costs of implementing and maintaining accreditation. There is some evidence to suggest that these systems yield public benefits, for example improved water quality and biodiversity (Chang and Kristiansen, 2006). Ultimately, environmental benefits from EMSs will only transpire if firms have an incentive or are required to adopt the system.

8.3.2.2. *Measuring ecological footprints*

Since 2007, there have been several attempts by stakeholders in the food industry to measure the ecological footprint (e.g., carbon emissions, water use) of food products through cradle-to-grave 'Life Cycle Assessment (LCA)' studies (see Peschel *et al.* (2014) for an overview of these studies). The aim of these LCAs is to determine the environmental impact of production, processing and transportation methods used to get food products to the end consumer. LCAs underpin recent retailer-driven eco-labelling programmes designed to provide consumers with information on the environmental 'footprint' of each food product in an effort to reduce the impact of food production and consumption on the environment. Footprint labels, certified by Carbon Trust, were first introduced by food retailer Tesco in the UK in 2009 (Upham, Dendler and Bleda, 2011). However, Tesco discontinued these labels in 2012 due to low uptake in the market by competitors and limited use by consumers (Peschel *et al.*, 2014).

A comprehensive study of the impact of carbon footprint labelling Upham and Bleda (2009) found the primary benefits of labelling the environmental footprint of food products were most likely to be enjoyed by upstream firms through emissions reductions, not by consumers. Furthermore, the main function of carbon and water footprint labels is actually to boost the image of the businesses participating in the scheme rather than communicating useful information to consumers or reducing the environmental impact of food production and consumption.

8.3.2.3. *Food sector 'sustainability' standards and rankings*

Firms interested in avoiding negative publicity can develop their own internal environmental indicators and communicate their activities through publicity. A recent example of this is the US food retail chain Whole Foods developing its own sustainable agricultural standards and food labelling programme, 'Responsibly Grown', which rates their suppliers based on issues such as the use of water and pesticides and waste management (Strom, 2014). Research suggests that standalone strategies can be risky in an environment where consumers and the public do not trust the company or its motives (Nyilasy, Gangadharbatla and Paladino, 2014).

Similar strategies are increasingly being used on other aspects of environmentally sustainable behaviour of food firms and it is clear why this sort of action compels behavioural change for firms wishing to protect their reputation. Recently the approach to assessing firms' behaviour is becoming broader and more comparative. For example, organisations such as Oxfam America produce an annual ranking of major branded food companies called 'Behind the Brands' (Oxfam America, 2014). This programme assesses companies on a number of social indicators, including environmental sustainability. Movement in rankings between 2013 and 2014 for that particular indicator suggests that these rankings can provide impetus to changing behaviour (Smith, 2014). In some cases, improving environmental indicators could prove easier than fixing other aspects of the ranking. Similarly, Greenpeace has pursued a grocery retailer ranking for seafood sustainability for some years in Canada and the US and improvements in the rank of particular firms are evident (Siegel, 2014).

Firms can also choose to work with other companies, NGOs and public agencies to develop industry-wide standards. A current example is the Global Roundtable on Sustainable Beef Production (Slama, 2014b). This is an organisation that includes retailers (e.g., Walmart), restaurants (e.g., McDonalds), cattle grower organisations and some public agencies and aims to 'advance continuous improvement in sustainability (including environmental) of the global beef value chain through leadership, science and multi-stakeholder engagement and collaboration' (Global Roundtable for Sustainable Beef, 2014). The fast food restaurant chain McDonalds was one of the leaders of this global initiative to improve its brand image and in response to competitive pressure to source more sustainable inputs (Slama, 2014a; Slama, 2014b).

Hahn and Pinkse (2014) discussed the tensions between a firm's desire to obtain private benefits from such cross-sector collaborations (essentially a competitive force) and the public benefits that these relationships might bring (essentially a positive externality).

One of their conclusions is that competitive behaviour amongst firms in such collaborations can enhance, but also limit, the potential of the private sector to mitigating environmental impact. Furthermore, this collective approach to developing and verifying industry-wide standards has been observed by some critics to be an attempt by industry to 'greenwash' stakeholders, including government and consumers (Akenji, 2014; Nyilasy, Gangadharbatla and Paladino, 2014).

As discussed earlier in the eco-labelling section, firms can also choose to work directly with NGOs who have established standards to be able to use their labelling/logos as part of the firm's environmental strategy (e.g., the Marine Stewardship Council). This strategy can be effective in avoiding the danger of being perceived to be 'greenwashing' the firm's activities. In one sense though, firms are then required to change their purchasing or production standards as the NGO changes their certification standards and potentially this is a significant cost for retailers dealing with multiple suppliers or agencies on a range of issues.

8.3.2.4. *Online food retailing*

In some cases consumers' food purchasing requirements are changing and increasingly time-strapped households are purchasing their groceries online rather than in an actual retail store. This is having a positive effect on the environmental footprint of major retailers, although the consumer driver appears to be convenience and not the environment. At its simplest level this change could reduce the footprint of grocery shopping by substituting fewer trips by a delivery van for many trips by many individual shoppers to many different stores for their purchases. There could in some cases also be environmental implications of shuttering some hypermarket grocery stores in favour of warehouses with lower demands on energy, lighting and even packaging.

Unfortunately, van Loon *et al.* (2014) point out that nothing is so simple and the environmental footprint associated with a move to online retailing is very complex and not necessarily positive due to travel trip considerations such as product failed deliveries, returns and trip chaining (even if one does not go to the grocery store there may have been multiple reasons for the trip that still require attendance).

8.3.2.5. *Food packaging and de-marketing*

Acceptance and design of food packaging is another area where food retailers and processors can play a role. Food packaging has an environmental impact itself as well as causing an environmental impact through an effect on the food it surrounds. Vanderroost *et al.* (2014) show that beyond the four basic functions of food packaging (protection, communication, convenience and containment) environmental sustainability can and will play an increasingly important role in packaging design. In their vision for intelligent food packaging of the future, they envision food packaging that can be reused, or recycled using a 'closed-loop process with zero loss in material' (p. 60).

Grönman *et al.* (2013) contend that the environmental burden of packaging disposal is small relative to the wastage that can occur from the food loss if packaging does not play its primary role competently. Consideration of the disposal of packaging (e.g., reuse or recycle) as well as reduction in food losses is paramount in the design of packaging and must be considered as a core element in the overall food product design. Clearly food processors and retailers can and do play a role in encouraging effective product and packaging design that enhances the environmental sustainability of the sector.

Kotler (2011) identifies trends in some industries towards 'demarketing' products — finding ways and encouraging consumers to conserve resources. This movement was originally seen in energy (electricity) and resource (water) markets. Recent concerns about food waste at the firm and household level may be part of the reason why demarketing strategies are becoming more popular in the food industry. An example of this is the case of TESCO UK ending 'buy one, get one' free promotions (Tesco PLC, 2014).

8.4. Summary and Conclusions: Do Food Industry Environmental Initiatives Lead to Positive Environmental Outcomes?

Food industry firms have undertaken a number of initiatives to address concerns expressed by consumers and customers, stakeholders (e.g., government and NGOs) and citizen activist groups about the impact that food production and food consumption is having on the environment. The aim of this chapter was to provide an overview of the different private-sector food system initiatives and developments that have attempted to privately address environmental issues. In addition to providing an overview of these initiatives, we discussed whether these systems have actually resulted in environmental benefits or if they are more marketing rhetoric or 'greenwashing' of consumers and customers.

Generally speaking, it is difficult to find conclusive evidence that private-sector initiatives designed to yield positive environmental outcomes do so directly. However, what is apparent from the literature is that various private strategies, which are underpinned by some type of auditable EMS or a set of production and process standards, can lead to production practices and consumption decisions which are more environmentally friendly. This is particularly true for those initiatives which are certified by a third party and become industry standards. For example, eco-labelling programmes, such as the MSC's 'certified sustainable seafood', which aim to provide consumers with information about the sustainability of fishing practices may not have impacted consumer behaviour. However, it has driven the seafood sector to adopt and conform to more sustainable fishing practices.

Further, it is also clear that many firms adopting environmental initiatives claim to be doing so because they are socially responsible while they are actually doing so to protect their bottom-line due to concerns such as firm or brand reputation, liability, market access, and market share. Putting aside true private-sector motivations, it does appear that, in many cases, firms perceive there to be benefits from adopting more environmentally sustainable management practices. This is perhaps the most important point when it comes to understanding the role of the private sector in ensuring food systems are environmentally sustainable: private-sector initiatives can lead to positive environmental outcomes.

Bibliography

Akenji, L. (2014). Consumer Scapegoatism and Limits to Green Consumerism, *Journal of Cleaner Production*, 63, pp. 13–23.

Aldersgate Group (2014). An Economy that Works. Available at: http://aneconomythatworks.org/content/uploads/2014/12/AETW-Report-LowRes.pdf [Acessed 15 December 2014].

Bacon, C. (2005). Confronting the Coffee Crisis: Can Fair Trade, Organic Specialty Coffees Reduce Small-Scale Farmer Vulnerability in Northern Nicaragua?, *World Development*, 33(3), pp. 497–511.

Barry, M., Cashore, B., Clay, J., Fernandez, M., Lebel L., Lyon, T., Mallet, P., Matus, K., Melchett, P., Vandenbergh, M., Vis, J.K., Whelan, T., Dilley, A., Peyser, J. and Kennedy, T. (2012). *Toward Sustainability: The Roles and Limits of Certification*, Resolve, Washington, DC.

Bernstein, S. and Cashore, B. (2007). Can Non-State Global Governance Be Legitimate? An Analytical Framework, *Regulation and Governance*, 1, pp. 347–371.

Bjorner, T.B., Hansen, L.G. and Russell, C.S. (2004). Environmental Labelling and Consumers' Choice. An Empirical Analysis of the Effect of the Nordic Swan, *Journal of Environmental Economics and Management*, 47, pp. 411–424.

Bradbear, C. and Friel, S. (2011). 'Food Systems and Environmental Sustainability: A Review of the Australian Evidence', *NCEPH Working Paper*. Australian National University, Canberra, pp. 1–56. Available at: http://nceph.anu.edu.au/files/Food%20systems%20and%20Environmental%20Sustainability%20A%20review%20of%20the%20Evidence%20NCEPHWorkingPaperOctober2011x%20%283%29.pdf [Accessed 9 December 2014].

Carter, N. (2007). *The Politics of the Environment: Ideas, Activism, Policy*, 2nd edition, Cambridge University Press, Cambridge.

Cary, J. Bhaskaran, S. and Polonsky, M. (2007). 'The Limitations of Market Driven Sustainability: The Case of Environmental Management

Systems for Food Production in Australia', *Australian Agricultural and Resource Economics Society 51st Annual Conference*, Queenstown, 13–16 February, AgEcon, St Paul, pp. 1–7. Available at: http://dro.deakin.edu.au/view/DU:30016375?print_friendly=true [Accessed 16 December 2014].

Cary, J.W. and Roberts, A.M. (2009). *EMS to Achieve Environmental Outcomes: Fantasy Land, Political Hope or Real Chance?*, 18th World IMACS / MODSIM Congress, Cairns, Australia 13–17 July. Available at: http://www.mssanz.org.au/modsim09/F12/cary.pdf [Accessed 9 December 2014].

Caswell, J.A. and Mojduszka, E.M. (1996). Using Informational Labeling to Influence the Market for Quality in Food Products, *American Journal of Agricultural Economics*, 78, pp. 1248–1253.

Chang H. and Kristiansen P. (2006). Selling Australia as 'Clean And Green', *Australian Journal of Agricultural and Resource Economics*, 50, pp. 103–113.

Darby, M.R. and Karni, E. (1973). Free Competition and the Optimal Amount of Fraud, *Journal of Law and Economics*, 16, pp. 67–88.

Delmas, M.A. and Grant, L.E. (2014). Eco-Labeling Strategies and Price-Premium: The Wine Industry Puzzle, *Business & Society*, 53, pp. 1–39.

De Pelsmacker, P., Driesen, L. and Rayp, G. (2005). Do Consumers Care About Ethics? Willingness to Pay for Fair-Trade Coffee, *Journal of Consumer Affairs*, 39, pp. 363–385.

Desai, N. and Ringler, C. (2013). 'Sustainable and Growing, But Also Food Secure?' in Fan, S. (ed.), *2012 Global Food Policy Report*, International Food Policy Research Institute, Washington, DC, pp. 29–38. Available at: http://www.ifpri.org/sites/default/files/publications/gfpr2012.pdf [Accessed 11 December 2014].

Euromonitor International (2014). The Top 10 Global Consumer Trends for 2014. Available at: http://blog.euromonitor.com/2014/01/the-top-10-global-consumer-trends-for-2014.html [Accessed 16 November 2014].

Farrell, C. (2014). M&S to Introduce LED Lighting to all Food Stores within Two Years. Available at: http://www.thegrocer.co.uk/home/topics/switch-the-lights/ms-to-introduce-led-lighting-to-all-food-stores-within-two-years/374212.article [Accessed 15 December 2014].

Gleim, M.R., Smith, J.S., Andrews, D. and Cronin, J.J. (2013). Against the Green: A Multi-Method Examination of the Barriers to Green Consumption, *Journal of Retailing*, 89, pp. 44–61.

Global Roundtable for Sustainable Beef (2014). Principles and Criteria for Global Sustainable Beef. Available at: http://grsbeef.org/DRAFTprinciples [Accessed 15 December 2014].

Godfray, H.C.J., Beddington, J.R., Crute, I.R., Haddad, L., Lawrence, D., Muir, J.F., Pretty, J., Robinson, S., Thomas, S.M. and Toulmin, C. (2010). Food Security: The Challenge of Feeding 9 Billion People, *Science*, 327, pp. 812–818.

Grebitus, C., Steiner, B. and Veeman, M. (2013). Personal Values and Decision-Making: Evidence From Environmental Footprint Labeling in Canada, *American Journal of Agricultural Economics*, 95(2), pp. 397–403.

Grönman, K., Soukka, R., Järvi-Kääriäinen, T., Katajajuuri, J.M., Kuisma, M., Koivupuro, H.K. Ollila, M., Pitkänen, M., Miettinen, O., Silvenius, F., Thun, R., Wessman, H. and Linn, L. (2013). Framework for Sustainable Food Packaging Design, *Packaging Technology and Science*, 26, pp. 187–200.

Grolleau, G. and Caswell, J.A. (2006). Interaction Between Food Attributes in Markets: The Case of Environmental Labeling, *Journal of Agricultural and Resource Economics*, 31(3), pp. 471–484.

Grunert, K.G. (2011). Sustainability in the Food Sector: A Consumer Behaviour Perspective, *International Journal on Food System Dynamics*, 2 (3), pp. 207–218.

Grunert, K.G., Hieke, S. and Wills, J. (2014). Sustainability Labels on Food Products: Consumer Motivation, Understanding and Use, *Food Policy*, 44, pp. 177–189.

Hahn, T. and Pinkse, J. (2014). Private Environmental Governance Through Cross Sector Partnerships: Tensions Between Competition and Effectiveness, *Organization & Environment*, 27(2), pp. 140–160.

Horne, R.E. (2009). Limits to Labels: The role of Eco-Labels in the Assessment of Product Sustainability and Routes to Sustainable Consumption, *International Journal of Consumer Studies*, 33, pp. 175–182.

Huffaker, R. (2014). 'Pursuit of Green Food Production', in de Gennaro, B.C. and Nardone, G. (eds.), *Sustainability of the Agri-Food System: Strategies and Performances*, Universitas Studiorum, Mantova, pp. 15–18. Available at: http://www.sidea.org/Lecce_2013_files/Atti%20Sidea_EBOOK.pdf [Accessed 11 December 2014].

Ipsos and London Economics Consortium (2013). Consumer Market Study on the Functioning of Voluntary Food Labelling Schemes for Consumers in the European Union, *Final Report EAHC/FWC/2012 86 04 to the European Commision Executive Agency for Health and Consumers*. Available at: http://ec.europa.eu/consumers/consumer_evidence/market_studies/food_labelling/docs/final_report_food_labelling_scheme_full_en.pdf [Accessed 12 December 2014].

Janssen, M. and Hamm, U. (2012). Product Labelling in the Market For Organic Food: Consumer Preferences and Willingness-to-Pay for Different Organic Certification Logos, *Food Quality and Preference*, 25, pp. 9–22.

Jones, P., Hillier, D. and Comfort, D. (2013). In the Public Eye: Sustainability and the UK's Leading Retailers, *Journal of Public Affairs*, 13(1), pp. 33–40.

Jordan, A., Wurzel, R.K.W., Zito, A.R. and Brückner, L. (2003). 'Consumer Responsibility-Taking and National Eco-Labeling Schemes in Europe', in Micheletti, M., Follesdal, A. and Stolle, D. (eds.), *Politics, Products and Markets: Exploring Political Consumerism*, Transaction, Somerset, pp. 161–180.

Kiesel, K., Buschena, D. and Smith, V. (2004). 'Consumer Acceptance and Labeling of GMOs in Food Products: A Study of Fluid Milk Demand', in Evenson, R.D. and Santaniello, V. (eds.), *Consumer Acceptance of Biotechnology Foods*, CABI Publishing, Cambridge, pp. 9–32.

Kotler, P. (2011). Reinventing Marketing to Manage the Environmental Imperative, *Journal of Marketing*, 75, pp. 132–135

Leadbitter, D. and Benguerel, R. (2014). Sustainable Tuna — Can the Marketplace Improve Fishery Management?, *Business Strategy and the Environment*, 23, pp. 417–432.

Leiserowitz, A.A., Kates, R.W. and Parris, T.M. (2006). Sustainability Values, Attitudes and Behaviors: A Review of Multi-National and Global Trends, *Annual Review of Environment and Resources*, 31, pp. 413–444.

Loureiro, M.L. and Lotade, J. (2005). Do Fair Trade and Eco-Labels in Coffee Wake Up the Consumer Conscience?, *Ecological Economics*, 53(1), pp. 129–138.

Loureiro, M.L., McCluskey, J.J. and Mittelhammer, R.C. (2001). Assessing Consumer Preferences for Organic, Ecolabeled, and Regular Apples, *Journal of Agricultural and Resource Economics*, 26(2), pp. 404–416.

Maloni, M.J. and Brown, M.E. (2006). Corporate Social Responsibility in the Supply Chain: An Application in the Food Industry, *Journal of Business Ethics*, 68(1), pp. 35–52.

Massoud, M.A., Fayad, R., El-Fadel, M. and Kamleh, R. (2010). Drivers, Barriers and Incentives to Implementing Environmental Management Systems in the Food Industry: A Case of Lebanon, *Journal of Cleaner Production*, 18, pp. 200–209.

Mazzanti, M. (2014). 'Does the Economy Need To Be 'Shocked' To Be Sustainable?' in de Gennaro, B.C. and Nardone, G. (eds.), *Sustainability of the Agri-Food System: Strategies and Performances*, Universitas Studiorum, Mantova, pp. 19–24. Available at: http://www.sidea.org/Lecce_2013_files/Atti%20Sidea_EBOOK.pdf [Accessed 11 December 2014].

Norm, B., Cerf, D. and Krishnan, R. (2011). The Consumer Effects of Environmental Impact Included in Labeling Information, *Journal of Consumer Marketing*, 28 (1), pp. 76–86.

Nyilasy, G., Gangadharbatla, H. and Paladino, A. (2014). Perceived Greenwashing: The Interactive Effects of Green Advertising and Corporate Environmental Performance on Consumer Reactions, *Journal of Business Ethics*, 125, pp. 693–707.

Oxfam America (2014). Behind the Brand: Scorecard. Available at: http://www.behindthebrands.org/en-us/scorecard [Accessed 15 December 2014].

Parkes, G., Young, J., Walmsley, S., Abel, R., Harman, J., Horvat, P., Lem, A., MacFarlane, A., Mens, M. and Nolan, C. (2010). Behind The Signs — A Global Review Of Fish Sustainability Information Schemes. Reviews In Fisheries, *Science*, 18 (4), pp. 344–356.

Pedersen, E. and Neergaard, P. (2006). Caveat Emptor — Let the Buyer Beware! Environmental Labeling and the Limitations of 'Green' Consumerism, *Business Strategy and the Environment*, 15(1), pp. 15–29.

Pereira, L.M. (2013). The Future of the Food System: Cases Involving the Private Sector in South Africa, *Sustainability*, 5, pp. 1234–1255.

Peschel, A.O., Grebitus, C., Steiner, B. and Veeman, M. (2014). 'Benefits to Retailers From Psychometric-Based Customer Targeting of Footprint-Labeled Products: A Latent Class Analysis,' *Working Paper*, Morrison School of Agribusiness, W.P. Carey School of Business, Arizona State University, pp. 1–34.

Ramirez, E. (2013). Consumer-Defined Sustainably-Oriented Firms and Factors Influencing Adoption, *Journal of Business Research*, 66, pp. 2202–2209.

Reardon, T., Timmer, C.P., Barrett, C.B. and Berdegué, J.A. (2003). The Rise of Supermarkets in Africa, Asia and Latin America, *American Journal of Agriculture and Economics*, 85(5), pp. 1140–1146.

Reinecke, J., Manning S. and Von Hagen, O. (2012). The Emergence of a Standards Market: Multiplicity of Sustainability Standards in the Global Coffee Industry, *Organization Studies*, 33 (5/6), pp. 789–812.

Roe, B. and Teisl, M.F. (2007). Genetically Modified Food Labeling: The Impacts of Message and Messenger on Consumer Perceptions of Labels and Products, *Food Policy*, 32(1), pp. 49–66.

Roheim, C.A., Asche, F. and Santos, J.I. (2011). The Elusive Price Premium for Ecolabelled Products: Evidence from Seafood in the UK Market, *Journal of Agricultural Economics*, 62, pp. 655–668.

Siegel, R.P. (2014). *Greenpeace Reviews Major Food Retailers for Sustainable Seafood Purchasing* [Online June 4, 2014]. Available at: http://www.triplepundit.com/2014/06/greenpeace-reviews-major-food-retailers-sustainable-seafood-purchasing/ [Accessed 7 December 2014].

Slama, J. (2014a). How to Make a Better Big Mac, *Chicago Tribune*, [Online, August 30, 2014]. Available at: http://www.chicagotribune.com/news/opinion/commentary/ct-perspec-mcdonalds-should-get-sustainable-0901-20140830-story.html [Accessed 16 December 2014].

Slama, J. (2014b). McDonalds Can Make History — And Rescue Its Brand — With Sustainable Food, *Huffington Post* [Online, September 3, 2014b]. Available at: http://www.huffingtonpost.com/jim-slama/mcdonalds-can-make-histor_b_5753098.html [Accessed 15 December 2014].

Smith, D. (2014). *An Update of the Behind the Brands Scorecard Reveals All But One of the Big 10 Food Companies are Making Improvements*, [Online, October 8, 2014]. Available at: http://politicsofpoverty.oxfamamerica.org/2014/10/food-companies-jockeying-for-sustainability-ranking/ [Accessed 9 December 2014].

Smith, K., Lawrence, G. and Richards, C. (2010). Supermarkets' Governance of the Agri-Food Supply Chain: Is the 'Corporate-Environmental' Food Regime Evident in Australia?, *International Journal of Sociology of Agriculture and Food*, 17(2), pp. 140–161.

Sønderskov, K.M. and Daugbjerg, C. (2011). The State and Consumer Confidence in Eco-Labeling: Organic Labeling in Denmark, Sweden, The United Kingdom, and The United States, *Agriculture and Human Values*, 28, pp. 507–517.

Strom, S. (2014). 'Whole Foods to Rate its Produce and Flowers for Environmental Impact', *The New York Times* [Online, October 15, 2014]. Available at: http://www.nytimes.com/2014/10/16/business/whole-foods-to-rate-its-produce-and-flowers-for-environmental-impact.html?_r=0 [Accessed 15 December 2014].

Sustainability (2011). Signed, Sealed ... Delivered? Behind Certifications and Beyond Labels. Available at: www.sustainability.com/library/signed-sealed-delivered-1#.VICtHDHF8wA [Accessed 10 January 2014].

Teisl, M.F., Roe, B. and Hicks, R. (2002). Can Eco-Labels Tune a Market? Evidence from Dolphin-Safe Labeling of Canned Tuna, *Journal of Environmental Economics and Management*, 43, pp. 339–359.

Tesco PLC. (2014). Reducing Food Waste. Available at: http://www.tescoplc.com/index.asp?pageid=590 [Accessed 15 December 2014].

Thompson, J. and Scoones, I. (2009). Addressing the Dynamics of Agri-Food Systems: An Emerging Agenda for Social Science Research, *Environmental Science and Policy*, 12, pp. 386–397.

Treves, A. and Jones, S.M. (2010). Strategic Tradeoffs for Wildlife-Friendly Eco-Labels, *Frontiers in Ecology and the Environment*, 8, pp. 491–498.

Tully, S.M. and Winer, R.S. (2014). The Role of the Beneficiary in Willingness to Pay for Socially Responsible Products: A Meta-Analysis, *Journal of Retailing*, 90(2), pp. 255–274.

Umberger, W.J. and Mueller, S. (2010). Is Presentation Everything? Using Visual Presentation of Attributes in Discrete Choice Experiments to Measure the Relative Importance of Intrinsic and Extrinsic Beef Attributes. *Agricultural and Applied Economics Association 2010 Annual Meeting*, Denver, Colorado, pp. 1–29. Available at: http://purl.umn.edu/61856 [Accessed 6 December 2014].

Upham, P. and Bleda, M. (2009). *Carbon Labelling: Public Perceptions of the Debate*, Report from the Sustainable Consumption Institute, University of Manchester. Available at: http://sciv2.iqmedialink.co.uk/uploads/carbonlabellingpublicperceptionsofthedebate.pdf [Accessed 15 December 2014].

Upham, P., Dendler, L. and Bleda, M. (2010). Carbon Labelling of Grocery Products: Public Perceptions and Potential Emissions Reductions, *Journal of Cleaner Production*, 19, pp. 348–355.

Vanderroost, M., Ragaert, P., Devlieghere, F. and De Meulenaer, B. (2014). Intelligent Food Packaging: The Next Generation, *Trends in Food Science and Technology*, 39, pp. 47–62.

van Loon, P., Deketele, L., Dewaele, J., McKinnon, A. and Rutherford, C. (2014). A Comparative Analysis of Carbon Emissions from Online Retailing of Fast Moving Consumer Goods, *Journal of Cleaner Production*, in press, pp. 1–9.

Waldman, K.B. and Kerr, J.M. (2014). Limitations of Certification and Supply Chain Standards for Environmental Protection in Commodity Crop Production, *Annual Review of Resource Economics*, 6, pp. 429–449.

Wessells, C. (2000). Ecolabelling and International Seafood Trade: The Role of Certification Costs and Consumers' Willingness to Pay, *Fisheries Economics Newsletter*, 50, pp. 44–49.

9. Payments for Environmental Services (PES) Schemes[1]

Gabriela Scheufele

9.1. Introduction

The environment can be managed to supply a variety of environmental services. The Millennium Ecosystem Assessment (2005) differentiates provisioning services (e.g., timber, food), regulating services (e.g., flood regulation, erosion regulation), cultural services (e.g., recreation, spiritual values), and supporting services (e.g., water cycling, soil formation).[2] Some types of services may be co-supplied such as soil erosion regulation and recreation. Others may be rival such as soil erosion regulation and timber production. Particularly in recent years, demand for a range of environmental services has been increasing. Yet,

[1]The chapter arises from research undertaken as a component of the project 'Effective Implementation of PES in Lao PDR', which is funded by the Australian Centre of Agricultural Research. Material from Research Report 1: Payments for Environmental Services — Concepts and Applications (Scheufele and Bennett, 2013) had been included.

[2]Millennium Ecosystem Assessment (2005) refers to 'ecosystem services'. This chapter treats the terms 'ecosystem services' and 'environmental services' as synonyms.

this demand growth has not been matched by an increase in supply as would be expected if markets were effective in linking potential sellers and buyers. Rather, the supply of a range of environmental services is in decline.

Markets fail to coordinate demand and supply if the costs of negotiating an exchange, the so-called transaction costs, are prohibitively high. Potential buyers and sellers refrain from trade if the transaction costs exceed the expected net returns that may be gained through a market exchange. The main driver for prohibitively high transactions costs are poorly defined and defended property rights to environmental services. If property rights are poorly defined, sellers bear the risk of not getting paid and buyers bear the risk of paying without getting the environmental services they wanted. With ownership in doubt, sellers also lack the legal right or ability to exclude anyone who does not pay for the provided environmental services. Those who do not pay cannot be prevented from accessing the environmental services. 'Free-riding' (enjoying benefits without any financial contribution to cover the costs) prevails among beneficiaries. Since producers would suffer a net loss, many non-excludable environmental services are undersupplied.

The demand for environmental services is often globally dispersed and is met by a large number of potential suppliers. This makes direct negotiations between individual buyers and sellers costly: the costs of engaging in an exchange may be too high for markets to emerge. For example, a large number of individuals in the international community may be interested in buying biodiversity protection from a large number of small-scale farmers practising slash and burn agriculture in tropical rainforests. However, in such a case, the costs of individually negotiated contracts would be too high for trade to be profitable for buyers and sellers.

As market-based instruments, PES schemes aim to establish the necessary conditions for sellers and buyers to engage in mutually advantageous trade so that supply can expand to match the growth in demand. To this effect, a PES scheme can be defined as a mechanism that seeks to establish and sustain a financial link between those with a demand for environmental services and those who are potential environmental service producers. This link may be established through one or multiple agents interceding between prospective buyers and sellers to facilitate an exchange. Agents external to the trade act as 'brokers' by performing tasks that involve transaction costs. By specialising in these tasks they have the capability of reducing transaction costs. This PES scheme definition adds to alternative definitions[3] by emphasising the importance of transactions costs as the main driver for the failure of markets in coordinating demand and supply and also the capability of agents in reducing these transaction costs through specialisation.

Numerous PES schemes have been developed around the world over the last few decades. There is evidence that they have the potential to stimulate environmental service production to meet growing public demand. Yet, few schemes have been designed such that they tap the potential of mimicking competitive markets for traded goods and services to improve their supply effectiveness[4] and economic efficiency.[5] Schemes that are ineffective in producing environmental services and fail to achieve gains in economic efficiency waste scarce resources that could have been used to generate net benefits elsewhere.

Tacconi (2012), based on Wunder (2005), sets out four desirable PES scheme characteristics: system transparency, supply additionality, payment conditionality and seller voluntariness. They are desirable in the sense that they support a PES scheme's potential to generate a social net benefit and avoid unintended distributional effects.

The first characteristic is system transparency. Tacconi (2012) follows Kolstad and Wiig (2008) to define transparency as '... the timely and reliable provision of information to all relevant stakeholders' (Tacconi, 2012, p. 33). The terms and conditions as well as the asso-

[3] Wunder (2005, p. 5) defines a PES scheme as '... a voluntary transaction where a well-defined ES (or a land-use likely to secure that service) is being 'bought' by a (minimum one) ES buyer from a (minimum one) ES provider if and only if the ES provider secures ES provision (conditionality)'. Tacconi (2012, p. 35) defines a PES scheme as '... a transparent system of additional provision of environmental services through conditional payments to voluntary suppliers'.

[4] Supply effectiveness refers to the power of a PES scheme to produce environmental services. It is driven by the number of participating sellers and the effectiveness of their supply actions in producing environmental services.

[5] An efficiency improvement is achieved if a scheme generates a net benefit to society.

ciated risks of PES participation need to be clear to potential buyers, sellers and agents in order to support supply competition (Midgley *et al.*, 2012), to build mutual trust (Muradian *et al.*, 2010) and to reduce (the perception of) corruption (Ferraro, 2008). Restricted supply competition and corruption limit a PES scheme's supply effectiveness, diminish efficiency gains and may cause unintended distributional effects. Transparency creates confidence in potential buyers and sellers that their investments will be beneficial. EcoTender in Australia (e.g., Eigenraam *et al.*, 2005) and the Vittel scheme in north-eastern France (e.g., Perrot-Maître, 2006) are examples of schemes that are characterised by a high degree of transparency.

The second characteristic is supply additionality. Additional supply means that the production of environmental services is additional to that which would have been produced in the scheme's absence (Tacconi, 2012; Wunder, 2007). The Vittel scheme in France (e.g., Perrot-Maître, 2006) and an extension of the existing Conversion of Cropland to Forest and Grassland Program (CCFGP) in the Sichuan Province in China (e.g., Wang *et al.*, 2012) are examples of schemes that have been successful in generating additional supply. Both schemes established a baseline and developed models to establish a quantitative link between supply actions and environmental service production. Yet, estimating the extent of additional supply may be challenging. As in the case of a PES scheme in Costa Rica, it may be difficult to disentangle the effects of the scheme from other policies (such as a ban on forest clearing) and from changes in economic conditions that make participating in the scheme comparatively more or less profitable for suppliers (Pagiola, 2008). If supply is not additional the costs of the scheme are borne without any associated additional benefits. Society forgoes the opportunity to allocate scarce resources (e.g., public funds) to stimulate the generation of additional benefits elsewhere. The scheme makes society as a whole worse-off. The Los Negros scheme in Bolivia (e.g., Asquith, Vargas and Wunder, 2008) is an example of a scheme challenged by securing additional supply. If very little additional supply has been generated, the scheme has mainly acted to redistribute wealth.

Individual sellers, but not necessarily society as a whole, have been made better off.

The third characteristic is payment conditionality. Payments are conditional if they are only made upon delivery of contracted environmental services or supply actions (Wunder, 2005; Tacconi, 2012). The CCFGP extension scheme in China (e.g., Wang *et al.*, 2012) and the Vittel scheme in France (e.g., Perrot-Maître, 2006) are examples of schemes that are characterised by a high degree of payment conditionality. Payment conditionality is essential to ensure that a scheme is effective in producing additional environmental services. If payments are not conditional, it is likely that sellers will fail to fulfil their commitments to supply. This will result in a small or no increase in environmental service production. The scheme in Lam Dong Province in Vietnam (Nguyen, 2011) is an example of a scheme challenged by enforcing the payment conditionality. Even though the payments were designed to be conditional on fulfilling responsibilities, interviews conducted by Burchards (2010) revealed that the sellers did not view the payments as truly conditional on the environmental service production (Phothisat, Khaopasurt and Lindros, 2013).

The fourth characteristic is seller voluntariness. If participation in the scheme is not voluntary, engagement may or may not make sellers better off (Tacconi, 2012). Sellers would only voluntarily engage in the scheme if their returns on participation outweigh their costs of production. The sellers' production costs are determined by their opportunity costs: the costs of using resources in their next best alternative use. The opportunity costs include the direct costs of production, the cost of entrepreneurship (in the form of a risk premium) and the transaction costs of engaging in the scheme. The Los Negros scheme in Bolivia (e.g., Asquith, Vargas and Wunder, 2008), PES in Costa Rica (e.g., Pagiola, 2008) and EcoTender in Australia (e.g., Eigenraam *et al.*, 2005) are examples of schemes that are characterised by voluntary seller participation. Voluntary sellers have an incentive to 'do it well'. If, on the other hand, participation is compulsory, sellers may be made worse-off. As a result, forced sellers who experience a net loss have a strong incentive to 'do a bad job' and the scheme would neither be expected to be effective in producing environmental services or to achieve efficiency gains. Insisting on voluntary buyers, however, may limit a scheme's applicability. It can leave it open to the problem associated with 'free-riding', if the environmental services produced under the scheme are public or common goods.

The remainder of this chapter discusses how PES scheme design choices influence their potential to be effective in producing environmental services and to secure gains in economic efficiency. Illustrative examples of past and current PES schemes are included to support this discussion.

9.2. Sellers, Buyers and their Agents

For a scheme to be successful in facilitating an exchange, the sellers need to have legal control over the production of the environmental services. In other words, they need to hold the property rights to the inputs required for environmental service production such as a land title (or land use rights) and, in consequence, the property rights to the produced environmental services. The legal control may be in the hands of an individual, a group or a government authority (Engel, Pagiola and Wunder, 2008). If the government has legal control over the production of environmental services, the government may be both a seller and an agent. For example, the government may act as a seller producing environmental services within a national park and, at the same time, as an agent representing the general public if the funds used for financing supply actions are sourced through compulsory taxation. If a group or community is empowered with the legal control over the production of environmental services, the distribution of costs and returns among the group or community members must be specified[6] and transparent. Otherwise, a scheme's supply effectiveness is expected to be low.

[6] For discussion on this topic see, for example, Fehr and Falk (2002), Sommerville *et al.* (2010), Kellert *et al.* (2000), Zabel and Engel (2010) and Milne and Niesten (2009).

Buyers pay for environmental service production and enjoy the generated benefits. More precisely, they purchase the property rights to the produced environmental services. Buyers are either voluntary or 'forced' buyers. Voluntary buyers are most likely to purchase environmental services that are excludable (private or club goods). The majority of buyers who purchase non-excludable environmental services (public or common goods) are 'forced' through taxation to address 'free-riding'. EcoTender in Australia (Eigenraam *et al.*, 2005) is an example, where the Victorian Government acts as the representative of the general public of Victoria buying environmental services on their behalf. Since funds to allow payments to be made are secured through tax payments, participation is compulsory for the buyers. Yet, not everyone is a 'free-rider'. Some buyers voluntarily purchase non-excludable environmental services. Examples are people who make donations to non-government organisations that aim to ensure biodiversity conservation.

The type of agent intervention required to facilitate a PES exchange depends on the driver(s) of the transaction costs. If the main drivers are poorly defined property rights to environmental services, a research institution may be able to lower the transaction costs to the point that trade becomes mutually profitable for sellers and buyers. The provision of scientific knowledge may be all that is needed to ensure an appropriate definition. For instance, a research institution may support the establishment of hydro-geological models that quantify the link between changed land management practices (supply actions) and improvements in water quality (environmental service) as observed in the Vittel scheme in France (e.g., Perrot-Maître, 2006).

Other cases require defending the property rights to environmental services to minimise 'free-riding'. The property right may be defended by the government who, through its power to raise funds through general taxation, 'forces' its tax-paying citizens to be buyers. Examples of this type of agent intervention are the CCFGP extension scheme in China (e.g., Wang *et al.*, 2012) and EcoTender in Australia (Eigenraam *et al.*, 2005).

This type of intervention is often complemented by assistance in the design, management and administration of the PES scheme. An example is the CCFGP extension scheme in China (e.g., Wang *et al.*, 2012), in which research institutions and government authorities assisted in determining the payment rates that facilitated efficiency improvements.

In some cases, agents act as 'brokers' by linking globally dispersed demand to large numbers of environmental service suppliers. For instance, a non-governmental organisation may mobilise demand through arranging to accept donations and transfer the payments to environmental service producers. By taking this step, the transaction costs may be lowered sufficiently to make an exchange advantageous for sellers and buyers.

Agent intervention causes transaction costs, which reduce efficiency gains achieved under a PES scheme. Agent intervention of any type is only warranted if the transaction costs of the scheme are less than the net returns buyers and sellers gain in the exchange. Otherwise, society as a whole is made worse-off and other policy instruments may be preferable to match environmental services demand with supply.

9.3. Payment Rate

Competitive markets for traded goods and services generate information on marginal costs of production and marginal benefits of consumption. A market price emerges through voluntary transactions of participating sellers and buyers who aim to maximise their individual net returns. At the 'market clearing price', market demand matches market supply. PES scheme designers face the challenge that markets, and thus information on market prices, do not exist for many non-excludable environmental services. The lack of markets is the very reason why PES schemes have been developed in the first place. This leaves two options: the payment rate is negotiated directly between buyers and sellers (facilitated by agents) or is determined by agents (who may consult the buyers and sellers).

A negotiated payment rate will be somewhere between the marginal costs of production (less any indirect marginal returns) and the marginal benefits enjoyed by the buyers. If this is not the case, neither the sellers nor the buyers have an incentive to participate. Trade will not take place. That is, directly negotiated payment rates ensure that the environmental service production generates a net benefit. The stronger the bargaining power of potential sellers (perhaps because there are small numbers of sellers who act together as a 'cartel'), the closer the payments will be to the marginal benefits enjoyed by the buyers. The stronger the bargaining power of the buyers (perhaps because of strong competition among sellers), the closer the payments will be to the marginal costs borne by the sellers. Few schemes employ a payment rate that is negotiated directly between sellers and buyers. The Vittel scheme in France (e.g., Perrot-Maître, 2006) is a rare example.

If the transaction costs of direct negotiations between sellers and buyers are prohibitively high, agents may step in and determine the payment rate on behalf of the buyers and the sellers. In that case, the payment rate the sellers receive is often set independently from the rate the buyers pay. The result is two payment rates (often including the costs of agent intervention) instead of a single payment rate that matches the 'market clearing price' at which demand matches supply.

One option is to set a uniform payment rate to sellers that is determined with little or no regard to marginal costs of production and marginal benefits of consumption. Such a payment rate may be input-based (payment per unit of supply action) or output-based (payment per unit of environmental service). The PES scheme in Costa Rica (e.g., Pagiola, 2008) is an example of a scheme that applies an input-based payment rate, where sellers receive a country-wide uniform payment per hectare of enrolled land.[7] A key difference between input-based and output-based payment rates stems from the possibility that the quantity of environmental service generated per unit of supply action may vary across sellers. In the extreme case (some) inputs used by (some) sellers may be ineffective in producing

---

[7]Two minor exceptions are a higher payment rate in the Rio Segundo catchment and a lower payment rate in the Rio Platanar catchment (Pagiola, 2008).

outputs. Schemes that apply input-based payment rates may be effective in achieving a high seller participation rate but they may be ineffective so that the participating sellers may not generate any environmental services through their supply actions. A scheme that is ineffective in producing environmental services generates a net loss to society, irrespective of the extent of PES participation.

If the payment rate (plus any indirect marginal returns) is smaller than the marginal costs for a substantial proportion of potential sellers, the scheme's supply effectiveness will be low. Sellers who would be made worse-off by engaging in the scheme have no incentive to participate. If participation is voluntary, such a payment rate will not achieve an economically efficient quantity of output. If the scheme was compulsory, forced sellers who experience a net loss will most likely 'do a bad job'. The efficiency improvements achieved under such a scheme will be small or negative. If, on the other hand, the payment rate is relatively large compared to the marginal benefits, the surplus to the buyers could be negative. If the scheme is voluntary, buyers would not participate. If, however, a government acts as the representative of the broader community and 'forces' its citizens (through its power to raise funds through general taxation) to be 'buyers', the scheme may still go ahead producing an inefficient quantity of output. Sellers who generate a net loss to society have an incentive to participate since the payment rate is greater than their individual marginal costs of production. It has to be stressed, though, that without collecting information on individual marginal costs and individual marginal benefits, PES scheme designers are ignorant of the discussed adverse effects of their design choices.

An alternative option is to set the payment rate to sellers equal to the monetary value of the marginal benefits of consumption. For example, all sellers participating in a PES scheme that aims to enhance biodiversity receive a payment rate equal to the marginal benefits enjoyed by the buyers that are generated per hectare of afforested area (input-based) or per percentage increase in the population of a certain indicator species (output-based). While the marginal benefits enjoyed from consuming environmental services are only known to the buyers, market and non-market valuation techniques can be used to estimate their monetary value (e.g., Barbier and Hanley, 2009). If the marginal benefits per unit of output are constant, an output-based payment rate will be uniform. Such a payment rate automatically ensures that none of the sellers is paid more than the generated marginal benefit per unit of output enjoyed by the buyers. Hence, sellers whose individual marginal costs are higher than the constant marginal benefits (the payment rate) have no incentive to participate voluntarily.

A special case is a payment rate set equal to the average benefits per unit of input generated across a wide group of heterogeneous sellers. The Lam Dong scheme in Vietnam (e.g., Nguyen, 2011) is an example. The scheme applied a payment rate set equal to the estimated average benefits per hectare of enrolled forest. Such a payment rate ignores differences in the effectiveness of inputs used to generate outputs. Sellers who perform highly productive supply actions generate more environmental services per unit of input than sellers who employ less effective inputs. Hence, the marginal benefits generated by the same quantity of inputs may differ across sellers. The first consequence would be that some sellers may produce very little or no output per unit of input. The second consequence would be that sellers who generate marginal benefits that are lower (higher) than the average marginal benefits generated across all sellers receive higher (lower) returns than they would if the differences in input effectiveness were recognised. A uniform payment rate (in the form of an average payment rate per unit of input) paid to all sellers independent of their individual contribution to the overall supply raises questions about fairness.

Yet another option is to set the payment rate equal to the marginal costs of production incurred by sellers per unit of input (or output). For example, all sellers participating in a PES scheme that aims to enhance biodiversity receive an (individualised) payment rate equal to their marginal costs per hectare of afforested area (input-based) or per percentage increase in the population of a certain indicator species (output-based). The payment rate can be set equal to individual marginal costs (individualised payment rate)[8] or to an average cost applied to all sellers (uniform payment rate).[9]

Schemes that apply a uniform payment rate reduce their supply effectiveness since, by construction, some sellers would face individual marginal costs that are higher than the average costs. These sellers have no incentive to participate in the scheme even though they might produce net benefits to society if included in the scheme. On the other hand, sellers whose individual marginal costs are lower than the average costs would extract producer surplus reducing the cost-effectiveness (from the perspective of the buyers or their agents) of the scheme.

Schemes that employ individualised payment rates are cost-effective (from the perspective of the buyers or their agents), given the estimated and true individual marginal costs coincide and the sellers do not earn any indirect returns. The entire surplus is secured by the buyers (or their agents). EcoTender in Australia (Eigenraam *et al.*, 2005) and the CCFGP extension scheme in China (e.g., Wang *et al.*, 2012) are examples of PES schemes that apply payment rates set equal to individual marginal costs. A high level of cost-effectiveness can help to reduce public expenditure for a given supply target or maximise the production of environmental services for a given budget. Reduced public spending in achieving supply goals increases the overall resources available to supply environmental services or other targets of government expenditure (e.g., education, health) elsewhere. However, cost-effective PES schemes deny sellers the opportunity to secure any net returns (ignoring any indirect returns). Whether or not schemes that employ individualised payment rates have the potential to achieve an efficiency improvement depends on the mechanism used to select the sellers.

---

[8] A concern advanced regarding individualised payment rates is perceived fairness; specifically, that not paying the same payment rate to all sellers may lead to social conflict or the rejection of the scheme (e.g., Nguyen, 2011; Muñoz-Piña *et al.*, 2008; Ferraro, 2008).

[9] Average costs of production may be estimated through market data or estimated elsewhere across a group of potentially heterogeneous sellers. Yet, it is unlikely that the so estimated average costs of production match their true value.

9.4. Seller Selection

One way to make a selection is to allow all sellers who meet a set of general eligibility criteria (perhaps based on the goals of the scheme and the policies driving it) to participate in the scheme ('all inclusive' approach). In some cases there is no choice. The environmental services may only be produced if all potential sellers within a catchment participate. The Vittel scheme in France (e.g., Perrot-Maître, 2006) is an example of such a case. The scheme aims to maintain a low nitrate concentration in the aquifer to enable the private water-bottling company Vittel (Nestlé Water) to comply with legislation defining 'natural mineral water' in its production. Since all farmers located within the spring catchment could have impacted individually on the nitrate levels in the aquifer, it was important to Vittel that all farmers participated. All farmers in the catchment had to be included to keep the nitrate levels at the desired level.

Yet, schemes may apply an 'all inclusive' approach even though a further selection may be feasible and economically sensible. The Lam Dong scheme in Vietnam (e.g., Nguyen, 2011) is an example of an 'all inclusive' scheme of that sort. 'All inclusive' schemes bear a risk of making society worse-off if sellers are included whose individual marginal costs are higher than the marginal benefits that are generated at the economically efficient level.

If the budget is insufficiently large to include all potential sellers, the need for further selection is clear. Schemes may cap participation by a bio-physical target or a budget constraint. The PES scheme in Costa Rica (e.g., Pagiola, 2008) is an example of a scheme that caps participation by a budget constraint. Budget constrained schemes are often combined with a 'first-come best-dressed' approach (those who apply first in time are selected over late-comers). It is unlikely that this approach achieves significant gains in efficiency because the timing of application is unlikely to be correlated with the net benefits generated by different sellers.

Alternatively, 'best-value-for-money' rankings may be used to select the sellers. The goal is to either minimise costs given a supply target or to maximise benefits given a budget constraint. Such rankings are often used in schemes that employ payment rates set equal to individual marginal costs of production. Individual marginal costs are only known to the sellers, they are 'hidden' from buyers and agents (Ferraro, 2008). A tendering process, also called procurement or reverse auction (Vickrey, 1961; Vickrey, 1962), is an effective mechanism to estimate these costs.[10] In a tender, potential sellers competitively bid to produce environmental services in return for a payment (e.g., Latacz-Lohmann and Van der Hamsvoort, 1997; Latacz-Lohmann and Schilizzi, 2005; Schilizzi and Latacz-Lohmann, 2007).

The competition created within a tender is expected to discourage strategic behaviour. Yet, a tender's incentive structure significantly influences whether or not it reveals the sellers' true marginal costs. In a tender that applies a 'paid-as-bid' rule all successful bidders are paid the individually requested amount per individually proposed bundle of supply actions. The requested amount is interpreted as their individual marginal costs at the proposed quantity of input they each propose. This implies that the sellers earn a zero economic profit if they reveal their true marginal costs. This raises questions regarding their motivation to participate. Attempts to explain their motivation include the prospect of securing informational rents (Ferraro, 2008) and of reducing income risks if PES payments are perceived more reliable than alternative investments.

Tenders often combine a 'paid-as-bid' rule with a 'best-value-for-money' ranking procedure. This combination forces bidders to make a trade-off between the magnitude of the proposed payment and the probability of being contracted.[11] This incentive structure reduces informational rents gained by sellers who inflate their true marginal costs — yet, they are not eliminated altogether (e.g., Ferraro, 2008). In a budget constrained scheme financed through public spending,

---

[10] Challenges to successfully conducting a tender include a lack of skilled participants and facilitators (Wang *et al.*, 2012; e.g., Eigenraam *et al.*, 2005) and insufficient competition among sellers including the potential for collusion (Latacz-Lohmann and Schilizzi, 2005).

[11] A discussion about the incentive structures of tenders that apply a 'paid-as-bid' rule is given by, for example, Holt (1980), Cox, Smith and Walker (1984), Milgrom (1989) and Milgrom (2004).

informational rents reduce the quantity of environmental services that can be purchased. If the available budget is smaller or equal to the budget required to purchase the economically efficient quantity, net benefits to society cannot be maximised.

One way to conduct a 'best-value-for-money' ranking is to take the ratio of the marginal costs of production and an environmental benefit index (EBI). An example is an EBI developed as a component of the Investment Framework for Environmental Resources (INFFER) (Pannell *et al.*, 2012). An EBI is usually based on a function of several attributes linking supply actions to environmental services. It aggregates the relative value of supply actions that are estimated in non-monetary terms by means of a scoring system into a single unit. However, the power of an EBI to express benefits enjoyed by the buyers is limited. First, it remains unclear if an EBI actually aggregates a bundle of environmental services in a way that reflects the relative merit of each individual environmental service. Second, an EBI is usually not based on public preferences. More often, it represents the judgements of experts and stakeholders. As a result, benefits estimated in terms of an EBI may not coincide with the benefits enjoyed by the wider society. This implies that an EBI may not embody information on the scheme's marginal benefits enjoyed by the buyers. Third, the benefits are not valued in monetary terms. This precludes the option to restrict supply by demand.

EcoTender in Australia (Eigenraam *et al.*, 2005) is an example of PES schemes that apply payment rates set equal to individual marginal costs estimated through tenders combining a 'paid-as-bid' rule with a 'best-value-for-money' ranking procedure as described above. Such schemes are likely to be cost-effective (from the perspectives of the buyers or their agents) if the opportunities to gain informational rents are limited.[12] Yet, the production of environmental services is unlikely to be economically efficient since the contracted supply is not restricted by demand, which remains unknown. It is not ensured

[12] Noting the higher transaction costs associated with the establishment of an EBI compared to 'all inclusive' or 'first-come-best-dressed' approaches.

that the benefits generated through supply actions are greater than the cost of production. Yet again, without collecting monetary information on both costs and benefits, PES scheme designers are ignorant of any adverse effects caused by their design choices.

Instead of using an EBI, proposals can be ranked by expressing their relative merit as a benefit–cost ratio, where not just the costs, but also the benefits, are valued in monetary terms using market and non-market valuation methods (e.g., Barbier and Hanley, 2009). The CCFGP extension scheme in China (e.g., Wang *et al.*, 2012) is an example of a scheme that ranked seller proposals by their benefit–cost ratios. The advantage of this approach is that marginal benefits can be compared directly with the marginal costs. Proposals that achieve a benefit–cost ratio greater than one would be ranked and included in the scheme until the budget has been exhausted (if the potential supply quantity is smaller than the economically efficient supply quantity) or until the economically efficient quantity of supply has been reached.[13,14] This approach ensures that sellers with proposals that deliver the highest net benefits are contracted and allows the identification and exclusion of proposals that would generate a net loss to society. Estimating monetary values causes the transaction costs to rise, which reduces any efficiency gains generated under a scheme.

Even though this approach ensures that the environmental service production initiated under the scheme generates a net benefit to society, the sellers earn a zero economic profit (ignoring informational rents and any indirect returns). The surplus is not shared between sellers and buyers. This raises questions about fairness, especially if potential sellers are low-income earners as is the case in many developing countries.

---

[13] The ranking procedure may be challenging if the inclusion of all proposals with a benefit–cost ratio larger than one exceeds the budget constraint and the lowest ranked proposals have equal benefit–cost ratios.

[14] The ranking procedure becomes more complex in the case of multiple environmental service types and if the marginal benefits of environmental service supply are diminishing.

9.5. The Road Ahead

Numerous PES schemes have been implemented around the world over the last decades. Some may have achieved cost-effective outcomes with little net returns earned by sellers, while others may have mainly redistributed wealth with only little effects on environmental service production. Many seem to have struggled to achieve or demonstrate efficiency gains.

Incorporating principles of competitive markets for traded goods and services more rigorously into PES scheme designs presents the opportunity to ensure that a PES exchange generates net benefits. One step in this direction is to set the payment rate equal to the 'market clearing price' sellers are willing to accept and buyers are willing to pay per unit of an environmental service. Such a payment rate would implicitly ensure that supply is capped by demand and that the surplus is shared between buyers and sellers depending on the price elasticities of demand and supply. The payment rate per unit of environmental service would be uniform. Yet, the payment rate per unit of supply action might differ across producers. More effective producers would receive a higher payment rate per unit of supply action than less effective producers.

The estimation of the 'market clearing price' requires information on production functions as well as on 'market' supply and demand. Production functions could be estimated by means of bio-physical models that establish a quantitative link between supply actions and environmental service production. 'Market' demand could be estimated in monetary terms using market and non-market valuation techniques. 'Market' supply could be estimated using tenders that yield information on individual marginal cost functions.

Collecting this information would cause the transaction costs to rise. If agents are unable to reduce the transaction costs sufficiently so that they are smaller than the net benefits generated through the exchange, the implementation of a PES scheme is not warranted. Other policy instruments may be preferable to match environmental service demand with supply.

Bibliography

Asquith, N.M., Vargas, M.T. and Wunder, S. (2008). Selling Two Environmental Services: In-Kind Payments for Bird Habitat and Watershed Protection in Los Negros, Bolivia, *Ecological Economics*, 65, pp. 675–684.

Barbier, E. and Hanley, N. (2009). *Pricing Nature: Cost–Benefit Analysis and Environmental Policy*, Edward Elgar Publishing, Cheltenham.

Burchards, G. (2010). *Payments for Ecosystem Services in Vietnam. A Comparative Case Study in the Context of REDD+*, A disseration submitted to the School of International Development, University of East Anglia.

Cox, J., Smith, V. and Walker, J. (1984). Theory and Behavior of Multiple Unit Discriminative Auctions, *Journal of Finance*, 39, pp. 983–1010.

Eigenraam, M., Strappazzon, L., Lansdell, N., Ha, A., Beverly, C. and Todd, J. (2005). *EcoTender: Auction for Multiple Environmental Outcomes*, Department of Primary Industry, Melbourne.

Engel, S., Pagiola, S. and Wunder, S. (2008). Designing Payments for Environmental Services in Theory and Practice: An Overview of the Issue, *Ecological Economics*, 65, pp. 663–674.

Fehr, E. and Falk, A. (2002). Psychological Foundations of Incentives, *European Economic Review*, 46, pp. 687–724.

Ferraro, P.J. (2008). Asymmetric Information and Contract Design for Payments for Environmental Services, *Ecological Economics*, 65, pp. 810–821.

Holt, C. (1980). Competitive Bidding for Contracts Under Alternative Auction Procedures, *Journal of Political Economy*, 88, pp. 433–445.

Kellert, S.R., Mehta, J.N., Ebbin, S.A. and Lichtenfeld, L.L. (2000). Community Natural Resource Management: Promise, Rhetoric, and Reality, *Society and Natural Resources*, 13, pp. 705–715.

Kolstad, I. and Wiig, A. (2008). Is Transparency the Key to Reducing Corruption in Resource-Rich Countries?, *World Development*, 37, pp. 521–532.

Latacz-Lohmann, U. and Schilizzi, S. (2005). Auctions for Conservation Contracts: A Review of the Theoretical and Empirical Literature, *Report to the Scottish Executive Environment and Rural Affairs Department*. Available at: http://www.scotland.gov.uk/resource/doc/93853/0022574.pdf [Accessed December 2014 (web-only publication)].

Latacz-Lohmann, U. and van der Hamsvoort, C. (1997). Auctioning Conservation Contracts: A Theoretical Analysis and Application, *American Journal of Agricultural Economics*, 79, pp. 407–418.

Midgley, S., Bennett, J., Samonty, X., Stevens, P., Mounlamai, K., Midgley, D. and Brown, A. (2012). *Enhancing Livelihoods in Lao PDR Through Environmental Services and Planted-Timber Products*, Technical Reports, Australian Centre for International Agricultural Research, Canberra.

Milgrom, P. (1989). Auctions and Bidding: A Primer, *Journal of Economic Perspectives*, 3, pp. 3–22.

Milgrom, P.R. (2004). *Putting Auction Theory to Work*, Press Syndicate of the University of Cambridge, Cambridge.

Millennium Ecosystem Assessment (2005). 'Ecosystems and Human Well-Being: Current State and Trend', in Hassan, R., Scholes, R. and Ash, N. (eds.), *Findings of the Condition and Trends Working Group of the Millennium Ecosystem Assessment*, Island Press, Washington, DC.

Milne, S. and Niesten, E. (2009). Direct Payments for Biodiversity Conservation in Developing Countries: Practical Insights for Design and Implementation, *Oryx*, 43, pp. 530–541.

Muñoz-Piña, C., Guevara, A., Torres, J.M. and Braña, J. (2008). Paying for the Hydrological Services of Mexico's Forests: Analysis, Negotiations and Results, *Ecological Economics*, 65, pp. 725–736.

Muradian, R., Corbera, E., Pascual, U., Kosoy, N. and May, P.H. (2010). Reconciling Theory and Practice: An Alternative Conceptual Framework for Understanding Payments for Environmental Services, *Ecological Economics*, 69, pp. 1202–1208.

Nguyen, Q.T. (2011). Payments for Environmental Services: An Analysis of the Pilot Project in Lam Dong Province, *Occasional Paper No. 5*, Institute for Global Environmental Strategies, Forest Conservation Livelihood and Rights Project, Kanagawa, Japan.

Pagiola, S. (2008). Payments for Environmental Services in Costa Rica, *Ecological Economics*, 65, pp. 712–724.

Pannell, D.J., Roberts, A.M., Park, G., Alexander, J., Curatolo, A. and Marsha, S.P. (2012). Integrated Assessment of Public Investment in Land-Use Change to Protect Environmental Assets in Australia, *Land Use Policy*, 29, pp. 377–387.

Perrot-Maître, D. (2006). *The Vittel Payments for Ecosystem Services: A 'Perfect' PES Case?*, International Institute for Environment and Development, London.

Phothisat, S., Khaopasurt, B. and Lindros, K. (2013). *Payment for Forest Environmental Services in Lao PDR*, Ministry of Agriculture and Forestry (Department of Forestry), Sustainable Forestry for Rural Development Project — Additional Financing, Vientiane, Lao PDR.

Scheufele, G. and Bennett, J. (2013). *Research report 1: Payments for Environmental Services: Concepts and Applications*, Crawford School of Public Policy, The Australian National University, Canberra.

Schilizzi, S. and Latacz-Lohmann, U. (2007). Assessing the Performance of Conservation Auctions: An Experimental Study, *Land Economics*, 83, pp. 497–515.

Sommerville, M., Jones, J.P.G., Rahajaharison, M. and Milner-Gullard, E.J. (2010). The Role of Fairness and Benefit Distribution in Community-Based Payment for Environmental Services Interventions: A Case Study From Menabe, Madagascar, *Ecological Economics*, 69, pp. 1262–1271.

Tacconi, L. (2012). Redefining Payments for Environmental Services, *Ecological Economics*, 73, pp. 29–36.

Vickrey, W. (1961). Counterspeculation, Auctions and Competitive Sealed Tenders, *Journal of Finance*, 16, pp. 8–37.

Vickrey, W. (1962). 'Auctions and Bidding Games', in Morgenstern, O. and Tucker, A.W. (eds.), *Recent Advances in Game Theory*, Princeton University Press, Princeton, pp. 15–27.

Wang, X., Bennett, J., Xu, J. and Zhang, H. (2012). An Auction Scheme for Land Use Change in Sichuan Province, China, *Journal of Environmental Planning and Management*, 55 (10), pp. 1269–1288.

Wunder, S. (2005). Payments for Environmental Services: Some Nuts and Bolts, *Occasional Paper No. 42*, CIFOR, Bogor, Indonesia.

Wunder, S. (2007). The Efficiency of Payments for Environmental Service in Tropical Conservation, *Conservation Biology*, 21, pp. 48–58.

Zabel, A. and Engel, S. (2010). Performance Payments: A New Strategy to Conserve Large Carnivores in The Tropics?, *Ecological Economics*, 70, pp. 405–412.

10. Exploring Private Roles in Environmental Watering in Australia and the US

Dustin Garrick and Erin O'Donnell

Recognition of the environment as a legitimate water use has been closely followed by questions about who should provide water for the environment, and how. This chapter examines the evolution of private roles in environmental water recovery in Australia and the US, two regions with arguably the longest history of reform experience to reallocate and manage water for riverine and groundwater dependent ecosystems degraded by overuse. In both regions, private non-governmental organisations (NGOs) have played important roles in the establishment and management of environmental water reserves, although these roles have shifted over time and in relation to public authorities. We compare the Australia and the US to understand which types of private organisations participate in environmental water, why and how.

These patterns of organisational and institutional development can be explained from multiple perspectives. Private roles have emerged for (at least) two reasons — reducing transaction costs and addressing governance deficits. Theories of transaction costs and environmental governance each offer a partial explanation. Together they can offer a more rounded explanation of the emergence, evolution and coordination of private and public roles. Transaction costs economics highlights issues of efficiency and the alignment between governance arrangements and the characteristics of environmental water transactions — both the acquisition and management of water holdings for the environment. Governance theory emphasises issues of legitimacy, accountability and the public trust, all of which impose transaction costs during the search, bargaining and enforcement of water transactions. Both perspectives provide 'partly rival, partly complementary' (Williamson, 1998) accounts of the evolution of environmental water organisations within a wider legal framework and system of property rights to water. Considering them together helps to identify the opportunities and limits for private provision of environmental flows.

In Section 10.1, we define the problem of environmental water as a public goods failure. We outline the main types and scales of organisational arrangements that have emerged to address this collective action dilemma: private NGOs, quasi-governmental organisations, and governmental organisations — each ranging from local to national in scale, with international (binational) examples developing. In Section 10.2, we present the history of environmental water organisations in Australia and the US in relation to two linked transactions: environmental water acquisition and management/delivery. In Section 10.3, we interpret these trends from two perspectives: transaction costs reduction and corporate governance. The final section offers brief reflections and implications.

10.1. The Problem of Environmental Flows Revisited: Public Goods and Private Roles in a Transaction Costs World

The problem of environmental flows needs to be understood within the wider context of competition for scarce and variable freshwater supplies. It must also be framed in terms of water's status as a complex economic good with interdependent public and private values (Hanemann, 2006; Libecap, 2005). First, the problem of environmental flows arises in the context of growing development and use of freshwater resources. By definition, the growth of consumptive human water uses for agriculture, cities, and energy production decreases the availability and impairs the quality of residual flows. The minimum flow regime (the pattern of base flows and flood pulses) needed to sustain freshwater ecosystem services varies geographically; however, it is rare to recognise and protect these environmental needs until critical thresholds are either approached or even breached. In this context, the problem of environmental flows is often a challenge of over-allocation and is closely associated with an increase in the scarcity value of water across competing uses.

In the Western US, semi-arid irrigation regions have dewatered stream flows in tributaries and groundwater-dependent wetlands. In the Colorado River Basin, for example, upstream development has reduced the Delta to less than 10 per cent of its historic extent. Outflows have been reduced, and eliminated completely in many years, until a recent binational private–public agreement restored base flows and flood pulses to the region (Flessa *et al.*, 2013). Chronic dewatering has also led to dry tributaries in sensitive fish habitat in many Western US rivers.

In the Murray–Darling River Basin in Australia, upstream diversions reduced outflows to 40 per cent of the modelled average at the Murray Mouth (Grafton *et al.*, 2013; Murray–Darling Basin Authority (MDBA), 2010). The problem of environmental flows as an over-allocation challenge can be traced to water's complexity as an economic good. Hanemann (2006) explores the hypothesis that 'water is different' as an economic good due its unique characteristics with diverse private uses, which depend on the maintenance of multiple public goods, including the freshwater ecosystem services that sustain consumptive uses. Human consumptive uses, e.g., for irrigation, are governed by exclusive property rights, one individual or group's consumption of water precludes others from doing so. Different forms of private or common pool property rights govern access, use, reallocation and management of these consumptive uses

(Schlager and Ostrom, 1992; Young and McColl, 2009). The establishment of diversion limits and tradable rights provides the enabling institutional framework and incentives for markets and transactions to reallocate water in response to shifting information and preferences.

In the Western US, a system of prior appropriation has developed, providing high security property rights to the first claimant to establish and maintain a beneficial use. Regulatory protections safeguard third parties from experiencing 'harm' due to water reallocation (Grafton *et al.*, 2012). These principles of equity and fairness have limited the extent of water trading and raised the transaction costs of market-based reallocation. However, several pockets of water rights reform have enabled water trade, with cities and environmental interests acting as catalysts for institutional reform and as buyers in emerging markets. Private NGOs have initiated citizens' petitions, court cases, and participation in watershed and catchment planning and rule-making to enable market-based reallocation and financing to secure water for the environment (Neuman, Squier and Achterman, 2006) (see Section 10.3).

By contrast, the Murray–Darling was characterised by the vestment of water ownership at the state level and issues of tradable entitlements to water users. Cap-and-trade water allocation reforms in the region have enabled an active market with up to 40 per cent of annual water allocations traded (Grafton and Horne, 2014). These reforms date back as far as the late 1960s moratorium on water licenses in South Australia. The Council of Australian Governments water reform package of 1994 led to an interim cap (1997). The cap accelerated the process of unbundling water and land rights and the development of easily accessed trading platforms underpinned by a framework of trading rules. About 20 years later, irrigators and environmental managers have adopted sophisticated risk management behaviour through water trade (Wheeler *et al.*, 2013). The development of the market preceded the broad commitments to environmental water recovery, however, illustrating a contrasting sequence of reform from the Western US. Indeed, the cap-and-trade reforms recognised unused historic licenses (sleepers and dozers) whose activation after the cap intensified pressure and provided an impetus for the ongoing transition to sustainable diversion limits now underway. In the Murray–Darling, environmental recovery lagged rather than led the development of water markets.

Despite these contrasting property institutions and cap-and-trade allocation reform trajectories, private interests have acted on behalf of the environment in both settings, although in different roles which have also evolved considerably over time. To understand the opportunities and limits of private roles in market-based environmental water recovery, it is important to acknowledge that environmental needs comprise a public good due to the high costs of exclusion and 'indivisibility' of benefits generated by their provision and maintenance — the notion that environmental flows generate benefits regardless of an individual's contribution. This creates incentives to free ride and hence the potential for a market and governance failure to provide environmental flows at socially desired levels. The standard responses — full privatisation and state control — form extreme points along a spectrum of institutional responses to the problem of environmental flows, each with their deficits and sources of inefficiency. In practice, a range of polycentric and public–private arrangements have emerged (Meinzen-Dick, 2007).

The complexity of water as an economic good increases the potential for conflict, uncertainty and associated regulatory barriers to trade, which together impose potentially high transaction costs. In this context, transaction costs refer to the resources required to define, manage, and trade property rights as well as to change property rights institutions (McCann, 2005; Marshall, 2013). Transaction costs comprise the 'economic equivalent of friction' (Williamson, 1985). This friction has the potential to prevent or slow otherwise beneficial reallocation of water, particularly for environmental needs whose benefits are diffuse, delayed and broadly distributed, while their costs are often local, concentrated and immediate (Harrison, 2013). Efforts to balance efficiency with other policy goals, such as legitimacy, accountability and fairness, are captured by the notion of adaptive efficiency, introduced by Douglass North (North, 1990) and adapted to the water allocation context as the 'sequentially more complex institutional innovations to reduce transaction costs' assessed over the long-term rather than a static assessment (Carey and Sunding, 2001).

What role does the private sector play in these sequentially more complex institutional innovations? How do these roles interact with public roles? Transaction costs economist and Nobel Laureate Oliver Williamson advanced the concept of the discriminating alignment as the governance arrangement matched to the characteristics of the transaction to achieve a transaction costs minimising result (Williamson, 1998). Environmental transactions can be decomposed into two separate, but linked, transactions: acquisition and management, e.g., delivery (Garrick *et al.*, 2012). Each can be described in terms of the transaction costs economics concept of asset specificity (Coggan, Whitten and Bennett, 2010). Asset specificity describes the potential to redeploy the technology and information used to execute a given transaction for future transactions, which depends on standardisation, frequency and other characteristics of the transaction. The complexity of environmental transactions, their relatively low frequency, and, hence, their high asset specificity, structure the opportunities and constraints facing private and public organisations in their efforts to reduce transaction costs.

Loehman and Charney have considered this private role in the Western US context to highlight how private and public roles have contributed to in-stream flow restoration and management activities (Loehman and Charney, 2011). Their review identifies 12 roles in protecting in-stream flows, ranging from identifying priority streams to monitoring stream flows and legal compliance. Three trends are noteworthy. First, private NGO groups were involved in 10 of the 12 functions identified. Second, public agencies were also active in all ten functions where private NGOs focused, although the entity taking the lead in any given function varied between public and private and from state to state, illustrating in part how the institutional environment shaped the public versus private roles. In Montana, for example, an emphasis on private leasing led to an active role for private entities in identifying priority streams and so on. Finally, the capacity in the private organisations has been minor relative to public investment, particularly in terms of staff, with the greatest disparity occurring in Washington where 120 state employees for environmental flows compare with 4.5 full-time staff in the state's private water trust. Loehman and Charney do not focus on transaction costs *per se*, but their conclusions are generally consistent with the notion of a discriminating alignment:

> The survey also indicated that there is complementarity in management activities: NGOs have a comparative advantage in working with local agriculturists to identify lease opportunities and efficiency opportunities, whereas state agencies have an advantage in monitoring, data collection, research and planning activities which require some continuity and consistency over time (Loehman and Charney, 2011, p. 890).

This conclusion not only supports the notion of transaction costs minimisation as one justification for private participation but also the specific advantages related to local engagement, time- and place-specific information, and the cultivation of trust and norms of reciprocity. In sum, private roles are critical to reduce transaction costs, but in a way that enhances legitimacy, accountability and perceptions of fairness.

10.2. Institutional and Organisation Innovations

The foregoing illustrates the interface of transaction costs and governance theory. This is well developed in the theory of the firm elaborated by Coase (Coase, 1960; Coase, 1937), but has not yet been widely applied in a sophisticated way to environmental water recovery (Crase and Gawne, 2011). Here we use the transaction as the unit of analysis (Commons, 1931) and define two linked transactions: acquisition and management (Tables 10.1a and 10.1b). Transactions refer to the transfer of a good or service across a technologically separable space (Williamson, 1985), but also to a social relation between buyer, seller, third parties and regulators, and

Table 10.1a: Project Cycle — Acquisition (Garrick, Lane-Miller and McCoy, 2011)

		US examples	Australian examples
Planning and prioritisation	Identify needs and prioritise projects	Federal Water Projects (*Secure Water Act*), State Instream Flow Programs (*Colorado Water Conservation Board*), Local and basin initiatives (*Northwest Power and Conservation Council — Subbasin Plans*)	Public policy (*Water for the Future*), Murray–Darling Basin Plan, state policies (*Our Water Our Future*), regional plans (*Northern Region Sustainable Water Strategy* (*SWS*))
Financing	Budgets (acquisition and ongoing administration)	Federal Water Projects (*California Environmental Water Account*), Statewide Programs (Environmental Water Account), Private Mitigation Funding/ Philanthropic Organisations	Federal government funding ($3.1b), state funding ($105m New South Wales (NSW))
Find sellers	Outreach	Private Water Trust (*individual sellers*), Quasi-governmental Watershed Organisations (*Deschutes water auctions*)	The Commonwealth Environmental Water Holder (CEWH) tender programme, NSW Riverbank purchase programme
Regulation review	Consider transaction impacts	State regulatory agencies	CEWH tender programme (staged application to minimise market impacts)

(*Continued*)

Table 10.1a: (*Continued*)

		US examples	Australian examples
Conflict resolution	Engagement and consultation	Administrative hearings (state regulation)	Murray–Darling Basin Plan engagement process
Holding of water rights	Legal transfer process	State regulatory agencies (most Western states); Exceptions in Montana with private holding allowed	CEWH (individual water access licences/water shares), Victorian Environmental Water Holder (VEWH) may convert into environmental entitlement
Monitoring	Contract compliance	Extensive monitoring by private water trusts and watershed organisations. Periodic monitoring by field-based officers of state regulatory agencies (watermasters)	A minimal formality in Australia
Evaluation and learning	Review and feed back into planning	Transaction reporting and accountability (*Columbia Basin Water Transactions Program* (CBWPT))	CEWH annual reports

brokers, all operating within a system of working rules and conflict resolution venues. We identify the organisational arrangements across the transaction cycle to understand private and public roles, as well as their possible configurations within public–private arrangements aiming for the joint outcomes of transaction costs minimisation and legitimacy.

Table 10.1b: Project Cycle — Management (Horne and O'Donnell, 2014)

		US examples	Australian examples
Policy	Long-term goals	*Clean Water Act* (indirect); Endangered Species Act (indirect)	Murray–Darling Basin Plan, National Water Initiative, Our Water Our Future
Planning	Identify values, assets, objectives, risks and prioritisation of actions	Instream flow planning (state-level); Statewide water plans (Colorado, California); Reservoir operation plan (various)	Multi-year environmental watering plans prepared by Catchment Management Authority (CMA)
Decision	Commitment to specific watering plan	Transaction level determination of stream reach (unregulated systems Storage operating plan (regulated systems)	CEWH annual watering plan, VEWH seasonal watering plan
Implementation	Use of water in accordance with plan	Adjustments to headworks; operations of canals to ensure delivery of water instream	Delivery of water to wetlands and provision of instream flows
Monitoring and reporting	Monitor water delivered and report on objectives	Monitoring individual transactions to ensure compliance (water is left instream) — both public and private efforts. Transaction reporting to ensure accountability with funders	CEWH annual report, VEWH annual environmental watering report, WFN project reports

(*Continued*)

Table 10.1b: (*Continued*)

		US examples	Australian examples
Evaluation	Monitor environmental response and adapt policy and planning	Accounting frameworks to assess biological impacts and ecological response (CBWTP)	CEWH Monitoring and Evaluation plan, Victoria's **Victorian** Environmental Flows Monitoring and Assessment Program (VEFMAP)

10.2.1. *Transaction 1: Acquisition*

Environmental water acquisition refers to the purchase or lease of water entitlements for the purpose of environmental protection or restoration. Environmental water uses include both in-channel and off-stream uses, typically for fisheries and wetlands, respectively. The institutional environment shapes the transaction cycle, and may prescribe specific regulatory processes. Nevertheless, a set of broad features can be identified in two categories — policy and implementation cycles (Garrick, Lane-Miller and McCoy, 2011; Garrick, Whitten and Coggan, 2013). In the former are the various elements of problem definition and policy enactment, primarily including the establishment of sustainable diversion limits, or minimum stream flows, as well as the reform of water rights systems to enable trade and to authorise the environment as a legitimate use. In the latter category (implementation cycle) are the contracting phases of the transaction, and associated searching, bargaining and enforcement, as they occur within the prevailing institutional setting. These steps include many of the components defined by Loehman and Charney and also in previous work by Garrick, Lane Miller and McCoy (2011), who identified planning and prioritisation, financing, cultivation and identification of willing sellers, regulatory review, conflict resolution, holding environmental rights, monitoring and enforcement (Garrick, Lane-Miller and McCoy, 2011; Loehman and Charney, 2011).

These functions imply a natural ordering between public and private. In the policy cycle, private NGOs have initiated petitions, court cases and so on, particularly in the Western US (Gillilan and Brown, 2013). The resulting legal frameworks have been a patchwork of statewide, e.g., Oregon, and programmes limited to specific sub basins, e.g., Upper Salmon of Idaho, although this varies considerably from state to state. For example, Washington's water acquisition programme has been driven by an active state regulatory agency, the Washington Department of Ecology, while Montana's in-stream leasing programme has been shaped by private initiatives.

In the implementation cycle, the non-profit roles have included all phases with particular emphasis on a role as an honest broker to cultivate willing sellers and assist them to navigate public financing opportunities and regulatory procedures (Sterne, 1997; Grafton and Horne, 2014; Horne, Purkey and Mcmahon, 2008). Increasingly, this private role has extended to both biological and legal compliance monitoring to ensure accountability and demonstrate the local and wider benefits of stream flow restoration, often by complementing the formal monitoring roles by the public regulatory agencies (Garrick *et al.*, 2009).

In Australia, state, interstate and Commonwealth public agencies and commissions have provided the impetus for market-enabling reforms and environmental water recovery. There has been more direct governmental oversight and implementation of water acquisitions initially at the state level with increasing interstate and Commonwealth efforts, culminating in the 2008–2017 Restoring the Balance programme administered by the Commonwealth Department of Sustainability, Environment, Population, Water and Communities (i.e., SEWPAC), the predecessor to the current Commonwealth Department of the Environment. However, environmental water management and delivery in Australia have exposed the importance of private and local roles in the implementation cycle, as noted below.

10.2.2. *Transaction 2: Management*

Management of environmental water refers to the delivery of water to specific locations (in-stream or via extraction to floodplain wetlands) and monitoring of water delivery (e.g., volume of water received, over what period, flow rates and areas of inundation) and environmental response (e.g., fish migration, bird breeding, vegetation growth) over the short and long term (MDBA, 2014). In the US, management varies based on the unregulated (typically in-stream) and regulated (both in-stream and off-stream) character of environmental flows. In the former, management principally involves the active monitoring of environmental water transactions to ensure legal compliance and document biological impacts associated with the net increases in stream flows contributed by the transaction. In most Western US states, a water master performs this role under the auspices of a regulatory agency or the courts, while private NGOs have become active in spot monitoring for legal compliance and accounting frameworks to document biological and ecological impacts of environmental water acquisitions brokered by private NGOs and underwritten by public funds. Regulated flows are associated with state and federal water projects and may involve special operating rules and therefore a prominent role for public agencies in delivery, with private NGOs involved in the associated planning, land use management and watchdog roles, as in the California Bay Delta, Walker Lake, Nevada and the Colorado River Delta flood pulse. In Australia, management can also include the sale of environmental water rights in order to generate the funds to purchase new environmental water in alternative locations, of different reliability or even to invest in complementary measures to enhance environmental outcomes of water delivery. As an example, the VEWH has successfully sold water allocations and re-invested those funds in the purchase of other water rights (VEWH, 2013). However, whilst this trade of existing environmental water creates additional flexibility for environmental water managers, it has been only rarely used.

10.2.3. *A typology of organisations*

Against this backdrop, environmental water organisations can be characterised along two dimensions — their public versus private character and their scale (Table 10.2). Government agencies are at the public end of the spectrum while water trusts, conservancies,

Table 10.2: Typology of Environmental Water Organisations

Character/Scale	Local and state	Federal and international
Public	• Catchment Management Authority • Local Environmental Water Officer • Water Master and Field Office • State Regulatory Agency	• Basin Authority • Commonwealth Government • Federal Water Project
Private	• Water Trusts • Conservancies • Other Conservation NGOs	• Binational Water Trusts

other forms of conservation non-profits, and catchment management organisations are either private non-profits or quasi-governmental organisations. They exist from the local to the national scales with the private tending to be more local and the public ranging from local to state and national, despite some notable exceptions with the emergence of a binational water trust in the Colorado River Delta.

10.3. History of Environmental Water Organisations

10.3.1. *US*

The emergence and evolution of environmental water management organisations in the US features two narratives. First, it has been a slow process. Decades of reform have been required to enhance in-stream flows within the prior appropriation system. Second, collaborative approaches have been needed to break the logjam of vested interests and inertia impeding change. On the other hand, market-based reallocation has been underpinned by collaboration (Siemann and Martin, 2007). Together these narratives demonstrate the explanatory power of combining transaction costs with the literature on environmental governance.

10.3.1.1. *Origins*

The history of environmental water recovery in the US dates at least to the state of Oregon's Minimum Perennial Flows Program of 1955, with programmes following in Washington, Colorado, Idaho and Montana in the 1970s. However, there are examples of in-stream flow protections for scenic waterfalls (Oregon) and lakes (Idaho) as early as 1915 and the 1920s, respectively (Neuman, Squier and Achterman, 2006). The Oregon *In-stream Water Rights Act* of 1987 marks the origins of the contemporary era of market-oriented environmental water acquisition. It was noteworthy for its establishment of water rights with in-stream flows as a beneficial use, a departure from previous requirements to have a physical diversion to establish beneficial use. Eligible in-stream uses include recreation, pollution abatement and conservation. It was also a milestone for authorising private organisations to purchase, lease, or gift established high security rights for conversion to in-stream flows (Amos, 2008), noting any 'person may purchase or lease all or a portion of an existing water right or accept a gift of all or a portion of an existing water right for conversion to an in-stream water right' (Oregon Revised Statutes, 537.348).

10.3.1.2. *Experimentations*

Six years after the Oregon *In-Stream Water Rights Act* was passed, a private transaction had yet to occur. The Oregon Water Trust was established in 1993 to pioneer private water acquisition efforts, becoming involved not only in the implementation of transactions but also the development of rules and procedures to govern these experiments (Neuman, 2004). The Deschutes Conservancy followed suit and offered another organisational model at the sub-basin scale; its governance relied on a multi-stakeholder board committed to a deep and broad local engagement, as well as a systematic approach to establish institutional frameworks for long-term and large-scale environmental water recovery. A third model relied on public acquisitions, principally by states and federal water projects. These three private models — state water trusts, quasi-governmental watershed conservancies, and state/federal agencies with stakeholder working groups — would bracket the range of experiments across the Pacific Northwest, and later the rest of the Western US. Water trusts were initially organised at the state level and have become more localised in their geographic focus or their organisation structure to promote field-based activities (e.g., the central Washington field office of the Washington Water Trust opening in approximately 2008). Initial transactions were characterised by high transaction costs and low frequency, as private entities navigated regulatory protocols, built local relationships, secured financing and developed monitoring criteria to ensure in-stream water rights were being met.

10.3.1.3. *Scaling up*

The promise of environmental water transactions became a reality by the early 2000s with almost 8.6 billion cubic meters restored from 1987 to 2007, principally using public financing (Scarborough and Lund, 2007). After the experimentation of the 1990s resulted in private water trusts in Oregon and Washington (and Montana in the early 2000s), local success stories raised questions about the potential to scale up activity to achieve local targets and basin-wide recovery. In 2002, the CBWTP was established under the auspices of Northwest Power and Conservation Council and Bonneville Power Administration's fish and wildlife programme in response to biological opinions issued to recover endangered salmon fisheries in compliance with the *Endangered Species Act*. The CBWTP was formed to harness local capacity within a regional framework and coordinated financing and reporting systems. In so doing, its objectives included efforts to support organisational capacity-building and reduce transaction costs through the exchange of technical expertise, cultivation of good practices, and adoption of public accountability measures, including a Basin-wide monitoring and accounting framework. The programme restored over four billion cubic meters over the life of transactions approved in 2013 alone (CBWTP, 2013).

The progress was not confined to the Columbia, nor even to the Western US. Garrick and colleagues noted over 24 programmes protecting approximately three billion cubic meters in active water protection, i.e., 'wet water', in the 2008–2009 period (Garrick, Lane-Miller and McCoy, 2011). Approximately half of the programmes were coordinated by private organisations, and all involved a private role across some phase of the transaction cycle. The CBWTP offered one prominent model of efforts to combine public and private roles to leverage the comparative advantages of each to reduce transaction costs for a given level of public accountability. However, no one size fits all cases, given the variation in federal roles (depending on whether a federal water project existed in the region) and the state allocation systems.

In the past five years, the dual mandates of reducing transaction costs and maximising legitimacy have yielded new regional, public–private arrangements in Nevada (Walker Lake), the Colorado River Delta, the California Bay Delta and a range of settings. In 2012–2013, the National Fish and Wildlife Foundation initiated its Western US environmental water transactions and restoration programmes, a sign of the growing network and community of practice.

10.3.2. *Australia*

Examining the history of Australia's environmental water management institutions also demonstrates the power of using both transactions costs and governance as a dual, complementary narrative. Australia has been actively delivering environmental water since 1980, when water was delivered to the Macquarie Marshes (National Water Commission, 2012). In 2004, a national agreement on water resource management committed all states to a programme of providing sufficient environmental water (Council of Australian Governments (COAG), 2004), including 500 GL for the Murray River under The Living Murray Program (Murray–Darling Basin Commission, 2007). Acquisition of water for the environment was largely the result of capping and regularising existing entitlements, with some small purchase programmes. In 2007, the Australian government committed $3.1b to purchasing water for the environment, and a further $5.8b for more efficient water infrastructure (Australian Government, 2010). This policy resulted in a massive environmental water acquisition programme at the federal level, as well as requiring the efficient management of increasingly large volumes of environmental water.

10.3.2.1. *Origins*

Early environmental water management was largely the responsibility of state governments, as environmental water was provided through a combination of river regulation and occasional entitlements in storage. The trigger for the shift to the modern environmental water management arrangements in Australia was two-fold: first, the severe and prolonged drought over south-eastern Australia from 2000 to 2010; and second, the emergence of an increasingly active water market across the Murray–Darling Basin. Private water rights had never been more important, or more valuable (National Water Commission, 2010). Environmental water managers needed to improve the efficiency of their operations, whilst still maintaining accountability, legitimacy and community support. This response resulted in the emergence of a range of environmental water management institutions, primarily within the Murray–Darling Basin (MDB).

10.3.2.2. *Scaling Up*

At the federal or basin scale, two new environmental water managers were created by the Commonwealth *Water Act 2007*. The MDB Authority is a statutory corporation, underpinned by Commonwealth legislation and an intergovernmental agreement between the Commonwealth and the states of the MDB. It retained ownership of water recovered through The Living Murray Program and sets the basin-wide policies for environmental water management. CEWH is a statutory entity, vested in a single employee of the Australian public service, supported by an office of staff within the Commonwealth bureaucracy (O'Donnell, 2012). The CEWH was created to streamline purchase capacities by enabling the Commonwealth government to efficiently buy water and to use economies of scale in coordinating the use of diverse water rights throughout the MDB. The CEWH had the additional objective of increasing transparency and clarity in environmental water management by focusing the decision-making within a single entity.

At the state level, NSW created Riverbank, a government agency designed to purchase water on the market efficiently, use this water for environmental benefits and sell water where necessary to help cover its operating costs (NSW Government, 2010). Again, this organisation serves a two-fold purpose: reducing the transaction costs of environmental water recovery and management, and providing greater transparency in management decisions. In Victoria, the VEWH aimed to give even greater transparency and legitimacy to environmental watering. The VEWH is a statutory corporation which holds all environmental water entitlements in Victoria. It was created in response to a lack of clarity in decision-making during the severe drought, and sought to depoliticise the process of using environmental water in difficult times (O'Donnell, 2012). Unlike all others in Australia, the VEWH was not created to acquire water, but to manage it efficiently and transparently.

10.3.2.3. *Experimentation*

At the local level, environmental water managers have been active for several decades. In NSW, the Murray Wetlands Working Group was formed in 1992, and given responsibility for managing two adaptive environmental water licenses, which enabled them to direct the watering events in their high-value wetlands (Murray–Darling Wetlands Working Group, 2014). Following the regularisation of water rights in 2004, NGOs emerged to obtain water for local environments. Healthy Rivers Australia (HRA), primarily active in South Australia, developed the process for receiving water donations under Australian tax law, reducing the cost of water donations (Garrick *et al.*, 2009). This was followed by other charities such as the Australian Conservation Foundation, who obtained donations of water and money for environmental watering of wetlands (Siebentritt, 2012).

Local NGOs provided a direct mechanism for community engagement with environmental water, through donation of water or money or via the provision of local knowledge as part of environmental watering activities. Following the massive investment by the Commonwealth government to purchase environmental water rights in the MDB (MDBA, 2012), most of the NGOs in Australia have shifted their focus from water acquisition to management of environmental watering activities. Organisations such as HRA, the Murray–Darling Wetlands Working Group and the Water for Nature (WFN) trust in South Australia are directly engaged in generating community support and engaging local constituencies. The value of these organisations can be seen by the recent decision of the CEWH to enter into a five-year agreement with WFN for the management of some of the CEWH's water.

Australia currently has a wide range of environmental water management organizations operating at local, state and federal/basin scales (O'Donnell, 2013). These organisations have emerged in response to the need to minimise the costs of environmental water acquisition and management, as well as providing accountable, legitimate and transparent environmental water management, with substantial local engagement.

10.4. Transaction Costs and Governance

> there may be no easy way to reduce transaction costs, and it may be necessary for CBWTP to accept that achieving in-stream goals may be more expensive than was previously envisioned, and seek greater financial resources to support the activity of QLEs [qualified local entities]. (Hardner and Gullison, 2007).

> The primary normative guideline for governance ... is legitimacy
> (Wolf, 2002, p. 40).

Legitimacy can be conceived in many ways, but one of the helpful distinctions is between input legitimacy (is the process acceptable to the affected people?) and output legitimacy (did the process solve the problem?) Hogl *et al.* (2012) argue that pathways to input legitimacy include access, equal representation, transparency and accountability, consultation and cooperation, and independence and credibility. Pathways to output legitimacy include support, acceptance, awareness and higher standards, coherent, shared strategies and robust outcomes. As environmental water managers seek to obtain and retain legitimacy and public support for environmental flows, these pathways to legitimacy have shaped the organisational response in both Australia and the USA, during both the acquisition and management phases.

The quest for legitimacy amidst contested public and private values has a direct impact on efforts to increase efficiency and reduce transaction costs. The third party evaluators of the CBWTP (noted in the quotation stated earlier) concluded that transaction costs reduction might prove difficult for in-stream flow goals. A longitudinal study of transaction costs in the Basin concluded that only 4 of the 11 sub-basins managed to decrease transaction costs across two study periods (2003–2007 and 2008–2010) CBWTP, 2013 and Garrick, 2012). The most cost-effective organisations included examples from a private statewide non-profit, a quasi-governmental river conservancy and the local field office of a state agency — in other words, examples from all three organisational types. The common thread was the commitment of the organisations to couple transaction implementation with ongoing efforts to reform the institutional environment for water trading, and to establish collaborative frameworks for planning and multi-stakeholder engagement to manage third-party impacts. In other words, long-term reductions in transaction costs depended on strategies to build legitimacy through effective governance arrangements.

10.4.1. *Acquisition phase*

Environmental water acquisition proceeded very differently in the western USA and the MDB, Australia. In Australia, water rights and water markets have emerged as government-backed institutions. Prior to 2007, most environmental water acquisition occurred via government programmes, and as water markets emerged as the most efficient mechanism to recover water for the environment, it was a natural extension of government's role to enter the market and purchase water. However, the ways in which it did so were heavily scrutinised and resulted in the statutory creation of identifiable environmental water management organisations (such as the CEWH and NSW's Riverbank) to create clear lines of accountability, and to ensure the acquisition programmes operated at arms' length from the relevant government ministers.

In the western USA, water purchases were essential to obtain senior water rights, and government purchasers were far less acceptable to water users. This created a real need for private organisations, and water trusts were established at the local or state level to seek out opportunities to acquire environmental water. Even after states such as Washington and Colorado had established government agencies with active acquisition programmes, there remained a need for NGOs to provide a buffer between water users and government and reduce risk of relinquishment proceedings. Initial discussions and even detailed negotiations with an NGO could be halted if a discrepancy between the paper value and the used value of the water right emerged, with no risk to the water user. NGOs helped to build public trust in the water transfer process. They continue to act as an honest broker between water users and state agencies, and are often referred to as the 'retail arm' of a state water acquisition programme.

Both jurisdictions relied on private organisations to enhance local community participation in water acquisition programmes. In the MDB, the Waterfind Environment Fund (later HRA) and the Australian Conservation Foundation 'Just Add Water' programme sought donations of water and money from the public, and offered a link to local environmental water needs (Siebentritt, 2012). In the western USA, private NGOs are often the face of environmental water recovery at the local level, seeking to enhance the legitimacy of the programme by ensuring win–win outcomes for local communities: keeping the irrigation business going, as well as restoring environmental flows.

10.4.2. *Management phase*

In Australia, legitimacy emerges as an even stronger driver behind the organisational response in the management of environmental water. The need for transparent, accountable decision-making for the use of environmental water during the severe drought (2000–2010) underpinned the creation of both the CEWH and the VEWH. They provided clarity of purpose as well as depoliticised evidence-based decisions, enhancing public trust in the difficult decision to use environmental water during the worst drought on record (O'Donnell, 2012). The MDBA, CEWH and the VEWH were also created to provide a single voice for the management and monitoring of large volumes of water across large scales, ensuring consistency and coherence, important pathways to output legitimacy. However, these large-scale government bodies distanced the public from the management process. NGOs have emerged and adapted to fill this gap. Where once NGOs focused on water acquisition, in Australia they are now much more prominent in management of environmental water, providing a necessary bridge between government bureaucracy and large-scale plans, and local communities (Commonwealth Environmental Water Office and Nature Foundation SA, 2012).

In the USA, the management phase is focused on monitoring outcomes. Both state agencies and NGOs are engaged in monitoring. NGOs have a critical role to play in monitoring the presence of water in-stream in accordance with the negotiated transaction, even when they no longer own the water right, because of the complaints-based system of water accounting: a water user complains to the accounting agency if the water is not available when required. In states where in-stream flows must be held by a state agency, there is often overlap between the agency holding the flows and the agency responsible for ensuring compliance with water rights. NGOs enhance public trust in this system, which would otherwise require government to regulate itself.

As environmental water programmes across the US have scaled up, there has been a corresponding increase in monitoring efforts. Bigger programmes operating on a larger spatial scale are introducing higher standards for environmental water transactions, and the monitoring of environmental response — an important pathway to output legitimacy. However, this can increase costs for local NGOs, and highlights the tension between effectiveness and community engagement.

10.5. Reflections

Demonstrating legitimacy ensures the sustainability of environmental water programmes, which are conceptually linked to the social values given to healthy rivers and groundwater dependent ecosystems (Hirji and Davis, 2009). These values change over time, and vary in response to local context. Good environmental governance must reflect this and, as a result, is often focused on demonstrating legitimacy through participation, accountability, transparency and openness (Arts, 2010).

Attaining legitimacy comes at a cost, however. Efforts to reduce transaction costs without building governance arrangements to enhance legitimacy are unlikely to achieve lasting success and adaptive efficiency. Despite the contrasting institutional environments of Australia and the US, the experiences in both regions illustrate that it is difficult to minimise transaction costs and maximise legitimacy simultaneously. Long term reductions in transaction costs depend on the investments in good governance and the emergence of private organisations to both access local information at low cost and cultivate trust and accountability. As such, private organisations are an essential link between large-scale, efficient and effective environmental water recovery and management, on the one hand, and local community participation, access and engagement, on the other.

Bibliography

Amos, A.L. (2008). Freshwater Conservation: A Review of Oregon Water Law & Policy, *Phase 1 Report prepared for the Nature Conservancy.* Available at: http://works.bepress.com/adell_amos/7 [Accessed 31 October 2014].

Arts, B., Appelstrand, M., Kleinschmit, D., Pülzl, H. and Visseren-Hamakers, I. (lead authors) *et al.* (2010). 'Discourses, Actors and

Instruments in International Forest Governance', in Rayner, J., Buck, A. and Katila, P. (eds.), *Embracing Complexity: Meeting the International Forest Governance Challenge, IUFRO World Series Vol. 27*, International Union of Forest Research Organisation, Vienna.

Australian Government (2010). *Water for the Future*, Department of Sustainability, Environment, Water, Population and Communities, Canberra.

Carey, J.M. and Sunding, D.L. (2001). Emerging Markets in Water: A Comparative Institutional Analysis of the Central Valley and Colorado-Big Thompson Projects, *Natural Resources Journal*, 41, pp. 283–328.

COAG (2004). *Intergovernmental Agreement on a National Water Initiative*, Council of Australian Governments, Canberra.

Coase, R.H. (1937). The Nature of the Firm, *Economica*, 4, pp. 386–405.

Coase, R.H. (1960). The Problem of Social Cost, *Journal of Law and Economics*, 3, pp. 1–44.

Coggan, A., Whitten, S.M. and Bennett, J. (2010). Influences of Transaction Costs in Environmental Policy, *Ecological Economics*, 69, pp. 1777–1784.

Columbia Basin Water Transactions Program (CBWTP) (2013). *Annual Report*. Columbia Basin Water Transactions Program, Portland, Oregon.

CBWTP, prepared by Dustin Garrick (2012). *Audit of Transaction Costs Trends 2003–2010*. Report of Columbia Basin Water Transactions Program, Portland, Oregon.

Commons, J.R. (1931). Institutional Economics, *The American Economic Review*, 21, pp. 648–657.

Commonwealth Environmental Water Office and Nature Foundation SA. (2012). 'Press Release: Commonwealth Works with Nature Foundation South Australia to Deliver Water', (October 24, 2012). Commonwealth Environmental Water Office and Nature Foundation SA, Adelaide.

Crase, L. and Gawne, B. (2011). Coase-Coloured Glasses and Rights Bundling: Why the Initial Specification of Water Rights in Volumetric Terms Matters, *Economic Papers*, 30, pp. 135–146.

Flessa, K.W., Glenn, E.P., Hinojosa-Huerta, O., De La Parra-Rentería, C.A., Ramírez-Hernández, J., Schmidt, J.C. and Zamora-Arroyo, F.A. (2013). Flooding the Colorado River Delta: A Landscape-Scale Experiment. *Eos, Transactions American Geophysical Union*, 94, pp. 485–486.

Garrick, D., Bark, R., Connor, J. and Banerjee, O. (2012). Environmental Water Governance in Federal Rivers: Opportunities and Limits for

Subsidiarity in Australia's Murray–Darling River, *Water Policy*, 14, pp. 915–936.

Garrick, D., Lane-Miller, C. and McCoy, A.L. (2011). Institutional Innovations to Govern Environmental Water in the Western United States: Lessons for Australia's Murray–Darling Basin, *Economic Papers: A Journal of Applied Economics and Policy*, 30, pp. 167–184.

Garrick, D., Whitten, S. and Coggan, A. (2013). Understanding the Evolution and Performance of Water Markets and Allocation Policy: A Transaction Costs Analysis Framework, *Ecological Economics*, 88, pp. 195–205.

Garrick, D., Siebentritt, M.A., Aylward, B., Bauer, C.J. and Purkey, A. (2009). Water Markets and Freshwater Ecosystem Services: Policy Reform and Implementation in the Columbia and Murray–Darling Basins, *Ecological Economics*, 69, pp. 366–379.

Gillilan, D.M. and Brown, T.C. (2013). *Instream Flow Protection: Seeking a Balance in Western Water Use*, Island Press, Washington, DC.

Grafton, R.Q. and Horne, J. (2014). Water Markets in the Murray–Darling Basin, *Agricultural Water Management*, 145, pp. 61–71.

Grafton, R.Q., Libecap, G.D., Edwards, E.C., O'Brien, R.J. and Landry, C. (2012). Comparative Assessment of Water Markets: Insights From the Murray–Darling Basin of Australia and the Western USA, *Water Policy*, 14, pp. 175–193.

Grafton, R.Q., Pittock, J., Davis, R., Williams, J., Fu, G., Warburton, M., Udall, B., McKenzie, R., Yu, X. and Che, N. (2013). Global Insights into Water Resources, Climate Change and Governance, *Nature Climate Change*, 3, pp. 315–321.

Hanemann, W.M. (2006). 'The Economic Conception of Water', in Rogers, P. P., Ramón Llamas, M. and Martínez-Cortina, L. (eds.), *Water Crisis: Myth or Reality?*, CRC Press, London, pp. 61–91.

Hardner, J. and Gullison, R.E. (2007). *Independent External Evaluation of the Columbia Basin Water Transactions Program (2003–2006)*, Hardner and Gullison Consulting, Amherst, NH.

Harrison, K. (2013). Federalism and Climate Policy Innovation: A Critical Reassessment, *Canadian Public Policy*, 39, pp. S95–S108.

Hirji, R. and Davis, R. (2009). 'Environmental Flows in Water Resources Policies, Plans, and Projects: Case Studies', *Natural Resource Management Series Paper 117*, The World Bank Environment Department, Washington, DC.

Hogl, K., Kvarda, E., Nordbeck, N. and Pregernig, M. (eds) (2012). *Environmental Governance: The Challenge of Legitimacy and Effectiveness*, Edward Elgar, Cheltenham.

Horne, A. and O'Donnell, E. (2014). Decision Making Roles and Responsibility for Environmental Water in the Murray–Darling Basin, *Australian Journal of Water Resources*, 18(2), pp. 118–132.

Horne, A., Purkey, A. and McMahon, T.A. (2008). Purchasing Water for the Environment in Unregulated Systems — What Can We Learn from the Columbia Basin?, *Australian Journal of Water Resources*, 12, pp. 61–70.

Libecap, G.D. (2005). The Problem of Water, *Workshop on New Institutional Economics and Environmental Issues*, Workshop on Environmental Issues and New Institutional Economics, INRA-ENESAD CESAER.

Loehman, E.T. and Charney, S. (2011). Further Down the Road to Sustainable Environmental Flows: Funding, Management Activities and Governance for Six Western US states, *Water International*, 36, pp. 873–893.

Marshall, G.R. (2013). Transaction Costs, Collective Action and Adaptation in Managing Complex Social–Ecological Systems, *Ecological Economics*, 88, pp. 185–194.

McCann, L. (2005). Transaction Costs of Pesticide Policies in Vietnam, *Society & Natural Resources*, 18, pp. 759–766.

Meinzen-Dick, R. (2007). Beyond Panaceas in Water Institutions, *Proceedings of the National Academy of Sciences*, 104, pp. 15200–15205.

Murray–Darling Basin Authority (MDBA) (2010). *Guide to the Proposed Basin Plan*, Murray–Darling Basin Authority, Canberra.

MDBA (2012). *Murray–Darling Basin Plan*, Commonwealth of Australia, Canberra.

MDBA (2014). 'Basin-Wide Environmental Watering Strategy', (Draft for public comment), Murray–Darling Basin Authority, Canberra.

Murray–Darling Basin Commission (2007). 'The Living Murray Business Plan: 25 May 2007', Murray–Darling Basin Commission, Canberra.

Murray–Darling Wetlands Working Group Ltd. (2014). 'About Us: History'. Available at: http://www.murraydarlingwetlands.com.au/about-us/history/ [Accessed 22 October 2014].

National Water Commission (2010). *The Impacts of Water Trading in the Southern Murray–Darling Basin: An Economic, Social and Environmental Assessment*, Commonwealth of Australia, Canberra.

National Water Commission (2012). *Australian Environmental Water Management: 2012 Review*, Commonwealth of Australia, Canberra.

Neuman, J.C. (2004). Good, the Bad, and the Ugly: The First Ten Years of the Oregon Water Trust, *The Nebraska Law Review*, 83, pp. 432–484.

Neuman, J.C., Squier, A. and Achterman, G. (2006). Sometimes a Great Notion: Oregon's Instream Flow Experiments, *Environmental Law*, 36, pp. 1125–1155.

North, D.C. (1990). *Institutions, Institutional Change and Economic Performance*, Cambridge University Press, Cambridge.

NSW Government (2010). *New South Wales RiverBank Business Plan Part A: Program Plan 2006–2011, Buying and Managing Water for the Environment* (2010 update), Department of Environment, Climate Change and Water, Sydney.

O'Donnell, E. (2012). Institutional Reform in Environmental Water Management: The New Victorian Environmental Water Holder, *Journal of Water Law*, 22, pp. 73–84.

O'Donnell, E. (2013). Australia's Environmental Water Holders: Who is Managing Our Environmental Water?, *Australian Environment Review*, 28, pp. 508–513.

Oregon Revised Statutes (1987). *Purchase, Lease or Gift of Water Right for Conversion to In-stream Water Right*, 537.348, Oregon State, Salem.

Scarborough, B.C. and Lund, H.L. (2007). *Saving Our Streams: Harnessing Water Markets: A Practical Guide*, Property and Environment Research Centre, Bozeman, Montana.

Schlager, E. and Ostrom, E. (1992). Property-Rights Regimes and Natural Resources: A Conceptual Analysis, *Land Economics*, 68, pp. 249–262.

Siebentritt, M.A. (ed.) (2012). Water Trusts: What Role Can They Play in the Future of Environmental Water Management in Australia? *Proceedings of a workshop held on 1 December 2011*, Water Trust Alliance and Australian River Restoration Centre, Canberra.

Siemann, D. and Martin, S. (2007). *Managing Many Waters: An Assessment of Capacities for Implementing Water and Fish Improvements in the Walla Walla Basin*, Report of the William D. Ruckelshaus Center, Seattle and Pullman, Washington.

Sterne, J. (1997). Instream Rights and Invisible Hands: Prospects for Private Instream Water Rights in the Northwest, *Environmental Law*, 27, pp. 203–243.

Victorian Environmental Water Holder (VEWH) (2013). *Annual Report 2012–2013*, Victorian Environmental Water Holder, Melbourne.

Wheeler, S., Garrick, D., Loch, A. and Bjornlund, H. (2013). Evaluating Water Market Products to Acquire Water for the Environment in Australia, *Land Use Policy*, 30, pp. 427–436.

Williamson, O.E. (1985). *The Economic Institutions of Capitalism*, The Free Press, New York.

Williamson, O.E. (1998). Transaction Cost Economics: How it Works; Where it is Headed, *De Economist*, 146, pp. 23–58.

Wolf, K.D. (2002). 'Contextualizing Normative Standards for Legitimate Governance Beyond the State', in Jürgen, R.G. and Gbikpi, B. (eds.), *Participatory Governance: Political and Societal Implications*, Leske + Budrich, Opladen, Germany, pp. 35–50.

Young, M.D. and McColl, J.C. (2009). Double Trouble: The Importance of Accounting for and Defining Water Entitlements Consistent with Hydrological Realities, *Australian Journal of Agricultural and Resource Economics*, 53, pp. 19–35.

11. Additional Parties in Environmental Markets: Motivation, Operation and Future

Anthea Coggan

11.1. Introduction

Government is becoming increasingly adept at designing and implementing market-based instruments (MBIs), policy tools that encourage certain behaviours through market signals rather than through explicit directives such as regulation (Stavins, 2003b), to enhance the provision of environmental goods and services from private parties. There is extensive literature discussing experience, type, design, costs and benefits of MBIs over more traditional command-and-control approaches to environmental management (see, for example, Hahn and Hester, 1989b; Hahn and Stavins, 1992; Jack, Kousky and Sims, 2008; Stavins, 2003a; Stavins, 2003b; Claassen, Cattaneo and Johansson, 2008; Pirard, 2012). This literature is heavily focussed on first-party traders (buyers and sellers) in environmental markets with less written on the existence and motivation behind government-created and privately emerging additional parties such as brokers and intermediaries who operate in this market and are often significant players in efficient and effective environmental trades.[1]

Highlighting the motivation for the emergence or creation of additional parties, their role in the operation of environmental markets as well as providing some examples of additional parties in environmental markets is the focus of this chapter. This chapter begins with a discussion of transaction costs as a driving force for additional parties. The beginning of this chapter also provides a reflection on the current state of the literature when it comes to linking additional parties to transaction costs in environmental markets and beyond. The second part of the chapter introduces the different types of additional parties that are currently operating or may emerge in environmental markets and provides examples of these additional parties where they exist in environmental markets. The chapter concludes with a discussion about the implications to trades and traders from the engagement of additional parties and where the future might lie for this type of environmental market participant.

11.2. Transaction Costs and Additional Parties in Environmental Markets

Regardless of whether a market emerges organically or is designed and implemented by government (which is more often the case in the supply of environmental goods and services from private entities),

[1] Additional parties may be private sector (referred to as emergent) or public sector (referred to as created) created and operated (in some cases government may create the additional party and outsource the operation of the additional party to a private party). Created additional parties occur where government has created a market system to achieve an outcome and has recognised that transaction costs may inhibit efficient and effective trades. In these cases it may be more cost-effective for government to create an additional party to inform trades and reduce transaction costs rather than make major changes to the newly established market. There are also many cases of additional parties created and operated by the private sector. Additional parties will emerge privately when they can profit from bringing specialist knowledge to trades. Exchange brokers are one type of additional party that has private and public sector operated additional parties.

markets for environmental goods and services are often characterised by high transaction costs. There are numerous definitions of transaction costs in the literature. These are well summarised by McCann *et al.* (2005), Allen (1999) and Wang (2007). In broad terms, transaction costs are the costs arising, not from the production of a good but from the transfer of this good from one agent to another (Niehans, 1971). Transaction costs are the cost of collecting information about the transaction, finding trading partners, negotiating the transaction and enforcing the exchange. Coggan *et al.* (2013a) suggest that for an environmental policy, transaction costs are experienced by the policy maker who designs and administers the policy and the private parties who engage with or are affected by the environmental policy. The policy administrator experiences transaction costs due to information collection activities to research and design a new policy, lobbying for a new policy, implementation, administration, monitoring and enforcing the policy. Private parties experience transaction costs due to the time as well as direct expenses incurred in learning about the policy, finding trading partners, preparing applications, negotiating and finalising contracts as well as conducting any required monitoring and reporting.[2]

Transaction costs are a key reason for the emergence or creation of additional parties in markets. The link between transaction costs and additional parties has been made in financial markets (Pollock, Porac and Wade, 2004), commodity futures markets (Ziegelbaeck and Breuer, 2014) and technology markets (Benassi and Di Minin, 2009). The link between transaction cost and additional parties has also been made in a number of environmental markets. All suggest that brokers emerge because the benefit of engaging the broker to the

[2]There are many definitions of transaction costs in the literature. These definitions range from considering transaction costs as the cost of affecting an exchange (Barzel, 1985) to definitions such as Coase's (1960) cost of carrying out market transactions. New Institutional Economists tend to refer to transaction costs as the costs to define, establish, maintain and transfer property rights (McCann *et al.*, 2005) as this captures the cost of the creation and change between institutions as well as the cost of exchange within an institution (Marshall, 2013). Transaction costs are defined and discussed by Garrett in Chapter 10 of this book.

primary exchange parties, through reducing transaction costs, whilst reducing the overall gains from trade, outweighs the cost of engagement of the additional party.

For environmental markets, Stavins (1995a), Stavins (1995b), Gangdaharan (2000) and Hahn (1987) explore the impact and extent of transaction costs and the emergence of brokers in the sulphur dioxide (SOx) trading programme. Gangdaharan (2000) demonstrates that transaction costs in the Regional Clean Air Incentives Market (RECLAIM), which operates to reduce emissions of nitrogen oxide (NOx) and SOx around Los Angeles by imposing factory mass emission caps, reduced the probability of trading during the initial years of the programme by between 30 per cent and 40 per cent. Hahn (1987) also suggests that the extent of internal rather than external trading further highlights the existence of transaction costs in this market. Stavins (1995b) notes that because there is no ready means for buyers and sellers to identify one another, buyers frequently pay substantial fees to consultants who help them search for available permits. Gangadharan (2004) notes that one broker charges a penny per pound traded from buyers and sellers or would only engage in transactions with a minimum fee of $200.

Woodward and Kaiser (2002), Woodward, Kaiser and Wicks (2002), Hahn (1987), King and Kuch (2003) and Hahn and Hester (1989a) explore transaction costs and brokers in water quality trading markets in the US. Hahn and Hester (1989a) highlight that transaction costs in the form of administrative requirements as well as uncertainty surrounding property rights were the key reasons why the Fox River water quality trading programme failed and had a significant impact on the quality and quantity of trades in other schemes. The high transaction cost experience of water and air quality permit trading in the US is contrasted with the programme of lead-right trading which occurred under the US Environmental Protection Agency's (EPA) leaded gasoline phase down. Under this programme there was a high level of trading which is attributed to the minimal administrative requirements and the fact that traders were already accustomed to making deals with one another which further reduced transaction costs (Hahn, 1987; Stavins, 1995b).

The Productivity Commission (2010) highlights that the growth and evolution of water quantity markets in the Murray–Darling Basin (Australia) was accompanied by the development of intermediary services such as brokers and links this growth directly to transaction costs. The Productivity Commission (2010) notes that by 2007, around 80 per cent of trades in water in the Murray–Darling Basin were managed by an intermediary. Further, in a Government tender to purchase water rights in the Murray–Darling, over half of the offers of supply were managed by brokers (Productivity Commission, 2010).

Additional parties such as brokers are also evident in carbon markets. In a study conducted by Landell-Mills and Porras (2002), carbon markets, more than other environmental markets, were characterised by the rapid emergence of ancillary services such as brokers and advisory services with private brokers mediating over 20 per cent of the recorded carbon market transactions. Finally, Landell-Mills and Porras (2002) and Coggan *et al.* (2013b) highlight the emergence of additional parties in biodiversity markets and link these to transaction costs. Landell-Mills and Porras (2002) highlight the search, negotiation and contracting transaction costs in biodiversity markets and how additional parties can reduce these costs. Coggan *et al.* (2013b) focus on transaction costs in biodiversity offset markets and seek to understand if and how additional parties reduce transaction costs that arise due to the nature of the goods (asset specificity), level of information available, types of trades (frequency and timing) and probity (especially for public additional parties).

11.3. Types of Additional Parties to Exchanges in Environmental Markets

With a specific focus on offset markets, Coggan *et al.* (2013b) highlight that there are six types of additional parties that tend to occur in environmental markets. These additional parties are: (i) information providers; (ii) exchange brokers; (iii) offset aggregators (referred to in this chapter as an advanced exchange broker); (iv) banks;

(v) additional parties emergent due to in-lieu-fee (ILF) offsets; and (vi) clearing houses. One extra type of additional party — trust funds — is added in this review. Each is described in the following sections with examples of the additional party operating in the market. Key features of each type of additional party are listed in Table 11.1 at the end of succeeding section to allow comparison.

11.3.1. *Information provider*

Information providers are an additional party to an environmental exchange who provide information to parties involved in this exchange. The information provider may focus on information provision about the market, about the environmental features of a particular piece of land and/or about how a company can fulfil environmental-related corporate social responsibility objectives.

There are many examples of additional parties operating in an information provision role in environmental markets. Stavins (1995b) highlights that information brokers regularly operate in the SOx trading programme in the US, conducting activities such as consulting with electrical utilities to help them understand their options as well as forecasting permit supply and demand. In carbon markets, intermediaries have been most active in exchange support through assessing offset exchange certification, insurance and compliance (Landell-Mills and Porras, 2002).

In biodiversity offset markets, additional parties may provide specialist services such as an environmental impact assessment or vegetation management plans which are required by the administering party to finalise an offset. Wotherspoon and Burgin (2009) highlight the potential that vegetation offset markets provide information provision intermediaries. Wotherspoon and Burgin (2009) suggest that private market ecologists can engage with offset schemes such as New South Wales' (NSW) BioBanking scheme[3] through activities such as

[3] More information about the NSW BioBanking scheme is available at www.environment.nsw.gov/biobanking/ [Accessed 5 December 2014]. More detail about offsets as an environmental policy is contained in the chapter written by Gillespie (Chapter 15).

Table 11.1: Key Features of Additional Parties

	Features				
Additional party type	**Additional party owns property**	**Additional party trades formalised and standardised credits**	**Additional party keeps a database of potential buyers**	**Additional party is responsible for the conservation site**	**Can it pool demand?**
Information broker	No	No	No	No	No
Standard exchange broker	No	No	No	No	No
Advanced exchange broker	No	No	No	Yes in some cases	Yes in some cases
Bank	Yes	No	Yes	Yes	Yes
Created from ILF	No	No	Yes	No	Yes
Clearing house	No	Yes	Yes	No	Yes
Trust fund	Yes in some cases	No	No	Depends on ownership. Often use a third party to manage land	Yes

assessment of ecological assets, conducting annual monitoring, decision-making around when BioBanking is appropriate and acceptable, input into the drafting and detail of the policy and related tools such as assessment tools as well as performing expert witness roles in dispute reconciliation when required.

11.3.2. *Standard and advanced exchange broker*

An exchange broker is an additional party who is contracted by buyers and/or sellers to mediate a transaction in environmental goods and services between the two parties. This form of additional party is often found in offset markets where they are classified as either standard exchange brokers or advanced exchange brokers (what Coggan *et al.* (2013b) refer to as offset aggregators). The standard exchange broker provides services which may include one or more of: assisting an offset buyer determine how to meet offset requirements (information provision and provision of specialist knowledge about government policy approval conditions and how to meet these); finding a seller of suitable goods and services which meet offset requirements (search activities); assisting in price negotiations; contract negotiation between buyers and sellers and between government and offset buyers; and monitoring and reporting on offset activities (Figure 11.1).

The advanced exchange broker provides the same services as the standard exchange broker but also holds a database of potential offset suppliers awaiting a buyer. Unlike a bank, the advanced exchange broker does not own any of these sites. In addition, unlike a clearing house, the potential offset suppliers do not yet have formalised offset credits. The advanced exchange broker operates by accepting payments for activities that a developer requires as offsets and securing these mitigation activities and offset sites (usually from within their database) at some time in the future (Figure 11.2). Recent amendments to the Queensland government's vegetation offset policy (Australia) (Queensland Government, 2011) to allow offset obligations to be discharged through a payment toa recognised

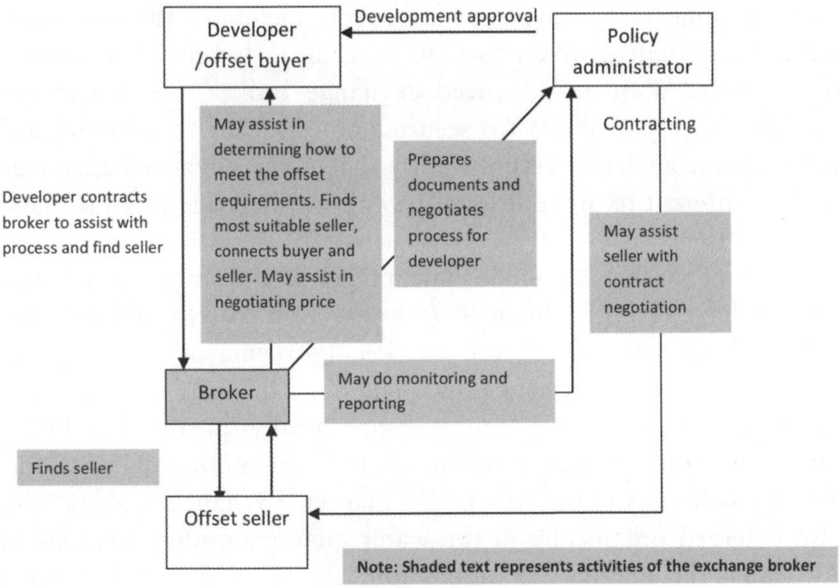

Figure 11.1: Specialist services of the standard exchange broker

Source: Adapted from Coggan *et al.* (2013b).

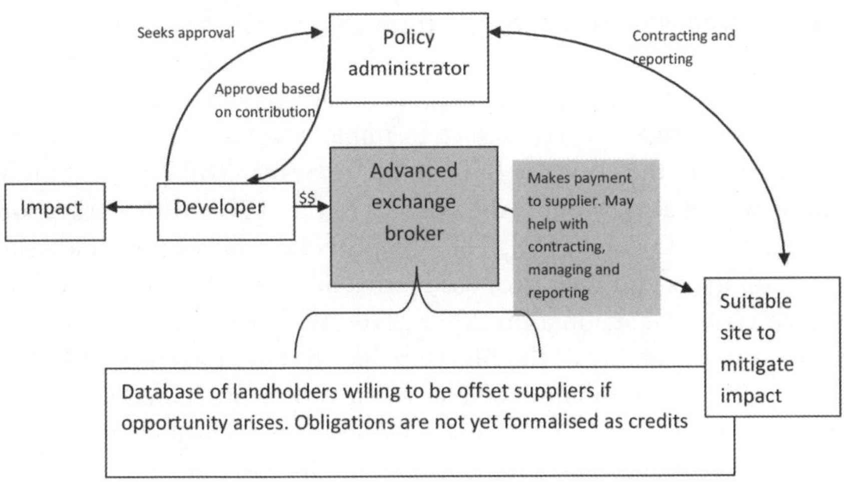

Figure 11.2: The advanced exchange broker

Source: Reprinted from Coggan *et al.* (2013b) with permission from Elsevier.

trust or obligation transfer to a broker, facilitates the use of an advanced exchange broker to assist in securing and finalising vegetation offsets. With an advanced exchange broker, developers can transfer the responsibility for securing an offset site to an additional party. The transfer of responsibility makes the advanced exchange broker different to an additional party generated due to an ILF system of offsets.

In some markets for environmental goods and services, exchange brokers have emerged due to high transaction costs, whilst in other markets, the creator of the market (government) has created exchange brokers to enhance the quality and quantity of exchanges. Exchange brokers have emerged organically in the US EPA's Emission Trading Program for criteria air pollutants (Stavins, 1995b) as well as in the RECLAIM market. Exchange brokers have also emerged organically in the water quantity trading markets in Australia (Productivity Commission, 2010) and are becoming increasingly involved in Australian-based biodiversity offset markets (Coggan *et al.*, 2013b, Wotherspoon and Burgin, 2009).

In some environmental markets, additional parties such as exchange brokers have been created by the market developer (usually government) to reduce the transaction costs and improve the quantity and quality of trade. The US New Jersey Pinelands transferable development rights scheme, where the government has taken a feeless brokerage role, is one such example (Stavins, 1995b). Another example from the US is the Bulletin Board System (BBS) of the South Coast Air Quality Monitoring District in the RECLAIM market for air quality (NOx and SOx). The BBS provides a list of potential sellers and buyers and their proposed terms of trade which reduces firm search costs (Gangadharan, 2004). Not all, however, are in agreement as to the ability of the BBS to reduce transaction costs (Ishikida *et al.*, 1998). Australian examples of Government created exchange brokers include the NSW BioBanking offset scheme, Victoria's BushBroker programme and EcoFund in Queensland.[4]

[4]More information on these schemes is available at www.environment.nsw.gov/biobanking/, www.depi.vic.gov.au (Bushbroker) and www.ecofund.org [All Accessed 7 December 2014].

11.3.3. *Bank*

A bank is an additional party who owns one or a number of environmental service supply sites and sells the services of these into one or many offset markets. The bank can be government organisations, private landholders, companies or non-government organisations with a specialist business focus to deliver offsets to multiple buyers or provide offsets to a single developer with multiple impacts (Fox and Nino-Murcia, 2005; Bendor and Brozovic, 2007) (Figure 11.3). One attractive feature of the bank in an offset market is that mitigation activities of the bank have at least commenced before the development impact, enabling a greater possibility of achieving the offset goal of no net impact of development in a timely fashion. In addition, because the bank owns the supply site, the bank takes on all the risk of delivering the environmental service which can further reduce transaction costs. In 2011, there were 90 active conservation banks in the US. At the same time there were 17 inactive banks and 19 banks which had been sold out (Madsen *et al.*, 2011).

11.3.4. *Additional party created from a system of ILF payments*

An ILF system operates by allowing a financial contribution by many parties to an additional party to cover the cost of the construction

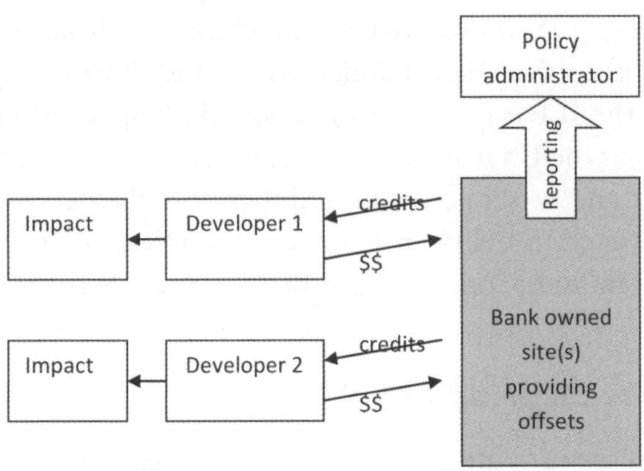

Figure 11.3: The bank form of additional party

Source: Reprinted from Coggan *et al.* (2013b) with permission from Elsevier.

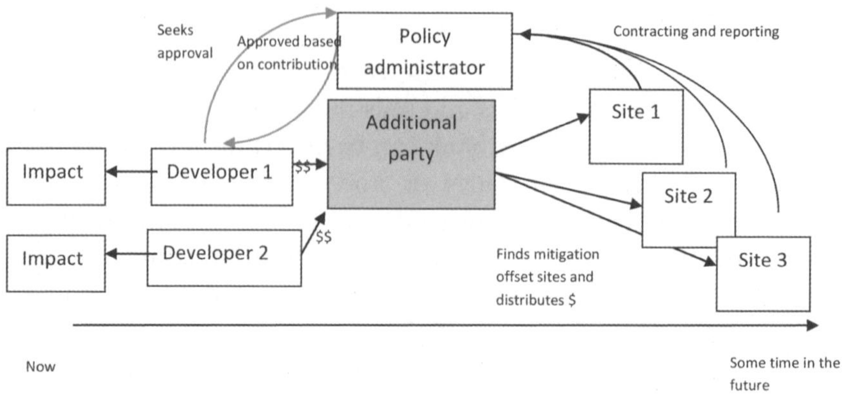

Figure 11.4: Additional party generated from ILF offsetting
Source: Reprinted from Coggan *et al.* (2013b) with permission from Elsevier.

and maintenance of privately owned future mitigation activities. In the case of the ILF, the additional party does not own the offset sites (which is the case of the bank form of additional party) but operates to find appropriate offset sites and manages the process to contract these as offset sites (Figure 11.4). The owners of the individual supply sites remain responsible for the delivery of the offset. By accepting payments from a suite of buyers, the ILF form of additional party can pool demand which can facilitate strategic investment resulting in increased environmental effectiveness, especially if environmental outcomes have minimum area requirements (such as the case with watershed protection, see Landell-Mills and Porras (2002)). One criticism of the ILF approach to manage the impact of development on wetlands in the US is the time lag that occurs between the development impact and offset activities and therefore the delayed ability for the ILF approach to deliver the no net loss objective of offset mitigation (Shabman and Scodari, 2004; Bendor and Brozovic, 2007).

11.3.5. *The clearing house*

Clearing houses provide transaction and settlement services to multiple transactors. This form of additional party is common in financial markets and is emerging as an additional party in environmental markets and especially for air quality credits (RECLAIM), water (the Idaho Clean Water Initiative for the Lower Boise River trading system)[5] and carbon trading (the proposed Emission Reduction Fund in Australia). The clearing house does not own property (and so it is different from a bank) but facilitates the process of trade for buyers and sellers often through one of two approaches.

The first operating approach of a clearing house may be by listing credits (standardised measures of improvements in native vegetation or carbon locked in by formalised agreements with government) and providing information which assists in the sale and settlement of credits (Figure 11.5). An example of this style of clearing house is the Native Vegetation Exchange (NVX) established to assist in vegetation offset trades under the Australian state of Victoria's Vegetation Management Framework (NVMF). For the NVX, all vegetation offset buyers and sellers are listed and a computer program finds the best vegetation match for a buyer or seller according to the Government's offset rules (Victorian Government Department of Sustainability and Environment, 2012). The second operating

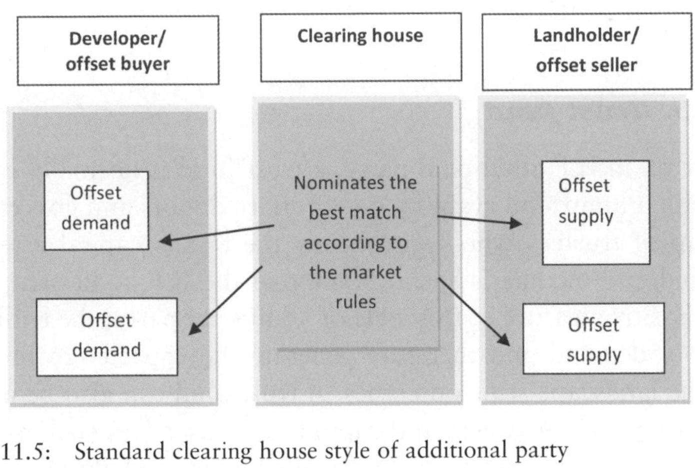

Figure 11.5: Standard clearing house style of additional party

Source: Reprinted from Coggan *et al.* (2013b) with permission from Elsevier.

[5] See www.envtn.org/Lower_Boise_River.html [Accessed 10 December 2012].

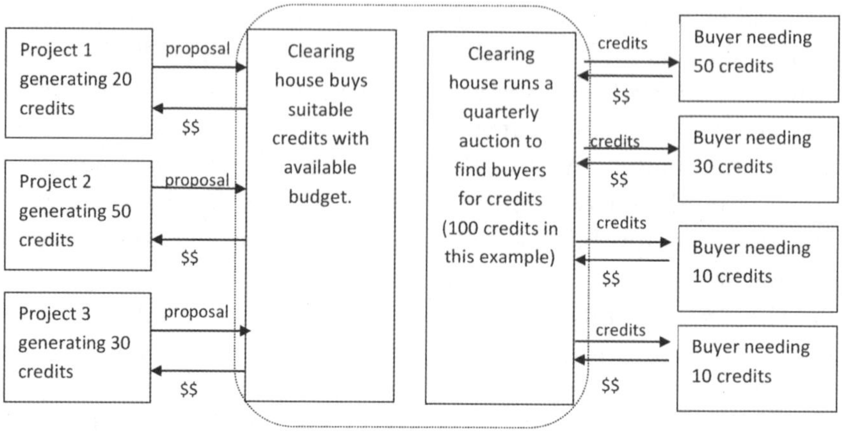

Figure 11.6: Clearing house with auction disposal of credits

approach common with clearing houses is to maintain an inventory of credits and hold an auction at regular intervals (quarterly or semi-annually) to discharge these credits to buyers (Figure 11.6). An example of this operating system is the Automated Environmental Credit Exchange, a joint venture with the Pacific Stock Exchange, operating within the RECLAIM market for air quality credits (Gangadharan, 2004).

11.3.6. *Trust fund*

Similar to an ILF additional party, a trust fund is normally capitalised with a lump sum grant by one or more donors and governed by a group of trustees who control how the trust's capital assets are managed and income is spent. Similar to the ILF additional party, and a positive feature of this style of additional party, the trust fund can pool demand and therefore generate the capacity to invest in strategic landscape scale outcomes. A trust fund can also be used as an intermediary to collect and capitalise on user fees such as is the case in watershed management (Landell-Mills and Porras, 2002). The trust may or may not own the conservation assets. Regardless of who owns the assets, it is common for a trust to pay an independent

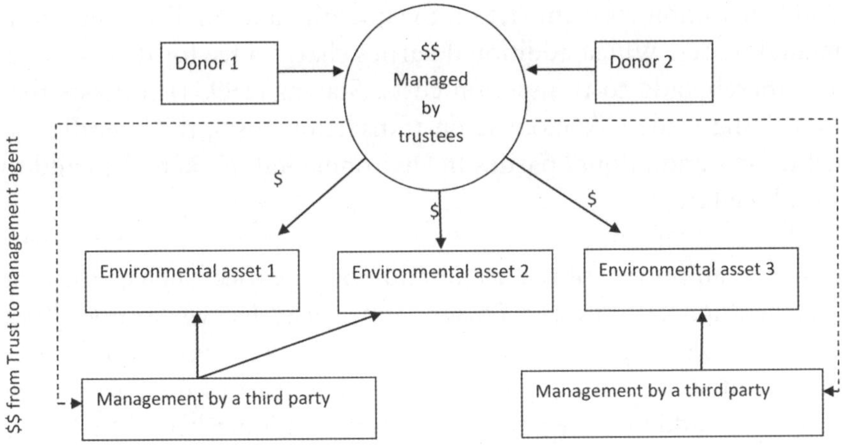

Figure 11.7: The Trust fund

third party to manage the physical assets (Figure 11.7). Trusts may be permanent, sinking, revolving or occur on- or off-shore. An example of a revolving trust fund is the Australian based Trust for Nature (www.trustfornature.org.au). This fund purchases land with conservation features on the open market, places legally binding conservation covenants on the land and re-sells the land on the open market. Profits from land sales go back into the revolving fund. The Trust for Nature is also operating as a standard and advanced exchange broker in the biodiversity offset market. Landell-Mills and Porras (2002) found that trust funds as additional parties were the most common form of intermediary used in biodiversity conservation exchanges.

11.4. Environmental Markets and the Future of Additional Parties

From the examples provided in this chapter it is clear that environmental markets are heavily influenced by parties additional to buyers and sellers of environmental goods and services. This indicates that traders in these markets continue to face high transaction costs and that transaction costs impact on the quantity and quality of environmental trades. Whilst additional parties charge a fee for their service, and thereby add to transaction costs, Stavins (1995a) suggests that by helping traders economise on transaction costs, the overall contribution of additional parties in environmental markets is to add to social welfare.

In some circumstances, government has created additional parties or is supportive of the use of additional parties (such as the case in vegetation offsetting in Queensland, Australia, where one offset option is to engage an additional party to broker or physically carry out the offset activities). There are two key reasons for government support of additional parties in environmental markets. The first is the fact that the use of additional parties in environmental markets may be a more cost-effective option to achieving trades and environmental outcomes compared to the cost of designing a market with lower transaction costs to the first-party traders. The second reason is the potential for additional parties to be able to achieve landscape scale outcomes from trades and therefore better environmental outcomes in the long run. This ability is highlighted by the evolution of wetland offsetting in the US. Initially developers requiring offsets under the *Clean Water Act* (1972) were required to make 'site specific' offset trades. When this was found to be resulting in an outcome that was less than the desired 'no net impact', the 1995 Wetland Mitigation Banking Guidelines were introduced which actively encourage the use of large scale established banks for wetland offsetting (Madsen *et al.*, 2011).

Given the ongoing interest in market based solutions to environmental problems and the fact that these markets are likely to continue to operate with high transaction costs; it would appear that the use of additional parties in environmental markets is set to continue. The nature of the additional party demanded by traders may vary over time as traders and markets mature. A first-party trader may only need to use information providers or standard exchange brokers for one-off or sporadic trades or if they are new to an environmental market. However, if these first-party traders find themselves making many trades to meet environmental obligations, a different type of additional party (perhaps a trust fund or bank) may be more cost-effective.

Bibliography

Allen, D. (1999). 'Transaction Costs', in Bouckaert, B. and De Geest, G. (eds.), *Encyclopedia of Law and Economics*, Edward Elgar, Cheltenham, pp. 893–926.

Barzel, Y. (1985). Transaction Costs: Are they Just Costs? *Journal of Institutional and Theoretical Economics*, 141, pp. 4–16.

Benassi, M. and Di Minin, A. (2009). Playing in Between: Patent Brokers in Markets for Technology, *R&D Management*, 39, pp. 68–86.

Bendor, T. and Brozovic, N. (2007). Determinants of Spatial and Temporal Patterns in Compensatory Wetland Mitigation, *Environmental Management*, 40, pp. 349–364.

Claassen, R., Cattaneo, A. and Johansson, R. (2008). Cost-Effective Design of Agri-Environmental Payment Programs: US Experience in Theory and Practice, *Ecological Economics*, 69, pp. 1777–1784.

Coase, R.H. (1960). The Problem of Social Cost, *Journal of Law and Economics*, 3, pp. 1–44.

Coggan, A., Buitelaar, E., Whitten, S.M. and Bennett, J. (2013a). Factors that Influence Transaction Costs in Development Offsets: Who Bears What And Why? *Ecological Economics*, 88, pp. 222–231.

Coggan, A., Buitelaar, E., Whitten, S.M. and Bennett, J. (2013b). Intermediaries in Environmental Offset Markets: Actions and Incentives, *Land Use Policy*, 32, pp. 145–154.

Fox, J. and Nino-Murcia, A. (2005). Status of Species Conservation Banking in the United States, *Conservation Biology*, 19, pp. 996–1007.

Gangdaharan, L. (2000). Transaction Costs in Pollution Markets: An Empirical Study, *Land Economics*, 76, pp. 601–614.

Gangadharan, L. (2004). Analysis of Prices in Tradable Emission Markets: An Empirical Study of the Regional Clean Air Incentives Market in Los Angeles, *Applied Economics*, 36, pp. 1569–1582.

Hahn, F. (1987). Economic Prescriptions for Environmental Problems: How the Patient Followed the Doctor's Orders, *Journal of Economic Perspectives*, 3, pp. 95–114.

Hahn, F. and Hester, G.L. (1989a). Where did all the Markets Go? An Analysis of EPA's Emissions Trading Program, *Yale Journal of Regulation*, 1, pp. 63–91.

Hahn, R.W. and Hester, G.L. (1989b). Marketable Permits: Lessons for Theory and Practice, *Ecology Law Quarterly*, 16, pp. 361–409.

Hahn, R.W. and Stavins, R.N. (1992). Economic Incentives For Environmental-Protection — Integrating Theory And Practice, *American Economic Review*, 82, pp. 464–468.

Ishikida, T., Ledyard, J., Porter, D. and Olson, M. (1998). *Implementation of a Combinatorial Market. The Experiments Behind the Automated-Environmental Credit Exchange (ACE)*, California Institute of Technology, California.

Jack, B.K., Kousky, C. and Sims, K.R.E. (2008). Designing Payments for Ecosystem Services: Lessons From Previous Experience With Incentive-Based Mechanisms, *Proceedings of the National Academy of Sciences of the United States of America*, 105, pp. 9465–9470.

King, D. and Kuch, P. (2003). Will Nutrient Credit Trading Ever Work? An Assessment of Supply and Demand Problems and Institutional Obstacles, *Environmental Law Reporter*, 33, pp. 10353–10368.

Landell-Mills, N. and Porras, I. (2002). Silver Bullet or Fools Gold? A Global Review of Markets for Forest Environmental Services and Their Impact on the Poor. *Instruments for Sustainable Private Sector Forestry Series*, International Institute for Environment and Development, London.

Madsen, B., Carroll, N., Kandy, D. and Bennett, G. (2011). *Update: State of Biodiversity Markets*, Forest Trends, Washington, DC.

Marshall, G. (2013). Transaction Costs, Collective Action and Adaptation in Managing Complex Social-Ecological Systems, *Ecological Economics*, 88, pp. 185–194.

McCann, L., Colby, B., Easter, K.W., Kasterine, A. and Kuperan, K.V. (2005). Transaction Cost Measurement for Evaluating Environmental Policies, *Ecological Economics*, 52, pp. 527–542.

Niehans, J. (1971). Money and Barter in General Equilibrium with Transaction Costs, *American Economic Review*, 61, pp. 773–783.

Pirard, R. (2012). Market-Based Instruments for Biodiversity and Ecosystem Services: A Lexicon, *Environmental Science and Policy*, 19–20, pp. 59–68.

Pollock, T., Porac, J. and Wade, J. (2004). Constructing Deal Networks: Brokers as Network 'Architects' in the US IPO Market and other Examples, *Academy of Management Review*, 29, pp. 50–72.

Productivity Commission (2010). *Market Mechanisms for Recovering Water in the Murray–Darling Basin, Final Report*, March, Canberra.

Queensland Government (2011). *Policy for Vegetation Management Offsets*, Department of Enviroment and Resource Management (DERM), Brisbane.

Shabman, L. and Scodari, P. (2004). 'Past, Present and Future of Wetland Credits Sales', *Discussion Paper 04–48*, Resources for the Future, Washington.

Stavins, R. (1995a). Transaction Costs and Markets for Pollution Control, *Resources*, Spring, pp. 9–20.

Stavins, R. (1995b). Transaction Costs and Tradeable Permits, *Journal of Environmental Economics and Management*, 29, pp. 133–148.

Stavins, R. (2003a). 'Experience with Market-Based Environmental Policy Instruments', in Maler, K. G. and Vincent, J.R. (eds.), *Handbook of Environmental Economics Volume 1*, Elsevier, Amsterdam, pp. 355–435.

Stavins, R. (2003b). 'Market-Based Environmental Policies: What Can We Learn From US Experience (and Related Research)?' *Discussion Paper 03–43*. Resources for the Future, Washington.

Victorian Government Department of Sustainability and Environment (2012). *Native Vegetation Exchange Trial: Landholder Frequently Asked Questions*, Melbourne.

Wang, N. (2007). Measuring Transaction Costs: Diverging Approaches, Contending Practices, *Division of Labour and Transaction Costs*, 2, pp. 111–146.

Woodward, R.T. and Kaiser, R.A. (2002). Market Structures for US Water Quality Trading, *Review of Agricultural Economics*, 24, pp. 366–383.

Woodward, R.T., Kaiser, R.A. and Wicks, A.-M.B. (2002). The Structure and Practice of Water Quality Trading Markets, *Journal of the American Water Resources Association*, 38, pp. 967–979.

Wotherspoon, D. and Burgin, S. (2009). The Consultant Ecologist's Role in the New South Wales (Australia) Approach to Biodiversity Offsets: "BioBanking", *Local Environment: The International Journal of Justice and Sustainability*, 14, pp. 61–71.

Ziegelbaeck, M. and Breuer, G. (2014). The Role of Market Makers in the Euronext Milling Wheat Contract, *Agricultural Economics (AGRICECON)*, 60, pp. 183–187.

12. Using Auctions for Conservation: The Australian Experience[1]

John Rolfe

12.1. Introduction

As in other Western countries, there have been substantial public concerns expressed in Australia about environmental losses and damages over the past 40 years. Most community and political attention has been focused on issues where there are immediate and directly consequential losses from human activity, such as the clearing of forests or losses of healthy waterways. Solving these issues involves decisions about which assets to protect, and the level of protection to provide. However, as environmental protection has become a more mainstream goal of society and government, an emerging issue of increasing importance is the selection of the mechanisms to employ to achieve the desired levels of protection.

[1] This chapter draws on the review by Rolfe, Whitten and Windle (2015). An earlier version of this chapter was presented at the 'Conservation Tenders in Developed and Developing Countries — *Status Quo*, Challenges and Prospects' Workshop in Boppard, Germany, in September 2013.

There are a number of different types of mechanisms that can be used to achieve environmental protection. For convenience, these can be summarised into four main groups: information and persuasion mechanisms; regulation; changes in property rights; and incentives (both positive and negative). There are several reasons why the choice of mechanism is important. Key reasons include variations between instruments in terms of effectiveness, opportunity and transaction costs, opportunities for free-riding, compliance effort, perverse incentives, and requirements for specialised knowledge. While regulatory mechanisms provide greater certainty about outcomes, they can also involve high administration and compliance costs, as well as generating adverse reactions and perverse outcomes. In contrast voluntary mechanisms tend to be better accepted but require more attention to design to ensure that targeted changes in behaviour and outcomes are achieved.

Achieving biodiversity protection on private lands can be difficult. Much biodiversity occurs on agricultural lands where management practices can have both positive and negative effects, but where there are large variations in the natural environment, agricultural production and the interactions between them. This means that the cost effectiveness of changing management practices can vary widely. While there may be public benefits to be achieved from improved conservation, the existence of private property rights, the difficulties of designing and enforcing regulatory mechanisms, and the political issues with imposing restrictions that generate private opportunity costs have led policy makers to consider voluntary approaches to generating improved environmental outcomes (Hanley *et al.*, 2012).

There are five broad types of voluntary mechanisms that are available to increase biodiversity conservation on private agricultural lands: mechanisms that change attitudes (e.g., education programmes); mechanisms that improve information (e.g., extension programmes); mechanisms that improve technology (e.g., research programmes); mechanisms that provide incentives to change behaviour (e.g., grants programmes); and hybrids of voluntary and regulatory programmes known as Market-based Instruments (MBI), with the latter group including conservation tenders and auctions. The two incentive-based groups (grants and conservation tenders), which provide financial incentives to landholders to change management and conservation practices, are known collectively as 'agri-environmental schemes', with the most prominent example being the Conservation Reserve Program (CRP) in the United States.

Incentive mechanisms have become popular in Australia to improve biodiversity conservation on private agricultural lands through the allocation of public funds. The Landcare programme was established in 1989 and provided small-scale funding support to landholders through a multitude of local cooperatives. This was supplemented in the mid-1990s by a move to 56 regional scale catchment management authorities or natural resource management (NRM) groups across Australia which ran conservation programmes and allocated public funds (Hajkowicz, 2009). While increasing the scale of funding programmes is likely to have reduced average administration costs, the use of simple grant mechanisms focused on input measures remained the same, so the cost-effectiveness of these funding programmes continued to be questioned (e.g., Pannell and Roberts, 2010).

In an effort to improve the efficiency of public funding mechanisms, conservation auctions were developed in Australia to address the problems of asymmetric information and cost-effective bid selection simultaneously. The first major conservation tender with public funds was the BushTender programme conducted in 2000–2001 to protect areas of native vegetation on private property in Victoria (Stoneham *et al.*, 2003). Since then, there has been substantial public investment, research and interest in these types of auctions to allocate public funding for environmental outcomes more efficiently (Hajkowicz, 2009). The range of approaches that has been used across a number of conservation tenders for a range of different environmental goods provides natural test conditions to identify how conservation tenders can be designed and conducted efficiently.

This chapter provides a review of conservation auctions that have been held in Australia between 2001 and 2012, and is structured as follows. A brief review of the underlying theory is provided in the next section, followed by an overview of the use of conservation tenders to protect biodiversity in Australia. This is followed in section four with an assessment of their design and performance, together with an evaluation of the key insights that have been generated.

12.2. Theoretical Background for Conservation Auctions

Conservation auctions involve competition for public funds, and are sometimes called conservation procurement auctions, conservation tenders or reverse auctions. The theoretical base for conservation auctions has been set out by Latacz-Lohmann and Van der Hamsvoort (1997, 1998) and Cason and Gangadharan (2004), with design and application issues described by Stoneham *et al.* (2003), Engel, Pagiola and Wunder (2008), Ferraro (2008) and Hanley *et al.* (2012) among others. Many reviewers have treated conservation auctions as a specialised case of Payments for Ecosystem Services (e.g., Engel, Pagiola and Wunder, 2008) or mechanisms to incentivise landholders (e.g., Hanley *et al.*, 2012), although many case study applications have focused more explicitly on conservation auctions.

The purpose of a conservation auction is to identify and secure the most cost-effective proposals for biodiversity protection and address problems of asymmetric information and complexity (Latacz-Lohmann and van der Hamsvoort, 1997, 1998; Cason and Gangadharan, 2004; Latacz-Lohmann and Schilizzi, 2005; Schilizzi and Latacz-Lohmann, 2013). In agricultural systems, asymmetric information occurs in two main ways. In the first, landholders have very specialised information about their enterprise and the potential changes in production and profitability that might be associated with management changes that public policy makers do not share. In the second, public policy makers may have specialised information about the biodiversity assets that need to be protected and the weight of community preferences for this to occur, that landholders do not share. Complexity arises because of variation in both agricultural systems and biodiversity assets, as well as the diversity of management actions and production system changes that can be used to improve protection. As the private costs and public benefits of conservation actions are poorly, if at all, correlated, it is difficult for policy makers to allocate public funds effectively unless some mechanism to identify appropriate policies and private costs can be identified.

A public procurement auction involves the public policy makers specifying the biodiversity assets and management actions of interest, with landholders submitting tenders reflecting their opportunity costs of supply plus a profit premium (bid-shading) (Schilizzi and Latacz-Lohmann, 2013). In a typical programme, landholders are invited to submit tenders to provide inputs or generate conservation outputs, each proposal is evaluated to identify the biodiversity and other benefits involved, the benefits are then summed into an overall benefits score, and then proposals are ranked by the ratio of the overall benefits score to the landholder bid amount. Funding can then be allocated to the most cost-effective proposals up to the point where the available funds are exhausted or some threshold rule is breached. The tender mechanism is essentially a one-sided auction with a single buyer and many sellers (hence the term procurement auction), so the standard theoretical basis for conservation tenders is in auction theory (Latacz-Lohmann and Van der Hamsvoort, 1997, 1998; Cason and Gangadharan, 2004).

Conservation auctions solve the twin problems of asymmetric information and complexity. The programme specification by the public policy makers addresses the second asymmetric information problem, and the revelation of private opportunity costs through the submission of bids addresses the first. The bid-shading (profit margin) provides an incentive for landholders to participate, but competition limits any excessive capture of rents by landholders. The call for proposals together with the profit motive provides an incentive for landholders to search for and nominate the most cost-effective means of achieving the required outcomes, addressing the complexity issue. Auctions for conservation outputs provide on-going incentives for landholders to search for innovations in management and provision, generating future gains and efficiencies. In this way, conservation auctions replicate both the market discovery process that matches buyers and sellers as well as the innovation incentives that generate economic progress.

Three major advantages of competitive auctions over fixed rate grants that are typical of many agri-environmental schemes can be identified (Latacz-Lohmann and van der Hamsvoort, 1998). The first is that issues of asymmetric information are reduced, the second is that the landholder bids are more likely to reflect the marginal value of the resources being used to produce the environmental outcome, and the third is that competition between landholders reduces the scope for rent-seeking bids. These advantages mean that competitive auctions are likely to be much more cost-effective than grant schemes at improving conservation on private lands (Latacz-Lohmann and van der Hamsvoort, 1997, 1998; Connor, Ward and Bryan, 2008; Windle and Rolfe, 2008; Rolfe, Windle and McCosker, 2009, Rolfe *et al.*, 2011). In other words, using conservation auctions allows more biodiversity to be protected for a given amount of public funds.

Within this broad theoretical framework, substantial opportunities exist to vary elements in the design, application and performance of conservation auctions. There are three key areas where application and performance can vary significantly: (a) the auction process (b) the evaluation of bids, usually through a 'metric' to summarise the biodiversity and other benefits and (c) the contract process, which captures the operation and enforcement of agreements with landholders once the successful bids have been selected. The involvement of human participants means that issues of knowledge gaps, learning effects, strategic behaviour, reactions to risk and uncertainty, perverse incentives and rent-seeking are potential behavioural issues that have to be considered, alongside the difficulties of ensuring landholder participation in often thin markets. On the administration or engagement side, variations in technical knowledge, administration capacity and engagement skills also exist. Together with the variation between case study situations, these factors mean that there are many reasons why conservation auctions may differ. Some elements of a competitive auction, such as those around landholder engagement and contracts, parallel tasks in a fixed grant and other payment-for-ecosystem schemes, so some reviews (e.g., Engel, Pagiola and Wunder, 2008; Hanley *et al.*, 2012) have covered the broader family of schemes to identify preferred options.

Drawing on auction theory for risk averse bidders, most designers of conservation auctions have focused on discriminatory, single round mechanisms (Latacz-Lohmann and Van der Hamsvoort, 1997; Stoneham *et al.*, 2003). The selection of discriminatory rather than uniform price bids means that successful bidders do not receive any surplus on top of their bid amounts, and that more can be purchased for a set amount of public funds. Holding only single round auctions means that bidders have incentives to reveal their true opportunity costs as they only have one bid opportunity. However, these designs rely on some key assumptions. The first is that bidders have close to perfect knowledge about their opportunity costs, as identified in the 'independent private values model' suggested by Latacz-Lohmann and van der Hamsvoort (1997) and Stoneham *et al.* (2003). Second, bidders do not learn how to behave strategically, as could occur in repeated or poorly designed auctions. Third, landholder proposals can be created independently from other bids.

Designing conservation tenders for agricultural producers provide very different challenges to other auction mechanisms (Rolfe, Windle and McCosker, 2009; Rolfe *et al.*, 2011). First, for most landholders, changing management systems to generate additional environmental benefits is peripheral to their production focus, and they may have limited understanding or interest in the trade-offs involved. Second, conservation auctions are an unfamiliar process, so there may be large uncertainties around bid construction, auction participation and contractual arrangements. Third, conservation auctions can be complicated by requirements to strategically align landholder proposals (e.g., for vegetation corridors) or ensure that threshold levels are reached (e.g., for species protection). Fourth, spatial factors often limit the number of landholders that can provide specific outcomes, leading to problems of thin markets or strategic holdouts. These factors mean that as well as meeting the standard challenges of auction, metric and contract design, designers of conservation auctions also have to generate adequate levels of landholder participation and ensure that landholders can construct bids accurately.

12.3. Overview of the Use of Conservation Auctions in Australia

From the late 1990s, Australian governments have provided significant investments into improved environmental management in agricultural areas, with a focus on the use of positive financial incentives and the formation of NRM groups to facilitate programmes and funding (Hajkowicz, 2009). By 2006–2007, general environmental expenditure by the Australian Government was $4b per annum (Hajkowicz, 2009), with funds allocated through strategic investments to protect biodiversity, limit weeds and pests, and address issues of salinity, soil erosion and nutrient movement.

It was during the period of rapid growth in public expenditures from the late 1990s that conservation auctions began to be applied, in part because of recognition that previous grant programmes were ineffectual or expensive (Stoneham *et al.*, 2003; Pannell and Roberts, 2010), or poorly scoped and targeted (Hajkowicz, 2009). Reasons for trialling auction mechanisms over fixed grant programmes have included a desire to improve the efficiency of the funding allocation process (Stoneham *et al.*, 2003), to improve participation and attract different groups of landholders, to provide incentives to search for efficiencies and to identify the opportunity costs for landholders to make management changes (Rolfe *et al.*, 2011).

The BushTender programme in Victoria in 2000 was the first major conservation auction scheme in Australia. It involved landholders in two regional areas being invited to submit proposals and bids to protect areas of native vegetation on their property (Stoneham *et al.*, 2003). The programme was widely viewed as innovative and successful, particularly because of the novel approach used to sum biodiversity benefits, the ranking of proposals in terms of cost-effectiveness, and the efficiency gains over a fixed grant approach.[2] As a result of this outcome, and concurrent with the large increase in public expenditure on environmental and conservation programmes, there was substantial interest in the use of conservation auctions and MBI more generally in Australia. In the following 12 years, approximately 60 different conservation tenders were conducted, most differing according to scale, purpose and funding source (Rolfe, Whitten and Windle, 2015). They are summarised in the following subsections, grouped by whether the focus of the different trials was to generate research knowledge, address a national priority, or address state or regional-level priorities.

12.3.1. *Research focused tenders*

As a part of the development process for large public funding programmes, there has been significant research attention on conservation auctions, largely through two federally funded MBI programmes. The research projects within these programmes spanned a number of environmental issues and potential control mechanisms, including a subset of conservation auctions. The first MBI programme ran from 2003 to 2005, and four of the projects were focused specifically on designing and testing conservation auctions (Grafton, 2005; Rolfe, Whitten and Windle, 2015):

- The 'Multiple-outcome auction of land use change' project extended the BushTender auction approach to include salinity, water quality, water quantity and biodiversity in the Goulbourn-Broken catchment in Victoria.
- The 'Auction for Landscape Recovery' project provided incentives for addressing diffuse source salinity and biodiversity outcomes against a regional biodiversity target in the Avon catchment in Western Australia.

---

[2] Stoneham *et al.* (2003) estimated that the conservation auction generated 25 per cent more biodiversity than a comparable fixed grants approach. Note, though, that a counterfactual to compare conservation auctions with fixed grants is difficult to establish precisely (Schilizzi and Latacz-Lohmann, 2007).

- The 'Catchment Care' project tested the use of conservation auctions by a regional NRM body in the Onkaparinga catchment in South Australia.
- The 'Desert Uplands' project tested the use of experimental workshops to generate coordinating bids for vegetation corridors in central-western Queensland.

Another four major research projects on conservation auctions were conducted in the second round of MBI from 2006 to 2008 (GHD 2009; Rolfe, Whitten and Windle, 2015):

- The 'Catchment Care' project in the Onkaparinga catchment tested different environmental benefit measures and auction design formats.
- The 'Bird-nesting project' in the New South Wales Murray Catchment tested the effectiveness of outcome-based contracts over input-based contracts.
- The 'Auction for landscape recovery' project in Western Australia extended the initial pilot to consider the effects of uncertainty and incomplete information.
- The 'Conservation tenders in the Burdekin' project in Queensland explored the trade-offs between the scope of a project and effects on landholder participation.

Evaluations of both MBI programmes were conducted: Round One by Grafton (2005) and Round Two by GHD (2009). The review process identified more caution emerging about conservation auctions over time. The results of the first round of MBI projects identified that not only were conservation auctions much more cost effective than fixed payment schemes and regulations, but they appeared to be more cost effective than other types of MBI that were tested (Cap-and-trade schemes, offsets, conservation insurance and leverage funds) (Grafton, 2005). As well, conservation auctions were preferred because of their fit with existing policy settings of positive incentives to change landholder behaviour (Grafton, 2005). However, the review of the second round of MBI projects was more circumspect. GHD (2009) noted that MBI (including auctions) needed to be designed and tailored to each specific case study, that more attention needed to be given to the underlying institutional framework, and that it was difficult to demonstrate that MBI were more efficient than other policy approaches.

12.3.2. *Programmes run by the Australian Government*

Concurrent with the conduct of the major research trials into market based instruments, the Australian Government led three separate programmes to conserve biodiversity with conservation auctions. The first of these, the Tasmanian Forest Conservation Fund, was established in 2005 to enhance conservation of old-growth and under-reserved forests on private land. Funding rounds were held over two years, with three separate rounds in the first year and one funding round alongside direct offers to landholders and a fixed price scheme in the second year. By the close of the programme in 2009 there were 88 successful bids for a total contracted area of 13,779 ha. Marsden Jacob and Associates or MJA (2010) reported that average bid prices increased during the rounds and appeared in the second year to be benchmarked by the concurrent fixed price offer, raising issues about programme design and the measurement of efficiency gains in repeated rounds.

In 2007, the Australian Government established the Environmental Stewardship Program through the major 'Caring for Country' initiative. The programme was designed to operate as a series of conservation tenders for specific high-value environmental assets where landholders would be contracted for up to 15 years to manage and preserve targeted areas. There have been four major environmental systems focused on to date: box-gum grassy woodlands in eastern Australia; multiple ecological communities in the central-west of New South Wales; peppermint box grassy woodland and iron-grass natural temperate grassland areas in regions of South Australia; and swamps of the Fleurieu Peninsula in South Australia. The box-gum grassy woodlands have received the most attention, with five funding rounds in 2008–2009 and 2009–2010, while the New South Wales ecological communities had only one funding round in 2010–2011, and the two South Australian projects both had funding rounds in 2010–2011 and 2011–2012.

In 2007 the Australian Government also established the Biodiversity Hotspots programme, with some funding allocated for stewardship payments for landholders that were to be allocated through a tender process. Most activity has been for the Mt Lofty initiative in South Australia through the 'Bush Bids' programme, where a conservation tender has been run over a five-year period.

12.3.3. *State and regional level programmes*

The majority of conservation auctions have been run by state governments or regional organisations.[3] Rolfe, Whitten and Windle (2015) identified 16 separate programmes that have been established, involving more than 50 separate conservation auctions. Most programmes have held multiple auctions in different regions, for different environmental goods, or over time. For example, the BushTender programme in Victoria involved 16 separate programmes held between 2001 and 2012, targeting different areas of native vegetation in regions of the State, while the Wimmera Catchment Management Authority in Victoria ran 12 conservation tenders from 2006 to 2012 involving a range of programmes, including River Tender, Habitat Tender and Buloke Tender. Some programmes only involved a single auction, such as the conservation auction to establish a vegetation corridor across the Desert Uplands in Queensland in 2006 (Rolfe, Windle and McCosker, 2009), but most, such as the Vegetation Incentives Program in Queensland, the Owens River Tender in Victoria, the Murray River Forest Tender in South Australia, the Liverpool Plains tenders in New South Wales and the Bush Returns programme in Victoria involved two or three separate auctions (Rolfe, Whitten and Windle, 2015).

[3] Details on many of these are available at: http://www.marketbasedinstruments.gov.au/ [Accessed 7 November 2014].

12.4. Discussion

12.4.1. *Design*

The majority of conservation tenders conducted used a discriminatory, sealed, single round bidding format, although some important variations on auction design can be identified from the Australian case studies. The first involves multiple bidding round auctions, which are often needed to coordinate actions from landholders across landscapes (Reeson *et al.*, 2011). Rolfe, Windle and McCosker (2009) report for the Desert Uplands vegetation corridor project that (a) multiple bidding rounds (three rounds) were held within the one auction; and, (b) participants were given some information about the location of other bids between bidding rounds to help encourage better linkage of vegetation corridors. Other variations on design include auctions based on outcomes to focus better on end-goals rather than input actions, the use of two-part bidding rewards with the use of involvement fees or contract bonuses to stimulate participation, and inclusion of multiple objectives in single auctions, including in combinatorial tenders.

The largest variation between conservation tenders in Australia relates to the associated metrics used to evaluate the bids, where there has been substantial experimentation around different bid structures and elements. Hajkowicz (2009) suggests that it is the use of metrics to quantify benefits that is one of the most clearly distinguishing features of conservation auctions compared to the more common grant schemes. One reason for the variation in metric design is the range of different environmental assets and outcomes that have been targeted, sometimes in a single auction process (e.g., Eigenraam *et al.*, 2007). Other reasons for variations are that metrics vary according to whether inputs, outputs or outcomes are being assessed, or whether the risks and uncertainties involved are accounted for in some way. For example, the benefits that are expected may be weighted to account for different risks and likelihoods that outcomes will be generated from the input actions that are to occur.

Metrics can be further differentiated by the design of predictive functions that Whitten *et al.* (2012) categorise into three groups. The first are based on condition indices, where the base score is given by an assessment of the vegetation of interest, and then other factors to account for management actions are included through additive or multiplicative processes. The Habitat Hectares score reported in Stoneham *et al.* (2003) provides an example of this approach. The second involves some form of multi-criteria based indices, where different elements are scored and then combined with weightings to generate a summary measure (e.g., Hajkowicz *et al.*, 2007). These are typically used to assess bids with multiple objectives. The third involves expected values, where there is more explicit focus on assessing the likelihood of future outcomes. These are more appropriate for outcome-based measures. All of these metric approaches have limitations because the benefits are assessed with arbitrary indices rather than some economic measure of the community values for the benefits; this restricts the approaches to some form of a cost-effectiveness measure rather than an assessment of the economic efficiency of the investments.

Contracts are the formal agreements that are required to ensure that all actions and payments occur. Hajkowicz (2009) notes that contracts for conservation tenders tend to be much more specific about the actions and inputs or outputs required than general grants programmes. Much of the attention on contract design has focused on the regulatory and institutional challenges in contracting for longer term agreements, and the effects of different contracting arrangements on incentives to participate (Comerford, 2013). The evidence is mixed: Moon and Cocklin (2011) and Comerford (2013) report that landholders involved in agricultural production prefer short-term conservation contracts over covenants or other restrictions on title and that non-producing landholders preferred the use of covenants and longer term mechanisms, while Miles (2008) and Blackmore and Doole (2013) reported that landholders preferred medium term contracts over short-term contracts.

12.4.2. *Performance*

The performance of conservation auctions in Australia can be assessed in a number of ways. Rolfe, Whitten and Windle (2015) note two important patterns when the location and timing of auctions are mapped across the country. First, although auctions have been conducted in all States in Australia, about half have occurred in Victoria. Second, the distribution over time shows a gradual increase in activity from the two BushTender auctions in 2001 to 2010 auctions in both 2009 and 2010, followed by a rapid decline to only one in 2012. Given the time required to support and design an auction, Rolfe, Whitten and Windle (2015) suggest that the real peak in support and funding occurred around 2007 and 2008, and hypothesise that the waning of support since then can be explained by changing governments and political imperatives. Other reasons may be that the difficulties of achieving high participation rates and the specialised design and management required for successful implementation have reduced bureaucratic support for these mechanisms.

While the number of conservation auctions that have been held in Australia is large relative to international comparisons, only a very small proportion of public funds allocated for environmental purposes has been allocated through auctions. Rolfe, Whitten and Windle (2015) estimate that approximately \$36m was allocated through conservation tenders in Australia between 2001 and 2012, assuming average expenditure per auction of \$623,000, while Doole, Blackmore and Schilizzi (2013) suggested that total expenditure could be as high as \$200m over that time period. Whatever the correct amount, they are very small compared to the estimates of annual public expenditure on agri-environmental schemes of more than \$1b per annum (Hajkowicz, 2009). On this basis, allocations through auction processes may amount to less than one per cent of public funding available for conservation purposes. This, together with the waning of activity, suggests that there has been limited attention in mainstream conservation programmes in Australia on efforts to improve the cost-effectiveness of programme allocations.

Attention has also been paid to the improvements in economic efficiency that have been generated by the use of conservation auctions over simpler grant mechanisms and other payment mechanisms. While almost all studies identify gains in cost-effectiveness, direct comparisons between conservation auctions and grant mechanisms are difficult to perform, so research evidence has been pursued in three main ways. One stream of analysis has focused on identifying heterogeneity in bid values and environmental benefits (e.g., Stoneham *et al.*, 2003; Connor, Ward and Bryan, 2008; MJA, 2010; Rolfe *et al.*, 2011; Rolfe and Windle, 2011b), as large variations in opportunity costs to produce environmental services indicates that substantial economic benefits can be gained from selecting projects on the basis of cost-effectiveness. A second stream of evidence relates to the potential variation in project selection between competitive tenders and other mechanisms; Rolfe and Windle (2011a) demonstrate that ranking by cost-effectiveness generates benefits over more traditional scorecard approaches. A third stream of evidence focuses on the cost effectiveness of different approaches such as between discriminatory and uniform pricing (e.g., Stoneham *et al.*, 2003; Cason and Gangadharan, 2005; Connor, Ward and Bryan, 2008; Rolfe and Windle, 2011a). However, it has proved difficult to assess accurately the cost-effectiveness of conservation auctions over grant schemes because it is difficult to establish an accurate counterfactual (Schilizzi and Latacz-Lohmann, 2007). Different schemes may attract different bids from landholders, and conservation tenders typically have higher design, assessment and administration costs because of the scientific assessment process (Lowell *et al.*, 2007).

12.5. Conclusions

The review provided in this chapter, as well as the more detailed evidence in Rolfe, Whitten and Windle (2015), show that while there have been substantial opportunities to use conservation auctions in Australia to improve the cost-effectiveness of public funds allocated to conservation works, the amount of use is small and in decline.

This is despite substantial evidence that conservation auctions deliver cost-effectiveness gains over simpler direct funding and grants schemes.

The limited role that conservation auctions have for allocating expenditure for environmental issues is puzzling. Some of the potential reasons include concerns by policy makers about the design skills needed to assess biophysical outcomes rigorously and to manage auction processes in thin markets. There may also be issues with the perceptions of government and catchment bodies about administration costs, transaction costs and competitive processes. A further reason may be that understanding of the cost-effectiveness gains may be limited, particularly when there is very little analysis of the cost-effectiveness of other grant mechanisms available for comparison. Public choice theory provides a final group of issues to canvass. Decision makers might not care about improving the efficiency of public spending, and have concerns about the transparency and loss of control that competitive auctions might bring to the process.

Bibliography

Blackmore, L. and Doole, G. (2013). Drivers of Landholder Participation in Tender Programs for Australian Biodiversity Conservation, *Environmental Science and Policy*, 33, pp. 143–153.

Cason, T. and Gangadharan, L. (2004). Auction Design for Voluntary Conservation Programmes, *American Journal of Agricultural Economics*, 86, pp. 1211–1217.

Cason, T. and Gangadharan, L. (2005). A Laboratory Comparison of Uniform and Discriminative Price Auctions for Reducing Non-Point Source Pollution, *Land Economics*, 81, pp. 51–70.

Comerford, E. (2013). The Impact of Permanent Protection on Cost and Participation in a Conservation Programme: A Case Study, *Land Use Policy*, 34, pp. 176–182.

Connor, J.D., Ward, J.R. and Bryan, B. (2008). Exploring the Cost Effectiveness of Land Conservation Auctions and Payment Policies, *Australian Journal of Agricultural and Resource Economics*, 42, pp. 303–319.

Doole, G., Blackmore, L. and Schilizzi, S. (2013). Determinants of Cost-Effectiveness in Tender and Offset Programs for Australian Biodiversity Conservation, *Land Use Policy*, 36, pp. 23–32.

Eigenraam, M., Strappazzon, L., Lansdell, N., Beverly, C. and Stoneham, G. (2007). Designing Frameworks to Deliver Unknown Information to Support Market Based Instruments, *Agricultural Economics*, 37, pp. 261–269.

Engel, S., Pagiola, S. and Wunder, S. (2008). Designing Payments for Environmental Services in Theory and Practice: An Overview of the Issues, *Ecological Economics*, 65, pp. 663–674.

Ferraro, P.J. (2008). Asymmetric Information and Contract Design for Payments for Environmental Services, *Ecological Economics*, 65, pp. 810–821.

GHD (2009). *National Action Plan for Salinity and Water Quality: Economics Evaluation Report for Round 2 of the National Market Based Instruments Pilot Program*, Report prepared for the Australian Government, Canberra.

Grafton, Q. (2005). *Evaluation of Round One of the Market Based Instrument Pilot Program*, Report to the National MBI Working Group, Australian Government, Canberra.

Hajkowicz, S. (2009). The Evolution of Australia's Natural Resource Management Programs: Towards Improved Targeting and Evaluation of Investments, *Land Use Policy*, 26, pp. 471–478.

Hajkowicz, S., Higgins, A., Williams, K, Faith, D.P. and Burton, M. (2007). Optimisation and the Selection of Conservation Contracts, *Australian Journal of Agricultural and Resource Economics*, 51, pp. 39–56.

Hanley, N., Banerjee, S., Lennox, G.D. and Armsworth, P.R. (2012). How Should We Incentivize Private Landowners to 'Produce' More Biodiversity?, *Oxford Review of Economic Policy*, 28, pp. 93–113.

Latacz-Lohmann, U. and Schilizzi, S. (2005). *Auctions for Conservation Contracts: A Review of the Theoretical and Empirical Literature*, Report prepared for the Edinburgh Scottish Executive Environment and Rural Affairs Department, The Scottish Government, Edinburgh.

Latacz-Lohmann, U. and Van der Hamsvoort, C. (1997). Auctioning Conservation Contracts: A Theoretical Analysis and Application, *American Journal of Agricultural Economics*, 79(2), pp. 407–418.

Latacz-Lohmann, U. and Van der Hamsvoort, C. (1998). Auctions as a Means of Creating a Market for Public Goods From Agriculture, *Journal of Agricultural Economics*, 49(3), pp. 334–345.

Lowell, K., Drohan, J., Hajek, C., Beverly, C. and Lee, M. (2007). A Science-Driven Market-Based Instrument for Determining the Cost of Environmental Services: A Comparison of Two Catchments in Australia, *Ecological Economics*, 64, pp. 61–69.

Marsden Jacob Associates (MJA) (2010). *Review of the Environmental Stewardship Program*, Report prepared for the Department of Sustainability, Environment, Water, Population and Communities, Canberra.

Miles, C. (2008). 'Testing Market Based Instruments for Conservation in Northern Victoria', in Lefroy, T., Bailey, K., Unwin, G. and Norton, T. (eds.), *Biodiversity: Integrating Conservation and Production*, CSIRO Publishing, Canberra, pp. 133–146.

Moon, K. and Cocklin, C. (2011). Participation in Biodiversity Conservation: Motivations and Barriers of Australian Landholders, *Journal of Rural Studies*, 27, pp. 331–342.

Pannell, D. and Roberts, A. (2010). Australia's National Action Plan for Salinity and Water Quality: A Retrospective Assessment, *Australian Journal of Agricultural and Resource Economics*, 54, pp. 437–456.

Reeson, A.F., Rodriguez, L.C., Whitten, S.M., Williams, K., Nolles, K., Windle, J. and Rolfe, J. (2011). Adapting Auctions for the Provision of Ecosystem Services at the Landscape Scale, *Ecological Economics*, 70, pp. 1621–1627.

Rolfe, J., Greiner, R., Windle, J. and Hailu, A. (2011). Testing for Allocation Efficiencies in Water Quality Tenders Across Catchments, Industries And Pollutants: A North Queensland Case Study, *Australian Journal of Agricultural and Resource Economics*, 55(4), pp. 518–536.

Rolfe, J., Whitten, S. and Windle, J. (2015). The Australian Experience in Using Tenders for Conservation, *Land Use Policy*, in press.

Rolfe, J. and Windle, J. (2011a). Comparing a Best Management Practice Scorecard With an Auction Metric to Select Proposals in a Water Quality Tender, *Land Use Policy*, 28, pp. 175–184.

Rolfe, J. & Windle, J. (2011b). Using Auction Mechanisms to Reveal Costs for Water Quality Improvements in Great Barrier Reef Catchments in Australia, *Agricultural Water Management*, 98, pp. 493–501.

Rolfe, J., Windle, J. and McCosker, J. (2009). Testing and Implementing the Use of Multiple Bidding Rounds in Conservation Auctions: A Case Study Application, *Canadian Journal of Agricultural Economics*, 57, pp. 287–303.

Schilizzi, S. and Latacz-Lohmann, U. (2007). Assessing the Performance of Conservation Auctions: An Experimental Study, *Land Economics*, 83, pp. 497–515.

Schilizzi, S. and Latacz-Lohmann, U. (2013). Conservation Tenders: Linking Theory and Experiments for Policy Assessment, *Australian Journal of Agricultural and Resource Economics*, 57, pp. 15–37.

Stoneham, G., Chaudri, V., Ha, A. and Strappazon, L. (2003). Auctions for Conservation Contracts: An Empirical Examination of Victoria's Bush Tender Trial, *Australian Journal of Agricultural and Resource Economics*, 47, pp. 477–500.

Whitten, S., Reeson, A., Windle, J. and Rolfe, J. (2012). Designing Conservation Tenders to Support Landholder Participation: A Framework and Case Study Assessment, *Ecosystem Services*, 6, pp. 82–92.

Windle, J. and Rolfe, J. (2008). Exploring the Efficiencies of Using Competitive Tenders Over Fixed Price Grants to Protect Biodiversity in Australian Rangelands, *Land Use Policy*, 25, pp. 388–398.

13. Agri-Environmental Schemes in Europe: Switching to Collective Action

Laure Kuhfuss, Philippe Le Coent, Raphaële Préget and Sophie Thoyer

This chapter focuses on the shortcomings of contract design of European agri-environmental schemes (AES), with special emphasis on the need for more collective actions. The AES financed by the Common Agricultural Policy (CAP) are mostly based on individual voluntary contracts signed between farmers and state authorities: farmers make a commitment to adopt pro-environmental farming practices and get a financial compensation in return, for a five-year period. However, the environmental outcomes of European AES have been disappointing. Evaluation reports point out, among other things, the weak rate of farmers' enrolment, especially in the most vulnerable areas. When environmental benefits increase non-linearly with environmental efforts, or require specific spatial configuration, low and scattered participation can be insufficient to trigger environmental improvements and public money is spent in vain. Moreover, it is well known that the adoption of new agricultural practices often follows an S-shaped curve and by encouraging the early adopters, one can accelerate the diffusion of desirable practices. This chapter therefore focuses on how European AES can be re-designed in order to include incentives for greater enrolment and more coordinated action without increasing their costs. It provides examples of how various member states have implemented such measures.

13.1. The Shortcomings of European AES

Agri-environmental measures (AEM) were initially introduced in the CAP in 1992 to try to limit the negative impact of agriculture on the environment. They are individual contracts signed with farmers who volunteer to implement pro-environmental farming techniques that go beyond legal obligations. Payment is calculated to compensate for additional costs and forgone farming revenue resulting from compliance with the contract. Over the 2007–2013 financial period, total payments made by the European Union (EU) for AES[1] amounted to EUR22.7b, and were supplemented by EU member states for an equivalent amount.

In practice, European policy-makers face the typical problem of information asymmetries in contract design: the compliance costs and the potential environmental benefits of farm management practices are highly heterogeneous across farms and are much better known by farmers, who keep this information private, than by the administrative service in charge of managing and controlling contracts. Since it would be too costly to tailor-make contracts to each type of farm, the vast majority of EU member states have chosen to propose standardised contracts with uniform effort-based (rather than outcome-based) payments, calculated on the basis of an estimation of average compliance costs at the regional or national level. In this context, farmers who face low adoption costs (either because they are located in favourable areas or because their farming practices are close to the recommended ones)

[1]Financial plan of the European Agricultural Fund for Rural Development (EAFRD) — axis 2 measure 214 (agri-environment).

tend to join the scheme whilst those whose willingness to accept (WTA) is higher than proposed contract payments do not participate and maintain their environmentally detrimental practices.

European AEM have been implemented under different strategies ranging from the 'wide and shallow' to the 'deep and narrow'. The former displays generally lower levels of environmental requirements, which can be easily reached by most farmers. Their objective is to favour large participation rates and promote or maintain 'good practices' that could be threatened by changing market conditions, or by land abandonment. They are often understood by farmers as a way to get an indirect income-support payment and have generally been criticised for their lack of ambition by evaluation reports commissioned by EU authorities. The latter are more demanding, and are usually targeted at specific areas and/or environmental issues. But they register very low participation and therefore display disappointing results, especially in areas which are most in need of environmental improvement. The European AES are thus confronted by three types of problems.

The first one is the risk of adverse selection (Dupraz *et al.*, 2003). Indeed, the selection of farmers is not made on the basis of their contribution to environmental benefits but rather on their compliance costs. This design leads to incentive compatibility problems which have been analysed by Quillérou and Fraser (2010) in the case of the UK *Conservation Stewardship Scheme*. Since compliance costs are not necessarily correlated to the effective production of high value environmental services, enrolled farmers are not necessarily those able to deliver the environmental services where they are most needed and valued.

The second problem is associated with the lack of additionality. Indeed, in a number of situations, AES generate windfall gains to farmers by paying them to adopt practices that they would have adopted anyhow, even in the absence of the scheme (Chabé-Ferret and Subervie, 2013). This leads to contracts which are not as cost-effective as they could be.

The third issue relates to coordination and threshold effects. Commonly-used uniform payment contracts, which rely on voluntary participation, do not include mechanisms to ensure spatial coordination of efforts at a landscape scale, although it is often essential to have a significant environmental impact (Goldman, Thompson and Daily, 2007). For example, the conservation of endangered species generally requires the creation or protection of natural habitats in the shape of corridors, patches, or mosaics that usually cut across several farms. The management of water quality issues is also better managed at the watershed level. Moreover, in a number of cases, the environmental state does not improve significantly as long as the global environmental effort (in terms of improved practices) has not reached a minimum level of intensity or has not been applied on a sufficient area in the zone of interest (Dupraz, Latouche and Turpin, 2009).

The three main shortcomings of these AES have been regularly pointed out by evaluation reports and research (Oréade Brèche, 2005; Barbut and Baschet, 2005; European Court of Auditors (ECA), 2011; Uthes and Matzdorf, 2013) to explain the disappointing environmental outcomes of AES in Europe: the insufficient participation of farmers; low levels of enrolled area in AEM which demand a greater environmental effort; and the lack of geographical targeting leading to the dispersion of contracts over large areas (Hanley, Whitby and Simpson, 1999; Yang, Khanna and Farnsworth, 2005; ECA, 2011) with the risk that environmental thresholds are not reached and public money is spent in vain with no (or insignificant) environmental benefits.

Responding to these criticisms in the Rural Development Regulation for the 2007–2013 period, the European Commission has opened the possibility for member states to adjust the national implementation of AES. In France, for example, territorialised agri-environmental measures (MAEt) were introduced in order to improve the cost-effectiveness of agri-environmental policies. Kuhfuss *et al.* (2012) analyse the advantages and limits of the main new features of these agri-environmental contracts. MAEt rely on a greater decentralisation of decision-making since their design is decided at the local level. This allows an easier control of the problem of information asymmetries and a better fit of contract characteristics to local environmental needs. They are also better targeted: priority areas are identified on the basis of their vulnerability to environmental issues (Natura 2000 areas, watersheds with acute water quality issues) and only farmers located in these areas are eligible for contracts.

Despite these institutional innovations, the French MAEt have not succeeded in increasing enrollment and improving significantly the ratio of environmental benefits to public money spent. More efficient solutions must be found.

13.2. Can Contracts with a Collective Dimension Improve AES Efficiency?

There is growing theoretical and empirical economic literature on the many reasons why farmers choose to enroll or not in an agri-environmental contract (e.g., Vanslembrouck, Van Huylenbroeck and Verbeke, 2002; Peerlings and Polman, 2009; Christensen *et al.*, 2011; Ma *et al.*, 2012). In a simplified analysis, it is assumed that farmers make their decisions based on the trade-off between the utility of contract payment and the disutility of the environmental effort provided.

Farmers WTA depends, therefore, on the level of restrictions imposed by the agri-environmental contract on farming practices. It also depends on the specific attributes of the contract such as contract duration, flexibility of technical constraints, and transaction costs associated with administration and control (Falconer and Saunders, 2002; Ducos, Dupraz and Bonnieux, 2009; Ruto and Garrod, 2009). Based on these findings, many recommendations have been made to improve the design of contracts and adjust them better to farmers' preferences and constraints. But one under-explored area of contract innovation is the collective dimension of contracts.

Introducing a collective dimension in contracts can help to respond to two shortcomings of traditional contract design: the lack of spatial coordination and the insufficient participation by farmers. This has been tested with laboratory experiments, simulation models and stated preference surveys.

13.2.1. *Improving spatial coordination and reaching environmental thresholds*

As emphasised before, current incentive contracts for ecological services in the EU are mainly implemented at the field/plot level. This generally results in more-or-less randomly scattered enrolled plots without any particular spatial pattern. Yet, ecological services, especially the biodiversity-related ones, are strongly influenced by landscape designs. Depending on the type of species targeted, the conservation of habitat in the shape of corridors, patches, or mosaics, is necessary in order to have a significant impact on biodiversity (Forman, 1995). It is therefore essential to include a landscape component in the design and implementation of conservation programmes (Goldman, Thompson and Daily, 2007).

Parkhurst *et al.* (2002) elaborated an incentive mechanism aiming at facilitating the enrolment of contiguous plots in a conservation programme. The principle of this mechanism is that landholders get a standard subsidy if they protect a plot, which is topped-up with an additional subsidy if the plot is contiguous to another plot (from the same or another landholder). This scheme, tested in decontextualised conditions in a laboratory with a pair of players, has very significant results on plot agglomeration. This result is improved if the experiment is run with stable pairs and with pre-play communication. This study provides encouraging results on the potential effectiveness of this incentive mechanism which, however, must be nuanced because:

(1) The level of agglomeration bonus used is unrealistically high;
(2) Plot shapes and distribution are much more complicated in real life; and
(3) A much larger number of landholders is usually involved.

Parkhurst and Shogren (2007) use the agglomeration bonus mechanism in a more complex laboratory experiment, which involves four players, a diversity of targeted shapes of conserved habitat and a more complex incentive scheme. In this configuration, the agglomeration bonus effect on the attainment of the targeted conservation shape is less clear than in the previous experiment, although coordination improves with players' experience. Other similar experiments provide insights on particular aspects of this mechanism: coordination is easier when groups are smaller (Banerjee, Kwasnica and Shortle, 2012) and pre-play communication can enhance coordination in the more complex setting proposed by Parkurst and Shogren (Warziniack, Shogren and Parkhurst, 2007).

Bamière, David and Vermont (2013), compare the effectiveness and efficiency of three different mechanisms for biodiversity protection: a classical AES-like subsidy mechanism, an auction system to allocate subsidies and an anti-agglomeration bonus. In this article, the objective is to ensure that plots conserved are as scattered as possible, which is particularly adapted for the protection of certain bird species. The efficiency and effectiveness of these three policy instruments are tested using an economic mathematical programming model (called OUTOPIE) which simulates farmer's behaviour as a profit maximiser under technical and administrative constraints. Results showed that the anti-agglomeration bonus has the best habitat conservation results.

Drechsler *et al.* (2010) compare the cost-effectiveness of an agglomeration payment and the classical homogenous payment system. They use a cooperative model to simulate farmers' behaviour and an ecological model that simulates the impact of both policy instruments on the conservation of the Large Blue Butterfly in Germany. In this context, the agglomeration bonus leads to cost savings of 30 to 70 per cent.

The production of environmental benefits does not always increase linearly with environmental efforts but rather presents thresholds and discontinuities (Perrings and Pearce, 1994; Muradian, 2001). In these cases, paying individual voluntary farmers to implement pro-environmental practices can be a waste of money if the sum of pro-environmental efforts is not sufficient. For example, risks of eutrophication of water bodies are reduced only if the water concentration of phosphorus and nitrogen falls below a certain threshold. Efforts of agricultural practices to reduce fertiliser leakage must be provided at a sufficient level at the watershed scale to attain this threshold. Individual agri-environmental contracts, as they are currently designed, cannot guarantee such results as there is no specific incentive to induce a minimum level of participation.

For these contexts, Le Coent, Préget and Thoyer (2014) analyse a conditional subsidy system in which farmers receive financial support only if they collectively reach the environmental threshold. Drawing an analogy between agri-environmental contracts and incentive mechanisms to improve the voluntary contribution to threshold public goods, they design a laboratory experiment to determine the effectiveness and efficiency of two types of incentive mechanisms: contracts with individual payments proportional to individual environmental efforts (similar to existing AES) and contracts with the same individual payments but conditioned to the attainment of a collective threshold of environmental efforts. In this experiment, individual environmental effort is represented by contributions to the public good and incentive payments by a partial subsidy of individual contribution to the public good. This mechanism presents the obvious advantage of spending public money only if the environmental threshold is reached but presents more risks for contributors as they are not guaranteed to ultimately receive the incentive payment. The results of the experiment (Le Coent, Préget and Thoyer, 2014), run with 220 subjects in the University of Montpellier, show that the incentive payments with collective conditionality improves efficiency and effectiveness. Besides the advantage that such a mechanism could represent in the case of environmental thresholds, it also suggests that incentive payments with collective features may interact with individual preferences for collective effort. This topic is developed in the next section.

13.2.2. *Improving participation — the role of social norms*

Another justification for collective contracts is that they provide incentives for groups of farmers to enrol, therefore initiating a dynamic of change and a more rapid diffusion of new practices through learning and imitation (Bikhchandani, Hirshleifer and Welch, 1998) on the one hand but also possibly through economies of scale in adoption costs (by sharing equipment for example). Behaviour is also a strong driver for the success of contracts. Literature in social psychology and behavioural economics shows that our utility level does not depend exclusively on our absolute level of consumption or wealth but also on how we compare ourselves relatively to others and how we perceive our position or rank in the social group to which we belong (Bernheim, 1994; Sustein and Thaler, 2008). People have social preferences for psychological reasons such as reciprocity, altruism, and aversion to inequality that determine their actions (Shogren and Taylor, 2008). These preference determinants, often called behavioural biases, may interact positively or negatively with the efficiency and effectiveness of policy instruments.

Decisions and choices can thus be guided by the willingness to obtain the same advantages as others, or more generally, to behave like others. In particular, it has been demonstrated that individuals value their conforming to the social norm. Social norms are usually sustained by feelings attached to the reputation and self-esteem generated by conforming to the common rule or behaviour, or the shame and guilt of not observing it. Therefore, individual behaviour can be influenced by the behaviour of other members of the community and, conversely, a change in aggregate behaviour can induce a change in individual behaviour (Dietz, 2002; Pretty, 2003).

A farmer can value the fact that his agricultural practices are similar to his neighbours' techniques. For example, Chen *et al.* (2009) have studied the effect of different factors on people's intentions of re-enrolling in a specific payment for environmental services scheme in China. They found empirically, using a choice modelling approach, that in addition to conservation payments and programme duration, the main driver of re-enrolment is the information that the neighbourhood is also intending to re-enrol. In other words, an already high level of participation can positively influence the choice of other farmers to participate. Chen *et al.* (2009) suggest that this result is explained by unconscious imitation, inter-personal comparison and a group's informal norms. Thus, the aggregate impacts of social norms at the neighbourhood level on the cost of AES can be substantial.

Additional evidence of the influence of other farmers' choices on individual stated preferences was found through an Internet survey, completed by 383 French farmers who participated in an AES in 2013 or before (Michaud *et al.*, 2014). The main objective of this survey was to collect farmers' opinions of this scheme in order to evaluate it before the new 2014–2020 Rural Development Program was designed. In the questionnaire, farmers were asked whether they would maintain the practices they had adopted under the scheme after the end of their contract. The survey was divided into three questionnaires addressed to three random groups of respondents. A control group was given no further information (treatment 1). A second group was given the information that, in a previous study (that actually was the pilot of this survey), 80 per cent of the respondents had stated that they would maintain their practices even after the end of the contract (treatment 2). The third and last group was given the same information but framed in a negative way (treatment 3): they were told that 20 per cent of the respondents in the previous study had declared that they would not maintain their practices if the contract was not renewed. The results showed that a significantly higher proportion of farmers in treatment 2 and 3 groups stated that they would maintain the practices they had adopted, compared to treatment group 1 (respectively 81 per cent and 79 per cent against 52 per cent). The information that a majority of farmers would not revert to their old detrimental practices was sufficient to trigger a more positive response concerning their own commitment to the new practices. However, the way this information was framed (positively or negatively) had no significant effect as there was no difference between groups 2 and 3. Even though these results were based on stated behaviours, it gave some evidence that collective incentive systems could be used to increase the influence of others' decisions on individual ones.

Building on these findings, Kuhfuss, Préget and Thoyer (2014) tested the efficiency of an innovative agri-environmental contract designed to increase enrolment rate without increasing public spending. The contract is a classical agri-environmental measure proposing a payment to farmers who switch to pro-environmental practices. But it includes an additional financial bonus, which is paid to each enrolled farmer only if the total enrolled area in the area of interest has reached a pre-defined threshold. The intent of such a conditional bonus is to signal that a greater participation rate in the AES will benefit all contractors through an additional payment. It can therefore provide an incentive to farmers to promote the AES and to encourage their fellow farmers to sign in as well. Despite this obvious advantage, it does not seem at first sight to be the right solution to reduce AES expenditures, since it may lead to more payments to farmers ... unless farmers' preference for such a contract results in greater participation for lower individual payments.

Farmers' preferences for such a conditional bonus were measured in a choice experiment on the reduction of herbicide use in wine growing. This choice experiment was carried out with a sample of 317 wine-growers in the Languedoc Roussillon region, located in the south-east of France. They were invited to select their preferred herbicide-reduction contract in different choice sets. One of the attributes of the contract was the inclusion (or not) of a conditional bonus. It was specified that a bonus of EUR30/ha/year of enrolled land would be paid in addition to the usual payment if 50 per cent of the area of the target territory were ultimately enrolled at the end of the five-year contract duration.

The analysis of farmers' stated choices showed that introducing a conditional bonus improved the probability to enrol and, for equivalent environmental effort intensity, it reduced the individual WTA by an amount which was on average six times greater than the amount of the expected bonus. This result hints that designing a contract with a conditional bonus could contribute to increasing enrollment without increasing expenditures.

The stated preferences of farmers in this survey were consistent with the hypothesis that farmers are more willing to provide environmental efforts when their neighbours also do so. One interpretation is that farmers want to make sure that their efforts do have a significant impact on water quality, an impact that cannot be

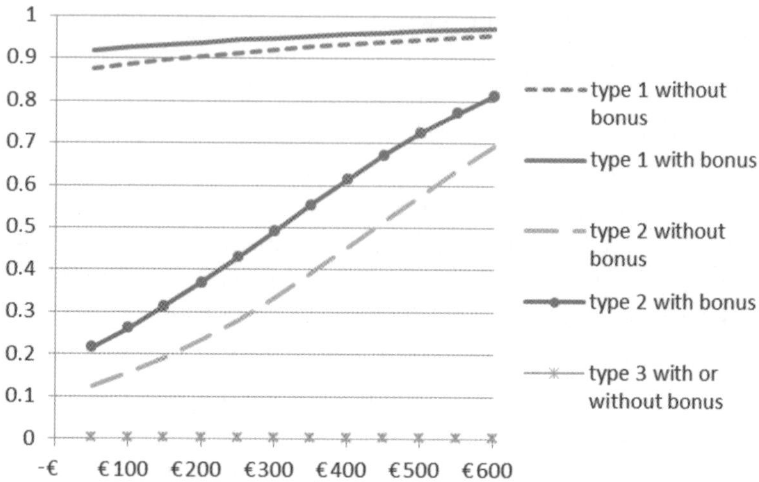

Figure 13.1: Probability to enrol with respect to individual payments proposed (example of a contract targeting at a 60 per cent reduction of herbicide use)
Source: Kuhfuss, Préget and Thoyer (2014), p. 136.

reached unless most famers in the same area also reduce their use of pesticide. Another interpretation is that they want to be reassured of their conformity to the choice of the majority. This collective bonus appears to be a tool that could encourage the emergence of a new social norm influencing the wine-growers' behaviour towards pro-environmental practices. Nevertheless, the results also revealed a high heterogeneity amongst wine-growers. There were three types of farmers, represented almost equally in the surveyed sample: those who were willing to change their practice even for a low payment (type 1 in Figure 13.1); those who were more reluctant but are very sensitive to the conditional bonus (type 2); and those who refused to join the AES, whatever the financial incentive proposed (type 3). This heterogeneity needs to be taken into account in the design of AES, since the conditional bonus will only help to improve efficiency when proposed to the second type of farmers.

All these research results indicate that contracts with a collective dimension can help improve their effectiveness. Let us examine how these contracts have been mobilised in the EU.

13.3. Strengths and Weaknesses of Existing European Contracts with a Collective Dimension

There are two broad categories of contracts with a collective dimension:

(1) Contracts signed with a group of farmers and involving a collective payment (community-based contracts); and
(2) Individual contracts with a payment condition linked to the behaviour or environmental results of a pre-defined group (conditional collective contracts).

13.3.1. *Community-based contracts*

Considering that the conservation and protection of landscapes and biodiversity would be more effective if handled by groups rather than by individual landholders, an obvious policy response is to help farmers to form effective collective action groups.

In the Netherlands, public policies have supported the creation of Environmental Cooperatives (ECs) since 1992. ECs are local farmer organisations, which often include non-farmers, who agree to work together in a coordinated way, and collaborate with various local and national agencies implementing conservation and landscape preservation projects (Renting and Van Der Ploeg, 2001). Franks (2011), using a case study cross-sectional analysis, identifies the advantages brought by ECs. The results of his survey show that ECs help to deliver more environmental gains, through encouraging higher participation rates and changing land managers' attitude towards the environment. This attitude change is partially due to the will of members to have an environmentally-correct attitude and to preserve their reputation within the EC. ECs can also increase participation to AES because they reduce a number of constraints. First, when farmers enrol in an AES they usually have to make substantial practice changes. Once they are enrolled, they may find themselves in a weaker position to renegotiate new AES contracts. Groups engaged in collective contracts through AES have a stronger position to negotiate, thereby reducing this 'hold-up' problem. Second, farmers may fear to enrol in AES programmes if they do not have a guarantee that others will also enrol, this is called the 'assurance problem' (Sen, 1967). By providing a discussion forum before committing in a collective contract, ECs may alleviate this fear.

There are now 150 of these cooperatives in the Netherlands and the Dutch government is planning to take a new step towards the development of this system. The ultimate objective is to channel most of agri-environmental support through these cooperatives. Besides the benefits of coordinated environmental effort, the Dutch government considers that this new organisation will drastically reduce implementation costs. They plan to use a front-door (contract between the state and cooperatives)–back-door (contract between cooperatives and individual farmers) contracting system whereby farmer selection, contracting and monitoring is managed directly by cooperatives.

In England, a recent policy measure also attempts to promote community-based agri-environmental practices. Following evaluations of agri-environmental policies, the White Paper on the natural environment published in 2011 by the British ministry of agriculture (**Department for Environment, Food and Rural Affairs** (DEFRA), 2011) has promoted an integrated approach to create a resilient ecological network across England. A review of the Environmental Stewardship Scheme (ESS) — the largest AES in England — was subsequently undertaken to better integrate landscape-scale conservation. To achieve this objective, specific incentive mechanisms were designed to encourage landholders to coordinate their conservation and agriculture practices through group approaches. The ESS has two types of contracts: a less demanding one, the Entry-Level Stewardship (ELS), and a more demanding one directed at priority species and habitats as well as a range of Heritage Ecosystem Services, the Higher Level Stewardship (HLS). One option aiming at facilitating landholders' coordination is included in the HLS: the HR8 'Supplement for Group action' option. The HR8 is a voluntary option targeted at protecting resources that require across-farms-boundaries actions. This measure helps funding costs for facilitating communal agreements among landholders such as the recruitment of technicians, for an additional subsidy of £10/ha/yr. This measure has been used in only 2 per cent of the existing HLS agreements, but with coverage of more than 10 per cent of the HLS contracted area. The measure has been adopted mostly in upland commons, although with a rather limited additional effect since there is already a history of collaboration among breeders in this area. It has, however, revived innovative initiatives in low-lands, such as bringing fragmented, high nature value sites within single management regimes (Franks and Emery, 2013).

Similar initiatives exist in Germany with the *Landschaftspflegeverbände* (Prager and Vanclay, 2010).

13.3.2. *Conditional collective contracts*

This type of contract is based on collective incentive mechanisms designed to trigger some form of cooperation (weak or strong) among individual farmers. They usually include a collective conditionality to release incentive payments that are made only if groups (the nature of that group varies depending on the context) respect certain conditions. Beneficiaries however remain individuals although amounts can vary depending on groups' performance. These collective conditions are usually used because of the discontinuous nature of the targeted objective (for example threshold effects in environmental issues), and of the need to increase participants' enrolment.

Dupraz, Latouche and Turpin (2007) study the optimisation of agri-environmental contracts in the presence of threshold environmental effects. The authors first develop a theoretical approach based on a principal-agent model in a context of information asymmetry on farmers' WTA payment for adopting pro-environmental practices. One of the conclusions drawn is that the establishment of a collective conditionality to trigger payments to farmers, for example, a minimum threshold of contracted acreage, avoids welfare losses because subsidies are spent only when environmental results are obtained. This approach has been implemented in the *Ille-et-Vilaine* Province, France, where the local administration promoted the use of grass strips along river banks to improve water quality.[2] A first experience of individual AES-like contracts had led to a very scattered and ineffective adoption of this practice. Public authorities therefore determined that a minimum threshold of 60 per cent of the riverbanks of the targeted streams had to be reached to trigger payments to farmers. Interviews with managers of this programme revealed that this threshold was reached for some of the targeted streams.

In the Alsace region, France, the European hamster (*Cricetus cricetus*) is considered an endangered species. Considering that the protection of this animal requires a minimum amount of favourable habitat, an incentive system with collective conditionality has been implemented since 2013. Applications for agri-environmental support must be submitted by a group of farmers. Farmers receive an individual financial compensation only if they are successful in converting or maintaining at least 22 per cent of their total area into a favourable habitat for the Alsacian hamster. Payment amounts are progressive. They increase by tier with the area protected (from EUR416/ha for 22 per cent of favourable habitat to EUR520/ha for the ceiling of 40 per cent of favourable habitat). In addition, the group is expected to collectively decide on the best location of favourable plots depending on the position of hamsters' burrows. It is too early to determine whether this system is more effective than an individual payment system but it shows that collective incentive systems are slowly being considered for implementation.

13.4. Conclusion

Individual agri-environmental contracts are still the dominant incentive mechanism used by the EU to support the adoption of pro-environmental farming practices. However, the advantage of introducing a collective dimension in contracts is increasingly

[2] A similar system is implemented in Oregon in the framework of the Conservation Reserve Enhancement Program (CREP) (Oregon Department of Agriculture (ODA), 2005).

explored in the literature. Better spatial coordination, management of environmental thresholds, initiation of collective dynamics of change are being implemented on a pilot basis in the field. The interest in such mechanisms has also started to be translated into agri-environmental policies. The newly approved 2014–2020 Rural Development Program confirms recent interest for collective delivery of environmental output. It includes the following provisions: 'groups of farmers and other land users' are mentioned as potential applicants and (final) beneficiaries under the agri-environment-climate part of the proposals for rural development (article 29). There are also broader possibilities for EU support for cooperative actions (rural development regulation, article 35), including coverage of the organisational costs. In France, the government has unveiled a policy measure that supports groups of farmers who intend to implement innovative projects for the improvement of sustainable farming systems, through the funding of so called '*Groupes d'Intérêt Économique et Environnemental* (*GIEE*)' which are groups of common environmental and economic interest.

There is also a potential for the use of these mechanisms in the growing number of private initiatives aimed at supporting the production of ecosystem services, such as biodiversity offsetting programmes funded by private operators or private initiatives to improve water quality (e.g., the Vitel case (Depres, Grolleau and Mzoughi, 2008)). The greater flexibility that these initiatives have on the definition of agri-environmental contracts, as compared to public policies, represents an opportunity to more quickly tap into the advantages of contracts with a collective dimension.

Bibliography

Bamière, L., David, M. and Vermont, B. (2013). Agri-Environmental Policies for Biodiversity When the Spatial Pattern of the Reserve Matters, *Ecological Economics*, 85, pp. 97–104.

Banerjee, S., Kwasnica, A.M. and Shortle, J.S. (2012). Agglomeration Bonus in Small and Large Local Networks: A Laboratory Examination of Spatial Coordination, *Ecological Economics*, 84, pp. 142–152.

Barbut, L. and Baschet, J. (2005). L'évaluation De La Politique De Soutien À L'agroenvironnement, *Notes et Études Économiques*, 22, pp. 37–68.

Bernheim B. (1994). A Theory of Conformity, *Journal of Political Economy*, 102(5), pp. 841–877.

Bikhchandani, S., Hirshleifer, D. and Welch I. (1998). Learning From the Behavior of Others: Conformity, Fads, and Informational Cascades, *Journal of Economic Perspectives*, 12, pp. 151–170.

Chabé-Ferret, S. and Subervie, J. (2013). How Much Green for the Buck? Estimating Additional and Windfall Effects of the French Agro-Environmental Schemes by DID-Matching, *Journal of Environmental Economics and Management*, 65(1), pp. 12–27.

Chen, X., Lupi, F., He, G. and Liu, J. (2009). Linking Social Norms to Efficient Conservation Investment in Payments for Ecosystem Services, *Proceedings of the National Academy of Sciences of the United States of America*, 106, pp. 11812–11817.

Christensen, T., Pedersen, A.B., Nielsen, H.O., Mørkbak, M.R., Hasler, B. and Denver, S. (2011). Determinants of Farmers' Willingness to Participate in Subsidy Schemes for Pesticide-Free Buffer Zones — A Choice Experiment Study, *Ecological Economics*, 70(8), pp. 1558–1564.

DEFRA (2011). The Natural Choice: Securing the Value of Nature, UK Government, London.

Depres, C., Grolleau, G. and Mzoughi, N. (2008). Contracting for Environmental Property Rights: The Case of Vittel, *Economica*, 75, pp. 412–434.

Dietz, R.D. (2002). The Estimation of Neighborhood Effects in the Social Sciences: An Interdisciplinary Approach, *Social Science Research*, 31(4), pp. 539–575.

Drechsler, M., Wätzold, F., Johst, K. and Shogren, J.F. (2010). An Agglomeration Payment for Cost-Effective Biodiversity Conservation in Spatially Structured Landscapes, *Resource and Energy Economics*, 32, pp. 261–275.

Ducos, G., Dupraz, P. and Bonnieux, F. (2009). Agri-Environment Contract Adoption Under Fixed and Variable Compliance Costs, *Journal of Environmental Planning and Management*, 52(5), pp. 669–687.

Dupraz, P., Latouche, K. and Turpin, N. (2007). Programmes Agri-Environnementaux En Présence D'effets De Seuil, *Cahiers d'Economie et Sociologie Rurales*, 82–83, pp. 5–32.

Dupraz, P., Latouche, K., and Turpin, N. (2009). Threshold Effect and Co-Ordination of Agri-Environmental Efforts, *Journal of Environmental Planning and Management*, 52(5), pp. 613–630.

Dupraz, P., Vermersch, D., Henry De Frahan, B. and Delvaux, L. (2003). The Environmental Supply of Farm Households, *Environmental and Resource Economics*, 25, pp. 171–189.

European Court of Auditors (ECA) (2011). Is Agri-Environment Support Well Designed and Managed? *Special Report No.* 7, pp. 1–75, Luxembourg publications office of the European Union. Available at: http://www.eca.europa.eu/Lists/ECADocuments/SR11_07/SR11_07_EN.PDF [Accessed 6 October 2014].

Falconer, K. and Saunders, C. (2002). Transaction Costs for SSSIs and Policy Design, *Land Use Policy*, 19(2), pp. 157–166.

Forman, R.T.T. (1995). Some General Principles of Landscape and Regional Ecology, *Landscape Ecology*, 10, pp. 133–142.

Franks, J.R. (2011). The Collective Provision of Environmental Goods: A discussion of Contractual Issues, *Journal of Environmental Planning and Management*, 54(5), pp. 637–660.

Franks, J.R. and Emery, S.B. (2013). Incentivising Collaborative Conservation: Lessons From Existing Environmental Stewardship Scheme Options, *Land Use Policy*, 30(1), pp. 847–862.

Goldman, R.L., Thompson, B.H. and Daily, G.C. (2007). Institutional Incentives for Managing the Landscape: Inducing Cooperation for the Production of Ecosystem Services, *Ecological Economics*, 64(2), pp. 333–343.

Hanley, N., Whitby, M. and Simpson, I. (1999). Assessing the Success of Agri-Environmental Policy in the UK, *Land Use Policy*, 16, pp. 67–80.

Kuhfuss, L., Jacquet, F., Préget, R. and Thoyer, S. (2012). Le Dispositif Des Maet Pour L' Enjeu Eau : Une Fausse Bonne Idée? *Review of Agricultural and Environmental Studies*, 93(4), pp. 395–422.

Kuhfuss, L., Préget, R. and Thoyer, S. (2014). Préférences Individuelles Et Incitations Collectives : Quels Contrats Agroenvironnementaux Pour La Réduction Des Herbicides Par Les Viticulteurs? *Review of Agricultural and Environmental Studies*, 95(1), pp. 111–143.

Le Coent, P., Préget, R. and Thoyer, S. (2014). Why Pay for Nothing? An Experiment on a Conditional Subsidy Scheme in a Threshold Public Good Game, *Economics Bulletin*, 34(3), pp. 1976–1989.

Ma, S., Swinton, S.M., Lupi, F. and Jolejole-Foreman, C. (2012). Farmers' Willingness to Participate in Payment-for-Environmental-Services Programmes, *Journal of Agricultural Economics*, 63(3), pp. 604–626.

Michaud A., Désolé M., Kuhfuss L., Préget R. and Thoyer S. (2014). Bilan De La Mise En Œuvre Des Maet En France (2007–2012). Synthèse des résultats d'une enquête nationale menée en 2013, p. 4, mimeo.

Muradian, R. (2001). Ecological Thresholds: A Survey, *Ecological Economics*, 38, pp. 7–24.

Oregon Department of Agriculture (ODA) (2005). The Conservation Reserve Enhancement Program — Partnerships That Benefit Oregon's Watersheds and Agriculture. Available at: http://www.oregon.gov/ODA/shared/Documents/Publications/NaturalResources/ConservationReserveEnhancementProgram.pdf [Accessed 6 October 2014].

Oréade-Brèche. (2005). *Evaluation des Mesures Agro-Environnementales*, Final Report, Auzeville. Available at: http://ec.europa.eu/agriculture/eval/reports/measures/fulltext.pdf [Accessed 6 October 2014].

Parkhurst, G.M. and Shogren, J.F. (2007). Spatial Incentives to Coordinate Contiguous Habitat. *Ecological Economics*, 64, pp. 344–355.

Parkhurst G., Shogren J., Bastian C., Kivi P., Donner J. and Smith R. (2002). Agglomeration Bonus: An Incentive Mechanism to Reunite Fragmented Habitat for Biodiversity Conservation, *Ecological Economics*, 41, pp. 305–328.

Peerlings, J. and Polman, N. (2009). Farm Choice Between Agri-Environmental Contracts in the European Union, *Journal of Environmental Planning and Management*, 52(5), pp. 593–612.

Perrings, C. and Pearce, D. (1994). Threshold Effects and Incentives for the Conservation of Biodiversity, *Environmental and Resource Economics*, 4, pp. 13–28.

Prager, K. and Vanclay, F. (2010). Landcare in Australia and Germany: Comparing Structures and Policies for Community Engagement in Natural Resource Management, *Ecological Management and Restoration*, 11, pp. 187–193.

Pretty, J. (2003). Social Capital and the Collective Management of Resources, *Science*, 302, pp. 1912–1914.

Quillérou, E. and Fraser, R. (2010). Adverse Selection in the Environmental Stewardship Scheme: Does the Higher Level Stewardship Scheme Design Reduce Adverse Selection? *Journal of Agricultural Economics*, 61, pp. 369–380.

Renting, H. and Van Der Ploeg, J.D. (2001). Reconnecting Nature, Farming and Society: Environmental Cooperatives in The Netherlands as Institutional Arrangements for Creating Coherence, *Journal of Environmental Policy and Planning*, 3, pp. 85–101.

Ruto, E. and Garrod, G. (2009). Investigating Farmers' Preferences for the Design of Agri-Environment Schemes: A Choice Experiment Approach,

Journal of Environmental Planning and Management, 52(5), pp. 631–647.

Sen, A. (1967). Isolation, Assurance and the Social Rate of Discount, *The Quarterly Journal of Economics*, 81, pp. 112–124.

Shogren, J.F. and Taylor, L.O. (2008). On Behavioral-Environmental Economics, *Review of Environmental Economics and Policy*, 2(1), pp. 26–44.

Sustein, C. and Thaler, R. (2008). *Nudge: Improving Decisions About Health, Wealth And Happiness*, Yale University Press, New Haven and London.

Uthes, S. and Matzdorf, B. (2013). Studies on Agri-Environmental Measures: A Survey of the Literature, *Environmental Management*, 51(1), pp. 251–266.

Vanslembrouck, I., Van Huylenbroeck, G. and Verbeke, W. (2002). Determinants of the Willingness of Belgian Farmers to Participate in Agri-environmental Measures, *Journal of Agricultural Economics*, 53(3), pp. 489–511.

Warziniack, T., Shogren, J.F. and Parkhurst, G. (2007). Creating Contiguous Forest Habitat: An Experimental Examination on Incentives and Communication, *Journal of Forest Economics*, 13, pp. 191–207.

Yang, W., Khanna, M. and Farnsworth, R. (2005). Effectiveness of Conservation Programs in Illinois and Gains From Targeting, *American Journal of Agricultural Economics*, 87(5), pp. 1248–1255.

14. The Role of Firms in Reducing Greenhouse Gas Emissions from Deforestation

Luca Tacconi

14.1. Introduction

Greenhouse gas emissions from forestry and other land uses — primarily from *deforestation*, and dominated by CO_2 — accounted for 12 per cent of total emissions over the period 2000–2009, amounting to an average of 4.03 Gt of CO_2 per year (Intergovernmental Panel on Climate Change (IPCC), 2014).[1] Forests are also important in relation to climate change because they are a significant sink of CO_2. Therefore, during the past decade, their role in the climate system has been at the centre of global negotiations about a climate change agreement. Those negotiations on a mechanism for Reducing Emissions from Deforestation and Forest Degradation (REDD+) have made steady progress since the 2009 meeting of the UN Framework Convention on Climate Change (UNFCCC). The fundamental idea

[1] Gt is the abbreviation for gigatonne, equivalent to one billion tonnes.

behind REDD+ is that developing countries would reduce forestry emissions (and increase carbon stocks in forests) in exchange for payments to cover at least the forgone financial benefits that are obtained through the conversion of forests to other uses, such as production of livestock and palm oil. Developing countries harbour large swathes of forests, where most of global land use change takes place.

REDD+ started gaining significant traction in international negotiations when the Stern Review, and later the Eliasch Review, pointed out that reducing emissions from forests was one of the most cost-effective ways of reducing global emissions, as well as one of the fastest ways because switching to less emission-intensive energy production systems appeared to be a long-term prospect (Stern, 2007; Eliasch, 2008). As discussed later in this chapter, progress on the implementation of REDD+ faces significant challenges that will need to be considered. This will be done in the context of the role of firms in deforestation, and as key actors involved in reversing that trend.

Over the centuries, deforestation was caused by the decisions of individual farmers. However, in recent decades, firms have become the most significant agents of deforestation, particularly in Asia and Latin America (e.g., Rudel, 2005; Fearnside, 2007; Nepstad, Stickler and Almeida, 2006), where the largest areas of forests are being cleared and degraded. Companies are involved in activities that clear land for:

(1) Agriculture, to produce commodities such as oil from palm and soy — oil crops accounted for most of the increase in cropped land in developing countries during the period from 1989–1991 to 2005–2007, amounting to 48 million ha (Alexandratos and Bruisma, 2012);
(2) Forestry, plantations to produce timber and fibre for pulp and paper; and
(3) Beef production.

Firms often also purchase the above products from smallholders for further processing and/or trade.

Finally, companies bring the finished products to consumers, mostly in developed countries, but increasingly also to developing country consumers. Given the role of firms in deforestation, we need to consider the part they may play in reducing deforestation. Can we expect them to change their practices voluntarily? Or are some pressures and/or incentives required?

To address these questions, this chapter begins by providing a sketch of academic perspectives on the relationship between corporate behaviour and the environment. This summarises the main strands of the literature on the drivers of corporate behaviour *vis à vis* the environment. Understanding those theories provides an understanding of corporations' potential priorities and behaviours. These are used in the following sections of the chapter to present a schematic framework to analyse firms' interests and behaviour in relation to forests. Then, the state of the development of REDD+ is summarised before the questions set out above are considered.

14.2. Firms' Decisions and the Environment

Several factors affect corporate decisions about the environment beyond the profit motive, which obviously is the major driving force of their activities. The management literature has categorised those factors in different ways, and it is beyond the scope of this chapter to present a comprehensive overview. Rather, it presents a broad picture of the research and the most significant factors. Relevant groups of factors include those internal to firms, external factors (often referred to as institutional), and positional factors (a term defined below that is not derived from the management literature, but it is used here for simplicity of exposition). Let us start with the external factors, as firms operate within the wider context, and internal factors need to be responsive to external ones.

To operate successfully, firms need to obtain so-called *licences to operate* from economic, regulatory and social stakeholders (Gunningham, Kagan and Thornton, 2004). This means that firms have to be responsive to the views of these three groups which include:

(1) Shareholders, customers, competitors, and business associations (economic stakeholders);
(2) Regulators, be they regional, national or international authorities; and
(3) The local and broader communities, non-governmental organisations (NGOs), and the media (social stakeholders).

Obviously, firms respond to the economic stakeholders as they are at the core of their operations. They also need to respond to regulators, given that not doing so may result, in the extreme, in the withdrawal of the necessary regulatory licences and the possible closure of the firm. Responding to social stakeholders' views may also be essential to the firms' operations when, for example, a lack of responsiveness could result in disruption to production (e.g., conflict with local communities that results in disruption to factories) or access to markets (e.g., NGOs carry out campaigns to boycott their products). The need to obtain the economic and social licences to operate is one of the reasons that firms may 'go beyond regulatory requirements to operate', which is the definition of corporate environmental responsibility (Gunningham, Kagan and Thornton, 2004). The influence of economic, regulatory and social contexts has been demonstrated by cross-country studies, for example, in relation to 15 Asian countries (Baughn and McIntosh, 2007).

Responses to the above-mentioned external factors vary across firms, given that they are also influenced by a range of internal factors that interact with the external ones (e.g., Banerjee, 2001). First, managers perceive and act upon external pressures in different ways at the plant level, depending upon plant- and parent-company-specific factors, including their track record of environmental performance, and the organizational structure of the plant (Delmas and Toffel, 2004). Apart from their decisions based on company specific issues, managers also influence firms' responses to environmental issues on the basis of their personal views, values, and attitudes towards the environment (e.g., Nilsson, von Borgstede and Biel, 2004). Other factors internal to companies that influence their environmental management decisions include the role of environmental and resource management activities in providing: competitive advantage; new market opportunities and innovation; enhanced corporate reputation (which can lead to greater competitive advantage and market opportunities); improved efficiency of operations; reducing costs; and reducing environmental risk (which translates into reduced business risk) (e.g., Dechant and Altman, 1994; Forte and Lamont, 1998; Porter and van der Linde, 1995). The ability of managers and firms to deal with external pressures in ways that suit firm-specific characteristics has also been emphasized as a significant internal (or resource-based) factor (Julian, Ofori-Dankwa and Justis, 2008). Whilst the above internal factors may be important, overall they will not be considered further in this chapter given the limited space available.

The concept of positional factors is used here to describe a firms production and market characteristics. A key production factor is the extent of a firm's dependence on inputs. This results in different levels of vulnerability (Julian, Ofori-Dankwa and Justis, 2008). In the present context, this may be exemplified by a logging company being completely dependent on accessing timber resources in the forest, whereas a furniture company may diversify away from timber into composite wood material or even non-timber material. Relevant market characteristics are a firm's visibility (Julian, Ofori-Dankwa and Justis, 2008), and the degree of concentration in the sector and, if companies are based in developing countries, whether they sell their products domestically or in developed countries (Özen and Küskü, 2008). The characteristic of visibility has been operationalized, for example by Julian, Ofori-Dankwa and Justis (2008), as being a public or private company, with the former being more visible. Obviously, even a private company could have high visibility if it had brand recognition. The degree of concentration of a sector increases the need for companies to differentiate themselves from their direct competitors (Özen and Küskü, 2008). There is a degree of overlap between the characteristics of visibility and sector concentration. Whether a firm sells its products in developing or developed country markets matters because the latter normally have higher environmental standards, both in relation to regulatory and social expectations.

Let us now consider REDD+ in some detail before addressing the role of firms in deforestation and reducing emissions.

14.3. REDD+

The aim of REDD+ is to reduce emissions of greenhouse gases from deforestation and forest degradation, and removing greenhouse gases from the atmosphere through the enhancement of forest management (represented by the '+' in the acronym) in developing countries. Whilst there has been steady progress in international negotiations, the practical implementation of REDD+ has seen rather limited progress. The lack of a global agreement on climate change means that there is no agreement on, and commitment to, specific targets for the reduction of emissions from deforestation and forest degradation. As a result, funding for REDD+ has been limited.

The Stern Review estimated the cost of halving deforestation at \$5–15b a year, whereas the Eliasch Review revised that figure to '\$17–33b per year (to 2030) if forest credits are included in global carbon trading' (Eliasch, 2008, p. 80). Over the period 2006–2017, a total of about \$10.94b has been allocated and pledged, and not necessarily spent, by developed country governments and international agencies, according to a database[2] that tracks 40 recipient countries. Even if it was accepted that that the level of funding requirements estimated by the Stern and Eliasch Reviews could be expected only after a global agreement was in place, it is instructive to note the following: at the 2009 UNFCCC meeting it was agreed that some \$30b would be allocated to developing countries to address a range of climate change financing needs, including 'substantial' funding for REDD+ (The Copenhagen Accord).[3] However, only

[2] REDD+ Database. Available at: http://reddplusdatabase.org/#graphs_and_stats [Accessed 5 August 2014].

[3] UNFCCCC. Available at: http://unfccc.int/files/meetings/cop_15/application/pdf/cop15_cph_auv.pdf [Accessed 5 September 2014].

about \$3b was actually allocated to REDD+ over that period.[4] It is also important to note that funds disbursed so far for REDD+ activities have been allocated mostly by donor countries to developing country governments for capacity building and preparatory activities. According to a database[5] that makes available information on REDD+ finance for 14 recipient countries, donors' commitments amount to about \$4.55b, with actual disbursements of around \$0.57b. Brazil, Mexico and Indonesia account for about 89 per cent of total received commitments, and 76 per cent of actual expenditure. Indonesia alone has received pledges of about \$2.44b, but so far has received \$102m. This is due, to a significant extent, to an agreement with Norway, which provides funding to set up the regulatory infrastructure for REDD+, but requires the actual reduction of emissions for most of the funding to be dispersed. Indonesia has not reached that stage.

Many pilot projects have been designed, and in some cases implemented, with funding from donor countries to test the practical implementation of REDD+ at the local level. These projects are not normally designed to deliver actual reductions in emissions. Rather they focus on testing methodologies, such as those related to monitoring and verification of emissions, and socio-economic approaches to sustaining livelihoods whilst reducing deforestation. There have been, however, some privately funded projects that have also focused on delivering actual emission reductions, which are then sold on the voluntary carbon market. Forestry emissions transacted in 2013 amounted to 22.6MtCO_2e, accounting for about 30 per cent of the total voluntary carbon market (76MtCO_2e). Voluntary forestry transactions were valued at \$94 m. The current volume and value of emissions traded on the voluntary market are a minute fraction of annual forestry-related emissions and the funds required to address them: about 0.56 per cent of the volume, and a similar percentage if

[4] REDD+ Database. Available at: http://reddplusdatabase.org/#graphs_and_stats. [Accessed 5 August 2014].

[5] Forest Trends REDDx Database. Available at: http://reddx.forest-trends.org. [Accessed 5 August 2014].

the Eliasch Review's lower estimate ($17b) was used. It is also useful to note that the volumes exchanged in the voluntary market are a fraction of trades on the European Union Emissions Trading Scheme (ETS), the main regulatory carbon market, which in 2013 amounted to about 9.3 $GtCO_2e$.

Apart from reflecting a lack of a global agreement on climate change, the slow progress in the implementation of REDD+ is also due to strong opposition from some influential NGOs, working in the social and environmental areas. The former are concerned about the possible exclusion of local people from forests, if their value increased as a result of reduced emissions being monetised and if companies and/or governments sought to lock up forests to capitalize on the new market.[6] Some environmental NGOs, such as Greenpeace, are opposed to REDD+. Their rationale was well summarised by one of its senior forest campaigners in a piece commenting on the upcoming deliberation of the Californian Air Resource Board about whether domestic companies will be allowed to invest in international forestry projects to off-set their pollution: 'When it comes to reducing California's climate emissions, should we allow companies to pollute our local communities, while paying our neighbours in Mexico to clean up the carbon? Should we gamble our climate policies on saving trees in other countries that can easily be destroyed by forest fires, just so that we can indulge in our own emissions instead of reducing them responsibly?' (Moas, 2014). The argument put is that companies should not be allowed to do that, because it is not guaranteed that forests will stand for the foreseeable future. NGOs such as FERN and Global Witness, had previously also welcomed the decision by the European Union to keep forestry credits out of the ETS at least until after 2020.[7]

It is now time to address, in this context of uncertainty, the questions that were set out in the Introduction.

---

[6] As an example see No-REDD. Available at: http://noredd.makenoise.org [Accessed 5 September 2014].

[7] Global Witness. Available at: http://www.globalwitness.org/library/commission-derives-credit-keeping-forests-out-carbon-market [Accessed 5 September 2014].

14.4. Firms' Activities Leading to Deforestation and their Role in REDD+

14.4.1. *Firms' interests related to forests and business characteristics*

A broad, schematic categorisation of firms whose operations are related to forests can be derived by using some of the key factors that characterise them, and affect their decisions, as described in Section 14.2. Table 14.1 groups the firms on the basis of broad sectors and more specific activities. It should be noted that the list of 'sectors' and especially 'activities' is not meant to be exhaustive, as that would be beyond the scope of this chapter. Rather, it focuses on those sectors/activities that are currently considered to be closely related to the main causes of deforestation.

In the forestry sector, logging activities are carried out by a large number of operators, ranging from very small, village-based groups to corporations operating in several countries. Those selling on the domestic market have low visibility, as a result of a relative lack of domestic consumers' interest in environmental issues and the large numbers of operators. Firms that export to other countries, particularly to Least Developed Countries (LDCs), have relatively low visibility for the same reasons. Even if some LDC-based corporations have at times come under the scrutiny of NGOs, visibility is set as Low in Table 14.1 because in the event of a successful NGO campaign to disrupt the operations of corporations, other small, less visible, operators could take the place of those larger companies. The situation is somewhat different for companies that target export markets in developed countries, given that there is more scrutiny by NGOs there, which also puts significant pressure on consumer goods companies to acquire timber from certified sources.[8] Despite those pressures, certification of sustainable practices only accounts for about 10 per cent of global forest cover and, even more significant,

[8] For example WWF. Available at: http://wwf.panda.org/what_we_do/how_we_work/businesses/transforming_markets/solutions/bettermarkets/timber [Accessed 5 September 2014].

Table 14.1: Business characteristics of the main sector/firm types with an interest in forests

Sector/Activity	Base	Resource dependency*	Profit source	Market	Concentration	Visibility
Forestry						
Logging	LDCs	Trees	Sale of logs	LDCs	Low	Low
	LDCs	Trees	Sale of logs	DCs	Low	Low medium
Pulp and paper	LDCs	Trees	Sale of pulp & paper	DCs & LDCs	High	Medium high
Emission offsets	DCs	Forest	Sale of offsets	DCs	High	Very high
Agriculture						
Beef	LDCs	Land	Sale of livestock	LDCs & DCs	Low	Low
Soy	LDCs	Land	Sale of soy	LDCs & DCs	Low medium	Low medium
Palm oil	LDCs	Land	Sale of palm oil	LDCs & DCs	Medium high	Low to high
Consumer goods	DCs	Primary commodities used in processed goods	Sale of consumer goods	DCs	High	High
	LDCs	Primary commodities used in processed goods	Sale of consumer goods	LDCs	Medium high	Low
Banking	LDCs	No dependency	Loans to companies	LDCs	Medium	Low
	DCs	No dependency	Loans to companies	DCs & LDCs	Medium	High

Note: * Refers to the dependency relationship with forest/trees, rather than considering the main input dependency of the Sector/Activity.
DCs: developed countries; LDCs: less developed countries.

it applies to minuscule areas in regions where deforestation takes place: Asia (2.1 per cent), Africa (1.1 per cent) and Latin America (1.6 per cent) (data from United Nations Economic Commission for Europe/Food and Agriculture Organization (UNECE/FAO), 2013).

Pulp and paper production is highly concentrated due to plant requirements for efficient and competitive production. Pulp and paper companies, particularly those based in Indonesia, have faced sustained campaigns by NGOs over their reliance on mixed species timber from forests. A campaign against the largest company in the world, Asia Pulp and Paper, driven to a significant extent by Greenpeace, led some 170 consumer goods companies — such as Adidas, Danone, Nestle, Mattel, McDonalds, National Geographic, and Uniliver — to source products elsewhere (Carrington, 2014). As a result, Asia Pulp and Paper has adopted a zero-deforestation policy and will work to preserve 'high conservation value' and 'high-carbon stock' forests.

Wilmar, one of the largest palm oil producers, has taken the same path as Asia Pulp and Paper by issuing a 'No deforestation, No peat, No exploitation Policy' at the end of 2013.[9] Palm oil production has been at the centre of attention of NGOs' initiatives because of its negative impacts on forests, particularly in Indonesia (Malaysia, the other major palm oil producer, cleared forests for that purpose well before Indonesia). The Roundtable on Sustainable Palm Oil (RSPO), whose members come from all different levels of the supply chain, from growers to retailers, as well as NGOs, was founded in 2004 and seeks to ensure that palm oil production does not cause deforestation. RSPO standards are used to certify areas that are planted without clearing forests. About 15 per cent of the total production came from certified plantations in 2013 (World Wide Fund (WWF), 2013). Initiatives similar to the RSPO have been initiated more recently for soy and beef production, which affect forests in Latin America. So far, the Round Table on Responsible Soy has certified 0.41 per cent

[9] WWF. Available at: http://www.wilmar-international.com/wp-content/uploads/2012/11/No-Deforestation-No-Peat-No-Exploitation-Policy.pdf [Accessed 5 September 2014].

of global production,[10] whilst the Global Roundtable for Sustainable Beef has not certified any produce yet.[11] The challenges faced by the two latter initiatives are even greater than those faced in relation to palm oil because of the less concentrated and visible nature of production. However, the challenges facing palm oil certification should not be underestimated given that production of this commodity is also not highly concentrated, and more and more smallholders are planting oil palm, further dispersing production of oil palm. And with the highest growth rates of population and income being found in developing countries, their demand for commodities will also grow faster in those less-environmentally sensitive markets.

In many cases, consumer goods companies in developed countries have reacted to NGOs' pressures by seeking to source their products from more sustainable sources, for example, as noted earlier in the case of the campaign against Asia Pulp and Paper. Industry associations have also responded, particularly The Consumer Goods Forum, which brings together some 400+ companies from around the globe — mostly from developed countries — with an aggregate turnover of some USD3 trillion. It adopted a zero deforestation policy in 2010.[12] More recently, the Tropical Forest Alliance, a new coalition of NGOs, governments and some global corporations, and including the above-mentioned Forum, has been formed with the objective of halting deforestation.[13] Two issues should be noted. First, whilst certified products may attract a (small) price premium in some cases, those products often account for a relatively small cost of production (such as palm oil used in products from soap to

[10] Available at: http://wwf.panda.org/what_we_do/how_we_work/businesses/transforming_markets/solutions/bettermarkets/farming/soy [Accessed 5 September 2014].

[11] WWF. Available at: http://wwf.panda.org/what_we_do/how_we_work/businesses/transforming_markets/solutions/bettermarkets/farming/beef [Accessed 5 September 2014].

[12] The Consumer Goods Forum. Available at: http://www.theconsumergoodsforum.com [Accessed 5 September 2014].

[13] Tropical Forest Alliance. Available at: http://www.tfa2020.com [Accessed 5 September 2014].

confectionery), hence using sustainably harvested products has a very low impact on the profits of consumer goods companies. Second, the consumer goods alliances mentioned above do not include many of the smaller companies, often based in LDCs and which process many products for their domestic markets that, as already noted, are not as environmentally sensitive as those of developed countries.

Multinational banks have also faced NGOs' campaigns for lending to companies that are engaged in deforestation activities. For example, a campaign was run recently against Deutsche Bank (and banks such as HSBC, Amundi, Rabobank were also mentioned) for providing finance to an Indonesian firm, Bumitama Agri, which, according to the campaign organisers, had been clearing forest without a licence to establish an oil palm plantation.[14] This is an interesting case because the Bumitama Agri is a member of the RSPO, and HSBC, which is the third largest global bank, was the first bank to adopt a forest policy aimed at avoiding the provision of funding to companies that are involved in deforestation (Environmental Impact Assessment (EIA), 2013). Multinational banks are more visible and have a large and a relatively environmentally conscious customer base. They are therefore concerned about NGOs' campaigns even if they affect a rather small share of their loans, as those campaigns present a broader reputational risk; even then, they face practical challenges in identifying risky customers as exemplified in the case of Bumitama Agri. However, smaller banks based solely in developing countries are less sensitive to environmental campaigns and could be an alternative source of funding for local companies that carry out deforestation activities. Therefore, funding for firms engaged in deforestation may still be able to access finances via the local banks.

So far we have not considered the role of firms involved in providing emission offsets (Table 14.1). There is a global voluntary carbon market that includes forestry emissions. However, its role is currently very marginal, as noted earlier. Let us consider, therefore, the role of emission offset activities within a more speculative discussion about

---

[14] Rainforest Rescue. Available at: https://www.rainforest-rescue.org/mailalert/946/indonesia-deutsche-bank-finances-deforestation [Accessed 5 September 2014].

the future involvement of firms in addressing forest conservation to achieve reduced emissions.

14.4.2. *The future of private forest conservation in developing countries*

Undoubtedly, at some point in the future, deforestation in tropical forests will come to an end as a result of economic and political development processes that have already been experienced by developed and some developing countries alike, as captured by the forest transition theory (Rudel *et al.*, 2005). However, some questions remain open: when will the transition be completed? How many emissions will have been released when that takes place? And how much biodiversity will have been lost by then? It is for these reasons that continued efforts to address deforestation need to be considered.

The initiatives taken by the private sector that were discussed earlier have often been stimulated and in some cases forcefully demanded by NGOs. These have resulted in reduced deforestation but are unlikely, as they stand, to lead to the sort of reductions that were envisaged by the Stern and Eliasch Reviews, and which are at the centre of the REDD+ mechanism. If all firms from developed countries (including the less visible ones) adopted no-deforestation policies, and the LDCs firms that export to developed countries did the same, there would still be LDCs firms that would continue to deforest to produce goods for developing countries' markets (which are the fastest growing ones), or who would buy those products from smallholders engaged in agricultural expansion, leading to deforestation, to sustain their livelihoods (Cacho *et al.*, 2014). It could be argued that one day the citizens of LDCs will become as environmentally sensitive as those of more developed countries, and would demand an end to deforestation, and/or smallholders would move to cities to find better-paid employment thus stopping land clearing. But that is what the forest transition theory is about, and those events may be decades away in many LDCs.

The two main options for reducing deforestation are government intervention and private sector activities. Governments have spoken for decades about the need to reduce deforestation, but, in practice, limited progress has been made in most cases as a result of limited direct government actions. Moreover, reducing deforestation is expensive and developed countries governments are not making available the financial resources required on the scale highlighted by the Stern and Eliasch Reviews. The private sector will take on a more significant role only if appropriate incentives to do so are present.

The only firms that are completely dependent on conserving forests as a whole to generate profits are those which deal with emission offsets (Table 14.1). The voluntary carbon market is highly unlikely to achieve a size large enough to make a significant dent into deforestation. Regulatory markets would either need to be created for forestry emissions credits, or they would need to be allowed into markets such as those of Europe or single state ones such as California. But the same obstacles that have so far limited the progress of REDD+ still lie ahead.

Without significant global commitments to reducing emissions, regional and/or domestic markets will not achieve a size sufficient to consider the inclusion of forestry emissions. If those commitments were to eventuate, there would still be significant resistance on the part of many NGOs to the inclusion of forestry emissions into those markets. The environmental NGOs that oppose it would need to consider whether their current position is actually helping the environment, if commitments to cut domestic emissions were substantial. The social NGOs that oppose REDD+ are rightly concerned about the impacts on the livelihoods of people living in, and around, forest. First, this argument highlights a contradiction in the rhetoric put forward by environmental and social NGOs in relation to forest conservation: the former often highlight how deforestation has negative impacts on local people as well as the environment, whilst the latter point out that forest conservation could negatively impact on rural peoples' livelihoods. Both arguments cannot stand, and they need to be addressed to clarify both the conservation and the business case for protecting forests. Second, the social NGOs that are not completely opposed to REDD+ correctly point out that rural people would need to be included in REDD+ activities in a way that benefits them; for example, emission offset companies could implement projects in partnership with local communities and share profits. Therefore, the social safeguards that have been developed through the international negotiation process would need to be tested in practice to see if they result in sufficient benefits for rural people, whilst enabling firms to operate effectively and efficiently.

14.5. Conclusion

In recent decades, globalization has resulted in firms becoming the prime agents of deforestation, particularly in the Asia and Latin America where the largest areas of forest are being cleared and degraded. The very large majority of firms operating in sectors related to forests in developing countries face an incentive structure that favours deforestation. The size of the voluntary carbon market is so small that it can only make a minuscule contribution to conserving forests. Therefore, corporate environmental responsibility activities aimed at reducing deforestation have been either forced onto firms by the NGOs' name-and-shame campaigns targeting large, often multinational, companies, or have arisen through the collaborative efforts between NGOs and companies to create sustainability certification schemes. All those initiatives have had some positive impacts. However, their limits have also been pointed out above. Appropriate market incentives need to be put in place to drive a change in firms' activities towards the reduction of forestry emissions. Those incentives may present some risks and drawbacks, but unless they are tested and eventually adjusted, firms and smallholders alike will continue their deforestation and forest degradation activities for several decades to come.

Acknowledgements

The work presented in this chapter is supported by a grant from the Australian Centre for International Agricultural Research FST/2012/040 'Enhancing smallholder benefits from Reduced Emissions from Deforestation and Forest Degradation in Indonesia'.

Bibliography

Alexandratos, N. and Bruisma, J. (2012). World Agriculture Towards 2030/2050: The 2012 Revision, *ESA Working Paper No. 12–03*, Food and Agricultural Organization of the United Nations, Rome.

Banerjee, S. B. (2001). Managerial Perceptions of Corporate Environmentalism: Interpretations From Industry and Strategic Implications for Organizations, *Journal of Management Studies*, 38(4), pp. 489–513.

Baughn, C.C. and McIntosh, J.C. (2007). Corporate Social and Environmental Responsibility in Asian Countries and Other Geographical Regions, *Corporate Social Responsibility and Environmental Management*, 14(4), pp. 189–205.

Cacho, O., Gonzalez, R., Milne, S. and Tacconi, L. (2014). Benefits and Costs of Deforestation by Small-Holders: Implications for Forest Conservation and Climate Policy, *Ecological Economics*, 107, pp. 321–332.

Carrington, D. (2014). Is APP's Zero Deforestation Pledge a Green Villain's Dramatic Turnaround? *The Guardian*, March 27, 2014.

Dechant, K. and Altman, B. (1994). Environmental Leadership: From Compliance to Competitive Advantage, *Academy of Management*, 8(3), pp. 7–20.

Delmas, M. and Toffel, M.W. (2004). Stakeholders and Environmental Management Practices: An Institutional Framework, *Business Strategy and the Environment*, 13(4), pp. 209–222.

Eliasch, J. (2008). *Climate Change, Financing Global Forests: The Eliasch Review*. Earthscan, London.

Environmental Impact Assessment (EIA) (2013). *Banking on Extinction: Oil Palm, Orangutans and the Certified Failure of HSBC's Forest Policy*, Environmental Investigation Agency, London.

Fearnside, P.M. (2007). Brazil's Cuiaba´-Santare´m (BR-163) Highway: The Environmental Cost of Paving a Soybean Corridor Through the Amazon, *Environmental Management*, 39(5), pp. 601–614.

Forte, M. and Lamont, B.T. (1998). The Bottom Line Effects of Greening, *Academy of Management*, 12(1), pp. 89–90.

Gunningham, N., Kagan, R.A. and Thornton, D. (2004). Social License and Environmental Protection: Why Businesses Go Beyond Compliance, *Law & Social Inquiry*, 29(2), pp. 307–341.

Intergovernmental Panel on Climate Change (IPCC) (2014). Working Group III contribution to the IPCC 5th Assessment Report 'Climate

Change 2014: Mitigation of Climate Change'. Available at: http://report.mitigation2014.org/drafts/final-draft-postplenary/ipcc_wg3_ar5_final-draft_postplenary_chapter11.pdf [Accessed 12 August 2014].

Julian, S.D., Ofori-Dankwa, J.C. and Justis, R.T. (2008). Understanding Strategic Responses to Interest Group Pressures, *Strategic Management Journal*, 29(9), pp. 963–984.

Moas, A. (2014). The Fallacy of Forest 'Offsets', *Capitol Weekly*, Available at: http://capitolweekly.net/forest-offsets-fallacy-carb/ (posted 17/7/2014) [Accessed 12 August 2014].

Nepstad, D.C., Stickler, C.M. and Almeida, O.T. (2006). Globalization of the Amazon Soy and Beef Industries: Opportunities for Conservation, *Conservation Biology*, 20(6), pp. 1595–1604.

Nilsson, A., von Borgstede, C. and Biel, A. (2004).Willingness to Accept Climate Change Strategies: The Effect of Values and Norms, *Journal of Environmental Psychology*, 24(3), pp. 267–277.

Özen, S. and Küskü, F. (2008). Corporate Environmental Citizenship Variation in Developing Countries: An Institutional Framework, *Journal of Business Ethics*, 89(2), pp. 297–313.

Porter, M.E. and van der Linde, C. (1995). Toward a New Conception of the Environment-Competitiveness Relationship, *The Journal of Economic Perspectives*, 9(4), pp. 97–118.

Rudel, T.K. (2005). Changing Agents of Deforestation: From State-Initiated to Enterprise Driven Processes, 1970–2000, *Land Use Policy*, 24(1), pp. 35–41.

Rudel, T.K., Coomes, O.T., Moran, E., Achard, F., Angelsen, A., Xu, J. and Lambin, E. (2005). Forest Transitions: Towards a Global Understanding of Land Use Change, *Global Environmental Change*, 15(1), pp. 23–31.

Stern, N.H. (2007). *The Economics of Climate Change: The Stern Review*. Cambridge University Press, Cambridge.

United Nations Economic Commission for Europe/Food and Agriculture Organization (UNECE/FAO). (2013). *Forest Products Annual Market Review: 2012–2013*. United Nations Economic Commission for Europe, Food and Agricultural Organization of the United Nations, Geneva.

World Wide Fund (WWF) (2013). *Palm Oil Buyers Scorecard: Measuring the Progress of Palm Oil Buyers*, World Wide Fund for Nature, Gland.

15. Mining Offsets in NSW

Robert Gillespie

15.1. Introduction

Conservation of biodiversity has public good characteristics and has primarily been provided by governments via the direct provision of protected areas and the regulation of economic activity that may have adverse impacts on the environment.

In New South Wales (NSW), Australia, approximately 7.1 million ha (8.8 per cent of NSW) are protected in public conservation reserves and managed by the NSW National Parks and Wildlife Service (NSW Environment Protection Authority (EPA), 2012). Private conservation schemes add to the conservation estate. Private conservation areas in NSW, including conservation agreements, wildlife refuges, property registration under the Land for Wildlife Scheme, conservation covenants and property vegetation plans in perpetuity, total 3.2 million ha or about 3.9 per cent of NSW (EPA, 2012).

Regulation through the development approval processes can help to prevent developments impacting areas of conservation value on private lands, through refusal of development applications where the development would cause unacceptable environmental harm or approval of development applications that have been modified to limit the potential harm. However, such approaches can result in considerable opportunity costs to society (i.e., forgone producer surplus benefits from the development) while doing nothing to improve the management of the private lands with conservation values or to prevent them from degrading.

Offset policies can remedy this situation. They can 'assist in achieving long term conservation outcomes while providing development proponents with the ability to undertake actions that have unavoidable impacts on biodiversity' (NSW Government, 2014a, p. 4). Offsetting (also known as set-asides, compensatory habitat and mitigation banks) is a policy instrument that enables some continued vegetation clearing to occur provided sufficient habitat can be protected, enhanced and/or established elsewhere (Gibbons and Lindenmayer, 2007). The concept of an 'offset' is based on the notion of 'strong sustainability': the stock of natural capital should not be permitted to decline as development takes place (Davies, 2013). Hence, any loss in natural capital at the development site must be 'offset' by a corresponding gain in natural capital elsewhere. Offset policies operate under an overall goal of 'improve or maintain' or 'no net loss'. Therefore offsets must provide at least as much conservation value as is lost, raising complex issues around whose value is relevant and how it should be measured. In the USA, over 40 assessment methodologies have been developed to determine the appropriate level of offsets (Hillman and Instone, 2010). Metrics used in Australia include 'habitat hectares' in Victoria and 'credits' in NSW (Bedford, Ellis and Simpson, 2009).

The outcome of offset policies in NSW is that considerable biodiversity conservation and ongoing management is now being undertaken by major developers, in particular mining companies. This chapter places offsets and Biobanking schemes within an economic context. It examines two policy frameworks for offsets in NSW: negotiated offsets as part of the development approval process; and, purchase of credits from the NSW Biodiversity Banking and Offsets (BioBanking) Scheme. The level of conservation being undertaken by mining companies under each policy framework is discussed. The non-participation of developers in the BioBanking

Scheme is explained with reference to details of the BioBanking Scheme's implementation.

15.2. Economic Context for Offsets

Minerals and ores from mining are private intermediate goods. They are traded in markets and used as factor inputs by firms to produce other goods and services. For instance, coal is used to produce steel and electricity, and gold is used in electronics, medicine, aerospace and jewellery. Production of minerals and ores provide economic value (producer and consumer surpluses) to society.[1] In a competitive market, the system of private property rights and the price mechanism (interaction of demand and supply) function together to produce market goods[2] at a level that maximises net benefits to society as a whole (Sinden and Thampapillai, 1995). However, markets fail with respect to mining because of poorly defined and/or defended property rights over some of the resources used, e.g., biodiversity, clean air, water and amenity. The resultant externalities cause a divergence between private returns and social returns and too much output is produced resulting in a deadweight loss to society.

Where a producer who creates an externality is required to pay a Pigovian tax related to the externality cost or compensate those who bear the externality cost, e.g., through Coasian bargaining, the externality cost will be internalised into the producer's costs and a Pareto-efficient level of production will occur. A requirement for

---

[1] At the project level, an individual (relatively small scale) mine, is a price taker. The supplier faces an elastic demand curve and hence there is no consumer surplus from the production of the good (Carson, 1991).

[2] Market goods can be measured, valued and have private property rights that are enforceability (ownership can be clearly defined), transferable (other persons can only use the good if its owner transfers the good to them in an exchange involving an incentive) and exclusive (all benefits and costs of using the good can only be experienced by the owner of the good) (Tientenberg, 1992).

developers to provide biodiversity offsets is a means of internalising the cost of an externality and is consistent with this economic framework.

Provided the community's values for the biodiversity offset are equal or greater than the community's values for the biodiversity lost from the development then, in aggregate, the community will be no worse-off with respect to biodiversity values. In economics, the community's value for conservation is measured by the aggregation of the community's demand or willingness to pay (WTP) for it.

One of the methods that can be used to elicit the community's WTP for biodiversity is choice modelling (CM). CM is a non-market valuation method (NVM) that uses questionnaires to describe a hypothetical policy scenario that will cause environmental, cultural and social changes. In a survey of the affected population, respondents are presented with a series of questions (choice sets), where each question shows the outcome of two or more alternative policy scenarios including a 'status quo' or 'no policy change' scenario. These outcomes are described in terms of different levels of a monetary attribute (cost) to be borne by the respondent and several non-marketed attributes. Respondents are asked to choose their preferred option from the array of alternatives. By observing people's choices between alternatives with differing levels of each attribute it is possible to determine the trade-offs respondents make between attributes. Because one of the attributes is specified in monetary terms it is possible to determine the implicit price of changes in the levels of different attributes.

An example of this economic approach to ascertaining the value of biodiversity impacted by a development and the value of biodiversity offsets is provided in Gillespie and Bennett (2012). This study utilised CM to examine the community values for the loss of endangered ecological communities (EEC) that would arise from continued coal mining at the Warkworth Mine in the Hunter Valley of NSW. The study design also facilitated the estimation of community values for offsetting actions such as planting of EEC in the region and protection of existing EEC in the region.

Using community values it was found that to offset the loss in community values from the clearing of 1 ha of EEC would require either:

- 4 ha of EEC planting (an offset ratio of 4.0:1); or
- 1.4 ha of protection of existing EEC in the region (an offset ratio of 1.4:1); or
- A multitude of combinations of planting and protection.[3]

The cost[4] of providing the level of offset that equates the lost values to the community from a development with the gained values to the community from improvements in habitat from offsetting actions is the relevant cost to be internalised and borne by development proponents. Offsetting actions can include restoration of degraded habitat, establishment of new areas of habitat and legal protection from future development.

A legal requirement for biodiversity offsetting provides the potential for the development of market exchange of offsets. Demand in such a market is created through requirements under the government's development approval process. Supply is generated by those who improve habitat through weed management, livestock exclusion and fire management, or establish new areas of habitat via tree planting. Buyers and sellers are potentially kept apart by transaction costs: the costs involved in collecting and understanding information regarding offsets and their owners/buyers.[5] Markets cannot form when there are high transaction costs because the gains available from trade are overwhelmed by the transaction costs that must be spent in order to achieve the trade. However, transaction costs can

[3] The offsets required by governments can be conveniently summarised by an offset ratio — the ratio of the area of the vegetation offset to the area that is cleared. However, care must be taken in their interpretation because offset areas can be of different qualities and result in the conservation of different attributes which are not reflected in a simple offset ratio.

[4] The cost is the opportunity cost of the land plus ongoing management costs.

[5] See Chapter 10 of this volume.

be lowered by the actions of 'brokers' who are specialists in the generation of information and hence, market facilitation.[6]

The process of developing a market for biodiversity offsets has been attempted in the state of NSW with the government acting as a broker. This followed the development of a similar scheme, BushBroker, in Victoria.

15.3. NSW Policy Context and Offsets Provided by Mining Companies

In NSW, there is requirement under the *Environmental Planning and Assessment* (*EP&A*) *Act*, *1979* for mining projects to be subject to an Environmental Impact Assessment (EIA)[7] process prior to decisions being made on whether they should be approved. This process includes a requirement to identify methods of mitigating, compensating or offsetting adverse impacts. Biodiversity offsets have increasingly formed part of the conditioning of consents/approvals where the project would adversely affect biodiversity. These conditions of consent in relation to offsets are directly negotiated with the NSW Government on a case-by-case basis.

While there is no public register of offsets in NSW, some indication of the scale of private conservation being undertaken by mining proponents can be obtained from individual mining companies. Coal & Allied Pty. Ltd. identifies that it has secured significant areas within the Hunter catchment as long-term biodiversity offsets for its recent projects. Figure 15.1 indicates offsets of over 27,000 ha for a combined disturbance footprint of less than 5,000 ha. This is an offset ratio of more than 5:1. In addition, Coal & Allied committed to a range of indirect offsets including investment in research projects and the contribution of land to conservation corridor projects.

[6] See Chapter 11 of this volume.

[7] EIA refers to 'the process of identifying, predicting, evaluating and mitigating the biophysical, social, and other relevant effects of development proposals prior to major decisions being taken and commitments made' (International Association for Impact Assessment, 1999, p. 2).

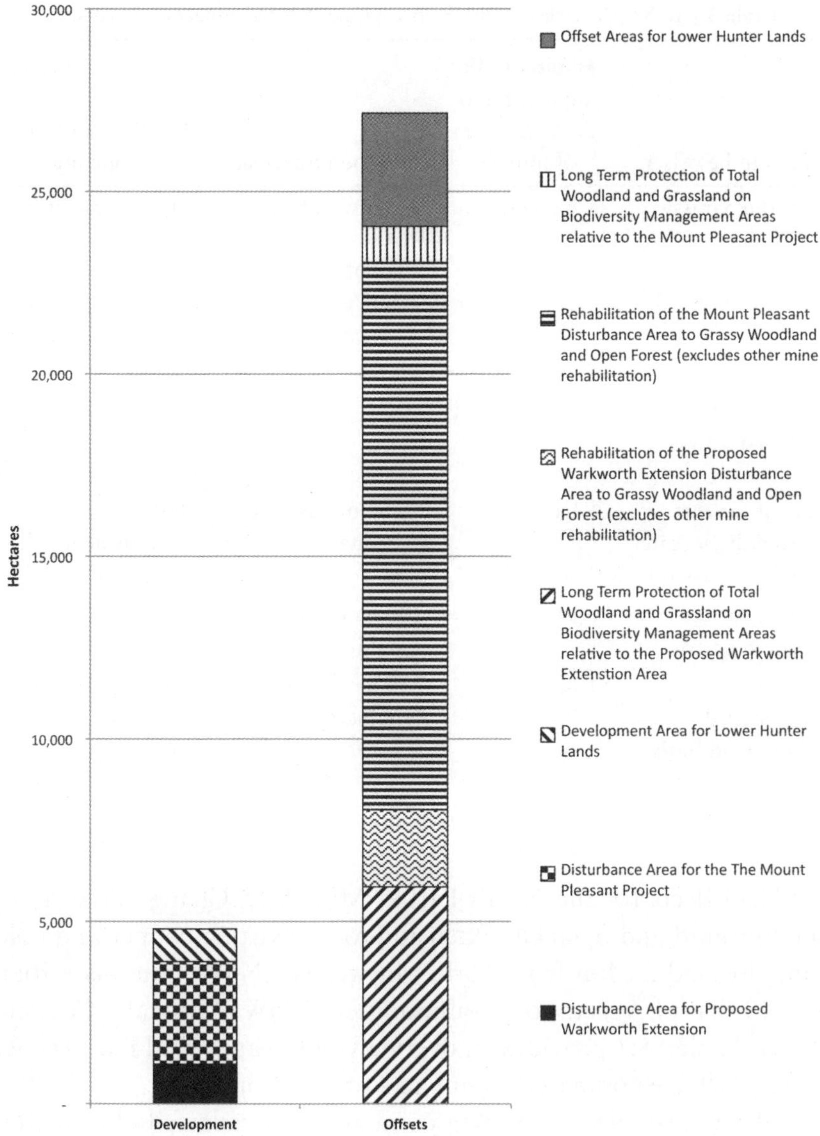

Figure 15.1: Coal & Allied development and offsets

Source: NSW Minerals Council (2014).

Table 15.1: North Parkes Mine Step Change Project impacts and offsets.

Values to be offset	Habitat to be impacted and likely size/area of impact	Kokoda offset site	20 year offset outcome
Grey Box Grassy Woodland	25 ha woodland 21 ha DNG	13 ha woodland 9 ha DNG (with active regeneration to woodland)	109 ha woodland
White Box — Yellow Box — Blakely's Red Gum Woodland	0.28 ha	2.2 ha	2.2 ha
Habitat for the regent honeyeater and swift parrot	66 ha	95 ha of equivalent habitat	191 ha of equivalent habitat
Habitat for the superb parrot	90 ha	206 ha of known habitat	206 ha of known habitat
Habitat for threatened woodland birds and bats	81 ha	236 ha of potential habitat	348 ha of potential habitat

Source: NSW Minerals Council (2014), p. 17.

The offsets for the North Parkes Mine Step Change Project, an underground and open cut extension to an existing copper and gold mine, located 27 km from Parkes in western NSW contains a total of 348 ha of vegetation communities (NSW Minerals Council, 2014). Table 15.1 provides an overview of the approved Biodiversity Offset Package compared to impacts of the Project.

Offsets provided by mining companies are primarily located on existing mining company landholdings or on land purchased from other landholders and managed directly by dedicated mining company staff, although in some instances offsets can be transferred to land management agencies. For example, the Mt Owen Mine, an open cut coal mining operation, established the 430 ha 'New Forest' in compensation for the clearing of 240 ha of Ravensworth State

Forest. The re-establishment of vegetation communities and habitats enabled the transfer of the New Forest to Forestry Corporation NSW in December 2003, and its incorporation into the Ravensworth State Forest where it has been designated for conservation (NSW Minerals Council, 2014).

The alternative approach to the provision of offsets is for the development proponent to acquire and retire biodiversity credits that have been established as part of the BioBanking Scheme under part 7A of the *Threatened Species Conservation* (*TSC*) *Act*, *1995*. This Scheme enables landholders to create biodiversity credits by undertaking management actions on their land that improve biodiversity values. These credits, once created and registered, can be traded (including being purchased by developers) and used as an offset against the impact of proposed development on biodiversity values. In the BioBanking Scheme, credits required by developers and generated by the management actions of landholders, are determined using the BioBanking Assessment Methodology (BBAM).

The NSW Minerals Council (2012, p. 7) identifies the potential benefits of this latter approach as:

- Allowing for consistent, quantitative assessment of impact sites and offset sites;
- Reduced negotiation of offsets;
- Provision of a reliable estimate of the cost of impacts of a development at an early stage, allowing for the consideration of different designs and offsetting arrangements; and
- Allowing private landholders to manage their land for conservation and developers to step away from this non-core business.

Notwithstanding this, in NSW most, if not all, mining (and other development) proponents have adopted the former approach (NSW Minerals Council, 2012).

At the time of the BioBanking Scheme review undertaken by the Office of Environment and Heritage or OEH (OEH, 2012), nine landholders had entered into BioBanking Agreements and obtained ecosystem and/or species credits (OEH, 2012), conserving approximately 450 ha of native vegetation and threatened species in perpetuity. Credits associated with 143 ha had been sold and retired (OEH, 2012). Excluding ecological mine site rehabilitation which is currently not recognised in offsetting schemes (NSW Minerals Council, 2014), the level of conservation achieved by negotiation in the approval process is more than ninety times the area of conservation that has been achieved via BioBanking.

The more market-driven BioBanking Scheme has therefore not delivered on its desired outcome.[8] Some of the reasons for this can be ascertained from a closer examination of the components of the NSW BioBanking Framework in the following section.

15.4. The NSW BioBanking Framework

15.4.1. *Introduction*

The NSW BioBanking Scheme is a voluntary, market-based scheme designed to help conserve biodiversity and build a market for the delivery of biodiversity service (OEH, 2012).

At its core is the BBAM that attempts to quantify, in non-monetary terms, the level of value (ecosystem credits and species credits) that a landholder generates from conservation actions that he undertakes on his property. Similarly, the BBAM also quantifies, in non-monetary terms, the level of value (ecosystem credits and species credits) that a developer needs to offset the impacts of a project. Buyers and sellers are free to negotiate the sale price of credits. However, credits must be priced to cover the costs of future management of BioBanking sites (including the cost of labour and site administration based on a third party undertaking management at a commercial rate (Department of Environment, Climate Change and Water (DECCW), 2009). The present value of those management costs (calculated using a set discount rate) from the sale of

[8] A similar outcome has resulted from the Victorian BushBroker Scheme where, after eight years of operation, 2,140 habitat ha (6,835 ha) have been protected with only 386 habitat hatraded (Jenni Thomas, BushBroker, Victorian Department of Environment and Primary Industries, *pers.coms.*, 26 June 2014).

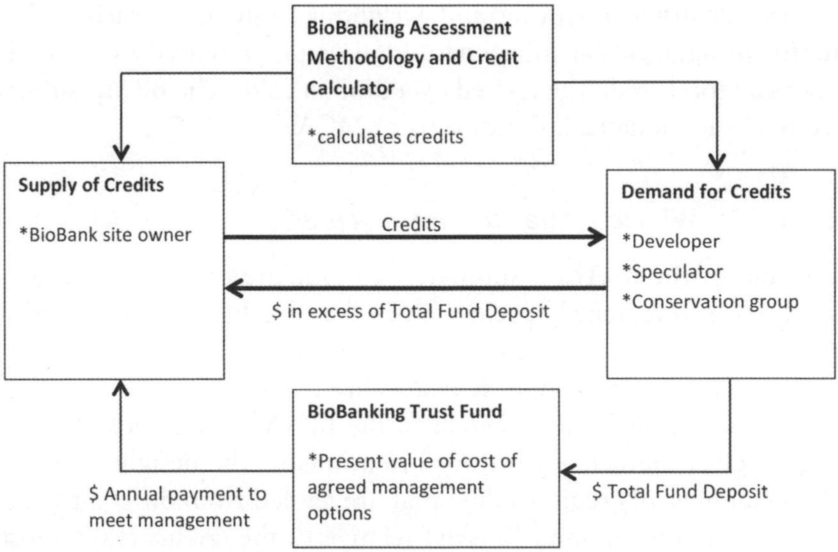

Figure 15.2: NSW Biobanking Scheme
Source: Based on DECCW (2007), p. 7.

credits must be deposited into a Biobanking Trust Fund. Money is returned from the BioBanking Trust Fund to the landowner annually to pay for agreed management actions. Any traded value of credits above the Total Fund Deposit accrues directly to the landowner. See Figure 15.2.

There are a number of fundamental issues with the operation of BioBanking that limit its ability to achieve its stated objective. These relate to:

- The BBAM that is used to estimate credits required by developers and credits obtained from landholders for management actions; and
- The operation of the market.

15.4.2. *BBAM*

The BBAM is a multi-criteria analysis (MCA) tool. It establishes a range of criteria for site value, landscape value and threatened species values, identifies a scoring and weighting system for each and a means of aggregation to estimate total credits required by a developer and total credits generated by a BioBank site. The BBAM suffers from all the fundamental problems of MCA.[9]

15.4.2.1. *Whose values are represented?*

The aim of the BBAM is ultimately to estimate the levels of biodiversity and threatened species values that are lost as a result of a development and the levels of values that are gained at a BioBank site by management action. It establishes credits as a non-monetary representation of value. Inherent in the BBAM (via choice of criteria, weights, mathematical transformations) is the designer's views of the number of credits (value) that are gained from different management actions on land (offsets) relative to the credits (value) lost from the impacts of a development site, rather than the views of the community. The marginal rate of substitution between development impacts and the outcomes of offset actions is therefore set by the designer and are unlikely to reflect the marginal rate of substitution of the community as would be indicated by NMV studies such as those estimated by Gillespie and Bennett (2012) for the Warkworth Mine.

As identified by the Productivity Commission (Baker and Ruting, 2014, p. 22):

> government-created markets are a complement, not an alternative, to non-market and other valuation. Unless valuation methods are used in the design of such a market, there is little reason to expect that the resulting price will reflect the value that the community places on the environmental outcomes achieved. This is because, without valuation, there is no reliable way to calibrate the demand side of the market to community preferences. In other words, government-created markets can put a price on environmental

[9] For a detailed discussion of the fundamental problems with MCA, refer to Dobes and Bennett (2009).

outcomes, but non-market valuation may be able to help ensure that this is close to the 'right' price.

15.4.2.2. *Subjective choice of criteria*

The criteria that economics would use to equate impacts with offset outcomes (i.e., determine the marginal rate of substitution between impacts and offset outcomes) is their community public good value, as indicated via the aggregation of individual preferences and estimated using NVM.

The approach used in the BBAM is MCA which has no single or overriding principle on which criteria or attributes are selected (Dobes and Bennett, 2009). Consequently, anything can be included in a MCA as a criterion, even if individual and community well-being is not impacted by it. In the BBAM, site value comprises ten attributes and landscape value comprises four criteria. However, different groups in society, even within the environmental field, may well consider different environmental attributes as relevant. The nature of MCA is that the inclusion or omission of criteria will result in different outcomes. In this case, different credit estimates for the impact of developments and the outcomes of offset actions and hence different marginal rates of substitution would be derived.

15.4.2.3. *Breaching of the principle of dimensionality*

MCA and the BBAM use a scoring and weighting system to aggregate different and incompatible units. In order to add or subtract, or to use some other mathematical operation to aggregate quantities, the quantities in question must have the same dimension (Dobes and Bennett, 2009). It is not possible to add 'total length of fallen logs' to 'number of trees with hollows'. Using an ordinal score system to represent levels of these attributes and then multiplication of this ordinal score by a weight (interval scale) and treating the result as a cardinal number that can be added to other cardinal numbers does nothing to correct the problem of incompatible dimensions. Any aggregation of the results is logically flawed (Dobes and Bennett, 2009).

15.4.2.4. *Appearance of objectivity*

> Despite the fundamentally flawed methodology that underpins MCA its proponents have developed mathematically sophisticated superstructures which may give the appearance of increasing its validity and rigour. However, no amount of sophisticated mathematics can compensate for fundamental flaws in the methodology (Dobes and Bennett, 2009, p. 24).

For example, the number of attributes used in MCA will affect the overall and relative scoring of attributes. This will change the number of credits generated by a management action or required by a developer, but only because of a procedural issue. Similarly, different mathematical procedures for converting unit measurements to scores and for applying weightings will also generate different levels of credits from a management action or a development. Which mathematical procedures are best is an arbitrary decision (Dobes and Bennett, 2009). If the mathematical procedures used result in developers requiring a higher level of credits for an impact (e.g., a high implied offset ratio or cost) participation in the scheme may be minimal. An alternative mathematical formulation could result in a lower level of credits required by a developer and/or a higher level of credits from management actions (e.g., a low implied offset ratio). The choice is highly subjective but inherently reflects what the builders of the BBAM consider a suitable trade-off.

The subjective nature of the BBAM is illustrated by the DECCW's previous proposal to modify the calculation of offsets by deleting Equation 9 and modifying Equations 10 and 11 within BBAM (OEH, 2009). Why not delete or vary other equations? The draft framework for assessing and offsetting state significant development (NSW Government, 2014b) also adjusts criteria, weights and mathematical formulations, presumably to make the credit calculations more likely to deliver outcomes that are politically desirable. For any particular case study, these modifications to the methodology would change the number of credits (and consequently implied value) attributable to different actions. So, unlike the values that the community hold for biodiversity, the non-monetary value of biodiversity as measured by the BBAM (and represented by credits) can now change with the stroke of a pen to suit politically driven requirements.

15.4.3. *Operation of the market*

The BioBanking Scheme is a means of creating a private market for biodiversity outcomes (credits) with the efficient operation of the market revealing the private cost of providing biodiversity outcomes. Mining, and other, proponents will buy credits if they can be obtained for a lower price than generating those credits themselves.

The efficient operation of the BioBanking Scheme requires a competitive market for biodiversity (credits) which is contingent on many buyers and sellers, a homogenous product, free market entry and exit and low transaction costs. Under these circumstances the interaction of supply and demand will determine an efficient level of buying and selling of biodiversity (credits). However, there are a number of issues with the market that is created by the BioBanking Scheme. These are discussed below.

15.4.3.1. *Credits are not homogenous*

BBAM is a methodology to convert all impacts to a common measure of non-monetary value (credit) and hence a homogenous product, albeit suffering the problems identified above with all MCAs. However, it cannot be used in relation to areas with high biodiversity conservation values (red flag issues — which are common for mining developments) and can only be used on 'like for like' impacts. Each credit has a credit profile defined by the catchment management authority subregion, vegetation type, vegetation formation, surrounding vegetation cover and patch size (OEH, 2012). In other words, the constructed product (credit) is not homogenous. It only represents biodiversity outcomes when used on similar vegetation communities or species. This has the effect of reducing the overall market scope for the credits from any given BioBanking agreement and creating numerous sub-markets.

15.4.3.2. *Supply costs impacted by the scheme*

In the operation of competitive markets, supply costs are determined by a supplier's minimum willingness to accept (WTA) compensation. In the long run this includes an amount sufficient to cover fixed and variable costs and a normal return on investment. In the biodiversity credit market, the supplier's WTA compensation is overridden in three ways. First, landholders are not able to suggest supply costs having regard to their opportunity cost of time. Their estimated marginal costs (in addition to their other land management costs of managing their property) of providing the required services must include the cost of labour and site administration based on a third party undertaking management at a commercial rate (DECCW, 2009).

Second, from the sale of credits the landholder must deposit into the BioBanking Trust Fund the present value of the estimated management costs. However, there is a mismatch between private discount rates of market participants (buyers and sellers) and the discount rate used to estimate the amount to be deposited in the BioBanking Trust Fund. An indication of the level of discount rate used in the market to convert future costs and benefits to present values is given by market interest rates. The discount rate used to convert future management costs to present values in the BioBanking Trust Fund and hence the level of payment required is set at 3.5 per cent (DECCW, 2009). This is lower than the market interest rate that generally prevails in the economy and certainly lower than individual private discount rates that have been found, using stated preference and revealed preference techniques, to be in excess of 20 per cent (Hausman, 1979; Ruderman, Levine and McMahon, 1986; Kovacs and Larson, 2008; Bond, Cullen and Larson, 2009). A low discount rate applied to the deposits in the BioBanking Trust Fund has the effect of increasing the management costs per credit. The difference between a 3.5 per cent BioBanking Trust Fund discount rate and a 7 per cent private discount rate is a doubling of the management costs. The difference between a 3.5 per cent BioBanking Trust Fund discount rate and a 10 per cent private discount rate is a near tripling of management costs.

Third, the development of a BioBanking Agreement between a landholder and the government entails considerable transaction costs. These are incurred when there is no guarantee that a landholder will be able to sell his biodiversity credits (OEH, 2012). This is a barrier to participation in the Scheme. OEH (2012) identifies the transaction costs at over $10,000 for formal assessment of a BioBank site. The Law Society of NSW (2012) identified transaction costs for assessing ecosystems and credits in accordance with the BBAM at between $20,000 and $50,000 per site and a time frame of 18 months.

15.4.3.3. *Demand for credits impacted by price of substitutes*

The demand for credits represents the developer's WTP for them. A number of factors influence the level of this demand. One of the important determinants is the existence and price of substitutes. BioBanking is a voluntary scheme. The alternative for developers is to arrange offsets via the development approval process. Any requirement for a biodiversity offset can then be met through direct negotiations with landholders. The scope of landowners who can be approached to secure this offset is only limited by those who own land with the desired characteristics. The supply costs for providing these offsets are not inflated by the rules of the BioBanking Scheme and hence this approach is likely to be cheaper in many instances.

15.4.3.4. *Supply and demand interaction*

The combination of supply and demand in the biodiversity credit market determines the market value of a credit. This is illustrated in Figure 15.3. In the absence of the supply cost enhancing characteristics of the BioBanking Scheme, the market price for a credit would be P* and quantity supplied would be Q*. Each of the supply characteristics of the Scheme identified above have the effect of shifting the supply curve (cost curve) to the left, reducing the quantity of credits demanded, (to Q1) and increasing the market price (to P1).

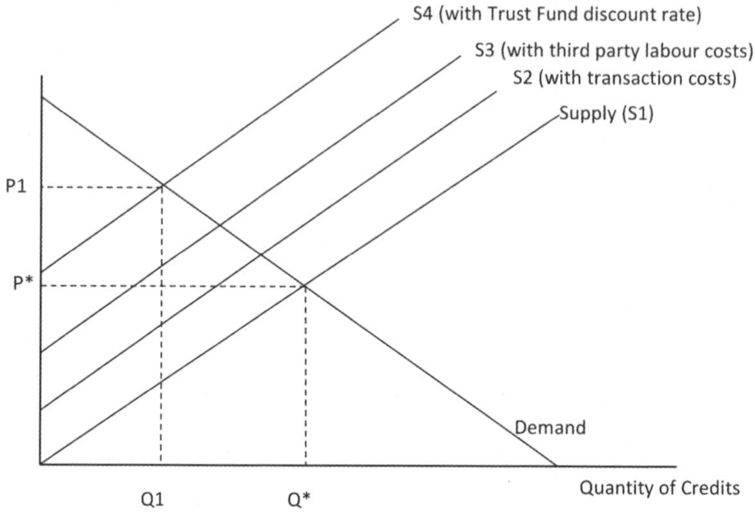

Figure 15.3: Interaction of supply and demand for credits

The number of credits required by the BBAM (designers' credit offset ratios) combined with the market price of a credit (cost of providing a credit), determined through the interactions of supply and demand, would appear to be greater than most developers are willing to pay, as evidenced by low participation in the BioBanking Scheme.

15.5. Discussion and Conclusion

Offsets policy is consistent with the concept of strong sustainability and the welfare economics notion of internalising the externalities so as to result in more efficient allocation of scarce resources. It allows decision makers to move away from the use of deontic rules in decision making to recognising that most developments will have some impacts and even the existence of significant impacts can be compensated. Allowing society to obtain benefits from development while ensuring other values are not diminished can enable the wealth of society to be increased.

In NSW, offsets policy has led to substantial areas of land being set aside and managed for conservation by the private sector. A key issue in the provision of offsets by the private sector relates to how value is determined — for impacted land and offset land — and hence what level of offset is required to ensure no net loss.

Approaches that have moved away from economic principles of supply and demand as measures of costs and benefits, respectively, and utilise more nebulous indicators of value such as credits or habitat hectares based on MCA, are inherently more subjective and can limit market participation. Ignoring the principles of competitive markets can similarly impact market participation.

The temptation of policy makers in NSW to adjust BBAM formulas for Major Projects to encourage greater participation in the BioBanking Scheme (NSW Government, 2014b) only serves to illustrate the subjectivity of the non-economic methods of establishing offset values.

The BioBanking Scheme in NSW (and elsewhere) could arguably be improved by:

- Using community values, determined using NMV methods, to inform the marginal rate of substitution (offset ratio) between development impacts and offsets;
- Relaxing of 'like for like' restrictions to create a more homogenous tradable product (credits) that better reflects the ability of individuals in society (and the community) to make trade-offs between many and varied goods and services;
- Removing supply side constraints, e.g., estimation of management costs based on third party suppliers, removing requirements for BioBanking Trust Fund Deposits or adjusting the discount rate to better reflect individual discount rates; and
- Adjusting administrative processes to reduce transactions costs for participants.

The provision and management of significant levels of offsets by the private sector (albeit not via the BioBanking Scheme) also highlights potential issues over management. Currently, offsets provided by mining companies as part of their conditions of consent are mainly managed by the mining companies themselves. This is not the core business of these entities. The NSW Government, in its Draft NSW Biodiversity Offsets Policy for Major Projects, is considering a system where credits are converted to a payment to be provided to an environmental management agency in government for the provision of more holistic conservation management. An alternative would be for the government to set offset ratios and strategic conservation objectives and auction the rights to the private sector to source and manage offset areas. A system where offsets are managed by the government or the private sector would still need to address issues around value and appropriate levels of offset, but may offer more strategic conservation benefits for the community and allow mining companies (and others) to focus on their core business.

Bibliography

Baker, R. and Ruting, B. (2014). Environmental Policy Analysis: A Guide to Non-Market Valuation, *Productivity Commission Staff Working Paper*, Commonwealth of Australia, Victoria.

Bedford, M., Ellis, M. and Simpson, C. (2009). Simple Modelling to Assess if Offsets Schemes Can Prevent Biodiversity Loss, Using Examples From Australian Woodlands, *Biological Conservation*, 142, pp. 2732–2742.

Bond, C., Cullen, K. and Larson, D. (2009). Joint Estimation of Discount Rates and Willingness to Pay for Public Goods, *Ecological Economics,* 68, pp. 2751–2759.

Carson, R. (1991). 'The RAC Kakadu Conservation Zone Contingent Valuation Study: Remarks on the Brunton, Stone and Tasman Institute Critiques', in Resource Assessment Commission (1991), *Commentaries on the Resource Assessment Commission's Contingent Valuation Survey of the Kakadu Conservation Zone*, Resource Assessment Commission, Canberra, ACT.

Davies, G.R. (2013). Appraising Weak and Strong Sustainability: Searching for a Middle Ground, *Consilience: The Journal of Sustainable Development*, 10(1), pp. 111–124.

DECCW (2007). *BioBanking: Biodiversity Banking and Offset Scheme: Scheme Overview*, DECCW, Sydney. Available at: http://www.environment.nsw.gov.au/resources/biobanking/biobankingoverview07528.pdf [Accessed 19 April 2014].

DECCW (2009). *BioBanking: Biodiversity Banking and Offset Scheme: Guide to Establishing a Biobank Site*, DECCW, Sydney. Available at: http://www.environment.nsw.gov.au/resources/biobanking/09336establishingbiobangsite.pdf [Accessed 19 April 2014].

Dobes, L. and Bennett, J. (2009). Multi-Criteria Analysis: 'Good Enough' for Government Work? *Agenda*, 16 (3), pp. 7–29.

Environmental Planning and Assessment Act 1979 (NSW). Available at: http://www.austlii.edu.au [Accessed 28 October 2014].

Gibbons, P. and Lindenmayer, D. (2007). Offsets for Land Clearing: No Net Loss or the Tail Wagging the Dog? *Ecological Management & Restoration*, 8(1), pp. 26–31.

Gillespie, R. and Bennett, J. (2012). Valuing the Environmental, Cultural and Social Impacts of Open Cut Coal Mining in the Hunter Valley of NSW, Australia, *Journal of Environmental Economics and Policy*, 1(3), pp. 1–13.

Hausman, J. (1979). Individual Discount Rate and the Purchase and Utilization of Energy — Using Durables, *Bell Journal of Economics*, 10(1), pp. 172–183.

Hillman, M. and Instone, L. (2010). Legislating Nature for Biodiversity Offsets in New South Wales, *Australia Social & Cultural Geography*, 11(5), pp. 411–431.

International Association for Impact Assessment (1999). *Principle of Environmental Impact Assessment Best Practice*, Institute of Environmental Assessment, Lincoln, UK.

Kovacs, K. and Larson, D. (2008). Identifying Individual Discount Rates and Valuing Public Open Space With State-Preference Models, *Land Economics*, 84(2), pp. 209–224.

Law Society of NSW (2012). *Submission to the BioBanking Review: Discussion Paper*, Law Society of NSW, Sydney. Available at: http://www.lawsociety.com.au/cs/groups/public/documents/internetpolicysubmissions/631975.pdf [Accessed 20 April 2014].

NSW Environment Protection Authority (EPA) (2012). *NSW State of the Environment 2012*, NSW EPA, Sydney.

NSW Government (2014a). *NSW Biodiversity Offsets Policy for Major Projects*, Office of Environment and Heritage for the NSW Government, Sydney.

NSW Government (2014b). *Draft Framework for Biodiversity Assessment: For Assessing and Offsetting State Significant Development and State Significant Infrastructure: NSW Biodiversity Offsets Policy for Major*

Projects, Office of Environment and Heritage for the NSW Government, Sydney. Available at: http://www.environment.nsw.gov.au/resources/biodiversity/1482draftfba.pdf [Accessed 20 April 2014].

NSW Minerals Council (2012). *Review of the NSW Biobanking Scheme 2012: NSW Minerals Council Submissions*, NSW Minerals Council, Sydney. Available at: http://www.nswmining.com.au/NSWMining/media/NSW-Mining/Publications/120713_EC_NSWMC-Submission_FINAL.pdf [Accessed 20 April 2014].

NSW Minerals Council (2014). *Environmental Offsets Inquiry*, NSW Minerals Council, Sydney.

Office of Environment and Heritage (OEH) (2009). Summary of Proposed Changes to the Biobanking Assessment Methodology. Available at: http://www.environment.nsw.gov.au/biobanking/summarytable.htm [Accessed 20 April 2014].

Office of Environment and Heritage (OEH) (2012). *BioBanking Review: Discussion Paper*, Office of Environment and Heritage, Sydney. Available at: http://www.environment.nsw.gov.au/resources/biobanking/20120062bbrevdp.pdf [Accessed 20 April 2014].

Ruderman, H., Levine, M. and McMahon, J. (1986). 'Energy-Efficiency Choice in the Purchase of Residential Appliances', in Kempton, W. and Neiman, M. (eds.), *Energy Efficiency: Perspectives on Individual Behavior*, American Council for an Energy Efficient Economy, Washington, DC, pp. 41–50.

Sinden, J. and Thampapillai, D. (1995). *Introduction to Benefit Cost Analysis*, Longman, Sydney.

Threatened Species Conservation (TSC) Act, 1995 (NSW). Available at: http://www.austlii.edu.au [Accessed 28 October 2014].

Tientenberg, T. (1992). *Environmental and Natural Resource Economics*, Harper Collins, New York.

16. Water Quality Trading

Suzie Greenhalgh and Mindy Selman

16.1. Introduction to Water Quality Trading

Across the globe, the water quality of rivers, streams and lakes is continuing to degrade, primarily because of land use intensification related to urban or agricultural development. In response to this degradation, governments are increasingly looking for policy mechanisms to halt and reverse this trend.

Regulating the sources of pollution that degrade water quality is a common approach used by many nations, such as the United States (US) through the *Clean Water Act*, Europe through the European Union Water Directive, and New Zealand through the *Resource Management Act*. Water quality trading is a complementary market-based mechanism used in some countries to provide regulated sources with flexibility on how they meet their regulatory obligation by allowing them to purchase an equivalent reduction in the regulated pollutant from another source. It has also been seen as a possible policy solution for mitigating the costs of achieving water quality goals (David *et al.*, 1980; Segerson, 1988). Most often, water quality trading is for nutrients (phosphorus and nitrogen), though some programmes have developed around other pollutants such as salinity and temperature.

Water quality trading leverages the differential abatement costs faced by different private-sector actors or sources of pollution (e.g., wastewater treatment plants, industrial facilities, urban developers, farmers) to create a market. Abatement costs vary between individual sources depending on their size, location, scale, management and overall efficiency, providing an arbitrage opportunity for regulated sources to meet their compliance obligations at lower cost (Greenhalgh and Selman, 2012).

There are two types of pollution sources: point sources (e.g., industrial facilities, wastewater treatment plants) whose discharges can be measured, and nonpoint sources (e.g., agricultural land and urban stormwater) whose discharges currently can only be estimated. In most instances, point sources are regulated using individual discharge permits or allowances, while the nonpoint sources are still largely unregulated; though some exceptions do apply (e.g., New Zealand where agricultural nonpoint sources are regulated).

The regulatory obligations that underpin water quality trading programmes are typically in the form of a catchment cap or limit based on the total pollutant discharges within a catchment or individual source permits or allowance limits for a pollutant discharge. Where an overall catchment cap is established, this cap is often allocated between sectors and then between individual sources in each sector.

This chapter outlines some of the key points of interaction between private sector actors and government authorities during the establishment and operation of water quality trading programmes. It does not delve into the theoretical basis for water quality trading, for which an extensive literature already exists (e.g., King and Kuch, 2003; Tietenburg, 2006; Horan and Shortle, 2011).

16.2. Water Quality Trading Programmes Globally

Individual water quality trading programmes operate in a number of countries around the world including the US, Canada, Australia and New Zealand. In the US, there are also 13 states that have or are in the process of developing state-level trading guidance, policy or rules (Willamette Partnership, 2012). As part of a 2012 assessment of water quality trading programmes (Greenhalgh and Selman, 2012), 63 water quality trading programmes were assessed. Of these, 33 were active[1] with the other 30 programmes either under consideration or development or were inactive. Of the 63, nine programmes were from outside of the US. There were two from New Zealand — Lake Taupo Nitrogen Trading Programme (active) and Lake Rotorua (under consideration); three from Canada — South Nation Total Phosphorus Management Programme (active), Lake Simcoe Watershed programme (under development) and Lake Winnipeg Basin (under consideration); and four from Australia — Hunter River Salinity Trading Scheme (active), South Creek Nutrient Trading Scheme (active), Murray–Darling Basin Salinity Credits Scheme (active) and the Moreton Bay Nutrient Trading Scheme (under consideration).

Some of the programmes, such as The Long Island Sound Nitrogen Credit Exchange Programme (US) and Hunter Valley Salinity Trading Scheme (Australia), focus only on point sources, as the discharges of these are relatively straightforward to measure, document and regulate. Others regulate point sources but include nonpoint sources as unregulated sources of nutrient reduction credits where point sources can purchase these credits to meet their regulatory compliance obligations. Two programmes that allow point source to nonpoint source trading are the South Nation Total Phosphorus Management Programme (Canada), which targets phosphorus, and the Pennsylvania Nutrient Credit Trading Programme (US), which targets nitrogen and phosphorus.

The Lake Taupo Nitrogen Trading Programme (New Zealand) is the only programme where nonpoint sources participate as a regulated source. In the Taupo catchment, agricultural nonpoint sources must maintain nitrogen losses at or below a target level determined

[1] While programmes may have finalised their trading programme design and trades can occur, this does not mean that actual trades have occurred.

by their highest nitrogen leaching year between 2001 and 2005.[2] In addition, a not-for-profit trust was established with government funding to permanently reduce the nitrogen load to the lake by 20 per cent. This reduction is being achieved through a mix of land purchase (and converting land use to low leaching activities) and purchasing nutrient discharge allowances (where farmers retain ownership of the land but change land use and receive a payment from the Trust) (Lake Taupo Protection Trust, 2014).

16.3. Key Areas of Interaction Between the Private Sector and Government

Setting the catchment cap and allocating the cap between sources of pollution, along with establishing the rules and regulations for the water quality trading programme itself, are the two key areas of interaction between the private sector and government. The first involves the negotiation and debate around the setting of the catchment-wide cap and how it is allocated between sources. The second involves establishing when and how trading is used to comply with regulatory obligations.

16.3.1. *Underpinning legal framework*

While the establishment of a catchment cap and the allocation of this cap to various sectors (e.g., agriculture, wastewater, urban stormwater), and then to individual sources, are not directly related to the trading mechanism, they are important components that underpin water quality trading. These caps, sector allocation and allocation to individual sources are often contained in a regulatory framework where individual sources are assigned discharge permits or allowances. Arguably, it is the establishment of the cap and then of the regulatory framework that underpins any trading programme that are the most contentious aspects, as they either immediately constrain

[2] http://www.waikatoregion.govt.nz/Community/Your-community/For-Farmers/Taupo/Nitrogen-trading-in-the-Lake-Taupo-catchment/ [Accessed 20 August 2014].

the activities of those in the catchment or will do so in the future. Trading is one mechanism that can theoretically reduce the compliance costs faced by regulated sources by providing flexibility in how they meet their regulatory compliance requirements.

16.3.1.1. *Catchment cap*

The underpinning regulations for existing water quality trading programmes have largely been driven by national or regional legislation that allows for the implementation of water quality caps or limits (either as catchment goals or water quality criteria) in individual catchments. For the private sector it is the stringency of the cap and its allocation (discussed in the following paragraph) that generates the debate. More stringent caps are likely to incur greater direct economic cost for the private and public sector, but lead to improved water quality, which has both direct and indirect benefits to the wider community.

Where the catchment cap is set at a level that still allows some increase in discharges then the debate is likely to be less contentious. This makes it easier to establish the cap, allocate the cap between sectors and sources and develop the rules for any complementary trading programme. There are also likely to be few, if any, trades occurring until the catchment cap and individual source discharge limits are reached. The Cherry Creek Trading Programme (Colorado, US), for instance, was established in 1997 in anticipation of future growth. However, it was not until 2006 that the first trades occurred and by 2009 four trades to offset increased loads had been made (Selman *et al.*, 2009).

Conversely, where a catchment cap is established with the aim of returning the targeted waterbody to a past water quality state or to maintain existing water quality, then the cap will be more stringent, the debate more controversial and, once operational, trades can be expected within shorter periods. The Lake Taupo Nitrogen Trading Programme has had 35 trades since 2009[3] while the Hunter River

[3]These trades are a mix of trades between the Trust and individual farmers and farmer-to-farmer trades.

Salinity Trading Scheme had approximately 980 trades between 2002 and 2012. Both programmes had quite stringent caps that required immediate actions by the regulated sources (Greenhalgh and Selman, 2012).

16.3.1.2. *Allocating the catchment cap between sources*

Allocating catchment caps between sectors and then to individual sources can also be highly contentious, especially where the cap requires sources to reduce their current discharge levels. This debate similarly affects both point sources and nonpoint sources as the allocation approach will determine the individual regulated compliance limits within which a source is required to operate.

There is no 'right' way to allocate a catchment cap (or sector allocation) between individual sources. Rather it is a decision that is likely to be based on the fairest and most equitable allocation. Of course, what is considered fair and equitable is likely to differ between owners of the different sources and other stakeholders involved in the debate. Once the implications of proposed allocation options are known, then it is likely there will be prolonged negotiations and assessments about which approach to adopt, as again the allocation option selected will have different financial implications for the individual sources. For some sources, it may mean they are required to reduce their discharges in the immediate term, while for others it may constrain their ability to grow (e.g., their ability to intensify land use or to increase discharge levels from industrial or wastewater treatment plants).

New pollution sources may also be treated differently where they either have to purchase allowances to operate in or enter a catchment or are given lower discharge allowances. For example, in Virginia (US) all new urban nonpoint sources are regulated and allocated a small discharge allowance of 0.45 lb P/acre/year (Virginia Department of Environmental Quality (DEQ), 2013).

In the case of the Pennsylvania Nutrient Credit Trading Programme there was a prolonged negotiation between the state agency tasked with establishing the guidelines and the wastewater treatment plants about how their permitted discharge levels would be determined for their National Pollutant Discharge Elimination System (NPDES) permits. Initially, the total permitted discharge was to be based on existing flows.[4] However, some plants felt they would be penalised as their treatment plants were designed and built for larger future anticipated flows (and therefore wanted allocations to be based on design flows) while others expected urban development to increase and would be required to meet these needs (and therefore wanted permits based on future projected growth).[5]

In New Zealand, where agricultural nonpoint sources are being regulated, debates over the allocation of the catchment cap to individual sources are equally as contentious. In the Lake Taupo Nitrogen Trading Programme, the forestry industry contested the use of an 'existing use' load (or grandparenting or grandfathering) on the grounds that they were disadvantaged by such an allocation as they had not intensified their land use and were now being penalised for that. This issue was negotiated with the regional authority for eight years culminating in an Environment Court[6] appeal. More recently, this debate is becoming more widespread as the National Policy Statement for Freshwater Management (NPSFW) (NPSFW, New Zealand Government, 2011, 2014) requirement to set limits in all catchments of New Zealand is being implemented.

A number of allocation approaches are being considered in New Zealand including grandparenting, catchment averaging, sectoral averaging, natural capital, equal allocation and nutrient vulnerability, to name just a few (Carren *et al.*, 2007; Daigneault *et al.*,

---

[4]The nutrient concentration level is the same for all treatments plants but the total load allocated to each plant is based on the flow multiplied by the nutrient concentration.

[5]The authors were part of the stakeholder group involved in the establishment of the initial trading guidelines for this programme and these observations are based on their personal knowledge of the process.

[6]The Environment Court in New Zealand is where all legal appeals are made to proposed environmental policy.

2012, 2013, 2014). The outcome of the discussions around the various allocation approaches for different catchments has often ended up in quite different places. For instance, in the Rotorua Lakes the regional council and stakeholders are currently proposing a sectoral averaging approach (Rotorua Te Arawa Lakes Programme, 2014) while grandparenting is being used for Lake Taupo. For the lower portion of the Hinds catchment in Canterbury existing land uses receive an allocation based on good management practices for the area while any land that changes use has a discharge limit of up to 27 kgN/ha/year (Canterbury Water, 2014); and in the Wanganui-Manawatu and Hawke's Bay regions a natural capital approach[7] is being used (Horizons Regional Council, 2013; Board of Inquiry, 2014).

The process of how these allocation approaches were determined also varies considerably between catchments; and reflects different relationships between the private sector and government agencies and also between different sector actors. The resulting allocation approaches in Taupo and Wanganui-Manawatu were determined using the typical 'consult and negotiate' planning process for New Zealand. Canterbury, however, reflects the new paradigm of collaborative governance recommended by the Land and Water Forum[8] (2012), and the Rotorua outcome is based on recommendations from a stakeholder advisory group.

It is important to note that even though water quality limits are being set for catchments across New Zealand, not all of these regulations are considering the use of a trading programme to provide flexibility for the regulated sources. Regardless, the debate and process to establish the allocation or leaching rate for individual sources are important considerations for trading programmes.

[7] A natural capital approach is based on the physical characteristics of the land or soil type. It reflects the land's productivity potential or, in some instance nutrient vulnerability, and is independent of existing land use.

[8] The Land and Water Forum brought together a range of industry groups, recreational and environmental NGOs, Maori, scientists and other organisations to develop a shared vision and a common way forward among all those with an interest in water, through a stakeholder-led collaborative process.

16.3.1.3. *Establishing the eligibility for non-regulated sources*

Some trading programmes, primarily those in North America, allow unregulated agricultural nonpoint sources to participate in markets as suppliers of credits. In this scenario, trading programmes establish eligibility criteria for agricultural nonpoint sources to ensure that reductions generated by these sources are additional to reductions that should have or would have happened anyway. If non-additional pollution reductions are allowed to generate credits or offsets for regulated sources, it could result in environmental backsliding or deterioration from business-as-usual water quality. Establishing the rules that determine nonpoint source eligibility can lead to intense debate among government agencies and agricultural and environmental interests. On the one hand, if eligibility criteria are too stringent, they run the risk of curtailing participation by nonpoint sources in trading, while on the other hand, if eligibility criteria are not stringent enough, they run the risk of undermining the environmental goals of the programme.

Eligibility for agricultural nonpoint sources is primarily determined using a 'baseline', which establishes an expected level of activity or environmental performance that the source must first meet before being eligible to participate in the trading programme. Project-timing and payment-stacking criteria are other types of eligibility criteria meant to address 'additionality' in water quality trading programmes (Maryland Department of Agriculture, 2008; Virginia DEQ, 2008; Electric Power Research Institute, 2012).

When developing agricultural nonpoint source baselines, trading programme developers typically consider several factors including:

- Regulatory requirements: Baselines should account for any regulatory requirements that the agricultural nonpoint sources may be subject to. In Maryland (US), for instance, agricultural nonpoint sources are subject to nutrient management regulations. These regulations require, for example, that livestock be excluded from adjacent streams, that there is a fertiliser/manure setback for fields adjacent to streams and that manure is incorporated within 48 hours of application (Maryland Department of Agriculture, 2013). A nonpoint source owner must be implementing these activities (as they apply to the operation) to be eligible to participate in the Maryland Water Quality Trading Programme (Maryland Department of Agriculture, 2008).

- Nonpoint-source catchment cap obligations: The baseline should reflect individual obligations for achieving the nonpoint-source sector cap allocation. However, unlike point sources, where the cap obligation is translated into individual discharge limits and generally codified in permits, there are often no obligations for individual pollution reduction established for nonpoint sources as part of the cap allocation. Thus it falls to the trading programme to establish a level of activity or environmental performance that approximates meeting the individual portion of the sector cap allocation.

As many trading programmes in the US have found, translating sector obligations to individual source obligations can be challenging as it involves interpreting sector load allocations that are often unclear or unreasonable in terms of expected level of implementation. For example, in Oregon, the Rogue River total maximum daily load (TMDL) for temperature establishes shade targets to represent 'system potential riparian vegetative conditions' (Oregon DEQ, 2008). Such a target is difficult to interpret and implement as a baseline condition for trading, as the baseline shading requirement for each landowner would be different and, furthermore, there would ostensibly be no additional shading practices the landowner could implement to generate credits.

In cases like these, some states have allowed trading programmes some leeway in the interpretation or timing of baseline requirements in order to establish a baseline that can be applied to an individual nonpoint source and still be consistent with cap obligations. In Wisconsin (US), for instance, the decision was made to phase in the baseline requirements by allowing nonpoint sources to generate short-term or interim credits for activities they have undertaken to comply with their TMDL obligations. Interim credits expire after five years, after which the eligibility baseline will be raised and only activities additional to the TMDL obligations will be allowed to generate credits (Wisconsin Department of Natural Resources (DNR), 2013).

- Trading programme requirements: In some cases, additional eligibility criteria are set by the trading programme itself. Pennsylvania's water quality trading programme, for instance, requires that agricultural participants in the programme have a nutrient management plan. Where no regulatory requirements or other obligations under a catchment cap exist, trading programmes may establish minimum eligibility criteria. This is to ensure that activities landowners should already be doing are not eligible to generate credits. Creating minimum eligibility criteria is also a way to prevent late adopters from profiting unduly from a water quality trading market.

The timing of projects is another aspect of eligibility that can spur debate among stakeholders. To ensure additionality, programmes often restrict eligibility to those projects involving new management practices. This in itself is challenging as there is a risk of excluding 'good actors' from participating in the programme. For instance, a landowner who has never implemented cover crops might generate eligible credits from adopting this practice, while another landowner who has consistently planted cover crops may not be eligible in the same trading programme. Many landowners disagree with early actors being excluded from water quality markets. In the Maryland Nutrient Trading Programme a compromise was reached where only new practices are eligible to generate credits, but all annual management practices are considered new and additional each year (Maryland Department of Agriculture, 2008). Thus, a landowner who implemented cover crops last year can still be eligible to generate and sell any reductions in nutrient losses from cover crops in the current year.

In the US, payment stacking and double counting, as they pertain to use of federal conservation payments, are usually a consideration for eligibility (e.g., Maryland Department of Agriculture, 2008; Virginia DEQ, 2008; Electric Power Research Institute, 2012). Payment stacking is where a single project is funded using multiple sources of revenue, e.g., federal conservation funds and market payments are used to fund a single project. Where this occurs it can be difficult to determine if the project is financially additional.[9] Payment stacking is relevant where there are large federal cost-share and incentive programmes available to the agricultural sector like those in the US. If landowners are receiving federal cost share or incentive payments to implement practices that are also being used to generate credits, it is unlikely these credits are financially additional.

Double counting is another concern where trading programmes allow credits from projects that receive federal conservation payments to be eligible. Federal cost-share payments are meant to incentivise projects that generate public environmental benefits and allowing these benefits to then be sold in a water quality trading market may constitute double counting. The debate among stakeholders (including private, public and NGOs) on the eligibility of credits generated with cost-share funding lies around wanting to incentivise the participation of agricultural nonpoint sources in markets and ensuring any eligible credits are additional.

To date three approaches have been taken in water quality trading markets in the US to address the issue of cost-share payments: (i) not allowing credits from projects that received federal cost-share or incentive payments to participate (e.g., the Maryland Nutrient Trading Programme and the Virginia Nutrient Trading Programme); (ii) only allowing landowners to sell the portion of the credits from cost-share projects that was financed by private investment, with the federal cost-share portion being ineligible (e.g., the Ohio River Basin Trading Pilot (Electric Power Research Institute, 2012) and Oregon

[9] Financial additionality, as with greenhouse gas markets, refers to whether a project or practice would or would not have been implemented in the absence of the market payment.

trading guidance (US Fish and Wildlife Service *et al.*, 2008); and (iii) placing no restrictions on the use of credits generated from cost-share projects in the market (e.g., the Pennsylvania Nutrient Trading Programme). While only the first approach assures financial additionality and avoids double counting, the proportional crediting approach has had the most traction in programmes in the US. It is argued that allowing for the mixing of funds on a project helps incentivise landowner participation and leads toward higher value projects,[10] while still minimising concerns about financial additionality and double counting.

16.3.2. *Development and operation of trading programmes*

A second area of interaction between the private and public sector is in the actual development, implementation and operation of trading programmes. The development and implementation phase is largely about engagement and negotiation, while during the operational phase the interaction is largely transactional. There are financial transactions between buyers and sellers and administrative transactions to amend permits or discharge allowances and to demonstrate compliance.

16.3.2.1. *Stakeholder processes*

As with any new policy approach, the type of interaction with stakeholders during the development/implementation of the rules

[10] For example, projects like riparian buffers or land use conversion may require higher payments to incentivise their adoption. Allowing the stacking of federal and market payments could result in higher adoption rates for these practices as was seen in the Clean Water Services (CWS) temperature trade (Oregon, US) in the Willamette/Tualatin Trading Programme. Federal incentive payments for riparian buffers, which were typically undersubscribed, were combined with payments from CWS to pay for the implementation of riparian shade practices that generated credits used towards CWS permit obligations for reducing stream temperatures. Temperature credits were discounted 2:1 in part to account for the government payment (Oregon DEQ, 2007).

and reporting of policy outcomes are important for how stakeholders perceive and respond to the policy. This often drives the level of trust between the private sector and government agencies.

Insufficient stakeholder engagement has created distrust in many programmes (Oregon DEQ, 2007; Greenhalgh and Selman, 2012). The South Nation Total Phosphorus Management Programme (Canada) had little initial outreach and this resulted in some farmers believing the programme was a 'license to pollute' for point sources. It took a further three years of stakeholder education and negotiation to address the farmers' issues before stakeholders were comfortable with the programme (World Resource Institute (WRI), 2007). Similarly, the lack of transparency around the Long Island Sound Programme (Connecticut, US) development meant legislation to establish the programme was not passed until a more open process was undertaken to redraft the legislation (WRI, 2007). In other programmes, there was substantial effort put into stakeholder engagement prior to programmes being established. Over 75 stakeholder meetings were held to inform stakeholders about trading before the Great Miami Trading Programme (Ohio, US) was developed. As a result, many stakeholders were fully supportive of the programme. In Lake Taupo (New Zealand) there was an initial rocky start to the development of water quality regulations and accompanying trading programme where farmers felt ill-informed about the scope of, and their contribution to, the problem.[11] After about eight years of engagement, consultation and legal proceedings, the underpinning regulation and trading rules for the Lake were finalised.

Another important component for some programmes has been local trading 'champions'. These champions, through their networks and the respect they have within their communities, have been able to generate grassroots enthusiasm for the development and implementation of trading programmes. This was an important ingredient for both the Great Miami Trading Programme and the South Nation Total Phosphorus Management Programme.

[11]Taken from interviews with farmers in the Taupo Lake Care Group, which was established to create a cohesive farming body to engage with the regulating agency during the development of the water quality plan for Lake Taupo (WRI, 2007).

16.3.2.2. *Regulatory agency buy-in*

Challenges around engagement and knowledge can also apply internally to staff within an administering agency and this can also hinder the development of trading programmes (Greenhalgh and Selman, 2012). In particular, a lack of understanding on how trading may fit within the relevant regulatory framework (e.g., US *Clean Water Act* or New Zealand's *Resource Management Act*) can result in a misrepresentation of trading concepts and legislative constraints during programme development.

Staff buy-in can also hinder development. This was seen in Michigan and Wisconsin in the US where trading advocates in senior management left the relevant administering agencies and the continued development of the trading programmes stalled. A different situation arose in the Cherry Creek and Chatfield programmes (Colorado, US). These programmes suffered resistance and suspicion from mid-level management because of the lack of additional resources made available to administer the programmes. This resulted in complex trade review processes and administrative hurdles, which discouraged trades.

16.3.2.3. *Transaction costs*

In the process of exercising trades, a number of transaction costs exist — such as the time taken for buyers and sellers to locate each other, or the time and cost of trade approval and verification procedures. Some costs relate to the requirements imposed by the administering agency while others may relate to the infrastructure (or lack of it) to support a programme. In the early days of water quality trading, high transaction costs were often noted as one of the key deterrents for programme participation (Rhonda Sandquist, Jackson Kelly PLLC, pers. com., 2008).

The trade approval processes for the Cherry Creek and Chatfield trading programmes in Colorado (US) are not standardised. This resulted in very lengthy approval processes where permits were often unnecessarily being rewritten and approved with each trade. Other programmes, though, have taken steps to try to streamline these processes to reduce transaction costs. Some programmes use a clearinghouse market structure (e.g., Long Island Sound Trading Programme, South Nation Total Phosphorus Management Programme, Great Miami Trading Programme), which means credits are verified before being available for sale. Others have created a market infrastructure so buyers and sellers can more easily find one another (e.g., the marketplace and registry used by the Maryland Nutrient Trading Programme[12] or the Hunter River Salinity Trading Programme, which has an online register and 24-hour credit exchange for scheme participants).[13] Others have a standardised credit and trade approval process (e.g., Pennsylvania Nutrient Credit Trading Programme and Long Island Sound Trading Programme).

Where non-regulated agricultural nonpoint sources can participate in a programme there are additional transaction costs involved. Again, administering agencies have attempted to reduce the cost of private-sector participation in programmes. Some programmes have reduced the costs of credit estimation and aggregation by leveraging government soil and water conservation staff to sign farmers up for the programme (e.g., Great Miami Trading Programme). Other programmes have standardised nonpoint-source nutrient leaching calculations (e.g., the Chesapeake Bay Nutrient Tracking Tool[14] used by the Maryland Nutrient Trading Programme; calculation spreadsheets used in the Great Miami Trading Programme; use of the OVERSEER® nutrient budgeting tool in the Lake Taupo Nitrogen Trading Programme) while others have provided consultants to help farmers and point sources with the trading process (e.g., The Deschutes River Conservancy assists farmers in the Willamette/Tualatin Trading Programme). In another example, The Pennsylvania Infrastructure Investment Authority (PENNVEST)[15] serves as central counterparty and clearinghouse for auction transactions in the Pennsylvania Nutrient Credit Trading Programme. They host the auctions for the

[12] http://www.marylandnutrienttrading.com [Accessed 16 September 2014].
[13] http://www.epa.nsw.gov.au/licensing/hrsts/index.htm [Accessed 21 August 2014].
[14] www.cbntt.org [Accessed 16 September 2014].
[15] http://www.pennvest.state.pa.us/portal/server.pt/community/nutrient_credit_trading/19518 [Accessed 21 August 2014].

sale and purchase of nutrient credits in the Susquehanna and Potomac catchments. Credit buyers and sellers contract with PENNVEST thereby reducing risk for buyers and sellers, which in turn helps create a stable trading market for nutrient credits in Pennsylvania.

These actions to streamline and standardise trading transactions are typically developed by administering agencies (usually government agencies) to reduce the costs for the private sector and municipalities to participate in markets, as well as to reduce their own administration costs.

16.4. Key Messages

As water quality trading programmes are emerging and maturing around the world, some key messages have become clearer. While trading programmes are still instruments of government, they have provided a flexibility mechanism that has enabled the private sector to more cost effectively meet regulatory obligations or to allow new growth. Trading has enabled regulated farmers in the Lake Taupo catchment in New Zealand to intensify their production to capitalise on high global milk prices by purchasing allowances from other regulated agricultural sources. In the Hunter River, mining companies are able to meet their regulatory requirements by trading salinity credits with other companies. This means that the environmental goal is being achieved while allowing the continued operation of many private-sector actors in these catchments.

Trading can also be seen as a mechanism to enable growth. In a number of areas in the US there is little allowance for urban growth within catchment caps. Effectively this means that new stormwater discharges are given a low allocation. Therefore, the only mechanism available to residential developers is to purchase allowances from a market. Without trading, new urban growth could not occur.

It should be noted, however, that the initial belief that trading programmes would be an effective mechanism to incentivise non-regulated agricultural nonpoint sources to reduce their nutrient losses voluntarily has not materialised to a great extent. In a related vein, trading programmes have not so far emerged as significant new funding sources for non-regulated sources to reduce their nutrient losses. The majority of trades have been between sources to meet regulatory compliance obligations rather than between regulated and unregulated sources.

What is also becoming increasingly clear is that, as water quality declines, the types and extent of efforts to maintain or enhance water quality are becoming more contentious. The response by government is often to regulate some or all sources of pollution. This process of establishing the regulation, and in some cases an accompanying trading programme, is often fraught, leading to very protracted stakeholder and legal processes. Those processes that are more inclusive and engaged with the full range of stakeholders early in the processes have tended to more quickly build trust in both the outcome and also the instruments, like trading, that have been developed to achieve the outcome.

In summary, water quality trading is proving to be a beneficial mechanism for the private sector to meet their regulatory obligations at a lower cost and to enable continued development in catchments where water quality limits are binding. Governments, through their provision of these programmes, are facilitating private-sector activity and participation in environmental protection while ensuring that public interests are protected through the establishment and achievement of water quality goals.

Bibliography

Board of Inquiry (2014). Final Report and Decisions of the Board of Inquiry into the Tukituki Catchment Proposal. Volume 1 of 3: Report and Decisions. Available at: http://www.epa.govt.nz/Publications/FINAL%20Report%20and%20Decisions%20-%20Volume%201%20of%203%20-%20Report%2018%20June.pdf [Accessed 19 September 2014].

Canterbury Water (2014). Ashburton ZIP Addendum Hinds Plains Area. Available at: http://ecan.govt.nz/publications/Council/hinds-zip-addendum-march-2014.pdf [Accessed 21 August 2014].

Carren, A., Clothier, B., Mackay, A. *et al.* (2007). '*Defining Nutrient (Nitrogen) Loss Limits Within a Water Management Zone on the Basis of the Natural Capital of Soil.*' *Appendix 6 to Farm Strategies for*

Contaminant Management. A report by SLURI, the Sustainable Land Use Research Initiative, for Horizons Regional Council, Palmerston North, New Zealand. Available at: http://www.horizons.govt.nz/assets/horizons/Images/one-plan-tech-reports-public/Defining%20nutrient.%20nitrogen%20loss%20limits%20within%20a%20water%20management%20zone%20on%20the%20basis%20of%20the%20natural%20capital%20of%20soil.pdf [Accessed 21 August 2014].

Daigneault, A., McDonald, H., Elliott, S. *et al.* (2012). Evaluation of the Impact of Different Policy Options for Managing to Water Quality Limits, *MPI Technical Paper 2012/46*. Available at: www.mpi.govt.nz/news-resources/publications [Accessed 21 August 2014].

Daigneault, A., Samarasinghe, O. and Lilburne, L. (2013). *Modelling Economic Impacts of Nutrient Allocation Policies in Canterbury: Hinds Catchment*, A report by Landcare Research for the Ministry for the Environment. Available at: www.mfe.govt.nz/issues/water/freshwater/supporting-papers/modelling-economic-impacts-of-nutrient-allocation-policies-canterbury.pdf [Accessed 21 August 2014].

Daigneault, A., Samarasinghe, O. and Lilburne, L. (2014). *Modelling Economic Impacts of Nutrient Allocation Policies in Canterbury: Selwyn–Waihora Catchment*. A report by Landcare Research for the Ministry for the Environment.

David, M., Eheart, W., Joeres, E. *et al.* (1980). Marketable Permits for the Control of Phosphorus Effluent into Lake Michigan, *Water Resources Research*, 16, pp. 263–270.

Electric Power Research Institute (2012). Pilot Trading Plan 1.0 for the Ohio River Basin Interstate Water Quality Trading Project. Available at: http://wqt.epri.com/pdf/ORB%20Trading%20Plan%208-1-12%20final.pdf [Accessed 19 September 2014].

Greenhalgh, S. and Selman, M. (2012). Comparing Water Quality Trading Programs: What Lessons Are There To Learn?, *Journal of Regional Analysis and Policy*, 42, pp. 104–125.

Horan, R.D. and Shortle, J.S. (2011). Economic and Ecological Rules for Water Quality Trading, *Journal of the American Water Resources Association*, 47, pp. 59–69.

Horizons Regional Council (2013). Proposed One Plan as Amended by Environment Court Decisions (May 2103): *Chapter 13 Discharges to Land and Water*. Available at: http://www.horizons.govt.nz/assets/publications/about-us-publications/one-plan-publications-and-reports/proposed-one-plan/Chapter13.pdf [Accessed 21 August 2014].

King, D. and Kuch, P. (2003). *Will Nutrient Credit Trading Ever Work? An Assessment of Supply and Demand Problems and Institutional Obstacles*, Environmental Law Institute 33-ELR-10352, Washington, DC.

Lake Taupo Protection Trust (2014). News and Events. Available at: http://www.laketaupoprotectiontrust.org.nz/page/lake_7.php [Accessed 5 September 2014].

Land and Water Forum (2012). Setting Limits for Water Quality And Quantity Freshwater Policy — and Plan-Making Through Collaboration. Available at: http://www.landandwater.org.nz/ [Accessed 21 August 2014].

Maryland Department of Agriculture (2008). Maryland Policy for Nutrient Cap Management and Trading in Maryland's Chesapeake Bay Watershed Phase II-A: Guidelines for the generation of agricultural nonpoint nutrient credits (Draft). Available at: http://www.mdnutrienttrading.com/docs/Phase%20II-A_Crdt%20Generation.pdf [Accessed 19 September 2014].

Maryland Department of Agriculture (2013). Maryland's New Nutrient Management Regulations: What You Need to Do to Comply. Available at: http://mda.maryland.gov/resource_conservation/counties/NMtimelineregsfinal.pdf [Accessed 19 September 2014].

NPSFW, New Zealand Government (2011). *National Policy Statement for Freshwater Management*. Ministry for the Environment, Wellington, New Zealand. Available at: http://www.mfe.govt.nz/publications/rma/nps-freshwater-management-2011/docs/nps-freshwater-mgnt-2011.pdf [Accessed 21 August 2014].

NPSFW, New Zealand Government (2014). *National Policy Statement for Freshwater Management 2014*. Ministry for the Environment, Wellington, New Zealand. Available at: www.mfe.govt.nz/publications/rma/nps-freshwater-management-2014/index.html [Accessed 21 August 2014].

Oregon Department of Environmental Quality (2007). Water Quality Credit Trading in Oregon: A Case Study Report. Available at: http://www.deq.state.or.us/wq/trading/docs/wqtradingcasestudy.pdf [Accessed 19 September 2014].

Oregon Department of Environmental Quality (2008). Rogue River Basin TMDL: Chapter 2 — Temperature. Available at: http://www.deq.state.or.us/wq/tmdls/docs/roguebasin/Rogue/Chapter2Temperature.pdf [Accessed 19 September 2014].

Rotorua Te Arawa Lakes Programme (2014). Setting Nitrogen Discharge Allowances. Available at: www.rotorualakes.co.nz/setting_NDAs [Accessed 21 August 2014].

Segerson, K. (1988). Uncertainty and Incentives for Nonpoint Source Pollution Control, *Journal of the American Water Resources Association*, 15, pp. 87–98.

Selman, M., Greenhalgh, S., Branosky, E. *et al.* (2009). *Water Quality Trading Programs: A Worldwide Overview*. WRI Issue Brief Note: Water Quality Trading No. 1, World Resources Institute, Washington, DC.

Tietenburg, T.T. (2006). *Emissions Trading: Principles and Practises*, 2nd edition, Resources of the Future Press, Washington, DC.

US Fish and Wildlife Service, National Marine Fisheries Service, US Environmental Protection Agency *et al.* (2008). Oregon Interagency Recommendations: Public Funds to Restore, Enhance, and Protect Wetland and At-Risk, Threatened and Endangered Species Habitats: Appropriate Uses of These Funds in Species and Wetland Mitigation Projects. Available at: http://www.fws.gov/oregonfwo/LandAndWater/Documents/PublicFunding-final.pdf [Accessed 19 September 2014].

Virginia Department of Environmental Quality (DEQ) (2008). Trading Nutrient Reductions from Nonpoint Source Best Management Practices in the Chesapeake Bay Watershed: Guidance for Agricultural Landowners and Your Potential Trading Partners. Available at: http://www.deq.virginia.gov/Portals/0/DEQ/Water/PollutionDischargeElimination/VANPSTradingManual_2-5-08.pdf [Accessed 19 September 2014].

Virginia Department of Environmental Quality (DEQ) (2013). Virginia Stormwater Management Handbook, Chapter 2. Available at: http://www.deq.virginia.gov/Portals/0/DEQ/Water/Publications/HndbkVolumeI.pdf [Accessed 25 September 2014].

Willamette Partnership (2012). In It Together: A How-To Reference for Building Point-Nonpoint Water Quality Trading Programs. Overview (Part 1 of 3). Available at: http://willamettepartnership.org/wp-content/uploads/2014/09/In-It-Together-Part-1_2012-07-30.pdf [Accessed 19 September 2014].

Wisconsin Department of Natural Resources (DNR) (2013). A Water Quality Trading How To Manual, 3400-2013-03, p. 33. Available at: http://dnr.wi.gov/topic/surfacewater/documents/WQT_howto_9_9_2013signed.pdf [Accessed 25 September 2014].

WRI (2007). *An Overview of Water Quality Trading*, Report prepared for the David and Lucile Packard Foundation and the Linden Trust for Conservation, World Resources Institute, Washington, DC.

Index